YOUNG ROMANTICS

YOUNG ROMANTICS

The Tangled Lives of English Poetry's

Greatest Generation

DAISY HAY

Farrar, Straus and Giroux • *New York*

Farrar, Straus and Giroux
18 West 18th Street, New York 10011

Copyright © 2010 by Daisy Hay
All rights reserved
Distributed in Canada by D&M Publishers, Inc.
Printed in the United States of America
Originally published in 2010 by Bloomsbury Publishing, Great Britain, as
Young Romantics: The Shelleys, Byron and Other Tangled Lives
Published in the United States by Farrar, Straus and Giroux
First American edition, 2010

Grateful acknowledgement is made to the following institutions for permission to quote from manuscript material: the Bodleian Library, Oxford; the Peabody Essex Museum, Salem, Mass.; the Luther Brewer Leigh Hunt Collection at the University of Iowa; and, at the New York Public Library, the Pforzheimer Collection of Shelley and His Circle and the Henry W. and Albert A. Berg Collection of English and American Literature.

Library of Congress Cataloging-in-Publication Data
Hay, Daisy, 1981–
    Young romantics : the tangled lives of English poetry's greatest generation / Daisy Hay.
    —1st American ed.
        p.   cm.
    "Originally published in 2010 by Bloomsbury Publishing, Great Britain, as Young Romantics: The Shelleys, Byron and Other Tangled Lives."
    Includes bibliographical references and index.
    ISBN 978-0-374-12375-8 (alk. paper)
    1. English poetry—19th century—History and criticism.   2. Romanticism—Great Britain.   I. Title.

PR590.H297 2010
821'.809—dc22

2009045650

www.fsgbooks.com

1   3   5   7   9   10   8   6   4   2

In memory of
Anne Mackenzie-Stuart

and for
Matthew

'The web of our Life is of mingled Yarn'

– John Keats to Benjamin Bailey, 8 October 1817

Contents

Author's Note

This book has a large cast of characters, some of whom share surnames, and several of whom share first names. Applying consistent naming conventions therefore presents certain practical and ideological challenges. In order to overcome these I have used the names most frequently used by the group themselves. Throughout, Percy Bysshe Shelley is referred to as 'Shelley', the name used by his mistress and his friends from 1814 onwards. Mary Wollstonecraft Shelley is referred to as 'Mary', the name by which she was universally known. More generally, following the conventions adopted in the group's letters and diaries, men are referred to by their surnames and women by their Christian names. In certain isolated cases the group themselves do not conform to this convention, and in these instances I have adopted their most frequently used alternatives.

The original spelling and punctuation of manuscript material has been retained, and mistakes and inconsistencies have been left uncorrected and unmarked by [*sic*], unless otherwise stated. Quotations from published primary sources follow the editorial conventions of particular volumes, which in most cases refrain from silent correction.

Preface

The Protestant cemetery in Rome stands at a distance from the grand sites of the rest of the city, just outside its old fortifications. To reach it on foot you have to trek along a road up past the Baths of Caracalla, through dusty and distinctly unlovely suburbs. I discovered this on the penultimate day of my honeymoon, as I marched my very new husband across Rome in the afternoon heat. We had been married for two weeks, but he already had good reason to think himself long-suffering, since although I had proposed the expedition to the cemetery, I had only a hazy idea about its location and had neglected to consult the scale on the map in our guidebook. While he gallantly agreed to my proposal, my husband was unconvinced about spending the little time we had left in Rome searching for the graves of long dead poets. The poets in question, however, were something of an obsession for me. They were the subjects of the PhD I had almost completed, and the book I was neglecting my PhD to research and write. They had become part of our lives, and their stories part of our story. Visiting their graves therefore seemed — at least to me — a strangely appropriate way to mark the beginning of our marriage.

I had read descriptions of the cemetery many times, and thought I knew what to expect. I knew that it wasn't really a Protestant cemetery at all, but historically the only spot in the city in which non-Catholics could be interred and that as a result Percy Shelley and John Keats, whose graves we were going to see, were buried alongside some

illustrious Orthodox Christians, Jews and atheists. I knew that Keats
lay in the old burying ground and Shelley, who died two years later,
in its western extension. But this did not prepare me for the contrast
between the traffic-blocked surrounding streets and the sudden, green
calm of the cemetery. I did not expect to feel so moved by this tranquil
world of overgrown paths, haphazardly arranged graves and indolent
stray cats, who lay sunning themselves at the base of the Pyramid of
Cestius.

   There was a further surprise in store. I had read that Shelley was buried
next to his friend Edward John Trelawny, an adventurer who arrived in
Italy during the last year of the poet's life. I knew that Keats too had a
graveside companion, Joseph Severn, who accompanied him to Rome
and nursed him through his final illness. But I did not anticipate the
emotional impact of seeing Shelley and Keats – both, in their different
ways, icons of solitary genius – buried next to their friends, alongside
men who were content to stand in their shadows. Even my sceptical
husband found himself moved by the shared burial sites. When we
returned to England two days later, memories of our visit spurred me
onwards to finish my PhD and to complete the biography that had
been illicitly germinating alongside my academic work for years.

———

This is not a biography of a particular person, nor does it tell the story of a
tightly coherent group of individuals. Instead, it explores the interlinked
lives of a group of writers, all of whom were characterised by their
youth, by their idealism, and by a particularly passionate engagement
with politics, art, and the romance of intellectual adventure. The stories
of these writers have been told many times before, but in a way that
downplays the significance of relationships in the shaping of individual
lives and a Romantic conception of creativity. This is largely because the
work of the most famous of these writers – Shelley, Keats and Byron –
frequently depicts both poet and poetic hero as isolated figures. In so
doing, it exemplifies many of the qualities which have come to define
the British Romantic movement. In different ways, the poetry of all
three asserts the supremacy of feelings and the imagination, attaches

much significance to an intuitive, visionary conception of nature, and presents artistic endeavour as an inherently solitary activity. This book looks beyond the image of the isolated poet in order to restore relationships to the centre of the Romantic story.

In common with other young writers whose lives were linked with theirs, Shelley, Keats and Byron were indebted to an earlier trio of Romantic poets, Wordsworth, Coleridge and Blake, whose work marked a striking break with the rational, Augustan poetry of the early eighteenth century. This break had a profound effect on literary culture in the decades following the French Revolution. Unlike Blake, whose work remained largely unread for decades after his death, Wordsworth and Coleridge were famous in their own time. Contemporaries of both poets were startled by the distinctiveness of their work, and by the new school of poetic thought they represented. Their example was both inspiring and troubling for the poets who followed them. The poetry of Shelley, Keats and Byron shared many of the concerns and ideas of their Romantic forebears, but it also demonstrated striking differences in outlook and opinion. This was in part the result of a significant generational gap between the two groups. Wordsworth and Coleridge started writing poetry in the 1790s, and their manifesto, *Lyrical Ballads*, was first published in 1798, when Byron, Shelley and Keats were aged ten, six and three respectively. Although Wordsworth and Coleridge would outlive the three younger poets and keep writing poetry and prose right through the period in which this book is set, their work was shaped by a different set of preoccupations and historical conditions to those that influenced their younger contemporaries. The first generation of Romantic poets were students of the French Revolution, an event which shaped all the poetry they subsequently wrote. Shelley, Keats and Byron, in contrast, produced their mature work in an intellectual landscape shaped by Napoleon's defeat at the Battle of Waterloo in 1815.

This was a landscape of reaction and repression. As the inevitability of Napoleon's fall became apparent, the victorious powers – Britain, Austria, Russia and Prussia – met in Congress at Vienna to decide how to divide up Europe. Across the continent, imperial monarchies regained control of peoples and territory. Austria took back its Italian city states, Russia was given Poland, and the Bourbons were restored to the French throne. For liberals and reformers throughout Europe this represented the final failure of the French Revolution: a revolution that had promised so much – representative government, the end of aristocratic rule – and delivered so little.

In Britain the end of a two-decade long war resulted in unprecedented problems of mass unemployment, as demobilised soldiers flooded the labour market. This coincided with the introduction of the Corn Laws, protectionist measures that kept the price of bread artificially high and provoked outrage among the growing ranks of urban poor. The result was a resurgence of a kind of popular political agitation not seen in Britain since the 1790s. Crowds gathered in huge outdoor meetings to demand the reform of Parliament and universal manhood suffrage, and the radical press grew in both size and power. Fear was fuelled by the activities of a small group of underground agitators who were committed to achieving revolution by violent means. One group of plotters attempted to take control of the Tower of London and the Bank of England; another planned to assassinate the entire cabinet in one fell stroke. The prospect of a revolution in Britain seemed very real.

Against this backdrop, poetry took on a new significance, as young, idealistic poets looked for ways to express their views about the plight of the people. Literary journals were quick to condemn works which ran counter to their opinions, or to praise poets whose work supported their viewpoint. Thus, in the hands of the younger generation of Romantic writers and their readers, poetry was transformed into a political weapon. Like William Godwin and Mary Wollstonecraft before them, this new generation turned to their art in order to proclaim both their independence and the depth of their political resistance.

Lord Liverpool's Tory Government responded to public unrest and eloquent literary opposition with a series of repressive bills which placed limits on free speech and movement and which were designed to stamp out radical publications. Habeas Corpus was periodically suspended and prosecutions for libel increased dramatically between 1817 and 1822. The Whigs were unable to mount successful challenges to this barrage of legislation, and instead became hand-wringing observers, prepared neither to ally themselves with those calling for reform, nor with an unpopular administration. Faced with such a weak parliamentary opposition, a number of liberal journalists stepped into the political vacuum to hold the government to account in the pages of the popular press.

Chief among these was the editor of *The Examiner*, Leigh Hunt, who stands at the centre of the circle of talented men and women this book explores. Over the course of the 1810s, Hunt's sphere of influence expanded, as first Byron and then Keats and Shelley gravitated towards him and, in the process, brought their own friends and relations into his orbit. It was Keats who articulated most eloquently the complexity of the group in which he found himself when he compared its chains of allegiance to a 'web . . . of mingled yarn', an analogy borrowed from *All's Well That Ends Well*. Shakespeare uses the metaphor to explore a series of delicate moral balances – 'The web of our life is of mingled yarn, good and ill together'[1] – but, in a different context, the image aptly describes the fragile yet powerful network which drew Shelley, Keats and Byron towards each other.

———

Writing about Shelley, Keats and Byron as figures in a web of social and intellectual allegiance is, at one level, counter-intuitive. Although, in the words of the literary critic Jeffrey Cox, 'we no longer necessarily view the romantic poet as the solitary singer declaiming alone on the mountain-top or sitting in isolation, pondering a bird's song',[2] the myth of the isolated artist has had profound cultural significance over the past two centuries.[3] In the Preface to *Lyrical Ballads* Wordsworth described poetry as 'the spontaneous overflow of powerful feelings' which 'takes its origin from emotion recollected in tranquillity'[4] and, in a single sentence, he pointed to a significant shift in the conception of the source of poetic inspiration. Shelley later extended and complicated Wordsworth's argument in his 'A Defence of Poetry', when he suggested that 'the mind in creation is as a fading coal which some invisible influence, like an inconstant wind, awakens to transitory brightness:

this power arises from within, like the colour of a flower which fades and changes as it is developed.'⁵ No more would the poet be inspired purely by God or his muse (as in Milton, invoking the aid of the Heavenly Muse to aid his 'adventurous song').⁶ Instead inspiration would stem from the soul of the individual.

Such statements about the source of inspiration transformed the way we think about creativity and genius. Creativity was repositioned as something internal and personal, and poetry – despite its political significance – as the product of an individual's communion with his own mind. The artist became an isolated figure, striving alone to create works of genius. Over the course of the nineteenth century, the lives of Shelley, Keats and Byron were recorded in a series of biographies which took their inspiration from this idea. These were largely respectable, semi-hagiographic accounts of noble lives, lived out without much recourse to friends and family. While the history of biography is far from straightforward, and this model of biographical writing was pioneered earlier, it nevertheless owed much to a Victorian emphasis on individualism that derived in part from the Romantic period.⁷ This emphasis, which led to the celebration of an idealised image of the individual as hero of his own life in single-subject, cradle-to-grave biographies, had a lasting effect on the genre.

Single-subject biographies can make for gripping, stimulating reading, and – especially in the hands of the great biographers who reinvigorated the genre in the final decades of the twentieth century – they present vividly contextualised portraits rich in detail, depth and colour. However, as the literary critic John Worthen has noted, while 'we write biographies of individuals as islands . . . we live as part of the main'.⁸ Living as part of the main was particularly important for Shelley, Keats and Byron, who, as they became friends with Hunt, became part of a group in which friendship was politically and philosophically significant. It is therefore ironic that their work should have helped to shape a conception of creative genius which downplays the interconnectedness of human existence.

This book is about a web of lives, within which friendships fade, allegiances shift, and nothing remains static for very long. The young Romantics were, in many respects, divided, but they were also united by their oppositional politics, by the depth of their convictions, and by their youth. (At the time this story begins Leigh Hunt, the oldest of the group's central figures, was twenty-eight, and Mary Wollstonecraft Godwin, the youngest, was fifteen.) They did not speak with one voice. But they *talked* to each other, in a conversation which transcended divisions of class and gender. They loved and hated each other. They were joined by shared ideals, but also by romance, sex and blood. They were friends, but they were also husbands, wives, brothers and sisters. Towards each other they were variously self-sacrificing, jealous, sympathetic, competitive, kind and cruel. The story of their tangled communal existence is, in many ways, as dramatic and as surprising as anything they ever wrote. It also sheds light on the creation of some of the most powerful writing in the English language.

PART ONE

Creating a Coterie

Husbands

On 3 February, 1813, Leigh Hunt began a two year prison sentence at Surrey Gaol in Horsemonger Lane, London. His crime was libel; his victim the Prince Regent. It was, by any standards, a harsh punishment, but Leigh Hunt was determined to bear imprisonment and separation from his family with fortitude. 'I must feel like a brother, a father and a husband, but I can still act like a man', he wrote. 'I have friends above price; I have done my duty; I am an Englishman setting an example to my children and my country; and it would be hard, under all these circumstances, if I could not suffer any extremity rather than disgrace myself by effeminate lamentation or worse compromise.'[1]

Surrey Gaol was nestled among the narrow streets of modern-day Southwark. It was one of the largest prisons in England and, like other county gaols, held a mixture of common criminals and debtors, who lived in and around the prison with their families. Its governor, Mr Ives, ran his establishment as a flourishing business, charging prisoners fees for ale, the services of prostitutes, the removal of chains, and even for release on acquittal by a court. Visitors formed an essential part of the prison economy, bringing the incarcerated food and money to pay fees as well as small home comforts – bedding, warm clothes – which made life inside more bearable.

A prisoner like twenty-eight year old Leigh Hunt offered the prospect of rich pickings for Ives and his staff. It was not uncommon for gentleman prisoners (largely white-collar criminals, guilty of offences such as libel, sedition and fraud) to serve out their sentences as guests of their gaoler, paying high rents to be accommodated in the master's house. Ives greeted his newest inmate with profuse expressions of pity and immediately offered him rooms in his own apartments. Hunt rejected this offer, on two grounds: he could not afford Ives's extortionate rent, and he objected to the gaoler's unctuous expressions of sympathy, which were as insincere as they were fulsome. As a result, he was allocated a cell previously occupied by Colonel Despard, an Anglo-Irish rebel found guilty of high treason, who had been executed on the roof of Surrey Gaol in 1803.

It was not a promising beginning to his sentence, and Hunt's first few days in gaol were dreadful. It was the sounds of prison life which distressed him the most: the noise of 'felons' chains, mixed with . . . horrid execrations or despairing laughter'[2] was worse than the sight of the felons themselves, and the scraping of cell keys turning in locks represented 'a malignant insult' to Hunt's 'love of liberty'.[3] A prison guard took him to see a woman about to be hanged for murdering her illegitimate baby, and Hunt was appalled that the gallows on which the woman was to be executed were 'brought out within her hearing'.[4] He was also revolted by the voyeuristic whisperings of the guard, and chastised him roundly for his behaviour. Ives and his staff soon learnt that Hunt was not a man to condone cruel or dismissive remarks about his fellow prisoners.

Hunt's brave talk boosted his morale but it did little for his health, which began to deteriorate under the strain of such an environment. Sympathetic members of the prison's board of magistrates agreed that, on health grounds, his bleak living conditions should be improved. His family were permitted to join him and two rooms were adapted for them in the old prison infirmary. The news that he was to be given a space of his own in which he could live with his wife and children spurred Hunt into action. The tradesmen who traipsed in and out of the prison selling their wares to its unfortunate inmates were joined by a team of decorators, who set about transforming the infirmary into accommodation fit for a gentleman.

Six weeks after the beginning of his sentence, Hunt was ready to receive visitors. His friends made their way through the dirty Southwark streets and the prison's dark corridors to find him settled in a riot of colour and comfort. He sat in splendidly appointed rooms, a fairy-tale king holding court in a bower of his own creation:

> I papered the walls with a trellis of roses; I had the ceiling coloured with clouds and sky; the barred windows were screened with Venetian blinds; and when my bookcases were set up with their busts, and flowers and a piano-forte made their appearance, perhaps there was not a handsomer room on that side of the water.[5]

Friends and admirers flocked to see him, some out of curiosity, but many more out of genuine affection. His cell became an unlikely literary salon, and a refuge – for both the prisoner and his visitors – from the cares of the world. Tradesmen brought good food and wine; special dinners were ordered, and Hunt and his companions talked late into the night until Ives or his underlings came to escort them off the premises. Hunt spent the hours between visits reading, writing, and landscaping his garden, a small patch of outside space attached to the old infirmary, which he made private with green palings and a trellis. He created flowerbeds around its edges, in which he planted flowers and saplings, and had the centre of his garden covered with grass turf. Here he walked with his young nephews and his son and played at battledore and shuttlecock with Jeremy Bentham, one of his more sporty visitors.

Leigh Hunt's name does not excite much attention today.[6] One of the reasons for this is that his best work was his most ephemeral: unlike his more famous friends he was not first and foremost a poet, but a campaigning journalist. He spent his youth cocooned in the bosom of his family, the adored, delicate youngest child of Isaac Hunt, a loyalist refugee from Philadelphia, and his wife Mary. His ancestors on his father's side were West Indian, and throughout his life his enemies would seize upon this, commenting in sly asides on his swarthy complexion, dark hair and thick lips. Isaac Hunt was a charismatic spendthrift, and some of Hunt's earliest memories were of the rooms at the King's Bench Prison where the family lived after Isaac was imprisoned for debt. He spent his schooldays at Christ's Hospital, then an unforgiving institution standing in the shadows of Newgate prison. In 1801, when Hunt was sixteen, his fond father arranged for the publication of his *Juvenilia*, funded by a group of eminent subscribers who supported Isaac because of his loyalist connections. It was most unusual to publish an author's *Juvenilia* before he had established himself as a significant literary voice, and the volume was a sign of Isaac's remarkable confidence in his son's abilities.

After *Juvenilia*, however, Hunt showed little sign of living up to his early promise, and he drifted aimlessly. His listless progress through late adolescence was marred by some of the curious contradictions in his character. Simultaneously self-confidently precocious and unsure of his own abilities, strong-willed and emotionally fragile, egotistical and selfless, he seemed almost overawed by his own potential. Eventually, his elder brother John, worried that his brilliant sibling was in danger of succumbing to their father's lackadaisical and irresponsible habits, took a hand in his future. John Hunt was nine years older than Leigh and the contrast in their characters was marked. He was hard-working, diligent, morally upright and an incisive judge of character. A highly responsible man himself, he bitterly resented Isaac's failures and the strain financial uncertainty placed on his delicate mother. He combined deeply held principles with business acumen and in 1808, when he was thirty-two and Leigh twenty-three, he spotted a gap in the politically polarised periodical market for an independent weekly newspaper. He had started newspapers before, to which Leigh had contributed on a part-time basis, but now John suggested a permanent partnership in which he would act as printer and Leigh as editor.

The resulting newspaper, *The Examiner*, bound the brothers together for almost two decades. Leigh shared his brother's principled devotion to political independence and to the cause of parliamentary reform and they worked well together, John providing the clear-headed common sense which ensured the newspaper was ready for printing by its Saturday deadline and Leigh the sparkling editorial comment columns which made its reputation. Leigh did not, however, share his austere elder brother's work ethic, and the carefree way he managed his own financial affairs was a source of considerable strain on their relationship. So too was Leigh's marriage in 1809 to Mary Anne Kent, which placed additional pressure on *The Examiner*'s resources. Leigh had met Mary Anne (known also as Marian and, ultimately, as Marianne) in 1802 when, as a directionless eighteen year old, he was introduced to the Kent family by a mutual friend who knew that Marianne's younger sister, Elizabeth, was eager to meet him. Elizabeth was only eleven in 1802, but she was bright beyond her years, had read and admired an essay by Hunt in the *Monthly Preceptor* and was keen to emulate his literary activities. Hunt was kind to the little girl, probably because he was attracted to her elder sister.

Hunt's courtship of Marianne was long and stormy, and dominated the adolescent years of both sisters. But by 1813, the year of his imprisonment, Hunt and Marianne were safely married and the parents of two small sons. Their household was chaotic, in marked contrast to that of John and his wife Sally. Leigh and Marianne moved in and out of London, between a series of rented cottages and apartments, scraping money together as they went along. John found his new sister-in-law's haphazard housekeeping exasperating, but his resistance to the marriage stemmed from more serious concerns. He feared for *The Examiner*'s future under the management of a domestically distracted editor, and doubted that the journal could support an additional family. He may also have worried that the presence of a flighty, disorganised, emotional wife would exacerbate Leigh's character flaws, and that Marianne would only make his brother more unreliable. She did not, however, have the detrimental effect on her husband's industriousness that John anticipated, and within two years of its foundation, *The Examiner* had become one of the most influential newspapers of the day.

From their motto ('Party is the Madness of the Many for the Gain of a Few') to their refusal to accept advertisements, the Hunt brothers proclaimed their independence at every turn. The paper's political position was liberal; its tone anti-establishment. It blamed the manifold weaknesses of government on the incompetence of those permitted to govern, on the unchecked problems facing the nation and, above all, on endemic corruption. In the first year of its life, the Hunt brothers' crusade against corruption brought them both widespread respect and a charge for libel when they made reference to a story circulating in London that the Duke of York's mistress, Mary Anne Clarke, had been selling military commissions. This libel charge only collapsed when the truth of the accusation against the Duke was laid bare by the scurrilous and extremely funny evidence given at the bar of the House of Commons by Mary Anne Clarke herself. Between 1808 and 1812 the Hunts faced two further libel actions. The first, levelled against an article on the 'headless state' of the government, was withdrawn just as the trial started. The second charge was more serious, and related to an article which condemned the practice of military flogging, comparing it unfavourably to the disciplinary methods used by Napoleon. On this occasion the Hunts were only acquitted thanks to the brilliance of their trial lawyer.

The libel cases against *The Examiner* greatly strained the Hunts' resources but the publicity engendered by legal action also brought the newspaper fame and new readers. Those who picked it up for the first time soon discovered that it was far more than a weekly political gazette. It included theatre reviews, columns on the fine arts, comment on contemporary manners, sketches of leading parliamentarians, and an impressive array of original poetry and literary reviews. It also carried verbatim reports of parliamentary proceedings, national and international intelligence, agricultural, law and police reports, a column on happenings at Court and current fashions, as well as an intriguing summary of 'Accidents and Offences', which described, in magnificent detail, some of the week's more bizarre domestic and local skirmishes. Nonetheless, its centrepiece was the political editorial contributed each week by Leigh Hunt. His columns chronicled the rise and fall of Napoleon, the progress of the British armies from the Spanish Peninsula to the Field of Waterloo, the scandals that enveloped the royal family and the government, the suffering of the labouring poor in the post-war years, and the long battle for parliamentary reform waged by a wide spectrum of reformers and radicals. Hunt kept up a constant attack on the government, his position moving from belligerence to despair.

At the beginning of 1811, King George III was finally declared mentally incapable to rule, and the Prince of Wales was appointed Prince Regent. *The Examiner*, like other reform-minded publications, greeted the prospect of a Regency with cautious enthusiasm, but by February 1811 Hunt was dolefully reporting that the Regent was little more than 'a mere signing and responding puppet'[7] who had failed to dismiss the tired Tory administration of Spencer Perceval and Lord Liverpool, bestowed sinecures on his friends, and held extravagant parties in a manner quite unsuited to his role as head of state. *The Examiner*'s anger against the Regent finally erupted in an editorial in March 1812. Reading reports of the Prince's activities in sycophantic journals, Hunt announced, one would never guess 'that this *delightful, blissful, wise, pleasurable, honourable, virtuous, true and immortal* PRINCE, was a violator of his word, a libertine over head and ears in debt and disgrace, a despiser of domestic ties, the companion of gamblers and demireps, a man who has just closed half a century without one single claim on the gratitude of his country or the respect of posterity!'[8]

A fourth libel writ was promptly issued against *The Examiner* by an outraged Attorney General. The Hunts had survived three previous libel actions and this time the trial judge, Lord Ellenborough, was taking no chances. The jury was hand-picked and 'packed' with men sympathetic to the Crown, and the result was never in doubt. Both Hunt brothers were sent to prison, Leigh to Surrey Gaol and John to Coldbath Fields in North London.

Lord Liverpool and members of his government may well have assumed that *The Examiner* was unlikely to survive the incarceration of its editor and printer. If so, they were destined to be disappointed. Instead of isolation, the Hunt brothers' sentence brought them new, powerful supporters and determined, congenial and interesting friends. In 1813 the circle which gathered around Leigh in prison included some important figures in English arts and letters. His regular callers included William Hazlitt, a painter and journalist beginning to make a name for himself as an essayist and literary commentator; Charles and Mary Lamb, the brother-and-sister co-authors of *Tales from Shakespeare*; and

Charles Cowden Clarke, son of a well-known Dissenting schoolmaster. He was also visited regularly by Thomas Barnes, a Christ's Hospital friend, the classical scholar Thomas Mitchell and Sir John Swinburne, whose nephew, Algernon, would scandalise Victorian society with the publication of his erotic libertarian poems. Henry Brougham, the lawyer who had unsuccessfully defended the Hunt brothers at their trial, was another frequent visitor, as was the painter Benjamin Haydon, an impetuous, religious, slightly wild-eyed twenty-seven year old. Haydon understood better than most how painful it was for Hunt to be cut off from London's theatres and exhibitions, and he arranged to have his great historical painting on the Judgement of Solomon transported to Surrey Gaol for Hunt to admire. He was, in 1813, among the most passionately loyal of Hunt's supporters, noting in his diary that 'Hunt's Society is always delightful – I don't know a purer, a more virtuous character, or a more witty, funny, amusing, enlivening man.'[9] Haydon visited Hunt throughout his time in gaol, wrote him long letters during his absences from London, and was a constant source of support and encouragement.

With the aid of such friends, the Hunts managed to keep *The Examiner* going so that it appeared every week of their two year sentence. Though John Hunt was accorded less freedom and his visitors were more restricted, a constant stream of *Examiner* employees scuttled back and forth between the newspaper's offices, John's cell at Coldbath Fields and Surrey Gaol, collecting editorials and instructions. And the group that began to form around Leigh Hunt acquired a life of its own in the pages of the newspaper. Thomas Barnes contributed a column on 'Parliamentary Criticism', and assumed responsibility for Hunt's theatre column. Charles Lamb wrote the early editions of 'Table Talk', a collaborative meditation on society and manners which appeared regularly from 1813. In 1814 William Hazlitt published the first of his regular contributions to the newspaper, in the shape of an article on Shakespeare and 'Posthumous Fame'. Benjamin Haydon supplied articles under the pseudonym 'E.S.'.

This cooperative endeavour had far reaching consequences. The act of keeping the paper going provided a focus for a group who were united in sympathy with Hunt and in opposition to his oppressors, and who could now announce their allegiance to him and the causes of free speech and liberty that he espoused in the pages of his journal. The harsh sentence handed down to the Hunts was an act of aggression by a politically motivated judiciary determined to clamp down on an outspoken liberal opposition. In response, the Hunts mobilised their friends to continue the professional activities and the private conversations disrupted by prison life. In the process, they ensured *The Examiner*'s survival. This was in itself an achievement, but it also provided their circle with an example of private lives lived for the public good, and it demonstrated that a group of friends could constitute their friendship and support of each other as an act of political resistance.

Leigh Hunt's most glamorous prison visitor was Lord Byron, who went to Surrey Gaol for the first time on 20 May 1813. Byron's anticipation of this visit has given us one of the most abiding images of the imprisoned Hunt:

> To-morrow be with me, as soon as you can, sir,
> All ready and dress'd for proceeding to spunge on
> (According to compact) the wit in the dungeon –
> Pray Phoebus at length our political malice
> May not get us lodgings within the same palace![10]

Byron was intrigued by Hunt, and he broadly agreed with the aims of *The Examiner*. While it might be surprising to find a peer of the realm sympathetic to a publication which campaigned against the injustices perpetrated by the House of Lords, Byron was no ordinary aristocrat. He was born in 1788, to Captain John 'Mad Jack' Byron and his wife Catherine Gordon. He hardly knew his father, an infamous Regency rake who abandoned his wife and son in 1790 and died in 1791. His childhood was dominated by the women who brought him up: his mother, who inculcated a sense of aristocratic entitlement in her son, and his nurse, whose Calvinist preachings had a profound effect on her imaginative charge. He was born with a deformed foot and the combination of painful treatments and his pronounced limp separated him from other boys and made him vulnerable to bullies. As a result he quickly learnt to defend himself and later recalled childhood fights from which he would emerge triumphantly proclaiming the family's motto: 'Crede Byron'.[11] His life changed dramatically in 1798 when his grandfather died and, aged ten, he became the sixth Baron Byron of Rochdale. On his elevation to the peerage, Byron moved with his mother to Newstead Abbey (his family's dilapidated ancestral seat) and then to London, from where he proceeded first to Harrow and then to Cambridge, where he made friends with a motley collection of young society roués. At Harrow he began a correspondence with his half-sister Augusta, the daughter of Mad Jack Byron and his first wife, Amelia D'Arcy.

By 1808, the year in which *The Examiner* was founded, twenty year old Byron had come down from Cambridge and was living in London, writing poetry and wining and dining with friends. These included John Cam Hobhouse, who would go on to a notable parliamentary career, Scrope Davis, a dandy and gambler, and Charles Skinner Matthews, who would drown himself in the Cam, tortured by his sexuality in one of the most repressively homophobic decades of the nineteenth century. Byron's first volume of poetry, *Hours of Idleness*, was published in 1807 when he was nineteen, and his second, *English Bards and Scotch Reviewers* (which appeared in 1809), was an incendiary attack on the literary and political establishment. The reaction to the poem was furious and it was savaged in both Whig and Tory journals. He spent much of 1810 and 1811 abroad, visiting southern Europe and the eastern Mediterranean, which would provide the backdrop for his Eastern Tales – *The Giaour*, *The Bride of Abydos* and *The Corsair* – and for the early cantos of *Childe Harold's Pilgrimage*.

The first two cantos of *Childe Harold's Pilgrimage* were published in 1812, and they sold out within a few days. Byron suddenly found himself the darling of the Regency drawing room: a star guest at parties, whose fads and fashions were copied by crowds of admirers. He was drawn into the 'Holland House' set, the aristocratic circle surrounding the Whig leader Lord Holland, under whose aegis he made his maiden speech in the House of Lords. One younger member of the Holland House set, Lady Caroline Lamb, was particularly charmed by Byron and embarked on a determined pursuit of him, which resulted in a brief liaison. It was Lady Caroline who labelled Byron 'mad, bad, and dangerous to know', although this is a phrase which could more accurately be applied to Caroline herself. The affair quickly cooled but Caroline's ardour for Byron did not. Lady Melbourne, Caroline's mother-in-law and Byron's confidante, suggested that her niece Annabella Milbanke might make him a suitable bride. In 1813, he started a correspondence with Annabella, and with the approval of Lady Melbourne made an offer of marriage which Annabella promptly refused. But the correspondence continued intermittently throughout 1813 and 1814 in a kind of shadow fencing match, with both parties simultaneously attracted and repelled by the perplexities of the other.

Early in 1813, Byron rediscovered an old acquaintance. Some years earlier his half-sister Augusta had married George Leigh, an impecunious and unsatisfactory army officer. When Augusta and Byron met again, after many years with little contact, the attraction was immediate. Their letters from this period make clear the strength of the affection between them and there seems little doubt that in the course of 1813 this developed into a sexual relationship.* When he first went to visit Hunt in Surrey Gaol, Byron was thus on the one hand conducting a strange epistolary romance with his putative bride, an ice maiden whom he would nickname (in ironic tribute to her mathematical abilities) the 'princess of parallelograms', and on the other becoming ever more entangled in a torturous affair with his half-sister.

---

* The paternity of Augusta's daughter Medora, born on 15 April 1814, has been the source of much speculation, and Medora herself would come to believe that Byron was her father. Byron, however, never demonstrated much concern for Medora, despite the closeness of his relationship with Augusta and the interest he would take in his other children – both legitimate and illegitimate. For a fuller discussion of Medora's paternity see Fiona MacCarthy, *Byron: Life and Legend*, pp. 214–15 and Michael and Melissa Bakewell, *Augusta Leigh*, p.115.

According to the poet Thomas Moore, who introduced Byron to
Hunt and accompanied him on his early visits to Surrey Gaol, Byron
was initially unsettled to find himself dining among Hunt's friends,
rather than as the honoured guest of a suffering writer. This faltering
start notwithstanding, Byron and Hunt's acquaintance developed
into friendship over the two years of Hunt's imprisonment. Hunt,
a little starstruck, was flattered by the attentions of an aristocrat and
celebrated poet. It reinforced his sense that he was suffering for a
noble cause, and that he was supported by all right-thinking members
of society. Indeed, Byron's visits bolstered Hunt's streak of vanity. He
began to have thoughts of reforming him and told Marianne that he
believed he could be of some use to the young peer. 'He is a young man
(24) evidently full, by his writings, of good natural feelings & a fine
improvable sensibility, but led away, I am told, by a town life.'[12] Despite
the fact that Byron, at twenty-five (not twenty-four as Hunt thought),
was only three years younger than Hunt, the older man viewed the
younger as a potential protégé, whose character he could help to form.
But although Hunt's attitude towards Byron was patronising, his
analysis of his contradictory character was astute. Byron was capable
of behaving appallingly, of being selfish, vain and egotistical. He was
also uncomfortably aware of his own failings, which led him to assert
his own importance and sometimes into vicious comment about his
adversaries. But he could be generous in his estimation of others and
had a talent for making and keeping friends.

For his part, Byron was forbearing in the face of Hunt's reforming zeal
and had considerable respect for him. Much later he would complain
that Hunt had been 'conceited into a martyr' by Surrey Gaol[13] but in
the months following their first meeting he was determinedly generous.
There was something about Hunt 'not exactly of the present age', he
wrote in his diary at the end of 1813, before remarking that 'he is,
perhaps, a little opinionated, as all men who are the *centre* of *circles*,
wide or narrow.'[14] Byron found much to admire in Hunt, and was
perhaps even a little envious: it was hard to avoid the fact that the
individuals who gathered around Hunt did so out of real friendship,
rather than a fascination with celebrity which brought crowds to the

Regency parties at which Byron made an appearance. But Byron was not blinded by the glamour of 'the wit in the dungeon', and he was, in his turn, astute about his new friend. Hunt could be vain, egotistical, sanctimonious and naïve; and his own letters bear witness to the fact that he rather enjoyed his position as sufferer-in-chief for free speech and reform. But he was also exceptionally brave. He refused to trade his sentence for the promise of future silence (an opportunity spurned by John Hunt as well); insisted on paying his own fine of £500, despite an offer by a repentant juror from his trial to pay it for him; and faced the horrors of incarceration in a hanging gaol with cheerfulness.

———

By April 1813, the living quarters provided for Hunt's family at Surrey Gaol were proving unsatisfactory. Two year old Thornton was a frail child, and his health declined quickly in the damp prison. Torn between the needs of her husband and son, Marianne decided that Thornton was in more danger than his father. Hunt and Marianne agreed that Thornton and baby John should be removed from prison while Thornton's health recovered, and Marianne took them to Brighton, where they stayed for much of 1813.

In her absence, Marianne's younger sister Elizabeth, now twenty-three years old, moved into the family's prison quarters to look after Hunt. Elizabeth, universally known as Bess, lived with Hunt at Surrey Gaol for much of 1813, making his tea, writing letters for him, helping him with his *Examiner* column, and presiding over his dinner parties. It was Bess who chased his friends out when he needed to work, who kept him writing when he was about to miss a publication deadline, who made sure he only wrote letters to his friends when he had time, and who read him to sleep when insomnia struck. It was Bess, the more intellectual of the sisters, who watched Hunt's weekly engagement with the world unfold in *The Examiner*, and who talked domestic and international politics with Hunt and his friends. While Marianne looked after two small children in a Brighton boarding house, Bess spent long, intimate days with her brother-in-law, talking, writing and entertaining.

Bess Kent is an enigmatic figure. We know she wrote voluminous letters, in which she laid her heart bare, but few have survived. We know that she wrote at least three books – two about flowers and trees and one for children, and that she planned to write another – but we know little about how she conducted her research, or how long these books took her to write. In the late 1810s and early 1820s she attempted to wean herself off opium, but there is little to indicate when she first developed this addiction. She made at least one suicide attempt and threatened to make others, but the circumstances surrounding them are a matter of conjecture. Several of her contemporaries commented on her appalling temper but only shadowy images of her survive. These suggest a woman of fierce intellect, who was more than capable of conducting business negotiations on behalf of her brother-in-law; a woman subject to ungovernable rages which made her periodically impossible to live with; and a woman with an immense capacity for affection, who looked after her sister's family devotedly.

This devotion to members of her family by Bess was repaid by a singularly enlightened attitude to her temper. Some indication of this appears in a letter dating from 1830, written by her half-sister Nancy to Marianne. Nancy describes her attempts to find new lodgings following the death of their mother. She recounts how Bess has insulted an old family friend, rejected all lodgings found, and 'as plainly as possible gave me to understand that she only wanted a convenient opportunity of destroying herself.'[15] Bess has made her stepfather Rowland Hunter furious, has had an irrevocable row with Hunt (Nancy wonders whether the suicide threats are an attempt to recapture his attention), and is making life miserable for all her family. Yet Nancy reproaches herself for her inability to be patient with her elder sister, and notes, in real perplexity, 'she is a very strange person. Sometimes when she is angry with me . . . [she] looks at me with an expression of malignity, that seems as if I were an object of actual hatred to her, and at others, she laughs and talks, and behaves . . . as one sister should to another.'[16] Nancy's letter was written some years after Bess's residence with the Hunts and postdates the period when Bess and Hunt were living together in Surrey Gaol by almost twenty years. But it does suggest that Bess suffered throughout her life from some form of manic depression. Nancy's letter is notable because, even without much understanding about the nature of depression, and without any diagnosis of a medical problem, it suggests that Bess's family understood that she somehow could not be held accountable for her phases of virulent nastiness.

The Bess of Surrey Gaol, however, was not going through one of her more destructive phases. She knew Hunt needed her, and this knowledge gave her the confidence to run his rooms like the hostess of a literary salon. She appears in Hunt's letters as a merry presence; and she was an object of some fascination to his friends. Most of them liked her, although some were made uneasy by her affectionate relationship with her brother-in-law. The painter Benjamin Haydon, for example, came to think that Hunt's 'smuggering fondness'[17] for her was positively disgusting, and was appalled by the public symptoms of their physical intimacy – an arm round a waist, heads too close together, a glance held for too long. Byron, in contrast, liked Bess and was charmed by her admiration for him. He found the sight of her and Hunt together arresting, and might have seen in their relationship a paradigm for an alternative kind of domesticity, where one lived in harmony with a woman to whom one was a little too closely related for comfort. Visiting Surrey Gaol had other advantages for Byron, not least that it provided an escape from the competing demands of Annabella and Augusta. It was a relief, once in a while, to slip away from society hostesses to sit with Hunt and Bess among the books and flowers, lapping up their admiration for his poetry, which they combined with a refreshing lack of interest in his rank.

Marianne was less convinced of Lord Byron's merits, related to her at length by Hunt and Bess in their letters. Reading descriptions of amusing evenings in Surrey Gaol with Byron did little to alleviate her loneliness in Brighton, and made her fearful that aristocratic admirers would distract Hunt from writing for *The Examiner*, on which her family's livelihood depended. While Hunt and Byron were close in age there was considerable social disparity between them, which Marianne perceived to be a problem. As a result, she remained stoutly unimpressed by the Byron of popular myth: a brooding, melancholic figure based on the hero of his *Childe Harold's Pilgrimage.*

Marianne's suspicion of Byron derived not only from her concern about his influence over Hunt, but also from her growing anxiety about the events taking place in Surrey Gaol in her absence. Thornton's health kept her in Brighton for longer than she intended, and she wrote increasingly worried letters to Bess, telling her to share the responsibility of looking after Hunt with her nephews and Kent cousins, and to think about returning to live with her parents. She also missed her husband badly. She coped with the prolonged separation by penning a steady flow of letters meant for Hunt's eyes only, in which she was quite explicit about how much she longed to be with him: 'fancy where you would like to have me most, and you will know what I dreamt about, &c. &c. &c!!!'.[18] Sometimes she sounded positively overcome with her own longing. She wanted, she told him, to 'take you dearly into [my] arms when you go to bed, and, and, you know what I mean . . . I must not think about it, if I do I shall grow outrageous.'[19] Hunt responded in kind, imagining that his arms were wrapped around her. 'I shall once more be clasped to one of the best hearts in the world, and have a bosom to rest upon, and a form to expatiate upon, that are all my own.'[20]

By the second year of Hunt's sentence Thornton had recovered sufficiently for Marianne to reassert her position as her husband's chief companion. She moved back into Hunt's cell, accompanied by Thornton and John, and Bess was sent home. Matrimonial relations were so well re-established that the Hunts' third child, Mary, was born in Surrey Gaol with Hunt acting as midwife, 'the hour having taken us by surprise'.[21] With Marianne and the children back in Hunt's rooms, his living arrangements gained the utmost respectability. Byron, busy with his own concerns, visited Hunt less frequently as 1814 wore on, although he continued to send books and kind letters. Perhaps the flower-filled dungeon was less fascinating when it was a disapproving wife, rather than an admiring sister-in-law, who presided over the coffee pots.

I am boiling with indignation at the horrible injustice & tyranny of the
sentence pronounced on Hunt & his brother, & it is on this subject
that I write to you. Surely the seal of abjectness & slavery is indelibly
stamped upon the character of England.

Thus wrote Percy Bysshe Shelley on 15 February 1813 to his friend and
bookseller Thomas Hookham. 'Surely', his letter continued, 'the public
for whom Hunt has done so much will repay in part the great debt of
obligation which they owe the champion of their liberties & virtues or
are they dead, cold, stonehearted & insensible, brutalised by centuries
of unremitting bondage . . . whilst hundreds of thousands are sent to
the tyrants of Russia, he pines in a dungeon far from all that can make
life to be desired.' He concluded his protest with a practical suggestion:
'I am rather poor at present but I have £20 which is not immediately
wanted. – Pray begin a subscription for the Hunts, put my name for
that sum, & when I hear that you have complied with my request I will
send it you.' [22]

Percy Shelley was twenty years old when he wrote this letter. It captures
his eloquence and his fervent hatred of tyranny and injustice, as well
as his conviction that the champions of individual liberties deserved to
be publicly celebrated. But it also captures the impulse to action which
was one of Shelley's essential features. From his youth he combined a
poetic sensibility with a belief in the power of political activism, and for
a political liberal he had a surprisingly aristocratic conviction that his
involvement in the Hunt brothers' predicament would be welcome. His
letter was also characteristic in that it combined the optimism of youth
with the world-weary tone of a much older man. At twenty Shelley had
in fact seen more of the world than many of his acquaintances and, like
Hunt, he had suffered as a result of his writing. However, he was still
searching for a cause to which he could nail his colours, and behind
the generosity of his offer to raise a subscription for the imprisoned
Examiner owners lay a touch of envy at Hunt's elevation to the role of
publicly acknowledged political hero.

Shelley spent much of his first two decades trying to become just
such a hero. Although barely out of adolescence at the time of Hunt's

imprisonment he was, in 1813, an ardent radical and anti-monarchist, bursting with ideas for the reformation of the world. Physically, he was rather odd, tall and slim to the point of limpness, with a high-pitched effete voice; but what he lacked in physical bulk he more than made up for in charismatic intensity. Among the earliest witnesses to this intensity were his school fellows at Eton, where he was sent by his landowning father when he was twelve. Initially he was bullied for his refusal to 'fag' for older boys, but the bullies soon discovered that, in spite of his feeble frame, Shelley was not a boy to succumb quietly to taunts. On the contrary, he could be terrifying when roused, and was quite capable of reciprocal acts of violence. He stabbed one tormentor's hand with a fork, and others remembered him as an almost unearthly creature, with flashing eyes, wild hair, and deathly white cheeks. Eventually the extremity of his reactions won him grudging respect, and he left school in 1810 the acknowledged leader of his contemporaries. From Eton he proceeded to University College Oxford. There, as at Eton, he developed a reputation for charismatic eccentricity, although this time he was not required to resort to violence to prove his worth. He was expelled from Oxford in 1811, when, on principle, he refused to admit to his authorship of a pamphlet (co-authored with his friend Thomas Jefferson Hogg) on *The Necessity of Atheism*.

A few weeks before his expulsion, Shelley wrote to introduce himself to Hunt, whose writing he greatly admired. It was a daring letter, written by an unknown undergraduate to an important political commentator some eight years his senior. Shelley told Hunt of his vision for 'a *meeting* of such enlightened unprejudiced members of the community, whose independent principles expose them to evils which might thus become alleviated',[23] and the pair met briefly at Shelley's urging. But their relationship did not prosper: Hunt was too busy to pay much attention to the wild schemes of an impetuous young man with little experience of putting his ideas into practice, and Shelley rapidly became distracted by the consequences of his expulsion and was unable to pursue the friendship. Less than a month after first writing to Hunt Shelley found himself alone in London, exiled from Oxford and, eventually, from his family home in Sussex.

Shelley's expulsion from Oxford represented a turning point in his life. His aristocratic childhood had not prepared him for outcast living. As far as his family was concerned it did not help that Shelley, like Hunt, considered himself to be a martyr to free speech, and that he combined the intransigence of youth with a deadly combination of idealism and aristocratic *hauteur*. But underneath the haughty persona he adopted during his dealings with his father – and, subsequently, with his father's lawyer – was a hurt and lonely young man.

Over the next few years, Shelley made many attempts to replace the three institutions – his family, school and university – which had failed him. As he moved restlessly about the country he tried to gather friends about him, or to put himself in places where he believed he would find like-minded people. Like the imprisoned Hunt, he was groping towards an understanding of the political and philosophical significance of friendship. But his existence in the years following his expulsion from Oxford was rootless and restless, and was less conducive to the creation of a meeting of the enlightened than Hunt's cocooned prison life. In the period of isolation which followed the breakdown of his relationship with his father he grew close to the family of John Westbrook, a merchant with two daughters, Eliza and Harriet. Harriet was a sweet-faced, slightly passive sixteen year old, very much under the thumb of her older sister. She responded to Shelley's stories of ill-treatment at the hands of his family and the authorities in Oxford with unquestioning sympathy and quickly came to think of him as a heroic outcast, fully deserving of her love. Shelley delighted in her admiration and her kindness and in August 1811 they eloped to Edinburgh, where they were joined by Hogg, Shelley's Oxford co-conspirator. From there Harriet and Shelley travelled to York, where they abandoned Hogg after he propositioned Harriet, and then to Keswick, where they met – and shocked – Coleridge's middle-aged friend Robert Southey, and where Shelley embarked on a correspondence with the radical political philosopher William Godwin.

Godwin's seminal contribution to English political thought, his *Enquiry Concerning Political Justice*, first appeared in 1793, the year after Shelley's birth. It was subsequently reprinted in revised editions throughout the 1790s. The significance of Godwin's work for a generation of radicals and reformers was beyond measure. *Political Justice* presented a philosophical framework through which the events in revolutionary France could be perceived, and it also provided a millenarian vision for the future of society. Godwin argued that all institutions which sought to limit the power of the human mind and its acquisition of knowledge – such as government, systems of punishment, religion and marriage – were evils which needed to be eradicated in order to achieve a state of 'perfectibility'. When Shelley learnt that Godwin was living in London with his family he was moved to write to him to ask for his friendship and to announce his allegiance to Godwin's principles. In the spirit of upholding these principles, he proclaimed his intention to move to Ireland, where he planned to play a heroic role in the struggle for Irish independence.

From Ireland, where Shelley distributed campaigning pamphlets and failed to make much impact on the independence cause, the Shelleys moved to Nantgwyllt in Wales, and from Nantgwyllt to Lynmouth, on the North Devon coast. From Lynmouth they moved back to Wales, and it was at their temporary home in the village of Tan-yr-allt that Shelley heard of Hunt's imprisonment. It was also in Tan-yr-allt that he composed much of his first important poem, *Queen Mab*. *Queen Mab* was an angry, avowedly political work, and in it Shelley was able, for the first time, to demonstrate for himself the political potency of poetry. In nine cantos of verse and in extensive accompanying notes, he explored the revolutionary idealism of the past, attacked monarchy, marriage and religion, and proclaimed his vision of an idealised atheistic republic. The poem was indebted to Godwin, as well as to Rousseau and the French *philosophes*. It grew out of Shelley's reading but was also influenced by his awakening perception of the rotten nature of contemporary society, manifested by the refusal of great institutions (Oxford) to permit independent thought; the sclerotic inability of the Irish to throw off the oppressive Anglo-Saxon yoke; and the poverty and hardship suffered by the Welsh villagers among whom the Shelleys lived. Like Godwin, Shelley fiercely objected to social, political and religious institutions which encouraged hypocrisy; and like Hunt he opposed all state attempts to limit individual freedom of thought and speech. As he moved around the country searching for companionship, Shelley refined and developed his philosophy, so that by the time of his twentieth birthday he was not just a Godwinian acolyte but a writer with well-developed ideas of his own.

Shelley finally met Godwin in the autumn of 1812, when he travelled to London with Harriet. There the young couple made several new friends, including Thomas Hookham, the bookseller who was privately printing *Queen Mab*, and an older poet, Thomas Love Peacock, who had already achieved some success. They were also introduced to Godwin's family. Understanding the complicated familial relationships in the Godwin household would have required some concentration from Shelley and Harriet. In 1796 Godwin had embarked on a relationship with Mary Wollstonecraft, author of *A Vindication of the Rights of Woman*, and a key figure in the circle of revolutionary thinkers and writers gathered around the radical publisher Joseph Johnson. Wollstonecraft already had an illegitimate daughter by an American merchant called Gilbert Imlay, whose desertion had caused her to attempt suicide by throwing herself off Putney Bridge. But Wollstonecraft found new happiness with Godwin. It was a transformative experience for both of them and, in 1797, the discovery that she was pregnant persuaded them to marry – despite Godwin's strictures against marriage in *Political Justice*. Their daughter, Mary Wollstonecraft Godwin, was born on 1 September 1797. But a little over a week later Wollstonecraft died of puerperal fever, brought on by the manual extraction of the placenta and subsequent infection and haemorrhaging.

If Mary Wollstonecraft had survived, her second baby would have received the same joyous love lavished on her daughter Fanny Imlay, described eloquently in her poignantly beautiful *Letters Written during a Short Residence in Sweden, Norway and Denmark*. But instead of being brought up by parents who were in love with each other and committed to a just and gentle education of their children, Fanny Imlay and Mary Godwin were left in the care of a forty-one year old man dazed by bereavement, who, over the course of an austere, hard-working life, had learnt few lessons about how to give and receive affection freely, and who had no idea how to care for small children. Kind friends looked after Fanny and baby Mary in the weeks following Wollstonecraft's death, but thereafter Godwin felt his inability to bring up the girls acutely.

In 1801, when Fanny was seven and Mary four, he remarried. His second marriage was pragmatic, and was designed to protect the children in his care, one of whom bore no blood relation to him at all. The second Mrs Godwin was a neighbour, Mary Jane Vial. Mary Jane referred to herself as 'Mrs Clairmont' – a surname she probably borrowed from the father of one of her two illegitimate children, Charles and Jane (who, in adult life, would always be known as Claire). In 1803 she bore Godwin a son, William, the only child in the Godwin ménage to know both his parents. Life in the Godwin household was thus far from straightforward. No child had the same pair of parents. Fanny was brought up by two adults to whom she was not related. She had never known her father, although she believed Godwin to be her natural father until sometime after her tenth birthday, and had only hazy memories of her mother, who died when she was three. But, from her teens, she could read about her childhood self in her mother's *Letters*, and, more disturbingly, would have known from reading Godwin's scandalous *Memoirs of the Author of A Vindication of the Rights of Woman* that her father Gilbert Imlay's desertion of her mother had led her to attempt suicide on more than one occasion. Mary, Godwin's own daughter, grew up with the knowledge that her birth had caused her mother's death, which was described in detail by Godwin in his *Memoirs*. But she also grew up as the favourite of Godwin, who was extremely proud of her developing intellect. Both girls were constantly reminded of their dead mother, whose portrait, painted by John Opie, hung in Godwin's study long after Wollstonecraft's death and his subsequent remarriage. And, along with their older step-siblings, Jane and Charles, both were expected to act like rational adults at all times. This could be unnerving for visitors. Coleridge, whose son Hartley was an occasional playmate of the Skinner Street children, found 'the cadaverous Silence of Godwin's Children . . . quite catacomb-ish'.[24]

When Mary was fifteen, Godwin wrote a letter to a correspondent
anxious to know how Wollstonecraft's educational theories were
working in practice. This letter reveals a good deal about the dynamics
of the household during the elder children's adolescent years. 'Of the
two persons to whom your enquiries relate', Godwin informed his
correspondent, 'my own daughter is considerably superior in capacity
to the one her mother had before. Fanny, the eldest, is of a quiet,
modest, unshowy disposition, somewhat given to indolence, which is
her greatest fault, but sober, observing, peculiarly clear and distinct
in the faculty of memory, and disposed to exercise her own thoughts
and follow her judgement. Mary, my daughter, is the reverse of her
in many particulars. She is singularly bold, somewhat imperious, and
active of mind. Her desire of knowledge is great, and her perseverance
in everything she undertakes almost invincible. My own daughter is,
I believe, very pretty; Fanny is by no means handsome, but in general
prepossessing.'

In the same letter, Godwin informed his correspondent of the
circumstances which had led to his second marriage. Noting that
the enquiry put to him related 'principally to the daughters of Mary
Wollstonecraft', Godwin conceded that 'they are neither of them
brought up with the exclusive attention to the system and ideas of
their mother.'[25] Neither he nor Mrs Godwin had time, he confessed,
for trying out 'novel theories', and in any case, Mary Jane was not
exactly a slavish Wollstonecraft adherent. Indeed, everyone who knew
the second Mrs Godwin agreed that she differed from her predecessor
in certain key respects. With a few notable exceptions, Godwin's
friends were uniformly rude about her, and the normally equitable
Charles Lamb castigated her for her 'damn'd, beastly vulgarity'.[26]
It cannot, however, have been easy to follow Mary Wollstonecraft.
All three girls – including, eventually, Mary Jane's own daughter,
Jane Clairmont – were ardent Wollstonecraftian disciples, which
strained their relationship with Wollstonecraft's successor. Mary, in
particular, resented many of her stepmother's rules and instructions,
and appears to have had little compunction about making her
displeasure clear. Mary Jane's lot was not made easier by the fact

that the family were always short of money. Godwin's position as
the godfather of radical political philosophy was not rewarded by
a steady income, and while the bookselling and printing business
which Mary Jane started, rather enterprisingly, in 1805 produced
some enduring works, it would ultimately prove to be disastrous. It
was this financial background which coloured Shelley's first meeting
with Godwin.

————

From the outset, Godwin was impressed by Shelley's intellect and was
appreciative of his admiration. Underlying the decision to befriend
him, however, was the knowledge that Shelley was a baronet's heir with
a relaxed attitude to the dispersal of his family's money. He might be
an impetuous youth whose ideas needed some refining, but he was
also in a position to extricate Godwin from his never-ending financial
difficulties. When the Shelleys visited Skinner Street in the autumn
of 1812 they were therefore made welcome. Godwin and the children
took to trim, smart little Harriet, and they were all rather fascinated by
the energy of the charming and unpredictable Shelley.

Shelley returned to Wales at the end of 1812 buoyed by the
conviction that in Godwin he had found at least one new friend.
He and Harriet moved to London the following summer, and there
Harriet gave birth to a baby girl, named Ianthe. But after Ianthe's birth
a shortage of money drove them first to the Lake District, and then to
Edinburgh. Accompanied by Harriet's sister Eliza, the young family
travelled northwards in Shelley's newly acquired travelling carriage,
dogged at every stage of their journey by bills and letters from angry
creditors, chief among them the harassed maker of their splendid new
coach. Travelling for days on end with a small baby and a disapproving
sister-in-law in tow was not, as Shelley and Harriet began to discover, a
recipe for marital harmony, and by the time they returned to the south
at the end of 1813 their relationship was fracturing under the triple
stresses of constant travel, new parenthood and financial insecurity. At
the beginning of 1814 Shelley took a house in Windsor, in which he
installed Harriet, Eliza and Ianthe. He did not stay there himself for

any extended period, but instead embarked once more on a peripatetic existence, moving between the houses of friends and temporary London lodgings. He continued to visit Windsor and, in spite of the strains, Harriet became pregnant for a second time. But he spent less and less time with his family as 1814 progressed and, by the summer, his occasional visits had ceased entirely.

This was because he was spending more and more time at the Godwins' house in Skinner Street. Godwin and Shelley were in constant contact during the first months of 1814, exchanging several letters a week. The subject of all these letters was money. Godwin's finances had reached a crisis point, and he desperately needed Shelley to provide some long-term financial support in order to release other loans and guarantees. In order to do so, Shelley had to raise funds on his expectations, and he and Godwin spent hours closeted with money lenders, hammering out the details of *post-obit* bond sales to financiers who would release cash against Shelley's entailed inheritance. Such a scheme for raising money was ruinously expensive, as William St Clair's meticulous research into the Shelley/ Godwin financial dealings has shown: in one case Shelley sold a *post-obit* bond of £8,000 and received a cash payment of £2,593–10s in return.[27] Shelley's cavalier dispersal of his inheritance greatly worried his family and his father, Timothy Shelley, reluctantly opened negotiations about an allowance for his son and the repayment of his debts – on condition that Shelley stopped selling his inheritance immediately.

In the early summer of 1814, a new reason for Shelley's frequent visits to Godwin's house appeared, when Mary Godwin returned to London from a long visit to Scotland. She was sixteen years old, beautiful, and extremely intelligent. She had made the long journey north by herself, had lived among strangers and made them her friends, and had acquired a wardrobe of dramatic tartan dresses which marked her out from her less exotically dressed sisters. She was also the daughter of Godwin and Wollstonecraft and thus represented a philosophical ideal. Shelley met her for the first time in May, and was enraptured. Writing to Thomas Hogg some months later he described his first feelings for her: 'how deeply did I not feel my inferiority, how willingly confess myself far surpassed in originality, in genuine elevation & magnificence of the intellectual nature until she consented to share her capabilities with me.'[28] Shelley was humbled by Mary: he had never met anyone who matched her in looks, character or parentage, and he felt acutely aware that her intellect far surpassed his own. But he also wanted to possess her, not just because she was beautiful and clever, but because of the radical union she represented.

There is no doubt that, at sixteen, Mary could have turned the heads of more than one wayward young philosopher. She could be funny, flirtatious and a tease, and she had a fine sense of drama and adventure. But she also had an air of reserve about her, which made it even more exciting when she revealed something of her passionate inner self to Shelley. She was, by the time Shelley met her, a highly independent young woman who had been sent away for her health, but also because her relationship with her stepmother was so fraught as to make her continued presence in Skinner Street tiresome for all concerned. In both looks and manners she presented a striking contrast to the more biddable Fanny, a quiet, slightly melancholic eighteen year old, who periodically tried to prevent the simmering tensions in Skinner Street from erupting into the rows she hated. Jane Clairmont, on the other hand, was nearly the same age as Mary and grew close to her stepsister after their parents' marriage. She was blessed with dark good looks, was a talented musician and linguist, and she now showed a pleasing eagerness to assist Shelley and Mary in their secret romance.

Mary was just as fascinated by Shelley as he was by her. He shared her devotion to the ideas of her adored father, as well as her love of drama; he was brilliant, quick and passionate, and he planned to reform the world. *Queen Mab* was a brave, inventive poem, which revealed in its author an alluring combination of talent, vision and rebelliousness. It was the poem of a man who could never be dull: cool and reasoned maybe, but also susceptible to fits of hyperactive over-excitement and to dreams and hallucinations. And all these qualities combined in someone who promised to rescue her family from financial disaster. Moreover, Mary had met very few young men, and Shelley reacted to her in the most flattering and unexpected way. It is hardly surprising that things moved as quickly as they did. The end of June and the whole of July were spent in a haze of developing passion. With Jane as a willing chaperone, Shelley and Mary stole walks and talks together, and on 26 June 1814, by her mother's tombstone in the overgrown graveyard of Old St Pancras Church, Mary declared her undying love for Shelley, while Jane loitered at a nearby grave.

Godwin became aware of the situation at the end of the first week of July. He reacted badly. Shelley was instructed to cease to call and Mary was 'talked' to – 'talk' signifying serious conversation in Godwin's diary.[29] This talk had little effect. Jane assisted Mary and Shelley by passing letters between them and their affair continued unhindered. Various accounts of this period suggest that events became rather dramatic: that Shelley burst into Skinner Street and threatened to kill himself unless Mary promised to love him for ever, and that the Godwin household was disrupted one night by a message from Shelley's landlord saying he had taken an overdose of laudanum. But these stories are recorded in mangled re-copying of the second Mrs Godwin's letters, and cannot be trusted. The events that are not in doubt are, in any case, quite theatrical enough. On 24 July 1814, a chaise bearing Shelley arrived at the corner of Skinner Street at five in the morning. Quickly and quietly, it picked up its additional passengers, and made its way along the old Roman road to Dover, from where boats departed for France. Passengers, not passenger – this was to be an elopement with a difference. There would be no marriage: Shelley was already married, and had left a wife and a baby daughter behind. And the occupants of the chaise were Shelley, Mary and her half-sister Jane.

Why was Jane in the Dover-bound chaise? There are several possible explanations. The simplest and the most convincing is that Jane was almost as dazzled by Shelley as was Mary, was thoroughly caught up in her stepsister's adventure, and in consequence refused to be left behind. She never liked to be excluded, and may well have resisted the suggestion that she should remain in England to explain Mary's disappearance to the Godwins. The prospect of returning to a penny-pinching existence in Skinner Street would, after all, not have been very attractive after the summer's excitement. It is also possible that

Shelley encouraged her to come, and that he anticipated a relationship between the three of them rather more fluid than Mary envisaged. All of them were caught up in a drama of their own making, and Shelley and Mary may have wanted an audience for their heady passion. Jane also spoke better French than the others, so her inclusion had certain practical advantages. It is certainly not the case, despite the testimony of documents redrafted by Jane in her old age, that she was duped into going with Mary – that she was tricked into entering the carriage and taken against her will to France. Probably her presence is best explained by a confluence of factors. Although they would cause much heartache in the years to come, the ties binding Mary and Jane were strong; and all three runaways were very young – too young to realise that the extent of Jane's involvement in her stepsister's affairs was emotionally and practically problematic. Shelley was twenty-one; Mary and Jane were both sixteen. And, as would rapidly become apparent, nothing about the elopement was very well thought through.

Their adventure lasted just over a month, and was characterised by intense discomfort from the outset. There were no passages to Calais to be had at Dover in any of the regular transports, so Shelley, Mary and Jane crossed the Channel in an open boat. The crossing was dangerously rough and water poured over the travellers. Mary was extremely seasick, which Shelley found rather romantic. 'She lay in my arms thro the night', he wrote in their joint diary, 'the little strength which remained to my own exhausted frame was all expended in keeping her head in rest on my bosom.'[30] Mary did not start making entries in the diary for some days, which suggests that she may have found the experience less exhilarating; but the boat eventually arrived in Calais, and the bedraggled party took rooms at an inn.

They were still in Calais twenty-fours hours later, when Mrs Godwin appeared, furious and anxious in equal measure. She promptly washed her hands of Mary, but made strenuous efforts to persuade Jane to come home with her. Jane wavered, agreed, talked to Shelley, and changed her mind, and Mrs Godwin was forced to return to England without either her daughter or stepdaughter. Having successfully disposed of their pursuer, the trio proceeded to Paris, where they discovered they had too little money to go any further. After a few days, Shelley managed to arrange a payment of £60 from his English bankers and they decided to continue on their journey through Europe. But because this was still a tiny sum of money, they opted to travel on foot.

The madness of this plan is another reminder of how young they all were. France in August 1814 was an inhospitable, dangerous place. Until the Allied entry into Paris four months earlier, much of continental Europe had been impassable for British tourists (apart from a brief period following the Treaty of Amiens) for almost two decades. Shelley, Mary and Jane were adventurous not just in their choice of transport (none) but in their determination to cross France at all. They were horrified by what they saw. 'The distress of the inhabitants', Mary wrote, 'has given a sting to my detestation of war, which none can feel who have not travelled through a country pillaged and wasted by this plague, which, in his pride, man inflicts upon his fellow.'[31] A little over twenty years earlier Mary Wollstonecraft had been in revolutionary Paris confidently awaiting the beginning of a new political dawn. Her daughter was now confronted by the bleak consequences of those revolutionary dreams: poverty, destruction, and violence.

Sobering political realities were matched by more practical problems. The donkey Shelley bought in Paris to transport their baggage proved unfit for the task. Jane was scared out of her own bed into Shelley and Mary's by rats and the overtures of an excessively friendly landlord. Shelley sprained his ankle, forcing them to hire a carriage which stretched their meagre funds badly. The driver they engaged then abandoned them, compelling them to make their own way over the Swiss border. All this made an arduous journey more difficult. Shelley was unable to walk, and Mary and Jane, who had lived most of their lives in London and were unused to the physical strains of walking day after day, found it a huge physical effort.

As they became increasingly tired, the disadvantages of eloping in a threesome became more apparent. When Shelley and Mary began a diary together, Jane responded by demanding paper so that she could start one too. Mary began to report walks taken by her and Shelley alone – without comment, but in a manner which suggests that snatched private moments were worthy of note. Jane wrote long descriptions of the scenery, interspersed with Wordsworthian meditations on the bountiful pleasures of nature. At one point Mary reported, rather cryptically, 'Shelley & Jane talk concerning J's character'[32] from which one can divine that Jane was spoken to for the good of her soul, probably because she was sulking about being left out of Shelley and Mary's private conferences and sight-seeing trips. At one point she took her revenge by taunting Mary when she refused to accede to Shelley's suggestion that they should bathe naked in a pool under the beady eye of the carriage driver. Shelley was an erratic travelling companion. One day he decided to adopt a beautiful little girl he saw on the road, and was surprised and put out when her father informed him she was not available.

By the time the trio finally crossed over into Switzerland, they had almost run out of money again. Shelley, in his indomitable way, took action. He wrote to his abandoned wife Harriet, asking her to join them on a strictly platonic basis, and to bring some money with her. He would, he promised, be her 'firm & constant friend . . . by whom your feelings will never wilfully be injured.'[33] Unsurprisingly, Harriet was not convinced by this promise, and refused to cooperate with Shelley's plans. She was pregnant with his second child, had no wish to become a member of his commune, platonic or otherwise, and did not feel inclined to courier papers and money across war-torn Europe on her errant husband's behalf. Her unaccountable failure to oblige made it impossible for them to stay in Switzerland any longer and they decided to return to England. Jane did not realise how poor they were and seems to have thought they were returning because Mary and Shelley had tired of adventurous hardship. 'Most laughable', she told her diary, 'to think of our going to England the second day after we entered a new house for six months – All because the stove don't suit.'[34] She herself had little interest in such mundane considerations as smoking stoves, and wrote a lofty dismissal of the decision in her diary. She had expected never to see 'dear England' again, and it was most disappointing to be made to leave the splendour of Switzerland just because the accommodation failed to please her bourgeois stepsister. There is something rather poignant about Jane's loftiness, which probably formed part of an attempt to dissociate herself from a decision from which she had already been excluded. It may also have allowed her to deny her own increasingly complicated feelings, which were becoming contradictory and unsettled after six weeks of being the odd one out in Shelley's company.

The trio started their homeward journey on 27 August, a month after their early morning escape from London. They travelled by water up to Germany and into Holland, and during long days on ponderous boats – which ranged from cargo packets to vessels which were little more than kayaks – they filled the hours by reading Shakespeare and Wollstonecraft, and by writing of their adventures in their diaries. At one point they amused themselves by talking against a fellow passenger, and seeing him off accordingly: 'we frightened from us one man who spoke English and whom we did not like by talking of cutting off Kings' heads.'[35] They arrived back in England on Tuesday, 13 September and were followed from Gravesend to London by one of the crew of the boat in which they had crossed from Holland, whose captain doubted their promises to return and pay up.

As they made their way towards London, all three now had to face several unpleasant facts. The first was financial. They had no money at all. When they arrived in London they had nowhere to stay and no means of getting rid of the boatman, who refused to leave their side until they paid him what they owed. Once again, in one of his more sublimely self-absorbed moments, Shelley turned to Harriet, who had moved back to her father's London house. While Mary and Jane sat outside the Westbrooks' establishment in a hackney carriage Shelley spent two hours inside with his estranged wife. He does not appear to have told her of the presence of his waiting companions, and eventually managed to convince her that she should settle his most pressing debt from the funds he had left for her. She agreed, the boatman was paid off, and Mary, Shelley and Jane were able to concentrate on the urgent business of finding lodgings for the night.

The second unpleasant reality that had to be faced was Godwin's reaction to the runaways. From the time that Shelley and Mary first told him they were in love, they had grappled with fierce paternal opposition. When they returned to London, he simply refused to see any of them. The failure of a beloved father to understand the strength of their feelings for each other would have been upsetting under any circumstances. But in *Political Justice* Godwin had made the following statement:

> Friendship, if by friendship we understand that affection for an individual which is measured singly by what we know of its worth, is one of the most exquisite gratifications, perhaps one of the most improving exercises of a rational mind. Friendship therefore may be expected to come in aid of the sexual intercourse, to refine its grossness and increase its delight. A friendship of this sort has no necessary connection with the cowardice which so notoriously characterises the present system of marriage, where each party desires to find in the other that flattering indulgence that overlooks every frailty, and carefully removes the occasions of fortitude.[36]

As far as Shelley was concerned, in leaving a wife he no longer loved to be with Mary he was simply acting in the spirit of Godwin's own philosophy and righting a wrong which occurred when Godwin himself took the cowardly step of marrying. Shelley was *living* the radical philosophy of *Political Justice*, and Godwin's ostracising of his adolescent daughters represented a terrible betrayal of both his and Godwin's ideals. Mary, meanwhile, had been brought up on a combination of *Political Justice* and Wollstonecraft's *Vindication*. Now, her beloved father was not only behaving hypocritically but was turning into the kind of oppressive patriarchal figure condemned by her mother.

Shelley's conviction that matrimony was a worthless institution also goes some way towards explaining his behaviour towards Harriet. His determination to be clear with his wife that he no longer loved her and his ardent expressions to her of his love for Mary formed part of his developing moral code. 'It would be generous', he told her, 'to consider with kindness that woman whom my judgement and my heart have selected as the noblest and the most excellent of human beings . . . My attachment to Mary neither could nor ought to have been overcome:

our spirits . . . are united. We met with passion, and she has resigned
all for me.'[37] By the late summer of 1814 Shelley genuinely believed
that in shaking off the bonds of matrimony when a relationship had
faltered he was living his life in accordance with a set of principles
which would reform the world. Moreover, he was acting as an example
to all would-be reformers. It is not surprising that Harriet did not see it
in this light. She was pregnant with Shelley's second child, and she was
receiving letters from her husband which were – no matter how fine the
philosophy underpinning them – spectacularly cruel. 'I was an idiot
to expect greatness or generosity from you', read one. 'In your heart it
seems you were always enslaved to the vilest superstitions, or ready to
accept their support for your narrow and worldly views.'[38] As an old
lady, Jane recalled one missive in response from Harriet, in which she
made a heart-rending cry for her husband's support: 'even beasts', she
had pleaded, 'stay by their kind when they are in a family way.'[39]

Mary and Jane's situation was, in some respects, almost as unenviable
as Harriet's, even though their plight was of their own making. Having
left the protection of their father, they were entirely dependent on
another man, on whom they had no legal claim. Shelley had a degree
of independence, by virtue of his sex and his position as his father's
heir. But for both Mary and Jane the practical consequences of the
elopement were potentially devastating, and bound them together in
a shared dependence on Shelley. Forced under the same roof by their
physical vulnerability, the close, sisterly relationship which sustained
them during the long years of their Godwin upbringing now began to
buckle under the strain of continued, inescapable companionship.

The problems of proximity were compounded by an isolation
which dated from the elopement. Shelley, Mary and Jane might have
crossed Europe, but they met few people on their travels. Nor did
they experience anything like the engagement with the politics of the
countries they visited demonstrated by Hunt from his prison cell in
The Examiner each week. Indeed, the further they travelled the more
inward-looking they became. It might have been fun to torment fellow
passengers with talk of cutting off the heads of kings, but this was a
poor substitute for political action.

On their return, they shuttled between temporary lodgings, and saw very few people. Chief among their limited number of callers were Thomas Hogg and Thomas Love Peacock. Throughout 1814 Peacock was in considerable sympathy with Harriet and he did his best to support her through Shelley's long absences. Perhaps for this reason, it took Mary and Jane a little while to warm to him. Shelley was also in regular contact with his bookseller, Thomas Hookham, and with various lawyers and money lenders, and Jane's brother Charles Clairmont visited occasionally. He did so in spite of a prohibition issued by Godwin, who, in addition to refusing the three admittance to his house, forbade them contact with his other children. Fanny and Charles defied him to act as illicit conduits for news from Skinner Street throughout the winter, but it caused poor Fanny considerable anxiety to disobey her step-parents. Peacock later remembered that winter as the most solitary period of Shelley's life, and it was equally so for Mary and Jane, thrown together by their exclusion from their family home.

In addition to bitter rows by letter with Harriet, money worries and estrangement from Godwin, there was another problem: seventeen year old Mary was pregnant, with a baby conceived earlier in the summer.[*] The combination of pregnancy and the vegetarian diet insisted upon by Shelley (who had praised vegetarianism in the notes to *Queen Mab*) made her ill and sleepy. As a result, Jane and Shelley spent long hours together. They sat up late at night talking about ideal communities, ghosts and spirit worlds. On one occasion Shelley spooked Jane into hysterics, and she had to be put to bed with Mary to calm her down.

---

[*] When Mary gave birth, on 22 February 1815, the child was described as a seven-months baby, but there is some doubt about this. Miranda Seymour suggests that Mary and Shelley first slept together on 27 June 1814, and the baby may have been conceived then, or shortly afterwards: 'Subsequent references by Shelley to . . . 27 June, as having been his true birthday (he was born on 4 August), suggest that this was the day on which he and Mary first made love. The discreet north-eastern corner of St Pancras churchyard would have seemed an appropriate setting, as if Mary Wollstonecraft were presiding over their union. Her grave was conveniently shaded by willows' (*Mary Shelley*, p.93). Mary's severe travel sickness during the journey to France supports this theory, as does the fact that her 'seven-months' baby survived its first few days, despite the fact that both the baby and Mary received only the most rudimentary medical care.

Shelley rather enjoyed the effects of his powers of invention on Jane;
Mary was less amused. 'Shelley and Jane sit up and for a wonder do not
frighten themselves',⁴⁰ she noted rather wryly in her diary a couple of
days later. And while Jane might have been easy to scare, she was not
easy to live with. An argument between her and Shelley caused him to
write huffily of 'Janes insensibility & incapacity for the slightest degree
of friendship'⁴¹ while Jane herself reported Mary saying seemingly
unkind things which made her feel deeply 'the imaginary cruelties I
conjured up'.⁴² As the winter drew on, Mary began to think about
finding alternative accommodation for her stepsister. But no solution
seemed to present itself and so the three of them spent their days
reading, quarrelling, sailing paper boats on the pond in Primrose Hill
and hatching mad schemes with Peacock to kidnap Shelley's younger
sisters from their school.

Any semblance of stability disappeared abruptly in mid-October
when Shelley's creditors set the bailiffs on him. In order to escape arrest
for debt he was forced to leave Mary and Jane in lodgings and to go
into hiding. He stayed with Peacock and then in a succession of dingy
hotels in the city and spent his days trying to arrange further loans and
his nights writing passionate letters to Mary. 'Know you my best Mary
that I feel myself in your absence degraded to the level of the vulgar
& impure', he told her before adding, rather coyly, 'Adieu remember
love at vespers – before sleep. I do not omit *my prayers*.'⁴³ Her letters
to him were equally heartfelt. She assured him of her love, and of her
intention never to vex him. She would learn Greek in order to please
him, she promised, noting that doing so might help her overcome her
desolation at her estrangement from her father. It all suggests that their
relationship was not exactly argument-free. For Mary – seventeen,
pregnant, impoverished, ostracised by her father, her lover in hiding
and with only a moody stepsister for company – life towards the
end of 1814 continued to look bleak. Until Shelley managed to raise
enough money to settle his debts, meetings with him were restricted to
snatched conversations on the steps of St Paul's, the occasional evening
together in a hotel, and Sundays together at home, since bailiffs were
not permitted to make arrests on the Sabbath. Shelley and Mary spent

their Sundays together in bed, getting up only to plan his movements and to eat. 'To sleep & talk', Jane noted sniffily in her diary, 'why this is merely vegetating.'[44] Jane does not seem to have taken kindly to being left alone while Mary spent evenings with Shelley, nor to being sidelined during snatched conversations in London squares. A diary entry following a meeting in Gray's Inn Gardens noting that 'I am much disappointed in Shelley to-day' is followed by a report of 'A letter from Shelley – putting all the fault of yesterday's Interview on me.'[45] Mary and Shelley's desire for privacy was natural, but it reinforced Jane's sense of emotional and physical exclusion. By the close of 1814, Shelley had become both the most fascinating and the most important person in her life, and when he disappeared with Mary, or criticised her behaviour, it mattered a great deal. Shelley might sit up late talking with Jane, and he might even enjoy the sexual frisson which stemmed from her ambivalent position in his household, but it was Mary's bed to which he retired.

Leigh Hunt spent 1814 confined to the few square yards of his prison rooms and garden, but the second year of his imprisonment was even busier than the first. As well as bringing out weekly editions of *The Examiner*, much of his time was given over to the composition of *The Descent of Liberty*, a masque (in the style of Milton's *Comus*) written to celebrate the allied victory over Napoleon in 1814. This was Hunt's first sustained attempt at representing his political views through poetry and constituted an important new development in his writing.

In *The Descent of Liberty* Hunt argued that political reform was a subject not only for the editors of newspapers but for all creative thinkers. In the 1790s, restrictions on free speech and political activity had acted as a creative spur for a whole generation of writers. This was the decade in which Wordsworth and Coleridge produced *Lyrical Ballads*, when Wollstonecraft wrote her *Vindication* and Godwin produced *Political Justice*. It was during this decade that Coleridge and Robert Southey formulated their ambitious plan for a political utopia, Pantisocracy, a society of equals to be founded in the United States.

Opposition proved fruitful for these writers, who produced their most influential and important work in a decade when they themselves were marginalised and vulnerable.

In the 1810s something similar happened to a new generation of intellectuals. *The Descent of Liberty* showed how a man who was oppressed through incarceration could reach out beyond the confines of political campaigning to find a new, literary readership, just as Shelley hoped to do in *Queen Mab*. Like *Queen Mab*, it also showed that poetry could be transformed into a vehicle for political protest. Although *The Descent of Liberty* celebrated the defeat of Napoleon, it had some strident criticisms to make of the victorious allied powers. But despite its subject – and because of its form – it was warmly received by periodicals who had previously taken very little interest in Hunt. While some of his political enemies were predictably unpleasant about his work, other commentators were quick to praise it. The *British Lady's Magazine*, not known for its support of radical journalists, was positively sentimental about him: 'Our readers will no doubt smile at the idea of a poet within the wall of a prison celebrating . . . the final triumph of Liberty, and descanting upon the blessings likely to ensue, with as much freedom and poetical spirits as if reclining at his ease upon the green bed of nature, with no other canopies than the oak and the heavens.'[46] Hunt's friends were equally complimentary. Thomas Moore thought the poem had the permanence of a portrait by Joshua Reynolds, and a joint letter to Hunt from Henry Robertson, William Havell and Charles Ollier (the last of whom would publish Shelley's work) described how they had met 'in solemn council' to read the work through. It left them, they reported, with 'such an impression of excellence on our minds . . . that we resolved thus to address you.'[47] The support and inspiration provided by Hunt's friends was crucial to the success of *The Descent of Liberty*. In it Hunt re-worked conversations with his visitors about the progress of European politics into poetry, and his letters for the winter of 1814 show that his supporters' encouragement of his literary activities sustained his creative energy and enthusiasm in less tangible ways as well.

From this point onwards Hunt increasingly used poetry as the vehicle for the expression of a political will. The effect of this was twofold. First, *The Examiner* became more eclectic and a significant number of poems sympathetic to its liberal aims began to appear in its pages. Second, Hunt's political activities ceased to be confined to the pages of *The Examiner* and began to reverberate through all areas of his literary life. These were important philosophical shifts for both newspaper and editor. Of course, there was nothing particularly original in the idea that art could be put at the service of politics. But the degree of integration envisaged by Hunt *was* new, as was the idea that a group of intellectuals, like those who contributed to the prison editions of *The Examiner*, could come from their different disciplines to work together in a way which would epitomise the ideals of reform and political resistance.

By the end of 1814, *The Examiner* was firmly established as the organ through which Hunt kept in touch with the world. Throughout the summer he had produced a series of brilliant commentaries on post-war Europe. He was dubious about the wisdom of exiling Napoleon to Elba and eyed the restoration of the Bourbons with undisguised scepticism, noting 'We confess indeed that if we could have *our* choice, we would have neither BONAPARTE nor BOURBON, whether limited in their power or not.'[48] He wrote a series of dismissive articles about the delegations of European leaders who came to London to discuss peace plans, and on the arrangements for their entertainment put in place by the Prince Regent; and provided his readers with a detailed analysis of Norway's position in the peace negotiations. He condemned the use of military torture and the Regent's ill-treatment of his daughter, Princess Charlotte of Wales, after her refusal to marry William of Orange. In the autumn he embarked on a long series of articles on the approaching Congress of Vienna, which seemed to offer an opportunity for the reformation of corrupt political systems across Europe – an opportunity which the Allied powers looked likely to squander.

As 1814 drew to a close Hunt seemed to have the whole of Europe under his gaze. No free man could have been more engaged with the cut and thrust of domestic and international politics. His sentence did not silence him as intended; instead it gave him the freedom to consolidate his thinking about the relationship between politics, literature and friendship. And throughout his sentence, his friends continued to work hard to make sure he knew he was neither deserted nor forgotten. Haydon wrote long letters from Paris when he arrived there shortly after the Peace, extracts from which were published in *The Examiner*. Charles Lamb visited regularly, sometimes struggling through rain and snow to get to Surrey Gaol, and often after he had worked long days in his office at the East India Company. Charles Cowden Clarke sent vegetables from his garden and eggs from his hens, and he too visited frequently, sometimes in the company of other members of his family. Thomas Mitchell and Thomas Barnes wrote often, as did Henry Brougham. In one such note Mitchell reassured Hunt that he thought of him whenever he opened *The Examiner*. 'I consider your paper . . . which I regularly see as a sort of weekly intercourse, & wish you could contrive in the Table Talk to introduce some kind of covert Bulletin, which unknown to the general reader, might combine to inform your absent friends of the state of your health.'[49]

The result was that by the end of his prison sentence Hunt had established 'sociability' as an important ideological principle. He did so in an experiment in living which elevated the rituals of friendship – communal dining, music making, letter writing, shared reading – so that, in Hunt's rooms in the old infirmary, these rituals took on a co-operative, oppositional significance. In *The Examiner*, such activities were given a public outlet, as conversations over dinner were rewritten in the collaborative 'Table Talk' columns, letters from friends were published and discussed in editorials, and as different members of Hunt's circle contributed theatrical and literary reviews which reflected the group's diversity as well as its coherence.

Hunt's enforced stillness pulled his friends and admirers towards him, positioning him at the centre of the group's emergent identity. The contrast with Shelley, restlessly moving about Europe and London, could hardly have been more marked. Shelley's search for companionship brought him profound isolation, which, from July 1814 onwards, he shared with Mary and Jane. But loneliness and failure did not dampen his political and philosophical ambitions, and he continued to work towards the creation of an association of ideal individuals which would match that meeting in Hunt's cell. Indeed, even as his own social circle shrank to a tiny, claustrophobic unit, Shelley remained determined to join the collegiate, literary world represented by *The Examiner*, and by Hunt and his friends. That determination would eventually bring him into contact with Hunt, even though at the end of 1814 he was too absorbed by the emotional ramifications of his domestic arrangements to seek out new acquaintances. In 1815, these arrangements would take on a further degree of complexity, postponing a meeting with Hunt still further. As Hunt passed his second Christmas in prison and Byron, after much vacillation, made his way northwards to marry his parallelogrammatical princess, Annabella Milbanke, Shelley, Mary and Jane, like Hunt and his friends before them, embarked on an experiment in living of their own.

Wives and Mistresses

'S & M talk in the morning. A note & present from Hogg to the own Maie . . . Clara & S walk to Hookhams & Westminster Abbey to Mrs Peacocks. Hogg comes in the evening',[1] wrote Shelley in the diary he shared with Mary on 1 January 1815. 'Clara' was Jane, who, over the course of the winter decided to rename herself, first Clara, and then Claire. She was tired of being plain Jane, of playing second fiddle to her brilliant elder stepsister, and her new glamorously alliterative name – 'Claire Clairmont' – signified her determination to assert herself. It was a conscious reinvention, and a sign of a new dynamic in her relationship with Shelley. While Mary remained at home, tied down by the late stages of her pregnancy, irritating Jane vanished, to be replaced by a rational, sympathetic, rather alluring Claire, who was only too happy to accompany Shelley on expeditions around London, and to talk to him for hours about his schemes for reforming the world.

On 1 January, the date of the diary entry, one such scheme – an experiment with the ideal of free love – took flight. It did so partly as a result of Jane's transformation, but also because of the presence in London of Shelley's friend Thomas Jefferson Hogg. Hogg had been expelled from Oxford alongside Shelley in the aftermath of the *Necessity of Atheism* scandal and, like Shelley, he was twenty-two at the beginning of 1815. He was serious, reserved and bookish, and had little of his friend's effortless magnetism. He was, however, more fortunate than Shelley in one respect, since he had an affectionate, sensible and practical father, who reacted to the expulsion decisively, removing his errant son back to his Durham home before enrolling him as a legal apprentice. John Hogg was concerned by his impressionable offspring's infatuation with Shelley and he seized the opportunity offered by the expulsion to separate the young men. But Hogg was not to be parted from Shelley so easily. It was only when he attempted to proposition Harriet during the Shelleys' brief 1811 residence in York that Shelley made a decisive break, which lasted until November 1812 when they met again in London.

By the end of 1814 Hogg had been admitted to the Middle Temple to train as a barrister and was living in London during the legal term. Mary and Claire were initially rather uninterested in him, but as he shook off his shyness they found him unexpectedly appealing. He had written a novel, *Memoirs of Prince Alexy Haimatoff*, an extended reverie on love, seduction and desire, and despite his lawyerly seriousness he had something of Shelley's rebelliousness. By January 1815, Hogg was spending much of his free time in their lodgings, where he would join late night talks about spirit worlds, ghosts, and 'making an Association of philosophical people'.[2]

It was perhaps predictable that Hogg should fall in love with Mary. He had some practice in losing his heart to women attached to Shelley, and Mary was beautiful and clever: a far more intriguing prospect than the conventional Harriet. Moreover, this time Shelley seemed predisposed to encourage his friend's interest. Accordingly, the little household entered into a risky emotional experiment. It would be a testing out of the Shelleyan idea that 'constancy has nothing virtuous in itself'. 'Love is free', Shelley wrote in the notes to *Queen Mab*. 'To promise for ever to love the same woman, is not less absurd than to promise to believe the same creed: such a vow, in both cases, excludes us from all enquiry.'[3]

While it is easy to view the events of January 1815 cynically, it would be short-sighted not to take Shelley's views on free love seriously. The key sentiment in the quotation from *Queen Mab* is not its denigration of monogamy, but its proposition that it excludes enquiry. Shelley wanted to push at the boundaries of monogamous relationships, but he did not wish to do so purely to satisfy his own libido. The claustrophobic community in which he found himself in January 1815 provided an ideal opportunity to test out an alternative model for human relationships. This model was not promiscuous, but neither was it wholly monogamous. The cast of experimenters must have seemed most suited to the task. Shelley and Hogg had some experience of sharing a woman before, although they had been hampered, in Shelley's view, by the deceitful way Hogg concealed his feelings for Harriet until his friend was temporarily absent, and by Harriet's distress at finding herself the object of Hogg's attentions. Since then, however, Shelley had developed his ideas about the limits of monogamy, becoming a more ardent Godwinian than Godwin himself, and Mary was no Harriet. She was an intellectual heavyweight, a disciple of Wollstonecraft who understood the value of throwing off social constraints on the behaviour of women. And Claire – well, Claire's role in the plan was rather unclear. But she undeniably evened up the numbers.

If it is important to take Shelley's pronouncements on marriage seriously, and to read them as a genuine attempt to free human behaviour from the shackles of social expectation, it is also important not to be too crude about what exactly he had in mind for his mistress and his best friend. In Mary, Claire and Hogg Shelley believed he had found three co-philosophers who understood the intellectual significance of ideal communities, an ideal first articulated in his 1811 letter to Hunt. Monogamy would only be practised if it reflected the genuine passions and desires of the parties involved, and restrictive social conventions would be ignored. Shelley's previous attempts to establish such a community had failed, but now he was surrounded by people who were all a little dazzled by the power of his convictions, and who were thus prepared to follow his lead and put his ideas into practice. The conditions in which they were living only made them more inclined to do so, for while the solitude of the winter gave Shelley time to reflect on the benefits of such an association, exile from Skinner Street predisposed Mary and Claire to align themselves with his ideals, in a gesture of filial defiance. Hogg, meanwhile, had long been willing to fall in with Shelley's wilder ideas.

On 1 January three things happened. First, Shelley and Mary talked, a fact duly recorded by Shelley in the joint diary. They did so in response to a letter from Hogg to Mary in which he declared his love for her. Then Shelley wrote a short note to Hogg telling him that 'Mary wishe[s] to speak with you alone, for which purpose I have gone out & removed Claire.'[4] Hogg did call in the evening, but if he also accepted Shelley's invitation to visit Mary alone, then she was unaware that such an invitation had been issued, and she wrote her own letter to him shortly after Shelley and Claire had left: 'As they have both left me and I am here all alone I have nothing better to do than take up my pen and say a few words to you – as I do not expect you this morning.' Her 'few words' thanked him for his expression of love, but suggested gently that she was not able to return his feelings fully. She reminded him how brief their acquaintance had been, and predicted confidently that their friendship would grow until they would be happier than the 'lovers of Janes world of perfection'. A 'bright prospect' was before them all, she told him reassuringly.[5]

Three days later, this 'bright prospect' had grown rather more luminous. Now Hogg received a missive informing him that 'Shelley & Jane are both gone out and . . . I do not expect them till very late – perhaps you can come and console a solitary lady in the mean time . . . You are so good & disinterested a creature that I love you more & more . . . but still I do not wish to persuade you to do that which you ought not.'[6] That Mary was attracted to Hogg is evident, but there is more than a straightforward come-hither in her letter. The impression given by both her correspondence with Hogg and her diary is that he provided a welcome relief from the boredom of the last months of her pregnancy. Shelley was out all day, visiting booksellers and negotiating with money lenders with the ever-faithful Claire at his side, and Mary had little to do except sit at home reading, and feel fat and unwanted. Her letter also indicates that Hogg was having more difficulty in throwing off the fetters of social convention than he cared to admit to Shelley. Shelley had encouraged a relationship between Mary and Hogg as part of a lofty experiment in ideal living, but Hogg was forced to weigh up his attraction to Mary against the deeply inculcated values of his upbringing. Harriet might have found this rather surprising, but for Hogg there was a difference between kissing his friend's wife in a moment of passion and embarking on a condoned affair with the same friend's mistress.

Nevertheless, by 7 January, the roles had reversed, and it was he who was encouraging Mary to move things forward. Now, confronted with the reality of his desires, Mary wrote to him in a slightly different vein. 'My affection for you although it is not now exactly as you would wish will I think dayly become more so . . . I ask but for time – time for which other causes besides this – phisical causes – that must be given – Shelley will be subject to these also.'[7] Her advancing pregnancy was an obvious reason to deny Hogg the kind of relationship he wanted, but there is something about Mary's letter which indicates it was not only this that caused her to prevaricate. It is possible that Hogg had become rather insistent in the few days since he and Mary began to discuss developing their friendship, and her letter does suggest that, despite her earlier protestations of affection, she remained unsure about both her own emotions and the path on which she and Hogg were embarked. Loneliness, rather than passion (philosophical or physical) motivated her to write to him on 4 January; now the prospect of dealing with that loneliness by sleeping with him was rather appalling. Philosophy aside, Mary may have found it hard to see how entering into a relationship with Hogg would draw Shelley closer to her – and it was Shelley who she wanted to relieve her loneliness; Shelley who she wanted by her side, rather than away on expeditions with Claire. She followed Shelley's lead as she invited Hogg's attention, but she did so for Shelley himself. And at some level, with a degree of insight not granted to the others, she must have realised that, philosophical protestations notwithstanding, sleeping with Hogg would only drive Shelley further away.

All the parties in this particular experiment were very young, and they were still learning how disruptive and unpredictable their own emotions could be. Some of this is evident in the final letter Mary wrote to Hogg before the birth of her baby. 'When . . . dearest Hogg I have my little baby with me what exquisite pleasure shall we pass the time – you are to teach me Italian you know & how many books we will read together but our still greater happiness will be in Shelley – I who love him so tenderly & entirely whose life hangs on the beam of his eye and whose whole soul is entirely wrapt up in him – you who have so sincere a friendship for him to make him happy.' She then broke off rather abruptly: Shelley and Claire had returned and 'are talking besides me which is not a very good accompaniment when one is writing a letter to one, one loves.'[8]

The fluctuations in Mary's feelings towards Hogg are particularly well-documented in the letters she sent him at the beginning of 1815. When we try and discover the true nature of the other important relationship in this 'Association of philosophical people' – that between Shelley and Claire – matters become more conjectural. No letters or diaries by Claire survive from this period, and Shelley's letters for the beginning of 1815 are scarce. As a result, the exact nature of their relationship during the early months of the year is puzzling. They evidently became close, especially after Claire put off her sulks with her old 'Jane' persona, and as Mary retreated to the bedroom, worn out by the strains of pregnancy and by a vegetarian diet which was probably inadequate. Mary's diary indicates that the pair spent many hours together out and about in London, and that this was an arrangement which made her feel lonely and unhappy. Shelley evidently welcomed – perhaps needed – Claire's attention. But for the period when Mary and Hogg were conducting their strange wooing of each other, there are few contemporary descriptions of the relationship between Shelley and Claire.

The best sources for this period are a series of unreliable letters, purportedly written by the second Mrs Godwin, but substantially redrafted by Claire in her old age, and these suggest that her chief attraction for Shelley may have been the constancy of her presence at his side and her willingness to acquiesce to his demands. The letters also suggest that she took considerable pride in his interest in her. She depicted herself in her drafts as an intellectual Cinderella, forced to toil over French and Italian texts, verses from Dante, and the histories of Edward Gibbon. She described how Shelley put a stop to her music, and required her to follow him around wherever he walked. Doing so got her into further trouble, she claimed, both with Shelley (because it left her with too little time to do her lessons properly), and with her jealous stepsister. Claire presented herself in these documents as naïve, and more than a little bit bullied by her tutor. Yet Shelley's bullying was presented as a sign of his interest in her, which Mary resented. And, although Claire herself might have resisted this interpretation of her papers, there is an undertow of erotic tension in her depiction of Shelley as dominant teacher and herself as submissive pupil.

The question of whether or not Shelley and Claire attempted to mimic Hogg and Mary's relationship during the early weeks of 1815 will probably always remain unresolved. A plausible argument can be made that Shelley pushed his friend and his mistress together in order to allow him to spend more time with her stepsister, but this underestimates the complexity of the philosophical and emotional issues at stake. At no stage does he appear to have actively rejected Mary in favour of Claire, and he was full of praise for his mistress in his letters to Hogg. It seems more likely that he turned to Claire briefly in search of admiration and companionship of the kind temporarily withdrawn by a housebound Mary. He would periodically turn to Claire again in the years to come, again at times when Mary, for various reasons, focused her attention elsewhere. Claire could never compete with Mary intellectually, and nor, probably, could she understand Shelley as did her stepsister, but she could accompany him on expeditions, listen to his schemes, and agree with his opinions.

For her part, Claire undoubtedly enjoyed being the object of Shelley's focus, but the episode, and its brief intensity, complicated her relationship with him, and made her presence even more disruptive for Mary. One remark made by Claire in old age also suggests that she was more alert to the damage Shelley's behaviour could do than the other evidence suggests. In one of the many notebooks in which he recorded his conversations with Claire, a retired American sailor called Edward Silsbee reported that Claire had told him of Mary coming into her room and 'putting her head on her [Claire's] pillow & crying bitterly saying Shelley wants her to sleep with Hogg – that he said Beaumont & Fletcher had one mistress.'[9] Claire's memoirs were unreliable, but this anecdote has a certain ring of authenticity about it – especially when read against the rather tortured ambivalence of Mary's letters to Hogg, and it also suggests that the costs of experiments in living were particularly high for the women involved. In the throes of a wearing first pregnancy, faced with the prospect of childbirth (and with the knowledge that her own birth had killed her mother), Mary already knew something of the physical price to be paid for free love. Faced with this realisation, and having seen her stepsister in distress, would Claire have embarked on her own precarious experiment in ideal living? It is possible that during a time of heightened emotions and insecurities Mary and Claire found themselves more in sympathy with each other than the sparse documentary record suggests.

On 22 February 1815 Mary gave birth to a girl, several weeks prematurely. Mary, Shelley reported in their diary, was 'perfectly well & at ease'; in contrast he was 'much agitated & exhausted'.[10] The baby defied expectations by surviving its first night, and for almost ten days Mary revelled in new motherhood. Shelley and Claire bustled about procuring a cradle and arranging more suitable lodgings; Fanny and Charles stole away to visit their new niece; and, in a conciliatory gesture, Mrs Godwin sent linen to keep the baby warm. But a few days later Mary awoke to find that her daughter – still unnamed – had died in the night. 'A miserable day', she wrote in her diary. Hogg was sent for, to comfort the bereaved mother and to help with arrangements for the burial. Mary was ill in the days that followed, and preoccupied by her loss. Shelley and Claire resumed their daily visits to money lenders and booksellers, and she was left alone to 'think of my little dead baby – this is foolish I suppose yet whenever I am left alone to my own thoughts & do not read to divert them they always come back to the same point – that I was a mother & am so no longer.'[11] It was Fanny who came through the rain to keep her younger sister company, and who defied Godwin's prohibition to do so.

On the surface, life settled quickly back into its usual patterns. Mary continued to stay at home while the others jaunted about town, tied down now by the lethargy of grief, rather than by an advancing pregnancy. Their days were still characterised by reading, talking, and by Shelley's endless financial negotiations. Hogg continued to haunt their lodgings, although he was sufficiently sensitive not to renew his sexual attentions to a grieving Mary. Mary herself now found the constant presence of Claire increasingly difficult to bear. Claire had not lost a child, and was able to continue her daily activities as cheerfully and as alluringly as ever. Before the death of her baby, Mary was able to cope with the petty trials of communal living; now her resilience was gone. The confidence she had shown in her early dealings with Shelley disappeared, and she became increasingly worried by the stability of her relationship with him and by his continuing interest in Claire.

Claire, on the other hand, was in many respects unchanged from the idealistic adolescent whom Shelley had met the previous summer. She was, if anything, more vivacious and confident, and, perhaps because of this, Mary came to view her as the symbol of all that was wrong with her life. Claire was no longer the supportive sibling, prepared to stand by her stepsister as she battled with Mrs Godwin, or eloped to France. Instead, she was a threatening presence who undermined Mary's relationship with Shelley. If she could be got rid of, then Mary and Shelley would have time to learn how to live with each other, unhampered by emotional distractions. Godwin's memoir of Wollstonecraft had described how their friendship had slowly matured into love, and how they came together with their eyes open, fully aware of the quirks and difficulties of character which made successful cohabitation a thing to be worked at, an ideal to be achieved. Mary knew her father's account of her mother's life intimately, and must have been struck at the contrast between her parents' relationship and the messy triangle in which she found herself. If it was even remotely possible that Shelley was slipping away from her, then there was an obvious solution. Claire had to go.

But go where? In mid-March, Mary re-opened conversations with Shelley about the possibility of finding alternative lodging for Claire. Shelley was reluctant to see her depart, although he understood Mary's desire for privacy, and he realised that they could not continue to live as a trio indefinitely. However, Claire refused to return to Godwin's house in Skinner Street, and so, Mary noted mournfully, 'our house is the only remaining place'.[12] Even if Claire had been prepared to return home, she might not have been welcome. Fanny's Wollstonecraft aunts

– her sole blood relatives – had a long-standing agreement with Godwin that they would take Fanny on as an assistant at the school they ran in Ireland once she was old enough to leave home. But their business suffered when Godwin's explicit memoir of their sister appeared, and they were well aware that recent events in Skinner Street could prove equally damaging to Fanny's (and their) reputation. While the Godwins refused to acknowledge the existence of their errant daughters, Fanny's good name might be maintained, but if Claire were to be readmitted to the family, this would suggest that her parents implicitly condoned her behaviour. In that case, Fanny's place in Ireland would have to be forfeited, since neither of the Wollstonecraft sisters could risk any more gossip about their already scandalous name. For Fanny's sake, both Claire and Mary had to be kept out of the family home. Since the options for Fanny's future were already severely limited, no one could afford to jeopardise her one prospect of respectable employment.

So Claire lingered on with Mary and Shelley. As winter turned to spring Mary's mood began to lift, and the round of daily events recorded in her diary became a little more light-hearted. With Hogg and Peacock, they spent afternoons making paper boats and sailing them, no longer on the pond at Primrose Hill, but on the wider expanses of the Serpentine. Claire and Shelley bought lottery tickets; Mary went to the British Museum with Hogg. Shelley opened up a fragile line of communication with Harriet, and a slightly more robust communication channel, established after the birth of the baby, remained open with Skinner Street. Although Godwin still refused to see any of them, the ban on Fanny and Charles visiting seems to have been quietly lifted, and they called several times in March and April. Shelley was locked in a legal dispute with his father about the arrangements for his inheritance, but despite this, and because of a new threat from the bailiffs, at the end of April he and Mary disappeared out of London, on a short excursion of their own. They spent a few nights in an inn in Salt Hill, now a suburb of Slough. Claire was left to look after their lodgings, and Hogg was not informed of their plans.

It was the first time Mary and Shelley had spent any significant time alone together, and Mary's correspondence with Hogg show that it made her much happier. She loved being in the country, and a few days alone with Shelley, during which they conceived a second baby, instilled in her a new confidence about the future. Her letters to Hogg suggest that the emotional turmoil of the past few months had begun to recede, and that greater security in her relationship with Shelley enabled her to respond to Hogg's renewed declarations of affection for her with more equanimity. Signing herself 'Runaway Dormouse' (Dormouse because she had spent most of the winter in bed), she sketched in their activities: 'Rain has come after a mild beautiful day but Shelley & I are going to walk . . . How delightful it is to read Poetry among green shades.' On their final day away she wrote cheerfully of their return: 'We shall try to get a place in the mail which comes into London about seven so you must rise early to receive the Dormouse all fresh from grubbing under the oaks.'[13] Even their perennial lack of money could not disturb her happiness. Hogg was directed, rather insouciantly, to 'send us some money as I do not think we shall have quite enough.'

In mid-May, Shelley finally reached an agreement with his father about his finances. He was given enough money to cover his debts and to permit him to settle some of Godwin's obligations, and an annual allowance of £1,000 a year was made over to him, out of which he agreed to award Harriet a separate allowance of £200 per year. It is one of the more remarkable features of Godwin's behaviour in the months following the elopement that he continued to demand money from Shelley even as he refused to admit either him or Mary and Claire to his house, and it is also considerably to Shelley's credit that he continued to provide financial support in return.[14] Financial security had manifold advantages. The threat of the bailiffs disappeared, and it became possible to pay for alternative accommodation for Claire. Since she could not return to Skinner Street, Shelley arranged for her to lodge in Lynmouth, the village where he and Harriet had stayed some years previously. On the eastern end of the North Devon coast, Lynmouth was far away enough even for Mary. Claire and Shelley spent a last day together, reported caustically by Mary. 'S. goes out with his friend . . . S. & the lady walk out . . . S. & his friend have a last conversation.' She had actually written 'S. & his friend indulge in a last conversation' but with Claire's departure imminent was able to cross this out and make a suitably magnanimous substitution.[15] The next day Claire was sped on her way by Shelley, who stayed out all afternoon after seeing her on to the coach. This made Mary anxious and she was relieved when he returned a little after 6 p.m. 'The business is finished', she wrote. 'I begin a new journal with our regeneration.'[16]

On 5 February 1815, readers of *The Examiner* picked up their Sunday papers to learn of the 'Departure of the proprietors of this paper from prison'. 'The first draught of free air', Hunt told his readers, 'may be allowed to make one a little giddy . . . there is a feeling of space and airy clearness about every thing, which is alternately delightful and painful.'[17] John Keats, an apothecary's apprentice and a friend of Charles Cowden Clarke, was moved by the release of Hunt (whom he had never met) to produce a sonnet, 'Written on the Day That Mr Leigh Hunt Left Prison', which imagined its subject 'free/ As the sky-searching lark, and as elate' straying 'In Spencer's halls . . . and bowers fair'.[18]

Keats was not the only aspiring poet to celebrate the end of the Hunt brothers' incarceration, and Hunt emerged from his prison cell a hero for a new generation of thinkers and writers. He had survived a vindictive punishment, and had ensured that his newspaper survived too. In fact, his newspaper not only survived but thrived and grew, as its editor's imprisonment brought it new readers and new writers eager to be part of its success. Nor was the continuation of *The Examiner* Hunt's only achievement during his stay in Surrey Gaol. He had completed *The Descent of Liberty*, embarked on a new long poem and consolidated his position as one of the country's leading liberal commentators.

There is no doubt that for Hunt the public man – editor, poet and friend of the liberal great and good – the months following his release in 1815 were a vindication. *The Examiner* became ever more self-consciously collegiate, with poems by Charles Lamb celebrating the beauty of Hunt's children, as well as articles by Hazlitt, Haydon and other Hunt admirers. Hunt's political writing was injected with a new level of urgency by Napoleon's escape from Elba, which also proved how right he had been to query the merits of sending him there in the first place. *The Descent of Liberty* was applauded in the press. Hazlitt arranged for the publication of *The Round Table*, a collection of essays co-authored with Hunt. Letters and volumes of poetry were exchanged with Wordsworth, who was both fourteen years older than the thirty year old Hunt and far more famous than any of Hunt's friends. Wordsworth called on Hunt in the summer of 1815 in the company of Benjamin Haydon, who was a fascinated witness to a meeting in which Hunt paid Wordsworth 'the highest compliments, & told him that as he grew wiser & got older he found his respect for his powers & enthusiasm for his genius encrease . . . I never saw him so eloquent as today.'[19] Haydon was himself a regular visitor, and he and Hunt spent long evenings arguing about the conduct of Napoleon and Wellington.

But in private the story was different. For two years, Hunt had been immured in a contained, even cosy space. His food and books were procured for him, his friends came to him, tradesmen's bills languished unpaid (after all, when one was already in prison, the consequences of debt were not so very serious). But on his release, he was expected to fend for himself and his family once more. The first step was to find somewhere to live. Hunt spent the first few days of his freedom staying with a friend near Surrey Gaol, but by the end of February the whole family were ensconced in lodgings in Maida Vale, a new development in west London. These lodgings were just round the corner from the house where John Hunt had installed his family, and Hunt movingly described his reunion with his brother in *The Examiner*. But the transition from Surrey Gaol to Maida Vale brought with it its own problems. The fine which both Hunts were required to pay proved crippling, and plunged Leigh into a spiral of debt on his release. As a result he now found himself living in cramped quarters (the fine made it impossible for him to rent a house) with his wife, his sister-in-law Bess, and his three children, Thornton, John and Mary. Marianne and Bess's cousin, Virtue Kent, also stayed with them intermittently.

Lack of space, however, was the least of Hunt's worries. For two years his world had consisted of two rooms and a small garden. On his release from prison he was overcome by agoraphobia. The crowded London streets terrified him. The sheer density of human bodies was shocking, and the cacophony of carriages and shouting barrow boys was as strange and dissonant as the sound of keys turning in locks had been two years before. The roads of Maida Vale were at least quieter than those of Southwark, but this didn't make it any easier for him to venture into central London and he was unable to resume his theatrical reviews or to visit his friends.

Agoraphobia narrowed Hunt's perspective on the world, which led in its turn to a shrinking of his ambition and his professional prospects. He seemed to age in the period following his release, and to lose some of the youthful fearlessness and optimism which characterised his earlier writing. The confidence he had gained from his triumphant imprisonment gave way to a new degree of vulnerability, which hampered his rhetorical and literary abilities. Since his family's financial survival depended on his ability to make *The Examiner* a success, this turn of events was particularly worrying.

Hunt set about re-establishing himself outside of prison by creating a space in which to work. Just as he had turned his cell in Surrey Gaol into a refuge from the horrors of prison life, he transformed one room in his new lodgings into a study which bore a startling resemblance to his prison bower. The books, busts, flowers and the piano were transported across London and installed in Hunt's new cocoon. He had the walls draped with green and white wallpaper and the furniture reupholstered to match. His new room was lily- rather than rose-themed, but in all other respects it was similar to his prison accommodation. His friends gathered around him, as he maintained the stillness of the previous two years. Everybody was remarkably understanding about the need to travel up to Maida Vale to help Hunt through his recovery – even Wordsworth, who by rights should have been visited by Hunt, as befitted his superior reputation, age and social status. Hunt sat in his green and white room drinking tea, entertaining his friends and writing his *Examiner* editorials. Nestled in a small, colourful space it was almost possible to trick himself into believing that he remained in prison, immured from the responsibilities and demands of freedom.

Hunt's study allowed him to maintain an illusion of continuity and safety, but the extensive redecoration inflated the housekeeping bills. Tucked away from the frightening outside world, he tried to focus on his writing rather than on domestic problems. But his fine made this impossible, as money worries now began to sour his relationships with people who had previously been supportive. His publishers, Gale and Fenner, tried to call in a loan, and received a stern rebuff. He was forced to make humiliating requests for money. Henry Brougham received a rather tortured letter in which Hunt conceded, 'You have seen me in the character of a lofty refuser of money: – I now come to you in a very different one.' He was indeed in an unenviable situation: in order to raise the funds to pay his fine and secure his release from prison, he had taken out a loan against the profits of *The Story of Rimini*, the long poem on which he was now working. But worries about money and the near breakdown which seems to have followed his release stopped him from finishing *Rimini*, and thus prevented him from realising the sums he had borrowed. Little wonder that he confessed to Brougham, 'when I was in prison, [I] longed for liberty; & now I am at liberty, it has almost renewed my prison.'[20]

Marianne was not a competent housekeeper but she was now operating in difficult circumstances. On the one hand, every new purchase and every food bill plunged the household further into debt. On the other, there were at least three adults and three children to feed, and the constant need to entertain friends exacerbated the problem. But the presence of friends was crucial to Hunt's rehabilitation, and to his ability to make any kind of living. Imprisoned in the house by his own mental fragility, he relied on visitors to bring him news of European events, to report on the theatre and parliamentary gossip. Hunt depended on his friends in less tangible, more creative ways too. It was their encouragement which had led to the completion of *The Descent of Liberty* while he was in prison, and he needed supportive friends to help him overcome the difficulties of finishing and publishing *The Story of Rimini*. In this instance, the necessary aid was provided by Byron, who was a faithful and regular visitor throughout the spring and summer of 1815. Indeed, Byron seemed to find Hunt's flowery study more appealing than his own grand home.

Visitors to Maida Vale would find him in Hunt's lodgings – flirting
with Bess, drinking tea in a green and white chair, riding Thornton's
magnificent rocking horse – while his new wife waited for him in the
carriage outside.

———

It was evident to all who saw them that the Byrons' marriage had soured
quickly. What was less obvious to casual acquaintances was that it started
badly too. Byron and Annabella were married on 1 January (the same
day on which Mary and Hogg embarked on their wooing of each other)
in the drawing room at Seaham, Annabella Milbanke's parental home.
Annabella wanted a large wedding, but her bridegroom insisted on a
private service and the only guests were the bride's parents and governess,
the vicar of Seaham and Byron's best man, John Cam Hobhouse.
Hobhouse was relieved that the wedding had gone off smoothly, since
Byron's demeanour on the journey north was hardly that of an eager
lover. Once the service was over, bride and groom departed for their
honeymoon at Ralph Milbanke's Yorkshire estate, Halnaby Hall. There
were no independent witnesses to their first journey together, and they
later gave distinctly different accounts of their conversation.

   When Annabella came to record her version of events, a little over a
year later, she recalled how 'as soon as we got into the carriage [Byron's]
countenance changed to gloom & defiance . . . He also told me that
one of his great objects in marrying me "though I said nothing of this
before" was to triumph over those who had pretended to my hand,
adding that there was no glory in gaining a mere woman of the world,
but "to *outwit* such a woman as you is something".'[21] According to
Annabella, the journey got worse and worse. At an inn on the road her
new husband 'turned to me with a bitter look & said, "I wonder how
much longer I shall be able to keep up *the part I have been* playing."'[22]
By the time they reached Halnaby he was abusing her mother and
attacking the size of his new bride's dowry.[23]

   Byron would later fiercely rebut Annabella's version of events,
claiming that he was 'put in the sulks' by the presence of Annabella's
maid in the carriage,[24] although both Hobhouse and Annabella

insisted that no one else travelled with them. Annabella's memoirs are, however, not much more reliable, since they had a specific function: to discredit Byron and to force him into agreeing to a separation and into relinquishing his claim on their daughter. But, regardless of which account one chooses to believe, it is clear that the start of the Byrons' marriage was anything but happy.

For this, both parties were to blame. In marrying Annabella, Byron allowed himself to be drawn into a relationship with a woman who fascinated him, but to whom he had little emotional attachment. His marriage to Annabella was a way of legitimising his position, of fending off the attentions of Lady Caroline Lamb, and of fulfilling his responsibilities to his name. He and Augusta had reached an impasse: she would not leave her husband, and neither of them was able to announce their relationship to the world. Perhaps Byron thought that with a wife established in his home, Augusta would be able to visit more easily; or perhaps he thought that his marriage would provide both him and Augusta with the opportunity they needed to end a relationship which, no matter how loving, could only be destructive and dangerous. Whatever the reason, he knelt in the drawing room at Seaham as a reluctant bridegroom, who had told Hunt just after his engagement that he was 'in all the misery of a man in pursuit of happiness'.[25]

It was not, however, as if he was marrying a woman who was head-over-heels in love with him. Annabella was the eldest daughter of Ralph and Judith Milbanke, and she met Byron during her second London season. Her decision to invite and to accept a second proposal of marriage from him in the autumn of 1814 seems to have stemmed from a variety of factors. She had not received other suitable offers; Byron was an aristocrat (and a mysterious poetic one to boot) and she thought she could reform the elements in his character which she found objectionable. But she was nevertheless uneasy about her engagement, telling a friend that she hoped 'you will rely more on the opinion which we have had <u>reason</u> to form than on the vague prejudices of the world.'[26] Her confident assumption that Byron would prove reformable was disastrous. Even allowing for exaggeration on her part, it is evident that the weeks spent at Halnaby for what Byron termed their 'treaclemoon'[27] were nightmarish for both of them. Annabella claimed that Byron refused to share the marital bed with her, that he greeted her the morning after their wedding night 'repellently, and uttered words of blighting irony: It is too late now. It is done and cannot be undone.' She described him pacing up and down the gallery at night with his dagger drawn, threatening suicide and cursing their marriage.[28] And she claimed he spent their time together dropping mysterious hints about the infamy of his past behaviour and in extravagant praise of Augusta.

By the time the Byrons returned to London their marriage was falling to pieces. In the early summer of 1815 Augusta arrived in London to take up an appointment as lady-in-waiting to Queen Charlotte, and stayed with her half-brother and sister-in-law at their ruinously expensive home in Piccadilly Terrace. The hellish scenes of the honeymoon were repeated with increasing frequency. Annabella, who fulfilled her wifely duty by becoming pregnant immediately after her marriage, later reported that she was driven to the edge of insanity by the constant presence of both Byron and Augusta: 'I must not . . . omit to state that my feelings were once – in London – so worked up by the continual excitement of horrible ideas . . . that in a moment when one of them became to my imagination *a fact* – I turned round to use a deadly weapon lying by – not against him, but against one whose treachery seemed at that instant revealed.'[29]

With tensions running so high, it is little wonder that Byron escaped with increasing frequency to Hunt's lily-themed study. The subject of their conversations, however, cannot have helped to dampen down the feverish atmosphere at Piccadilly Terrace. Byron and Hunt met several times over the summer to talk about Hunt's poem, *The Story of Rimini*. The poem retold the tragic romance of Dante's Paolo and Francesca, the brother and sister-in-law lovers of Canto V of the *Inferno*. On publication it was condemned for its celebration of incest, even though the relationship between its protagonists was no closer than that between Hunt and Bess. Byron made comments on the manuscript of *Rimini*, suggested cuts, and queried some of Hunt's more verbose expressions,[30] and in return Hunt dedicated the poem to him. Throughout their joint work on the *Rimini* manuscript, Hunt displayed a characteristic combination of condescension and neediness. At one point he thanked Byron for his suggestions and informed him that 'I shall avail myself of the objecting ones for alteration in some instances, and if I do not do so in the greater number, you will do me justice enough to believe that it is not from mere vain rejection, but in vindication of a theory which I have got on the subject.'[31]

Byron was a touchy and difficult man, and it is perhaps surprising that he put up with Hunt's manner so patiently. There were, however, rewards for doing so. Byron had always found Hunt's domestic ménage fascinating. At Surrey Gaol his hostess had been either Bess or Marianne, but now both sisters were living in cramped conditions under the same roof, sharing responsibility for looking after Hunt and the children. It was no coincidence that once work on *Rimini* was complete Byron began his own celebration of incest in *Parisina*, written during the second half of 1815, and both *Rimini* and *Parisina* suggest that Hunt and Byron found the presence in their households of Bess and Augusta intellectually stimulating and erotically suggestive. One wonders what Annabella made of it all. At one point, she seized upon the manuscript of *Rimini*, which was at Piccadilly Terrace while Byron edited it, and copied out Hunt's description of a difficult husband, perhaps to console herself with the thought that other women suffered as she did. 'He kept no reckoning with his sweets and sours;/ He'd hold a sullen countenance for hours'[32] must have read as an all too accurate description of Byron himself.

As 1815 progressed, however, the opportunities for intimate discussions in Maida Vale receded. By May, Hunt's health was so bad he was forced to apologise to his readers for the meagre matter of *The Examiner*, and the restoration of the Bourbon monarchy led to a series of gloomy editorials about the way in which the European powers had squandered their post-Waterloo chance for reform. In the autumn the Hunts moved from Maida Vale to Hampstead, and while the move had a beneficial effect on Hunt's agoraphobia, the transition from lodgings to house did nothing to alleviate the pressing money problems which were now dominating family life. By the end of the year, Hunt's literary and political reputation was as glorious as it ever would be. But in his private life, money, an ever-increasing family and tensions between a newly pregnant Marianne and her sister combined with his own ill health to make life out of gaol more difficult than it had been during his imprisonment.

With Claire safely in Lynmouth, and with their financial worries alleviated, Shelley and Mary were free to do as they pleased. They disappeared from London and embarked on a tour of the West Country, although their precise movements in the early summer of 1815 are not known. Shelley was unwell at one stage and as a result they certainly spent some time in London, where he sought the advice of Sir William Lawrence, an eminent physician who would become a trusted friend. Lawrence's calm good sense exercised a beneficial influence over Shelley, who suffered from periodic and debilitating abdominal pain. Since he was predisposed to hypochondria, this made him intensely anxious. He was also experiencing consumption-like symptoms, and believed the disease would kill him. But by midsummer his health had recovered sufficiently to enable him to make plans for the future, and he began looking for a suitable home for him, Mary, and the baby due to be born at the end of the year.

In August, Shelley's house-hunting produced a result, and he and Mary installed themselves in a rented house near Windsor. Their new home was a snug, square little building in the hamlet of Bishopsgate, at the eastern entrance to Windsor Park, and it was larger and more comfortable than the London lodgings they had shared with Claire. For the first time in their life together they had a house to themselves, and the move – and a second pregnancy – signified a new level of permanence in their relationship. A pattern of reading, writing and talking was established. Hogg visited intermittently, and there was no Claire to disturb the peace and quiet. Mary's letters from this period do not survive, but in her biographical notes to Shelley's poems, published in 1839, she described the 'several months of comparative health and tranquil happiness'³³ of their Bishopsgate residence. Shelley's friend Thomas Love Peacock had moved to the Georgian village of Marlow, and he frequently made the long walk along the Thames to Bishopsgate, staying for several nights at a time with Shelley and Mary. In relaxed, congenial circumstances, Mary and Peacock gradually grew to like each other, a process made easier by their mutual respect for the other's intellect.

At twenty-nine, Peacock was seven years older than Shelley, and, since their meeting in 1812, had become a close friend and adviser to the younger man. He was a poet of some repute and a brilliant – and entirely self-taught – classical scholar, who exercised a powerful influence over Shelley's reading of Latin and Greek texts. He had no independent income, however, and was struggling to maintain both himself and his elderly mother on his literary earnings. But, like Harriet and Godwin, he was a beneficiary of Shelley's financial negotiations with his father and, from 1815 onwards, accepted an annuity from Shelley of £120 per year to act as his agent and business adviser. The annuity enabled Peacock to establish a permanent home in Marlow and over the course of the winter Mary came to value his energy and his robust practical streak, both of which did much to stir Shelley out of melancholic brooding on his health.

Peacock persuaded Shelley to give up his diet of bread, butter, and 'a sort of spurious lemonade'[34] and to start eating meat again, which helped to improve his pallid complexion. He offered the young couple a certain level of practical protection from their creditors, as he assumed responsibility for Shelley's financial negotiations. He was frequently sceptical about some of Shelley's wilder ideas and he acted as a calming influence, introducing a new element of domestic equilibrium into their previously turbulent life together. And his presence brought a new level of focus to the household's joint reading, as he directed their attention towards the classical texts he had taught himself to love. He came to realise that Mary was a more suitable partner for Shelley than Harriet, and that she contributed a great deal to his happiness. This did not alter that fact that he felt Harriet had been treated very badly, but he did concede that 'Shelley's second wife was intellectually better suited to him than his first.' He also understood how important her support was to Shelley, noting 'that a man, who lived so totally out of the ordinary world and in a world of ideas, needed such an ever-present sympathy more than the general run of men.'[35]

The benefits of Peacock's friendship with Shelley and Mary

were reciprocal. While he provided them with practical and moral support, they repaid him by welcoming his presence at their fireside and including him in their conversations and literary pursuits. For the first time in his life, Peacock found himself part of a circle from which he could draw both emotional and intellectual support. The fruits of this became apparent in the second half of 1815 as he finished *Headlong Hall*, the first of the satirical works which would make his name. *Headlong Hall* and the novels which followed it were comedic arguments, in which plot was made subservient to debate and dialogue.[36] The conversations of this period would be played out and reworked in Peacock's subsequent novels, *Melincourt* and *Nightmare Abbey*, both of which simultaneously celebrated and criticised the friends from whom he derived his inspiration.

Peacock opened Shelley and Mary's eyes to the beauty of the Buckinghamshire countryside, and to the intellectual and aesthetic possibilities of Thames-side living. In his 1810 poem, *The Genius of the Thames*, he had explicitly linked the river with politically reformist ideals. The Thames was the place 'Where peace, with freedom hand-in-hand,/ Walks forth along the sparkling strand/ And cheerful toil, and glowing health/ Proclaim a patriot nation's wealth.'[37] Such ideas were most inspiring, and they had a powerful effect on Mary's stepbrother, Charles Clairmont, who visited Bishopsgate shortly after Shelley and Mary's arrival there. Charles was a pleasant twenty year old, brimming over with ideas for his future, all of which involved substantial funding from Shelley. This could be trying and Peacock took Charles off on day-long walks by the river in order to give Shelley and Mary some time alone. Charles was delighted by his new surroundings, and in mid-September the combination of his infectious enthusiasm, Peacock's expertise and Shelley's restless energy prompted the group to embark on a boating expedition up the Thames. They acquired a sturdy open boat which the three young men rowed in turn while Mary sat demure in the prow, admiring the shifting scenery.

As they rowed they discussed history, literature and politics with the eager conviction of the principled young. A flavour of their conversation survives in a letter Charles later wrote to Claire. He recounted a day spent wandering through the quadrangles and winding streets of Oxford, during which they visited Shelley's old rooms at University College. Charles's account suggests they worked themselves up into a fine frenzy about the behaviour of the university authorities: 'We visited the very rooms where the two noted Infidels Shelley & Hogg . . . poured with the incessant & unwearied application of an Alchemyst over the artificial & natural boundaries of human knowledge; brooded over the perceptions which were the offspring of their villainous & imprudent penetration & even dared to threaten the World with the horrid & diabolical project of telling mankind to <u>open its eye</u>.'[38] Charles's images are strikingly similar to those which would appear in *Frankenstein*. Mary was evidently listening carefully, filing away snippets of conversation for future use.

After Oxford they rowed further upstream to Lechlade where, buoyed by their success, they hatched grand plans for continuing up to the source of the Thames, and then into Wales and up to the Lake District. More practical considerations prevented this: the fee for passing through the Severn Canal was £20, and the river became so shallow they were obliged to lift the boat out of the water and turn around. 'We have all felt the good effects of this jaunt', Charles reported, 'but in Shelley the change is quite remarkable; he has now the ruddy healthy complexion of the autumn upon his countenance, & he is twice as fat as he used to be.'[39]

For the first time in two years, Shelley had enough time and money to write for sustained periods. In the autumn of 1815, he embarked on his most ambitious poetic project since *Queen Mab*, completed some three years previously. This was *Alastor; or, the Spirit of Solitude*, a poem which demonstrated a new level of intellectual maturity in its writer. *Alastor* is a less angry poem than *Queen Mab*, but it presents its complicated arguments with a virtuosic subtlety absent from the earlier work. It tells the story of a poet who leaves his home to wander the world. His visionary meanderings end in his death – a death mourned by nature, and by the poetic voice who relates his fate.

In the Preface, also written that autumn, Shelley described how *Alastor* 'represent[ed] a youth of uncorrupted feelings and adventurous genius led forth by an imagination inflamed and purified through familiarity with all that is excellent and majestic.'[40] But, he continued, 'the picture is not barren of instruction to actual men. The Poet's self-centred seclusion was avenged by the furies of an irresistible passion pursuing him to speedy ruin.' *Alastor* was thus, at one level, an indictment of selfish solitude: 'those who love not their fellow-beings, live unfruitful lives, and prepare for their old age a miserable grave.' But Shelley's announcement of the centrality of human sympathy is complicated by a simultaneous acknowledgement that the 'power which strikes the luminaries of the world with a sudden darkness and extinction' also awakens them 'to too exquisite a perception of its influences.' Thus, although it involves the abnegation of community, those who seek truth are endowed with both knowledge and a powerful intensity of perception. Even though the poet-wanderer of *Alastor* has rejected all human contact, his death is still mourned, both by the narrator and by nature itself:

> It is a woe too 'deep for tears', when all
> Is reft at once, when some surpassing Spirit,
> Whose light adorned the world around it, leaves
> Those who remain behind, not sobs or groans,
> The passionate tumult of a clinging hope;
> But pale despair and cold tranquillity,
> Nature's vast frame, the web of human things,
> Birth and the grave, that are not as they were.

Alastor reflected a dilemma which was beginning to formulate itself in Shelley's mind, and which would preoccupy him, in one form or another, from this point onwards. This was a dilemma of solitude and sociability, about whether the poet needed companionship or isolation in order to produce great work. In *Alastor* Shelley was influenced by Wordsworth (whose *Ode on Intimations of Immortality* provided the source for too 'deep for tears'), and his Lake poet contemporaries. He was reacting to the disappointments of both post-Waterloo Europe, and to the inability of the first generation of Romantic poets to respond to the final failure of the French Revolution represented by the Bourbon restoration. Wordsworth, Coleridge and Southey had betrayed their youthful radicalism and had retreated into solitude and political apostasy, only to re-emerge as puppets of a corrupt administration. Shelley parodied their solitary solipsism through the figure of the self-absorbed poet-wanderer, while demonstrating the importance of poetic influence, in his self-conscious indebtedness to Wordsworth's early poetry. *Alastor* showed too the influence of Peacock – who suggested its title – and Mary, with whom Shelley discussed Wordsworth's failures. It was Mary who recorded the scathing reading note on Wordsworth's *Excursion* in her diary: 'much disappointed – He is a slave.'[41] And the circumstances of the poem's composition supported its argument: Shelley was able to write again when he was settled among close friends and intellectual kindred spirits. And yet – could a poet really achieve greatness supported by others? Didn't the development of powers of intense perception ultimately involve a rejection of society? Wasn't the search for knowledge in the end a solitary one? *Alastor* asked all these questions, and refused to answer any of them.

By the end of 1815, *Alastor* was complete. The autumn had been highly productive and for the first time, Shelley had succeeded in gathering a harmonious community of kindred spirits about him. The Bishopsgate version of this community was less avowedly political than the ideal communities of his imagination, but it provided him with an opportunity to think seriously about how poetry might provide a more subtle and philosophically ambitious vehicle for reforming the world than campaigning political prose. Buoyed by the support of his friends, in January 1816 he sent *Alastor* to John Murray, and asked him to become his publisher. His request met with instant rejection: Murray was quite uninterested in publishing *Alastor*, the work of a young man who had previously produced only the scandalous *Queen Mab*.

Leigh Hunt, who also sent work to Murray in January 1816, had more success, and a reluctant Murray was persuaded by Byron to publish *The Story of Rimini*. The difference in the fortunes of Hunt and Shelley was the direct result of Byron's patronage, since Murray would never have agreed to publish Hunt's work without Byron's persuasion. Byron's friendship provided Hunt with powerful literary support, something notable by its absence from Shelley's life. But this balance of power, and the role played by Byron in the lives of Shelley and Hunt, was about to change dramatically. The catalyst for this change would be Claire.

3

Sisters

Claire put on a brave face about her expulsion to Devon, maintaining in her letters that she lived in a state of 'constant tranquillity'.[1] Lynmouth was a 'dear little spot' and Claire was 'enraptured' by her escape from the 'turmoil of passion and hatred' created by Shelley and Mary's elopement. 'I am perfectly happy', she boasted to Fanny. She lived in a cottage covered in jasmine and honeysuckle, the countryside was full of delightful walks, and the town's gentleman landowners were absent from their homes – and so, Claire's letters suggested, could not disturb her peace by falling in love with her. Poor Fanny, still trapped in Skinner Street, could have been forgiven if Claire's enthusiastic descriptions of her peaceful life made her envious. It seemed as if Claire had once again fallen on her feet when she abandoned Shelley and Mary's cramped lodgings in favour of a charmed existence by the sea.

This was certainly the reaction Claire hoped for from her sisters, but the reality of her situation was rather different. Perched on the coast, cut off inland by the high ground of Exmoor, Lynmouth was little more than a fishing village, and Claire was a stranger to the area. Shelley and Harriet had lived in Lynmouth for a few months in 1812, and it is likely that Shelley arranged bed and board for Claire with the landlady who previously housed him. But he did no more than attend to her basic needs and, once she arrived, Claire was left to fend for herself. She had little to do except sew and read, and letters took weeks to arrive. It is not surprising that, in spite of the honeysuckle covered cottage, in later life she burned with resentment at the way she had been treated. 'Hatred and persecution let loose their destroying hounds upon me in the very dawn of life', she told Mary in 1835. 'But a mere child I was driven from all I loved into a solitary spot . . . day after day I sat companionless upon that unfrequented sea-shore, mentally exclaiming, a life of sixteen years is already too much to bear.'[2] Long days alone by the sea gave Claire plenty of time to contemplate the events of the previous year, and the predicament in which she now found herself. She envied Mary her relationship with Shelley and the life she had with him; but she had no wish to share Shelley with her stepsister. The emotional peril of attaching herself too closely to Mary and Shelley was all too evident. As a result, Claire seems to have decided that once she left Devon, she would arrange matters very differently.

Claire's movements in the second half of 1815 are something of a mystery, with the exception of a brief period in October when she travelled to Ireland with her brother Charles. At the beginning of 1816, however, she was finally permitted to rejoin Shelley and Mary in order to assist at the birth of Mary's baby – a healthy little boy, named William, after his grandfather. But shortly after William's birth she left the Shelleys and appears to have established herself in separate lodgings in London. She had learnt the hard way that a dependent sister was all too likely to be used, had no control over her own destiny and no way of forging an independent existence. She was determined not to put herself in such a position again.

———

Had she known Claire, Bess Kent might have sympathised with her predicament. In January 1816, Bess too was living with her sister and a brother-in-law to whom she was uncomfortably close. In 1816, Hampstead, the location of the Hunts' new home, was surrounded by fields and open countryside. Socially it bore little resemblance to the millionaires' village it is now, although the arrival of Hunt and his friends marked the beginning of its gentrification. The Hunts' cottage was in a small hamlet a short distance from the centre of the village. Known as the Vale of Health, the hamlet consisted in 1815 of fewer than fifteen cottages. Walking through the Vale today, it is noticeable how enclosed it is, cut off from the rest of Hampstead by a narrow, tree-lined lane, and surrounded by the steeply rising banks of the heath on three of its four sides. It is therefore ideal for someone with agoraphobic tendencies, and it is little wonder that Hunt came to identify so strongly with the area. Helped by a new sense of physical security, and by expeditions on to Hampstead Heath itself, he slowly began to reintegrate himself into the world from which he had retreated, making trips to the theatre and to *The Examiner* offices.

Although the move to Hampstead eased Hunt's agoraphobia, it did not diminish its impact on his life and work. During his incarceration in Surrey Gaol and his self-imposed confinement in the lily room in Maida Vale, the idea of 'home' took on a new significance for Hunt. Domestic pleasures had saved him from the bleakness of prison life, and had comforted him in the frightening weeks following his release. Now he increasingly came to view domesticity itself as a crucial source of inspiration. Accordingly he set about transforming the cottage's parlour into yet another bower – another room which would be the physical and emotional heart of the place. The busts, books, and piano were installed, alongside portraits and the customary flowers. The green and white furniture was moved up from Maida Vale, and Hunt was surrounded once more by the objects and colours he loved. The room was tiny – just big enough to seat two people – but this suited Hunt perfectly. The Hampstead version of his prison rooms soon allowed him to retreat not just from the world, but from the emotional dramas of his own household.

These dramas started early in 1816, with the publication of *The Story of Rimini*, which tells the tale of Dante's Francesca, who is trapped in a passionless marriage, and finds solace in the arms of her brother-in-law, Paulo. Hunt was unapologetic in his depiction of the sensual pleasures of a forbidden relationship: 'Paulo turned, scarce knowing what he did,/ Only he felt he could no more dissemble,/ And kissed her, mouth to mouth, all in a tremble . . ./ The world was all forgot, the struggle o'er,/ Desperate the joy. – That day they read no more.'³ Such descriptions won much praise from his friends. Hazlitt thought the poem full of 'beautiful and affecting passages', and told Hunt, rather slyly, 'you are very metaphysical in character and passion, but we will not say a word of this to the ladies.'[4] Haydon reported that after reading it 'every nerve about me seized with trembles',[5] and Charles Lamb that it had given both him and his sister Mary 'great delight'. They agreed, he continued, 'in thinking it superior to your former poems.'[6]

Few of the literary journals concurred. Unkind comparisons between Paulo and Francesca's relationship and Hunt's own living arrangements proved irresistible, and Bess's position in Hunt's household became the subject of public comment. This made her situation extremely difficult. It was one thing to be living in her sister's house, with no means of contributing to the household funds other than by providing free childcare. It was quite another matter when her relationship with her brother-in-law became a matter for public discussion. That it did so was partly the result of a misguided intervention by Hunt's friend Charles Cowden Clarke. Some of the early reviews of *Rimini* confined themselves to condemning Hunt's morality and refrained from explicitly linking his ideas with his domestic arrangements. The *British Lady's Magazine*, which had greeted *The Descent of Liberty* a year earlier with effusive praise for Hunt, merely noted its 'repugnance' at his choice of subject. The *Eclectic Review* was worried that the poem would 'do some hurt to the cause of morality'.[7] In response to these early reviews Cowden Clarke published an anonymous pamphlet defending *The Story of Rimini*, in which he alluded to the rumours circulating about Hunt in such a way as to give them further credence. 'Suppose', he asked, 'Mr. Hunt . . . were a gambler, an adulterer, or a debauchee . . . what would all this have to do with the merits, or demerits of his poem?'[8] The pamphlet demonstrated Cowden Clarke's loyalty to Hunt, but his restatement of the innuendo directed towards his friend did little to damp down public speculation. The rumours rumbled on, until they were given explicit voice in *Blackwood's* and, bizarrely, in *The Examiner* itself.

Under a guise of concerned morality *Blackwood's* noted that the publication of *The Story of Rimini* was followed by mysterious accusations about Leigh Hunt's 'domestic relations'. Since his readers did not understand his unashamed 'love of incest', *Blackwood's* noted, they started to speculate about his private life, 'till at last there was something like an identification of Leigh Hunt himself with Paulo, the incestuous hero of Leigh Hunt's chief Cockney poem.'[9] *Blackwood's* reproduced a letter which informed Hunt that he was spoken of as a perfect tyrant, who devoted himself to the sensual gratification of his passions. The worst charge was that 'a sister of Mrs Hunt's resides with you, who is the mother of at least one child, of which you are the father.' Hunt not only printed this letter in *The Examiner* but responded to it in kind:

> An assailant of all the women that came in his way! A tyrant to his wife! And the father of children by her sister! ... the whole of these charges are most malignantly and ridiculously false, so as to make those who are in habits of intercourse with him alternately give way to indignation and laughter.[10]

It was typical of Hunt's bravado that he should confront the rumours head on, but it did nothing to damp down speculation about Bess's place in his household, which became so intense over the next two years that she would eventually be obliged to lodge with her brother instead. As public scrutiny intensified, Marianne and Bess argued with increasing seriousness and frequency. Hunt hated their rows and responded by retreating to his study, while his friends attempted to reconcile the sisters to each other. Their efforts met with little success.

The difficulties caused by Bess's presence in Hunt's household were exacerbated by the fact that she was much more than an unpaid live-in housekeeper, and her situation was thus more complicated than that of the many unmarried women who lived with siblings at the beginning of the nineteenth century. Bess's intellectual abilities, her engagement with Hunt's work and his complex reaction to her presence in his household increased her importance while rendering her position more ambivalent. She was certainly no mere skivvy for her sister. She acted as Hunt's agent, carrying money to and from his publishers and negotiating with them on his behalf.[11] Notably it was she, rather than Marianne, who accompanied Hunt on the rounds of social visits on which he embarked once he overcame his agoraphobia. This was surprising, since Hunt and Marianne's relationship remained close despite Bess's presence. But Bess and Marianne represented different things for Hunt. Marianne was the mother of his children, the hostess at his fireside and the companion of his bedroom, and she thus represented the internal, domestic, homely existence which meant so much to him. Bess, in contrast, mediated between Hunt and the outside world, as she dealt with his publishers, discussed politics and literature with him, and accompanied him to the houses of his friends. Both women were therefore essential to Hunt's happiness, but this did not make their problematic living arrangements – or their own relationship – easier.

It was Bess rather than Marianne who accompanied Hunt on his frequent visits to the home of Vincent and Mary Novello. The Novellos were a hospitable, talented, principled couple, who had been introduced to Hunt by mutual friends around the time of Hunt's release from prison. Novello was born in 1781, to Italian and English parents. Banned because of his Catholicism from holding official posts, he spent twenty-five years as organist at the Portuguese Embassy Chapel, to where fashionable crowds flocked to hear him play. His playing became so famed that eventually George IV, in spite of his anti-Catholic views, offered him the position of private organist at the Pavilion in Brighton. Novello declined this offer, probably because it did not accord with his deeply held beliefs about the importance of making music accessible.

In 1813, Novello helped to found the London Philharmonic Society to promote the performance of classical music. Later, in 1829, assisted by his son Alfred, he founded the publishing house which still bears his name. The central principle of Novello and Company was that music should be made available to all and not just those who could travel to London to hear it. Novello spent his life working towards this goal, and his scores were arranged and priced so that popular works could be performed by groups of friends in the parlour, as well as by professionals in the concert hall. This represented a radical democratisation of high culture, and demonstrated the strength of Novello's allegiance to liberal ideals.

Novello's wife Mary Sabilla Hehl was herself a formidable character. Nicknamed 'Wilful Woman' by Hunt, she gave birth to eleven children, and wrote numerous articles and essays, as well as a full length collection of stories, *A Day at Stowe Gardens*. One of her friends compared her admiringly to Mary Wollstonecraft, and the comparison is apt, since, like Wollstonecraft, she had strongly held views about the best way to bring up her children. Unlike Wollstonecraft, she had the opportunity to put her views into practice. Both Vincent and Mary Novello believed that their children should be treated as friends rather than as subservient dependents and the descriptions of their unorthodox parenting methods feel startlingly contemporary. They were rewarded with great public devotion from their offspring. Their eldest daughter, another Mary, recalled the delightful mornings following her father's evening concerts, when all the children piled on to his bed while he read to them and ate his breakfast: 'First came the "looking at the pictures"; then, the multiplicity of eager enquiry they elicited; then, the explanation, then, the telling of the subject of the book; then, the account of its author; then, the final glory of seeing *V. Novello's children, 240 Oxford Street*, written in the blank leaf, or cover, at the beginning.'[12]

The Novello household was swelled by the presence of Mary Sabilla's sister, who lived with them for some of the time during the 1810s. The similarity of this arrangement to that of Hunt's household illustrates that it was not Bess's presence which infuriated his critics but the idea that the relationship between Hunt and Bess was illicit and immoral. The Novellos, however, were perfectly happy about the fact it was Bess rather than Marianne at Hunt's side during the evenings they spent together, and it may be that, like Byron before them, they found Bess the more lively and interesting sister. Bess and Hunt passed many evenings in the comfortable Oxford Street sitting room, where, in the company of the friends and temporary lodgers who sought refuge in the Novellos' happy home, they gathered around the piano to sing and exchanged jokes and literary gossip by the fire.

Congenial evenings at the Novellos' could not mask the fact that, by mid 1816, the Hunt family finances were in a desperate state. Hunt's letters during this period show him frantically trying to sell copyrights to his work and searching for somewhere cheaper to live. He even went as far as to suggest that Thomas Moore (the poet who had brought about his meeting with Byron) should lodge with them in an attempt to reduce their household bills. Since the cottage was already overcrowded with three adults and three children (a fourth, Swinburne, would be born to Marianne that August) it was perhaps fortunate that Moore declined Hunt's offer. It is to Hunt's credit, however, that despite his own problems he remained alert to the dramas and crises in the lives of his contemporaries. In the spring of 1816, it was Byron who was in difficulty, and in need of support.

In January that year, Annabella Byron left her husband at Piccadilly Terrace and travelled to her parents' home in Durham. She took with her a baby daughter, just over four weeks old. Annabella undoubtedly suffered a great deal in the year after she married Byron, and her sufferings increased after Augusta's arrival in London in the early summer of 1815. Although some of the more extravagant claims she subsequently made can be discounted, she was well aware that her husband cared more for his half-sister than he did for her. She dealt with this by convincing herself that Byron was suffering from some kind of mental illness and was not in full possession of his faculties. In the weeks following her arrival in Durham, she told her parents about some of the scenes which had taken place at Piccadilly Terrace and, horrified by what they heard, they instigated separation proceedings. From the outset they were chiefly concerned that Annabella should retain custody of her daughter. In an era when children were absolutely the property of their father, this necessitated painting Byron as the villain of the piece.

Byron initially refused to believe that Annabella herself had any wish for a separation, and was convinced they would be reconciled. This belief was shattered when Annabella threatened to reveal the true nature of his relationship with Augusta unless he relinquished his claim on both her and baby Ada. In London, the separation proved a fertile topic for scurrilous speculation. News filtered out that Annabella was threatening to reveal the terrible truth of Byron's crimes to the world. Even though details of these crimes remained scarce, gossip quickly centred around the nature of Byron's connection with Augusta, and, even more damagingly, around rumours – probably true – about his relationships with young boys. The threat of bailiffs, scandal, and a potential prosecution for homosexual activity made Byron's continued presence in England untenable, and he made plans for a prolonged stay on the continent. He and Augusta were snubbed at a party and in April the periodical press launched a sustained attack on him following the distribution of 'Fare Thee Well', a short poem in which he bid Annabella a bitter and very public goodbye.

Throughout, Hunt provided support in both public and private. In the *Examiner* he condemned those in the press who sought to make titillating gossip from a private tragedy and defended Byron's honour and reputation.[13] Along with Hobhouse, Hunt spent nights at Piccadilly Terrace, providing Byron with bachelor society. Years later, after their friendship had faltered badly, Byron would remember Hunt's kindness during this period, reportedly telling Thomas Medwin 'when party feeling ran highest against me, Hunt was the only editor of a paper, the only literary man, who dared say a word in my justification. I shall always be grateful to him for the part he took on that occasion.'[14] In the torrid days of March and April the easy conviviality of male company suited Byron far better than the whispers and finger pointing of society parties.

Unbeknownst to Byron, however, he was shortly to be subject to a very different kind of company. In the early spring of 1816 Claire Clairmont did something extraordinary. Out of the blue, she wrote Byron a letter, in which she offered herself to him fully and freely:

If a woman, whose reputation has yet remained unstained, if without either guardian or husband to control she should throw herself upon your mercy, if with a beating heart she should confess the love she has borne you many years, if she should secure to you secrisy & safety, if she should return your kindness with fond affection & unbounded devotion could you betray her, or would you be as silent as the grave?[15]

The writer of this letter was a complete stranger to Byron, but he was not the man to ignore such an approach. Claire was admitted to Piccadilly Terrace, where she charmed and flattered Byron into a state of pleasantly bewildered acquiescence. She chose her persona carefully, presenting herself as an independent woman with literary aspirations. She reinforced her liberal credentials by telling Byron of her friendship with Shelley, whose *Queen Mab* Byron admired. Claire was determined to attract Byron's attention and, for a brief period, she succeeded. With Claire leading the way at every turn the pair flitted from London one Thursday evening to spend the night at an inn. 'There we shall be free & unknown', she told Byron. 'I have arranged everything here so that the slightest suspicion may not be excited.'[16] In order to ensure a degree of respectability Claire brought Mary to Piccadilly Terrace to introduce her to Byron, although she warned him not to keep Mary waiting in the hall as he did Claire, since 'she is accustomed to be surrounded by her own circle who treat her with the greatest politeness.' The word 'circle' had been substituted in this note for 'coterie', suggesting that Claire didn't want to sound as though she were excluded from Shelley's social world.[17] Her letters to Byron grew ever more passionate as the date of his departure from England approached. 'Now do not smile contemptuously & call me a "little fool" when I tell you I weep at your departure', she begged. 'Pray write. I shall die if you don't write.'[18]

What possessed Claire to act in this way, and how was it possible for her to fall for Byron in such a short time? The answer to these questions probably lies in her exile in Lynmouth, where she had ample opportunity to brood on her position. Whatever Claire felt towards Shelley, and however flirtatious he had been with her, it was clear that she would not succeed if she competed for his affections with Mary; and the hazards of becoming too close to him were obvious. Yet she now knew that she could – intermittently – hold the interest of a poet. Claire was both competitive and wounded and Byron – famous, brooding, brilliant – was a much bigger catch than Shelley, of whom few people had heard. Mary and Shelley had known each other for less than three months when they eloped together and Claire was a close witness to their relationship. She now had no difficulty in convincing herself that she was in the grip of an equally grand passion. Mary's example also suggested that romance could bring with it independence – in her case, from the Godwins. Claire wanted a similar degree of autonomy, both from her mother and stepfather and from Mary and Shelley themselves. A relationship with Byron might allow her to break away from both households in favour of an existence in which she could play the part of the romantic heroine, rather than that of an insignificant dependant. Claire had been part of Mary's story since their childhoods, and she now wanted a story of her own. Shelley and Mary had made a life together outside the confines of marriage: Claire saw no reason why she and Byron should not do the same. Throughout her life she would demonstrate her capacity for rapid emotional shifts and her decision to fall in love with Byron combined matters of the heart and a Shelleyan ideology of free love most satisfactorily.

Unfortunately Byron did not see matters in this light. For him, the situation was straightforward: an unattached girl of indeterminate class and unconventional views had thrown herself at him and offered him sex. He was still married to Annabella, so there was no suggestion that a relationship with Claire would be anything more than a brief diversion before he left England. He had had affairs before, both with high-born ladies who understood the rules of the game, and with actresses who likewise understood the code of the green room. As he prepared for his departure, he grew less interested in an increasingly demanding Claire. By the time he left England her letters, with their constant repetitions of her unhappiness at his impending absence, had simply become irritating.

However, in another extraordinary act, which had implications for all those around her, Claire decided to follow him. She knew Byron was planning to travel down the Rhine valley into Switzerland so she proposed to Shelley and Mary that they should all embark on a new European adventure. Beset by arguments with both Godwin and his father about money, Shelley agreed. He was, by this time, restless and bored with the quiet life he and Mary were leading. He was also keen to meet Byron, the most famous poet of the age. Friendship with Byron was a glamorous and exciting prospect, but Shelley – ever in search of sympathetic friends – must also have hoped that he would be an intellectually stimulating companion. So it was that on 3 May, Shelley wrote to Godwin from Dover, explaining that he was taking Mary out of the country once again. A few days later Claire wrote to Byron from Paris, informing him that she would be joining him in Switzerland. From two different directions, Shelley, Byron and their respective parties began their gradual convergence on Geneva.

Shelley, Mary and Claire arrived first. This time they travelled through Europe by carriage, memories of sore feet, the wisdom of additional years and the presence of baby William making a re-enactment of their 1814 European odyssey out of the question. The journey through France, newly subjugated by the restoration of the Bourbon monarchy, led Shelley to write nostalgically to Peacock of England, 'a free country where you may act without restraint & possess that which you possess in security.'[19] The emphasis here on possession is notable: Shelley never advocated violent revolution, but his sense of entitlement to his property and inheritance nevertheless sat uneasily with the radical philosophy of *Queen Mab*. Mary was acutely aware that Britain had played a significant role in the reinstatement of the monarchy in France and felt this was reflected in their treatment at the inns in which they stayed. 'Nor is it wonderful', she told Fanny, 'that [the French] should regard the subjects of a government which fills their country with hostile garrisons, and sustains a detested dynasty on the throne, with an acrimony and indignation of which that government alone is the proper object.'[20] Claire was more focused on the romance of Switzerland, 'the land of my ancestors' (she believed her father to be the Swiss Charles Gaulis, one of her mother's 'husbands'). After ten days on the road they arrived in Geneva, and settled themselves at the Hotel d'Angleterre in Sécheron on the outskirts of the city. There was no sign of Byron, but Claire was relieved to find letters directed to his travelling companion waiting at the post office.

Byron was in fact pursuing a leisurely progress through Belgium and the Rhine valley. He was accompanied by a young doctor, John Polidori, who was being paid by the canny John Murray to keep a diary of his travels with Byron. Polidori seemed a sensible appointment when Byron was preparing to leave England, but he turned out to be moody and difficult. Byron's journey was made more uncomfortable by his decision to travel in a huge carriage modelled on the one used by Napoleon. The carriage broke only a few days into the journey, delaying the travellers on the road between Ghent and Antwerp. They limped on to Brussels, where they stayed for a few days while Byron visited the field of the Battle of Waterloo and the carriage underwent repairs. They then proceeded slowly through Germany, visiting the castles of the Rhine en route, but were forced to halt again when Polidori became ill. Byron found a diversion in the shape of a chambermaid, with whom he had a 'ludicrous adventure' and whose looks 'made me venture upon her carnally'.[21] A more serious diversion was his writing: he had embarked on a third canto of *Childe Harold's Pilgrimage*, transforming the scenes through which he travelled into an evolving narrative of European exile. Like his creator, the central figure of the third canto of *Childe Harold* is an outcast, driven from his native land. As he travelled further away from England, Byron reshaped the poem which had brought him fame into an indictment of the society which had first lionised and then rejected him. A moving, beautiful lyric to Augusta and stanzas in which he mourned his separation from his daughter did nothing to damp down speculation about his private life when the poem was published at the end of 1816.

Ten days after the Shelley party installed themselves in the Hotel d'Angleterre, Byron's travelling carriage finally rolled into Sécheron. Exhausted and more than a little irritated with Polidori, Byron entered his age in the hotel register as 100, causing Claire, who had been watching the comings and goings at the hotel (*the* destination for all English travellers) to despatch a note to his room: 'I am sorry you are grown so old, indeed I suspected you were 200, for the slowness of your journey. I suppose your venerable age could not bear quicker travelling. Well, heaven send you sweet sleep – I am so happy.' She instructed Byron to reply under cover of a note to Shelley, but no response was forthcoming.[22] Billets-doux from an importunate young woman who failed to understand the rules of aristocratic *affaires* did not improve the mood of a man who had been travelling for weeks with only Polidori for company. Two days later Claire wrote again to complain of his treatment of her. 'I have been in this weary hotel this fortnight & it seems so unkind, so cruel, of you to treat me with such marked indifference.'[23]

Claire did have her meeting with Byron, although not the romantic reunion she envisaged. The encounter took place a few days after Byron's arrival, as Shelley, Mary and Claire bumped into Byron while he and Polidori were climbing out of their boat on to the lakeside quay. Everyone was shy and Polidori was so ill at ease he abandoned his patron entirely, taking the boat back on to the lake until all danger of interaction had passed. But later that day Shelley and Byron furthered their acquaintance. Shelley, Polidori reported succinctly, was 'separated from his wife; keeps the two daughters of Godwin, who practise his theories; one L[ord] B[yron]'s.'[24]

———————

Shelley and Byron quickly became friends. On the surface, it was an unlikely pairing. Byron, at twenty-eight, was jaundiced and embittered about being hounded out of England, in contrast to the idealistic, enthusiastic twenty-three year old Shelley. Byron was also a famous poet of superior rank, while Shelley was heir to a mere baronetcy, and was still struggling to get his poetry published. But their friendship flourished in spite of these differences. Each recognised and respected the other's talent, and each knew something of life as an outcast. Before long the two parties moved out of the gossipy Hotel d'Angleterre, Byron to the Villa Diodati, on the shores of the lake, and the Shelley group to a small chalet named Montalègre about ten minutes walk away from Diodati. A regular daily pattern emerged. Shelley and Byron would breakfast together, sometimes in the company of Mary. Mornings spent reading gave way to afternoon expeditions on the lake, as Shelley and Byron discovered a mutual passion for boating. Sometimes they took to the lake again in the evenings, taking Mary, Claire and Polidori with them. Occasionally they would land and walk along different parts of the shore, Byron hiding his limp by loitering behind the rest, trailing his sword-stick through the grass. Mary later recalled evenings when the wind buffeted the boat and, while she rejoiced in their 'contest with the elements', Byron would add to the drama by singing Albanian songs – which mostly consisted of 'strange, wild howls'.[25]

It was the kind of situation in which Shelley thrived. Like Mary, he loved the feeling of battling against the weather, and Byron combined theatrical exoticism with a formidable intellect. They spent their boating afternoons and evenings arguing about poetry, love and the relationship between place and inspiration. This was a more glamorous version of the 1815 Thames boat trip with Peacock and Charles Clairmont, and it bolstered Shelley's confidence to realise that he was influencing Byron's thinking and the direction of his poetry. It was also a sign of how far he had come – socially and intellectually – since he had sat with Mary and Claire on Rhine barges reading and teasing his fellow travellers. Then he had been entirely alone in the world: now he was a friend and confidant of Byron, an older, celebrated poet. Shelley loved boats, and throughout his life he would solidify friendships by embarking on shared nautical projects. The boat he hired with Byron for expeditions around Lake Geneva symbolised their friendship, their joint commitment to the Swiss landscape, and the inspiration they drew from each other. Shelley could hardly have presented more of a contrast to Hunt, cultivating friendship and inspiration in a series of enclosed, claustrophobic rooms.

When boating was over Byron and Polidori joined Shelley's party for tea and conversation, either in the drawing room at Diodati or in the less grand confines of Montalègre. Little William – now six months old – was shuttled between the two houses; looked after by his mother, his aunt and the nursemaid who travelled to Geneva with them. Byron seems to have consented to a very brief renewal of his liaison with Claire. After all, she was available and all too eager and, as he told his friend Douglas Kinnaird some months later, 'if a girl of eighteen comes prancing to you at all hours – there is but one way.'[26] Polidori developed a crush on Mary, but she treated him like a younger brother. It was particularly galling to be told this was how she thought of him a few days after he jumped from a wall in an effort to impress her, spraining his ankle badly in the process (at the advanced age of twenty-one, Polidori still seemed younger than worldly-wise, eighteen year old Mary). Mary herself was most contented by the life she was leading. A few days before Byron's arrival she wrote to Fanny of her delight at her new surroundings: 'We do not enter into society here, yet our time passes swiftly and delightfully. We read Latin and Italian during the heats of noon, and when the sun declines we walk in the garden of the hotel, looking at the rabbits relieving fallen cockchaffers, and watching the motions of a myriad of lizards, who inhabit a southern wall of the garden . . . I feel as happy as a new-fledged bird, and hardly care what twig I fly to, so that I may try my new-found wings.'[27] She liked Byron and found the combination of his and Shelley's company stimulating. It was a shame that Fanny responded with dreary, slightly sentimental letters and that Godwin's finances continued to cause anxiety, but it was hard to engage with the woes of the Skinner Street inhabitants when one was hundreds of miles away watching lizards in a sun-drenched garden.

One of the better known facts about this most famous of literary summers is that nothing stayed sun-drenched for very long. In one of Mary's most anthologised letters she described the freak weather which put an end to the Swiss sunshine.

> Unfortunately we do not now enjoy those brilliant skies that hailed us on our first arrival to this country. An almost perpetual rain confines us principally to the house; but when the sun bursts forth it is with a splendour and heat unknown in England. The thunder storms that visit us are grander and more terrific than I have ever seen before . . . one night we enjoyed a finer storm than I had ever before beheld. The lake was lit up – the pines on Jura made visible, and all the scene illuminated for an instant, when a pitchy blackness succeeded, and the thunder came in frightful bursts over our heads amid the darkness.[28]

Boating expeditions became impossible, so the group retreated inside to talk and read. Shelley and Byron discussed Plato, Rousseau
and Wordsworth, and Shelley tried to convince Byron that the disappointment of Wordsworth's apostatical later work should not obscure the genius of his early creations. In July the two poets disappeared
off on a jaunt of their own around Lake Geneva, visiting Clarens, the
setting of Rousseau's great novel *Julie*, and touring the house in which
Gibbon had completed his *Decline and Fall*. Mary and Polidori read
Tasso together and the whole group spent one evening reading German
ghost stories and Coleridge's *Christabel*. Polidori, who had written his
doctoral thesis on somnambulism, discussed 'principles' with Shelley,
and 'whether man was to be thought merely an instrument'. Elsewhere
he reported that Shelley and he talked, 'till the ladies brains whizzed
with giddiness about idealism.'[29]

It is altogether too tempting to shape a neat narrative about
where these conversations were leading. Mary did exactly this in her
Preface to the 1831 edition of *Frankenstein*. There she described how
Byron decreed that everyone should write a ghost story. She recalled
her embarrassment when no ideas came to her, and the evening in
which Byron and Shelley discussed the work of Erasmus Darwin 'who
preserved a piece of vermicelli in a glass case, till by some extraordinary
means it began to move with voluntary motion' while she sat 'a devout
but nearly silent listener'. She went on to dramatise the night which
followed, describing how she saw 'the hideous phantasm of a man
stretched out and then, on the working of some powerful engine, show
signs of life, and stir with an uneasy, half vital motion.'

Finally, she described the triumphant moment in which she was able
to announce to the others she 'had thought of a story'. Shelley was
accorded praise for encouraging her to develop her story into a novel,
and she concluded her account with the following valediction:

And now, once again, I bid my hideous progeny go forth and prosper.
I have an affection for it, for it was the offspring of happy days, when
death and grief were but words, which found no true echo in my heart.
Its several pages speak of many a walk, many a drive, and many a

conversation, when I was not alone; and my companion was one who, in this world, I shall never see more.[30]

This narrative of creativity has become nearly as famous as the novel whose creation it describes, and it has received almost as much critical attention from generations of scholars who have sought to unpick the complicated chain of influences which underpinned Mary's extraordinary first novel. We now know that the events which led to the composition of *Frankenstein* were less cohesive and dramatically satisfactory than Mary's Preface suggests and that the reading and conversations of the whole of the Swiss summer played their part in the novel's development. But it is also the case that in *Frankenstein* Mary brought together ideas which had been germinating for years. The summer of 1816 provided an ideal context in which to knit these ideas together, but conversations about ghosts and galvanism were by no means solely responsible for her novel.

In the companionable atmosphere of the Villa Diodati, Mary began to synthesise Godwin's narratives of historical perfectibility, Wollstonecraft's visions of parental responsibility, and Shelley's materialist philosophy of the origins of life (a philosophy which owed much to Erasmus Darwin). She did so in an imaginative response which incorporated years of reading, a new understanding of the power of electricity (gained from watching the lightning reverberate around the lake) and a claim for the importance of creative community. It also incorporated images which had been bubbling away in her conversations for several years. Charles Clairmont's 1815 letter to Claire in which he described Shelley and Hogg poring over the artificial and natural boundaries of human knowledge' gives one indication of the kind of imagery delighted in by the Shelley circle at the time; a similar glimpse into a shared linguistic register survives in one of Claire's early letters to Byron, in which she informed him that 'the Creator ought not to destroy his Creature'.[31] These images and turns of phrase, developed and used communally over a period of years, would all find their way into *Frankenstein*.

Frankenstein, like Shelley's *Alastor*, is a critique of selfish, isolated creativity. It tells the story of a young man who creates a living being from human remains, only to discover the limits of his power over his creation. Frankenstein brings about his downfall through an act of self-aggrandising creation which is characterised by his failure to consider the social ramifications of his actions. He rejects the communal, institutional context of the University of Ingolstadt to lurk in charnel houses and his attic room in pursuit of personal glory. *Frankenstein* condemns much of what Byron's *Childe Harold* represents: isolation, self-indulgence and an abnegation of social responsibility. It is Mary's manifesto for the idealised community of enlightened individuals she and Shelley attempted to assemble, first in the winter of 1814, then more successfully at the house in Bishopsgate in 1815. Her description in the elegiac Preface of the process by which *Frankenstein* came into being may elide some details, but it champions a method of endeavour in which ideas reach fruition through 'many a walk, many a drive, many a conversation' – a method entirely absent from the novel itself. Indirectly, through its representation of the possibility of what might have been, her novel is a celebration of the communal, inspiring summer in which it emerged.

Shelley played a key role in the development of *Frankenstein*. Together he and Mary discussed its plot, its intellectual antecedents and its emerging form. He acted as her agent, searching for a publisher and correcting some of the proofs, and he edited her drafts, making many emendations and revisions in the process. His script is interlinked with hers in the pages of the *Frankenstein* manuscript, transforming it into a powerful symbol of cooperative creativity. Many of Shelley's changes concerned tone and style, but some were thematically substantive and they reveal surprising things about the dynamic of Mary and Shelley's relationship.

Shelley's alterations consistently emphasised *Frankenstein*'s insistence on the necessity of a socially responsible pursuit of knowledge. He highlighted Frankenstein's naïve enthusiasm for alchemy; an enthusiasm which isolates him from the University of Ingolstadt and contributes to his downfall. In several places Shelley added whole sentences to the narrative. For example: 'The ambition of the enquirer seemed to limit itself to the annihilation of those visions on which my interest in science was chiefly founded. I was required to exchange chimeras of boundless grandeur, for realities of little worth.'[32] Shelley's language – 'annihilation', 'grandeur', 'little worth' – points towards the extent of Frankenstein's delusional attachment to his visions, and suggests he perceives modern science as a violent destroyer of dreams. Another Shelley addition, in which Frankenstein's investigations lead him to see 'all the minutiae of causation as exemplified in the change from life to death, and death to life',[33] increases his responsibility for his own downfall. Frankenstein's neatly weighted rhetoric makes the shift from life to death seem inconsequential, and it is only through the murders of his own family that he comes to realise his mistake.

Shelley's involvement in shaping Frankenstein's rejection of the Romantic solitary creator (a figure epitomised by his own Alastor) is striking. Shelley was a good editor: he strengthened and sharpened Mary's critique of selfish genius, but did not seek to impose his own ambivalence about the creator's need for both solitude and sociability on to her work. Through the creation of a manuscript with two hands, in which the second hand consistently emphasised the value of social responsibility, Mary and Shelley established an alternative model for creative endeavour to that practiced by Frankenstein himself. Since the early 1970s Shelley has been alternately praised and censured for his work on Frankenstein, his supporters attributing the novel's power to his pen, and his detractors condemning his alterations as an act of patriarchal oppression.[34] But the manuscript supports neither view. The novel's greatness lies in the intensity of its plot and in its virtuosic response to Wollstonecraft, Godwin, Darwin and Shelley himself, whose alterations are those of a sympathetic and careful reader, rather than of a man attempting to impose his intellectual philosophy on to a woman's work. In fact, the Frankenstein manuscript reveals co-operative Romantic sociability at its best: equitable, constructive, sympathetic and incisive. It is a testament to the characters of both Mary and Shelley – and to the strength of their relationship – that they worked so well together.

While Mary formulated her ideas into the beginnings of a novel, Byron and Shelley directed their shared reading and conversations into poetry. For Shelley, the intellectual impact of touring Lake Geneva worked itself into his 'Hymn to Intellectual Beauty', the poem in which he made his first sustained attempt to formulate a version of neo-Platonism modulated through both Rousseau and Wordsworth. Conversations about the first generation of Romantic poets influenced his second major poem of the summer, 'Mont Blanc', in which he rewrote Coleridge's conception of a Christian sublime (articulated in the elder poet's 'Hymn before Sunrise, Written in the Vale of Chamouni') so that the sublime was transformed into a symbol of the limits of human knowledge. Both he and Mary were most impressed by Byron's work, and watched the progress of *Childe Harold's Pilgrimage* eagerly. One evening Shelley read Mary the early sections of the poem's third canto in their little bedroom at Montalègre after the others had gone to bed, and thereafter she associated the canto with listening to Shelley's voice as she watched the sky darken over Lake Geneva and the mountains.

Byron reformulated Shelley's conception of Platonic love and his plea for the importance of Wordsworth's early work in important and troubling ways in the third canto of *Childe Harold*. Here, inspired by the example of the younger man, Byron found himself exploring love and its symbiotic relationship with nature in a way which was quite distinct from anything he had previously written. Later he would disown this moment in his intellectual development, reportedly telling a companion that 'Shelley, when I was in Switzerland, used to dose me with Wordsworth physic even to nausea',[35] and he would reject Shelley's philosophy in the fourth canto of *Childe Harold's Pilgrimage*, announcing to Hobhouse, 'I have parted company with Shelley and Wordsworth. Subject matter and treatment are alike anew.'[36] But his later embarrassed dismissal of a brief moment of Shelleyan enthusiasm does not detract from the significant role Shelley's views played in the development of Byron's poetic voice. Nor was Shelley the only person to influence his thinking over the course of the summer. He would later tell one of his biographers that Mary was exceptionally clever, and, like Shelley, he found the thought of her parentage rather alluring.

'Mrs Shelley is very clever, indeed it would be difficult for her not to be so; the daughter of Mary Wollstonecraft and Godwin . . . could be no common person.'[37]

Claire played little part in the intense exchange of ideas and literary opinions which dominated the summer. Although she may have started a ghost story like the others, she limited her literary activities to the copying out of the third canto of *Childe Harold's Pilgrimage*. This task had its advantages, in that it gave her daily entry to the Villa Diodati at a time when Byron was increasingly reluctant to see her, but it hardly put her at the centre of the group's intellectual exchanges. Meanwhile, the goings-on at Diodati were a fertile topic for gossip and speculation. The local hotelier did a brisk trade in sailing trips on the lake during which shocked English visitors could inspect the washing drying outside Byron's villa for evidence of female inhabitants – telescopes were thoughtfully included in the ticket price. John St Aubyn, who had settled in Geneva shortly before Byron's arrival, reported the peer's presence to a friend, remarking that he was accompanied by an 'actress and another family of very suspicious appearance'.[38] Polidori noted in passing that Mary was referred to by them all as 'Mrs Shelley', but this clearly did little to allay speculation about the nature of the Shelley ménage. In July Shelley, Mary and Claire removed themselves from Geneva for a little while and travelled to Chamouni, the village from which intrepid tourists could explore the Mont Blanc glacier. By the time they returned to Montalègre it was necessary to confront Byron with a development which Claire (and Shelley) had known about for some time. At eighteen, Claire, like Mary before her, was faced with the practical consequences of free love: she was pregnant with a child conceived with Byron before his departure from London.

Together, Claire and Shelley slowly worked their way towards an understanding with Byron about the baby's future. These negotiations were difficult, and they disrupted the intellectually stimulating con-versations which had characterised the summer. As soon as he knew she was pregnant Shelley took on responsibility for Claire, and, during his lake voyage with Byron, spent one evening at an inn where he made a new will, in which Claire was left £6,000 for herself and £6,000 in trust for any other person she cared to name (proof, if any were needed, that she took Shelley into her confidence early on). But Claire's child would be Byron's to do with as he pleased, a legal imbalance which was matched by the disparity in their respective incomes. Claire had no independent means; Byron was a wealthy man. Eventually Shelley, Claire and Byron agreed that Byron would send for the child when it was old enough to leave its mother and that Claire would have the right to see it when she desired. This arrangement would turn out to be unsatisfactorily vague, but it must have seemed to Claire to be preferable to Byron's first suggestion, which entailed her handing her baby over to his half-sister, Augusta Leigh. Since Byron had occupied at least one evening by dropping hints to Claire about the dark and depraved nature of his relationship with Augusta, it is not surprising that she thought this suggestion repugnant. Shelley found himself in the position of mediator between Claire and Byron, which strained his relationship with both of them. For her part, Claire was made acutely aware of the social disparity between her and the powerful man to whom she had given her heart.

By the end of August the creativity of June and July had faded, to be replaced by tension and uncertainty about a future in which Claire and Byron were inextricably linked. Byron was joined by more friends – Matthew 'Monk' Lewis (the author of one of the period's most notorious gothic novels), Scrope Davis and John Cam Hobhouse. These London society bucks made Shelley feel marginalised and loosened his bond with Byron still further. On 29 August, Shelley, Mary, Claire and William left Geneva for England, carrying with them the manuscripts of the third canto of *Childe Harold*, 'Mont Blanc', 'Hymn to Intellectual Beauty', the beginnings of *Frankenstein*, and some shorter poems by Byron. It had, by any measure, been an astoundingly productive summer.

They arrived back at the end of the first week in September and made their way to Bath, where they settled for the winter. After a summer of poetry and good conversation, England and an English autumn proved to be rather a shock. The stormy weather which fired up Mary's imagination that summer had a grimmer consequence in Britain and elsewhere in Europe. Fanny's account of England's state of 'evil' and 'misery'[39] might have been dismissed as Fanny-ish gloom when read in a sunny garden but now they were back on English shores the accuracy of her description became apparent. The harvest had failed, food prices had risen, and there was much distress among the poor and labouring classes. Shelley was shocked by what he saw, telling Byron that 'the whole fabric of society presents a most threatening aspect'. He was relieved to note that 'the people appear calm, & steady even under situations of great excitement; & reform may come without revolution.'[40] It is interesting to note that, again, the Shelley who wrote this held views which were distinctly more moderate than those of the Shelley of *Queen Mab*. Claire also wrote to Byron, describing the distress she and Shelley witnessed on their walks in the Bath countryside, but her letter went unanswered. Once again, Shelley, Mary and Claire were thrown together in an uncomfortable threesome. They were tied to Bath and each other by the necessity of keeping Claire's pregnancy secret from Skinner Street, cut off from their friends and surrounded by frequent reminders of how badly the poor were suffering. Happy evenings by Lake Geneva with Byron and Polidori seemed like little more than a dream.

———

The 'national distress', and the failure of the government to alleviate it, dominated Hunt's *Examiner* editorials in the autumn of 1816. He called on the 'Sinecurists' – officials with comfortable government jobs – to lower taxes, and praised aristocrats who contributed to funds for poor relief. Like Shelley, Hunt was worried by the prospect of a revolution ('We do not believe there is any necessity for Revolution in this country, though we are more and more of the opinion, if possible, that there is much for Reform'), but he did concede that 'Revolutions are reckoning days with the abuses of the Great' and that some kind of 'reckoning' was overdue.[41] Although he deplored the state of the country, Hunt realised that national distress presented political opportunity and *The Examiner*'s strictures against corrupt and overpaid parliamentarians grew almost as loud as they had been before the imprisonment of its editor and printer.

In October Hunt made a new friend, when Charles Cowden Clarke

introduced him to John Keats. Keats responded joyfully to the news that
a meeting with Hunt had finally been arranged, telling Cowden Clarke
''t will be an era in my existence',[42] and the attraction between the two
men was immediate. Keats was almost twenty-one when he met Hunt,
and had just finished his medical training. In July 1816 he qualified to
practice as a surgeon and physician and was admitted to the Society of
Apothecaries. As his biographer Andrew Motion has noted, this was a
considerable achievement in one so young.[43] But qualifying brought
home to Keats the tensions in his life between the professional path
on which he was placed and the poetry he was tentatively beginning to
write. Even while he worked towards membership of the Royal College
of Surgeons he was exploring the different directions his life might take.

Hunt – always more perceptive about the talents of others than
about his own poetry – was quick to recognise Keats's potential and
to encourage him to write and develop his ideas. Keats found Hunt a
cheerful, sympathetic listener who understood the difficulties facing
a young poet and who, at the advanced age of thirty-two, had the
experience to help him negotiate the pitfalls of the literary world. A first
formal visit stretched into a series of calls and before long Keats was a
frequent visitor at Hunt's Hampstead cottage, sometimes staying for days
at a time, sleeping night after night on the sofa in Hunt's parlour. Charles
Cowden Clarke recalled one evening spent in the company of both:

> The occasion that recurs with the liveliest interest was one evening when
> . . . Hunt proposed to Keats the challenge of writing, there, then and
> to time, a sonnet 'On the Grasshopper and the Cricket'. No one was
> present but myself, and they accordingly set to. I, apart, with a book
> at the end of the sofa, could not avoid furtive glances every now and
> then at the emulants. I cannot say how long the trial lasted. I was not
> proposed umpire; and had no stopwatch for the occasion. The time,
> however, was short for such a performance, and Keats won as to time.
> But the event of the after-scrutiny was one of many such occurrences
> which have riveted the memory of Leigh Hunt in my affectionate regard
> and admiration for unaffected generosity and perfectly unpretentious
> encouragement.[44]

Sonnet writing competitions were one way in which Hunt and Keats exchanged ideas, with Hunt recommending a poetic form he had always championed, and then praising Keats's response to that form. He showed Keats a model for poetic endeavour in which poetry was occasional, spontaneous and celebratory and in which simultaneous composition was a tool for literary experimentation.

Huntian values permeated the poetry Keats now began to produce with increasing intensity. In his first major poem, 'Sleep and Poetry', Keats drew inspiration from the private world of Hunt's cottage, as he celebrated its sounds, sights and colours. In the tiny study ('Round about were hung/ The glorious features of the bards who sung/ In other ages'), Keats saw images of 'fauns and satyrs taking aim/ At swelling apples' and, in tribute to Marianne and Bess, 'two sisters sweet/ Bending their graceful figures till they meet/ Over the trippings of a little child'.

'Sleep and Poetry' celebrated the transformative effect of a night spent surrounded by Hunt's household gods: books, paintings, flowers. But it was also a statement of the importance of poetic retreat from society, and of a balance between conversation and silence. The poem ends at the point at which 'the chimes/ Of friendly voices had just given place/ To as sweet a silence, when I 'gan retrace/ The pleasant day, upon a couch at ease.' A day spent with Hunt inspired Keats to write, but poetry could only be formulated in peace and quiet, once conversation had died away. From the very beginning of his acquaintance with Hunt, Keats explored the problematic tension between sociability and solitude, both of which had a profound influence on his early poetry. 'Sleep and Poetry' evokes an ideal balance between companionship and loneliness, but Keats would struggle to maintain this balance – which was crucial to his development of an independent poetic voice – as his friendship with Hunt progressed.

Within a few days of their first meeting, Keats was admitted to the inner ranks of Hunt's circle, which at this point numbered among its members Charles Cowden Clarke, Benjamin Haydon, John Hamilton Reynolds (another young poet encouraged by Hunt), William Hazlitt, the Novellos and Charles and Mary Lamb. Keats's early delight at being part of the group is evident in his letters and poems from this period, but his presence in Hampstead was not without its problems. Days and nights spent in Hunt's study were days and nights away from his medical training. And his presence destabilised some already fragile relationships, most notably that between Hunt and Haydon.

In the autumn of 1816, Haydon's feelings about Hunt became deeply contradictory. In September he was writing of his gratitude for Hunt's friendship, proclaiming that 'the Hunts have been to me such friends that nothing but Death shall ever disjoin us', but by October they were arguing about religion, with Hunt claiming that poetry was always in advance of religious thinking, and Haydon accusing Hunt of denying the sublime beauty of Christian doctrine because of a cowardly fear of 'being roasted or pitchforked or punished'. Hunt, he decided, was a remarkable man: intellectually alert and capable of immense sympathy, and he admired his capacity for affection. But he criticised his tendency to encourage 'inferior people about him to listen, too fond of shining at any expense in society, too apt when another is beginning to divide attention by exhibiting more knowledge to stop it by a joke which is irresistible – a love of approbation from the darling sex bordering on weakness.' In November, an analysis which began as an attempt to understand Hunt's weaknesses sharpened into stringent criticism. 'Such is the morbid sensibility of his temperament that the supposition he can be guilty of Sin gives gloomy pain & he must be kept in a continual excitement of pleasure & voluptuousness by amorous poems & bodily sensations to keep himself in a state of ordinary every day comfort.'[45]

This shift, from approbation to criticism, was attributable to several things. Haydon's perplexed grappling with Hunt's oddness and with the qualities which made him simultaneously loveable and infuriating was not unique: other friends and acquaintances were equally puzzled by Hunt. But Haydon's obsessive accounts of Hunt's relationship with women, of his amorousness and need for physical affection, were particular to him, and were symptomatic of his preoccupation with the women in Hunt's life, by whom he was alternately attracted and repelled. These women – and Bess in particular – played a key role in the souring of Hunt and Haydon's friendship. This culminated in Haydon dispatching a furious missive to Hunt railing against the treatment meted out to him by Marianne, who had suggested that he would make a suitable husband for her sister:

> For these seven years that I have been honoured by the sneers of Mrs Hunt, every body has told me of them, from your oldest friends to your newest acquaintances, and have asked me the reason! I never gave one, tho' perfectly aware they proceeded from my having resisted an attempt of your wife and her mother to entrap me into a marriage with Miss Kent . . . It was always irksome to me to visit your family after that transaction, and I have ever endeavoured by every minor attention to soften the anger I saw but ill concealed, whenever I was present.[46]

Here as elsewhere Haydon protests too much. He was obsessed by Bess, and by her relationship with Hunt, which he considered at length in private diary entries: 'he likes & is satisfied to corrupt the girl's mind without seducing her person, to dawdle over her bosom, to inhale her breath, to lean against her thigh & play with her petticoats, and rather than go to the effort of relieving his mind by furious gratification, shuts his eyes, to tickle the edge of her stockings that his feelings may be kept tingling by imagining the rest.'[47] This particular diary entry was written after an evening in which Hunt made Haydon furious by being rude about Christianity, and it presents a vivid picture of the continuing closeness between Hunt and Bess. But his agitated cataloguing of the 'sickly pukings' of Hunt's 'lechery' reveals as much about Haydon's own fascination with Bess's bosom, thighs, stockings and petticoats as it does about her relationship with her brother-in-law.

In addition, the suggestion that Haydon was poorly treated by the Hunts is not supported by the many references during the previous 'seven years' to his love and affection for both Hunt and Marianne. His reaction to a ham-fisted attempt at matchmaking was overblown and his references to Bess's 'power' and her 'ill concealed' anger towards him are vindictive enough to suggest the extent of his preoccupation with her. The passing of time did little to subdue Haydon's morbid fascination with Hunt's household. Over a decade later he would work himself up into another fury about the Hunt women and write an article for *Blackwood's* in which he lampooned Marianne and Bess as drunken nose-pickers. He subsequently withdrew the article in a fit of remorse, but not before the proprietors of *Blackwood's* derived much malicious enjoyment from his anguished spite.[48] And in marginal annotations to a biography of Byron, written at some point after 1824, he returned once more to the subject of Hunt, Bess, and his relationship with them. He maintained that Bess 'pretended to be dying for me', and that she was made 'hysterical' by his rejection. He conflated his memories of the Surrey Gaol years with the period following Hunt's release from prison to argue that Hunt became interested in Bess as he comforted her following Haydon's refusal of her advances: 'Hunt, in trying to console her, got interested himself – and as I was positively a witness once to the grossest conduct, while she played on the Piano forte before him – I fear as they were alone for weeks in Prison – they went further – I think nothing but such an act, could have so completely altered Hunt.' He proceeded to suggest that only such immorality could account for *The Story of Rimini*, '& all its feelings', apparently forgetting his own admiration for the poem at the time of its publication.[49]

At the point that he wrote these comments, Haydon had convinced himself that Hunt, Byron, Shelley and Godwin were co-conspirators in a plot to bring revolution to Britain, and that they were only thwarted because they 'shocked the Country by their opinions on sexual intercourse'. But at the time it was in fact the arrival of Keats, rather than Hunt's sexual immorality, which really changed the relationship between Hunt and Haydon. Haydon was among the first of Hunt's circle to extend friendship to Keats and he quickly became a devoted admirer of the young newcomer. Keats was flattered by the attention, and before long the two men were breakfasting and spending evenings together, often in the company of John Reynolds, who rapidly attached himself to Keats. Hunt was not invited to join them. Keats wrote sonnets in praise of Haydon, and Haydon responded by suggesting Keats's poetry should be shown to Wordsworth. Inspired by this example, Reynolds, once one of Hunt's most ardent followers, was moved to write his own sonnet in praise of Haydon, because, he informed him, 'I really *feel* your Genius.'[50]

Writing sonnets in praise of one's friends was an activity pioneered by Hunt, and it was now being used as a way to assert allegiance and strengthen the ties of a coterie from which he was partially excluded. Haydon was able to move away from Hunt because Keats provided him with an alternative focus. And in this new circle it was Haydon who was the centre of attention, and who positioned himself, as Hunt had done before him, as the older, wiser artist basking in the admiration of a group of clever young men.

———

On 1 December 1816, *The Examiner* published an article entitled 'Young Poets'. Buried amongst a discussion of Bonaparte's residence on St Helena and a diatribe against *The Times* ('this paper is a nuisance which ought to be abated'), the article, by Hunt himself, drew the attention of the newspaper's readership to the work of 'three young writers, who appear to us to promise a considerable addition of strength to the new school'. This 'new school of poetry', Hunt proclaimed, 'began with something excessive, like most revolutions, but this gradually wore away; and an evident aspiration after real nature and original fancy remained, which called to mind the finer times of the English Muse.' The 'old school' of French, artificial, neo-classical poetry (exemplified by Alexander Pope) had been a target of Hunt's criticism since his *Feast of the Poets*. His three young writers would build a new English poetry and would demolish the flimsy efforts of the eighteenth-century poets to resurrect the grandeur of Milton and Spenser. These three poets were Keats, Reynolds – and Shelley.

Throughout the tumultuous events of 1814–1816, Shelley had retained his respect for Hunt. The same admiration which caused him to boil with indignation when the proprietors of *The Examiner* were sent to prison prompted him to write to Hunt in 1816, when his own literary fortunes were at a low ebb. The summer with Byron convinced Shelley of the importance of publicity, and made him realise that his work could never reform the world if it did not reach an audience. Over the course of the summer Byron talked of Hunt's generosity with much enthusiasm, and when Shelley returned to England it was to find that *The Examiner*'s literary column was growing ever more influential. Encouraged by Byron's example and conversation, and frustrated by his own failure to achieve public recognition, Shelley sent Hunt his 'Hymn to Intellectual Beauty'. It was a bold step, which was to have important personal and professional ramifications for both men. But, at first, it seemed as if Shelley's attempt to thrust his work forward had failed. Hunt promptly lost the manuscript of 'Hymn to Intellectual Beauty' and, to Shelley's disappointment, the poem remained unpublished.

However, Hunt did at least read 'Hymn to Intellectual Beauty' before he mislaid it in the piles of paper in his study. He was impressed by what he saw and, in his 'Young Poets' article, he praised Shelley as a 'striking and original thinker'. He commended Reynolds too, although he censured him for being too ready to imitate Wordsworth and for poetic details 'too overwrought and indiscriminate'. But, Hunt concluded, Reynolds was still young, and only in want of 'still closer attention to things as opposed to the seduction of words, to realise all that he promises.' Keats, the youngest of them all, had 'not yet published anything except in a newspaper; but a set of his manuscripts was handed us the other day, and fairly surprised us with the truth of their ambition, and ardent grappling with Nature.' Hunt concluded by insisting that his praise for all three poets was justified: 'we really are not in the habit of lavishing praises and announcements . . . [but] we have no fear of any pettier vanity on the part of young men, who promise to understand human nature so well.'[51]

Hunt's 'Young Poets' article is remembered now as the first piece of writing to anticipate the canonisation of Shelley and Keats. It also had room for brief praise of Byron (who, in the third canto of *Childe Harold*, had 'taken his place where we always said he would be found, – among the poets . . . who go directly to Nature for inspiration'), so it is often read as an early proclamation of the powers of a new generation of Romantic poets. But when the article is resituated among the complex, shifting dynamics of the Hunt circle in the autumn of 1816 'Young Poets' appears primarily as an assertion of power. Hunt used the article to reposition himself at the centre of the circle of writers and sympathetic thinkers who gathered around him after his release from prison. In praising Keats and Reynolds in *The Examiner* Hunt was reclaiming them as his: *his* protégés, *his* discoveries. In the short term, it worked. Keats was delighted by the article, by public recognition of his talents and his place in a new poetic canon. Along with his burgeoning friendships with literary men 'Young Poets' gave him the confidence, at the end of 1816, to give up his medical training for good and to devote himself to poetry.

In Bath, Shelley was equally delighted by Hunt's article, which more than made up for his failure to publish 'Hymn to Intellectual Beauty'. The unexpected public praise boosted his confidence, in a bright moment in a dark and difficult autumn. While Shelley shuttled back and forth between Bath and Peacock's house in Marlow, from where he was looking for a more permanent residence, Mary and Claire lived quietly, reading, attending lectures, writing letters and walking through Bath's Georgian crescents. Mary worked on the first draft of *Frankenstein*, building on the ideas and conversations of the summer, and both she and Claire took drawing lessons. In September Claire was left in charge of William while Mary joined Shelley and Peacock in Marlow. From Bath, Claire attempted to assert her presence in the group through a series of instructions: 'tell Peacock from me to make his Book "funny"'; 'Don't over walk Shelley & pray <u>make</u> him get a great coat'; 'pray write & say when you will be home'.[52] Mary was still in Marlow four days after receiving this last command, so she evidently felt no urgent need to hurry back to her stepsister.

Shelley and Mary returned to Bath at the end of September to find the periodicals advertising the third canto of *Childe Harold's Pilgrimage*. Shelley was taken aback to learn that Byron's poem was already in print. He had delivered Byron's manuscripts to John Murray on his return from Switzerland and in the process presented himself to Murray as Byron's de facto agent. He therefore felt snubbed when he learnt that the poem had been published without his involvement. He did not understand that Murray had no intention of letting such a valuable

commodity as a new Byron poem be tainted by the obscure author of
Queen Mab. Byron himself connived at this: although he asked Shelley
to oversee publication, he was more than happy to let Murray organise
matters as he wished. For Shelley, the episode symbolised his renewed
exclusion from literary circles. After a summer during which he had
felt himself to be an intimate of Byron's, this was a blow. Meanwhile a
'stupid' letter arrived from Fanny, disturbing their peace still further.[53]

Fanny's 'stupid' letter was a cry for help, not for herself, but for her
adopted parents. She criticised Mary for thinking unkind things about
their stepmother ('I know that she has every good <u>will</u> and wish for you
& your child') and Shelley for failing to help Godwin out of the financial
mire in which he now found himself. 'Is it not your and Shelley's duty
to consider these things?' she demanded. 'And to endeavour to prevent
as far as lies in your power giving [Godwin] unnecessary pain and
anxiety?'[54] Six days after writing this, quiet, melancholic Fanny, who
had tried so hard to keep her family together, equipped herself with an
overdose of laudanum and wrote a second letter, this time to Godwin
himself. This note was written from a Swansea inn:

> I have long determined that the best thing I could do was to put an end
> to the existence of a being whose birth was unfortunate, and whose life
> has only been a series of pain to those persons who have hurt their health
> in endeavouring to promote her welfare. Perhaps to hear of my death
> will give you pain, but you will soon have the blessing of forgetting that
> such a creature ever existed as[55]

The note ended abruptly: someone – possibly the kindly owner of the
inn – tore the signature off in order to avoid a formal identification
of the body. Fanny was identifiable only by the initials embroidered
into her stays, and by a watch Mary and Shelley brought her from
Paris. With no signature on her note the Godwins were spared the
humiliation of having their daughter publicly named as a suicide. After
the inquest, Fanny's body was interred in an unmarked grave.

Shelley, Mary and Claire knew that they had played a part in Fanny's misery.[56] They had abandoned her, first in 1814, when she was excluded from their early morning flight to Europe, then in 1816, when they departed once again without warning. She was left to arbitrate between two warring parties and knew herself to be the object of some derision in the Shelley household. Her small kindnesses – walking through the rain to visit Mary after the death of her baby girl while Shelley and Claire were occupied elsewhere – were insufficiently appreciated, and her relationship with her Wollstonecraft aunts suffered as a result of Mary and Claire's impropriety. It is clear she longed to be involved in their lives from her letters of the summer of 1816, which asked eagerly for details of Byron's character: 'for where I love the poet I should like to respect the man'.[57] In September she wrote wistfully of Mary's 'calm contented disposition, and the calm philosophical habits of life which pursue you, or rather which you pursue everywhere.'[58]

But all hints that she might join them for a while, that she might be relieved for a few days of her constant anxiety about Godwin, went unnoticed. We know much less about Fanny than we know about Mary and Claire, but there is no suggestion that she was any less shrewd. She may have been quieter and more obedient, but she was well aware of her Wollstonecraft heritage, and thanks to Godwin's *Memoir*, of her mother's attempts to kill herself. She probably recognised that she had inherited Wollstonecraft's depressive tendencies, from which death seemed the only escape. Fanny's mother showed through example that attempting suicide was not dishonourable; that it was a legitimate act for a woman who had felt she had nothing else to live for. Mary and Claire paid their homage to Wollstonecraft by living: by running away, and by loving men to whom they were not married. Fanny paid hers by dying.

When news reached Bath of a first, desperate note from Fanny (in which she announced her intention to 'depart immediately to the spot from which I hope never to remove')[59] Shelley left immediately to find her and stop her. He followed her to Swansea, from where he returned with the 'worst account'.[60] Godwin forbade him from travelling back to Swansea to claim her body and embarked on a campaign of disinformation so effective that Charles Clairmont, journeying through Spain, only heard of her death six months later. Claire told Byron that Shelley's health was damaged by the horror of it all, but it was a particularly cruel blow for Mary. She had been the main recipient of Fanny's melancholy letters, and she failed to provide the answers and consolation which Fanny evidently needed. Moreover Fanny was her half-sister, in contrast to Claire, who was no blood relation, and they had spent their infancy together. Both knew themselves to be daughters of Wollstonecraft, something Claire rather resented (she later claimed that Fanny was pretentious about her mother).[61] With Fanny dead, Mary found herself the sole inheritor of the Wollstonecraft legacy, of a name to which scandal and opprobrium were attached.

In the weeks following the suicide, Mary sought distraction in work, and she drafted the first four chapters of *Frankenstein* at great speed. She was pleased with the results, telling Shelley (who was house hunting again) 'I have also finished the 4 Chap of Frankenstein which is a very long one & I think you would like it.' But in the same letter, she expressed more pressing concerns about their future living arrangements. She dreamt of 'A house with a lawn a river or lake – noble trees & divine mountains that should be our little mousehole to retire to' but all she really wanted was 'a garden & <u>absentia Clariæ</u>.' Give me this, she told Shelley, 'and I will thank my love for many favours.'[62]

Mary's wish for a home in 'absentia Clariæ' would grow in the years that followed into an all-consuming desire. In the autumn of 1816 it was brought on by her own misery and by the descent of the pregnant Claire into perpetual gloom. Poor Claire had ample reason to be miserable. She was eighteen, eight months pregnant, entirely without means to support herself and was being ignored by the father of her child. She dispatched pitiful letters to Byron, in which she begged for news and complained of her solitude. If he could not love her, she pleaded, could he at least love their baby? After all, the idea of a child deserted by its father was too melancholy for words. 'My love is quite a gentle one', she protested, 'but if you are afraid of me who would rather die than do you the least harm, the moment I've read your letter I will either enclose it back to your dear self again or give it into Shelley's keeping till you return.'⁶³ But it was not fear of exposure which prevented Byron from writing to Claire. He might have been momentarily attracted by her forwardness, but he regarded her letters as nagging and sentimental almost from the outset. He left Geneva in September and, after sacking Polidori, travelled over the Alps to Italy in the company of his friend John Cam Hobhouse. By Christmas he was in Venice, where unsuitable Italian ladies, including the wife of his landlord, provided ample distraction. He soon grew bored of reading Claire's missives and instructed her, via a letter to Shelley, to stop writing to him. 'My hopes are therefore over', she replied. 'I will not write to teize you again.'⁶⁴ Her plan to acquire a poet of her own had backfired disastrously, and with it her hopes of independence.

For Shelley, the unexpected validation of his work in *The Examiner* provided a welcome relief from domestic misery. Hunt wrote to him to draw his attention to 'Young Poets', and must also have mentioned his financial distress, since Shelley then sent a substantial sum of money to help him out of his difficulties. This sounds rather crass – to praise a wealthy young poet and then to inform him of one's poverty – but Hunt was taken aback by the gift, and promptly sent Shelley £5 in interest. With equal promptness Shelley returned the £5, citing his ability to help Hunt, Byron's long-held admiration for him ('I cannot doubt that he would not hesitate in contributing at least £100 towards extricating one whom he regards so highly from a state of embarrassment') and suggested that Hunt spend the money on 'some little literary luxury' for himself.

In the correspondence which followed the article's publication Shelley described himself to Hunt as an outcast mocked by all those who knew his work. He spoke too of how social exile had affected his sense of poetic vocation:

Perhaps I should have shrunk from persisting in the task which I had undertaken in early life, of opposing myself, in these evil times & among these evil tongues, to what I esteem misery & vice; if I must have lived in the solitude of the heart. Fortunately my domestic circle incloses that within it which compensates for the loss. – But these are subjects for conversation, & I find that in using the privileges which you have permitted me of friendship, I have indulged that garrulity of self-love which only friendship can excuse or endure.[65]

A few days later, Shelley left his 'domestic circle' to visit Hunt. Mary recorded in her diary that Shelley was 'pleased with Hunt'[66] and he returned to Bath much gratified by the attentions of his new friend. Hunt was equally pleased with Shelley and their relationship got off to a bright new start, each of them intrigued by the character and ideas of the other. Shelley slotted comfortably into Hunt's household and revelled in fireside conversations in the colourful study. Hunt offered him sympathy and kindness, as well as intellectual debate of the kind he had not experienced since parting from Byron.

For Hunt, it was refreshing to meet a man who did not need guidance and advice about how to pursue his poetic vocation, and who had no stake in the fraught cliques which were forming among his friends. Shelley was no Keats: he would not be blinded by the admiration of the likes of Haydon, or led away to other social groups by fulsome compliments. Recognising this, Hunt never attempted to patronise Shelley, despite their eight-year age gap. Instead, he treated him as an equal from the outset, and during Shelley's first visit to Hampstead he and Hunt discovered the luxury of mutually respectful friendship, free from underlying tensions about age, class, or disparity of intellect.

Within a few days, however, Hunt's friendship became crucial to Shelley. Back in Bath, he received a letter from his bookseller Thomas Hookham, telling him that Harriet's pregnant body had been found in the Serpentine. He set out immediately for London, determined to learn the circumstances of Harriet's death and to claim his two children, four year old Ianthe and two year old Charles. When he arrived, however, he met stiff opposition from Harriet's family. Shelley had no intention of leaving the children with the Westbrooks, who he believed would turn them against him and fill their minds with the poison of bourgeois hypocrisy, but Harriet's sister Eliza and her father John would not give up her offspring to the atheistic radical who abandoned her during her second pregnancy. Faced with this impasse, both sides began to prepare for a custody battle in the courts.

If Harriet Shelley has not appeared very much in this narrative it is because she was effectively excluded from Shelley and Mary's lives from the spring of 1815 onwards. After Shelley abandoned her she moved back with her children to her father's house. Divorce was impossible, but without it she had no hope of re-establishing herself in domestic respectability, and no hope of ever again being the mistress of her own establishment. In the September before her death she left the children with her sister Eliza, and information about her thereafter is scarce. At some point she must have realised that she was pregnant, which may well have contributed to her decision to end her life. The identity of her unborn child's father is not known, but it is unlikely to have been Shelley.[67] In her suicide note Harriet begged Shelley to leave their daughter with her sister Eliza, and to be careful of their son:

> As you form his infant mind so you will reap the fruits hereafter. Now comes the sad task of saying farewell – oh I must be quick. God bless & watch over you all. You dear Bysshe. & you dear Eliza. May all happiness attend ye both is the last wishes of her who loved ye more than all others. My children I dare not trust myself there. They are too young to regret me & ye will be kind to them for their own sakes more than for mine. My parents do not regret me.[68]

It was the second such note Shelley had read in as many months. In the days following Harriet's death Hunt was a constant source of support. Shelley stayed at his house in Hampstead, propped up by his 'affectionate attentions'. 'Leigh Hunt has been with me all day', he reported to Mary, '& his delicate & tender attentions to me, his kind speeches of you, have sustained me against the weight of the horror of this event.'[69] Hunt's kindness went further than sympathetic speeches, and he offered to take charge of Shelley's children and prepare them for a new life with their father. In the light of his pressing financial obligations and his own noisy and ever-growing brood this offer was truly generous. But Eliza Westbrook declined to hand over the children and ignored Shelley's suggestion that she should make an appointment with Hunt to do so.

Shelley and Hunt's friendship had begun in the spirit of mutual admiration, but it was now strengthened by crisis and adversity. Harriet's death drew them together and thus brought about a unification of their separate worlds. It was an important moment for them, their families and their friends. From this point onwards, their friends would meet each other in a kaleidoscopic series of shifting configurations, all of which had Shelley and Hunt at the centre. And all these configurations had their roots in the dark days of December 1816, when Shelley and Hunt joined forces in a battle for Shelley's neglected children.

At the end of December Mary left William with Claire and travelled to London. On the penultimate day of the year, she and Shelley were married at the city church of St Mildred's, in the presence of a beaming Godwin, who was allowed to believe that Claire remained in Bath for some unidentified reason related to her health. Shelley thought that marrying Mary would strengthen his case against the Westbrooks; Mary found that after two and a half years of exile she was re-admitted to her family home. 'The ceremony so magical in its effects was undergone this morning',[70] Shelley told Claire, rather dismissively. But despite his tone, he too felt the benefits of these 'magical effects'. Marriage ended his exile from Skinner Street, regularised his relationship with Mary and removed some of the stigma attached to little William's birth. It also legitimised the baby Mary conceived around the time of the wedding: her third pregnancy in two and a half years.

By the end of 1816, Mary and Shelley were fully integrated into both the Hunt and the Godwin households. Mary was reconciled with her father, and despite the disparity in age and education, she found common ground with Marianne Hunt. Both were married to men battling conventional prejudice with their pens; both had to cope with troublesome sisters; and both were newly pregnant. Shelley was the new star in Hunt's firmament; he was confident he would win his custody battle; and he received his first favourable notice in the press. Hunt's financial problems were temporarily relieved by Shelley's generosity; Shelley praised *Rimini* and his political writing; and Keats also entered his life. It was a different story for the women outside this charmed coterie, especially those troublesome sisters, Claire and Bess, each trapped in her own way in a no-man's land of social indeterminacy. But the year ended well for Mary and Shelley, and for Marianne and Hunt, ensconced in a circle of friends.

4

Children

Shelley initially expected to be able to claim his children quickly, and he was taken aback by the actions of Harriet's family. John and Eliza Westbrook began to assemble documents for their court case: letters which revealed how Shelley had neglected Harriet, and extracts from *Queen Mab* which demonstrated its author's atheistic and republican views. But Shelley had wealth and precedent on his side. In English law children were assumed to be the property of their father, and while Shelley's views were unorthodox, his antecedents were impeccably aristocratic. At the beginning of January he and Mary returned to Claire in Bath to make arrangements for the future. Claire's baby was almost due; Mary was pregnant again, and it seemed more than likely that they would soon need to make room in their home for Ianthe and Charles. Their Bath lodgings were not suitable for such a rapidly expanding brood, and house-hunting took on a new urgency. Shelley bought a lease on a house in Marlow, and made preparations for a spring move.

On 12 January 1817, Claire gave birth to a baby girl. It was Byron's right to name her, so, in the absence of any instructions from him, Claire temporarily called her Alba, in a tribute to Byron himself, whom the Shelleys affectionately nicknamed 'Albe'. From the start Claire was a devoted mother and she found her infant daughter a constant source of surprise and delight. Absorbed in her baby, she wrote few letters, and any diary she kept during this period has not survived. But the diary she started a year later was filled with references to her 'darling'; to baths and games and walks with 'my Da'. Claire would later eradicate these references, but the ink she used to obscure her words has faded. As a result, it is once again possible to read the record of her happy experience of motherhood.

Byron was informed of the birth of his daughter by both Mary and Shelley. Through Mary he received messages from Claire: 'she sends her affectionate love to you and begs me to say that she is in excellent spirits and as good health as can be expected.'[1] From Shelley he received a brief description of his daughter: 'a creature of the most exquisite symmetry . . . betraying, even at its birth, a . . . sensibility very unusual.'[2] Byron greeted the news of an illegitimate addition to his family in typically laconic fashion. Although he was more than ready to cast aspersions at Claire ('is the brat *mine*?'),[3] he was lazily pleased to hear he had gained a pretty daughter. He was, however, quite uninterested in making plans for the future of his by-blow. By the time news reached him of Alba's birth he was in Rome and was absorbed in Italian scenery, Italian women and his current literary project, a drama entitled *Manfred*.

The presence of Claire and her baby did little to make Shelley's household more orthodox. This mattered when his morals were under scrutiny in a courtroom, but Byron remained unhelpfully silent. Shelley's custody battle commenced on 24 January and dragged on into February and March. The case was heard by the Lord Chancellor, Lord Eldon, who was unsympathetic to Shelley, and was inclined to read *Queen Mab* and Shelley's early prose pamphlets as signs of his inherent depravity. Shelley returned to London and spent much of his time closeted with his lawyers and Godwin, thinking of arguments which would undermine the Westbrooks and blacken Harriet's name.

It was a relief to be able to retreat from the painful legal dispute to Hunt's cottage, where the constant stream of visitors offered plentiful distraction. Shelley found himself plunged into Hunt's circle and he relished the opportunities for debate and the exchange of opinions it offered. It was a group quite unlike any he had known. For a start, it was bigger and more complicated. Hunt, Haydon, Keats, Reynolds,

Lamb, Cowden Clarke, Hazlitt and Novello all met regularly, but in different configurations and at different points. Within the group there were factions and rivalries, and its leading members frequently clashed over differences in politics, religion and character. Haydon possessed an explosive temper; Hazlitt frequently found Hunt infuriating and spent hours arguing with him about politics and literature. One such argument, about monarchy and republicanism, started after supper one evening and lasted until three in the morning, ending only when the participants fell into an exhausted sleep. Keats and Reynolds periodically took offence at Hunt's proprietorial pride in their work, especially when they felt he was attempting to claim the credit for their success. As Haydon, Cowden Clarke and Hunt argued away the hours and Keats and Reynolds affected poses which were simultaneously overawed and supercilious, Lamb and Novello watched the emotional dramas of their younger friends with amused – if faintly baffled – detachment.

Shelley found the clash of ideas and egos highly stimulating, and he enjoyed the fluidity of the group, which was intermittently swelled by Horace Smith (whose *Rejected Addresses* had taken London by storm several years before), Bryan Waller Procter (another young poet, and an ardent Hunt disciple), and by Novello's own eclectic group of friends. It was an artistically varied set. Novello was a musician; Haydon a painter. The writers in the group were authors of poetry, essays, political journalism and drama. Shelley's lawyer Basil Montagu sometimes joined the party so that the professions as well as the arts were represented. Mary Lamb, Mary Novello and Bess Kent, meanwhile, were strong-minded women, who contributed to discussion and debate on their own terms in a circle which was, nevertheless, shaped by the preoccupations and the friendships of men.

Hunt's delight at Shelley's presence in his circle was boundless, but others were irritated by the change it wrought in Hunt. Keats found himself displaced in his mentor's affections and was suspicious of Shelley, interpreting his advice that Keats should postpone publication of his poems (advice which was kindly meant and which was drawn from Shelley's own scarring experiences with *Queen Mab* and *Alastor*) as a patronising denigration of his abilities and his background. Haydon was revolted by hearing Shelley 'hold forth to Mrs Hunt & other women present . . . on the wickedness and absurdity of *Chastity*', but he was even more disgusted that Hunt championed Shelley's ideas without having the courage to put them into practice. Shelley at least acted on his principles, while Hunt merely defended them, content with a 'smuggering fondle'.[4] Meanwhile Bess – the object of Hunt's fondles – found herself edged out of Hunt's inner circle, first by the advent of Keats and then by Shelley. She became increasingly miserable.

The tension caused by Shelley's prolonged stay in Hampstead erupted one evening during a dinner party at the house of Horace Smith, when Hunt and Shelley baited the deeply religious Haydon about Christianity. Shelley quoted lines from *Cymbeline* which suggested religious doubts on the part of Shakespeare, and Hunt laughed at the literalism of his friend's religious belief. He masked his mockery with ironic sympathy for Haydon's predicament, telling him there was 'no disgrace in acknowledging an error'. At the end of the evening, as Marianne and Bess were getting ready to go home, Hunt 'looked at them both with an air of interest' and, guessing something of Haydon's tortured preoccupation with Bess, asked 'are these creatures to be damned?'

The onslaught reduced Haydon to enraged incoherence, and he devoted several pages of his diary to a furious account of the evening. He was particularly angry that he had been laughed at and humiliated in front of Marianne and Bess (whose giggles, he claimed, incited Shelley to ever more offensive rhetorical heights), and he delivered damning verdicts on his assailants. Hunt, he prophesied, would 'go out of the World the dupe of his own sophistications, the victim of his own vanity, with the contempt of his enemies, and the sorrow of his Friends.' Shelley was no dupe, but an immoral hypocrite: 'Shelley said he could not bear the inhumanity of Wordsworth in talking of the beauty of the shining trout as they lay after being caught . . . Ah, thought I, you have more horror at putting a hook into a fish's mouth than giving a pang to a Mother's bosom. He had seduced Mary Wollstonecraft's daughter &

enticed away Mrs Godwin's own daughter, to her great misery. He has now married the former, but this only shews the nature of his mind.'[5]

Other evenings were more convivial. Several descriptions survive of parties at the Novellos during which the guests gathered around the piano to hear Novello play and Hunt sing. Mary Cowden Clarke (Novello's eldest daughter) later recalled these evenings, 'where poets, artists and musicians, friends of the master of the house, met in kindly, lively converse . . . Keats, with his picturesque head, leaning against the instrument, one foot raised on his knee and smoothed between his hands; Leigh Hunt, with his jet-black hair and expressive mouth; Shelley, with his poet's eyes and brown curls, Lamb, with his spare figure and earnest face; all seen by the glow and warmth and brightness of candlelight.'[6] Charles Lamb described such evenings, too, in one of his Elia essays. His version focused on the food – the beer and cheese which comprised an informal supper. It focused too on the glory of Novello's music, and on the virtues of the 'pleasant-countenanced host and hostess'.[7] In between music and food Novello, Hunt and Lamb swapped puns and told jokes. For Shelley, accustomed to the more cerebral humour of Peacock and Hogg and Byron's scathing wit, the joviality of such evenings was an entirely new experience.

Reading descriptions of these evenings now, they can sound rather contrived and smug. But this obscures the fact that the evenings had a serious political and philosophical purpose, first elaborated by Hunt during his time in Surrey Gaol. In the 1790s Godwin and his contemporaries formed coteries within which they could exchange and disseminate ideas partially protected from an ever-present threat of espionage. Now, following their example, Hunt developed his conception of sociability as an oppositional idea, as an instrument for binding together individuals with shared ideals. When he and his friends argued about politics and religion, they kept alive debates which were being stifled by a government determined to restrict the free exchange of opinions. *The Examiner* and other newspapers were vulnerable to repressive new laws, particularly after a stone was thrown through the window of the Prince Regent's carriage and the government seized the opportunity to threaten gagging acts and suspend Habeas Corpus. But as long as reformist ideals continued to be discussed in private, no laws could prevent their gradual spread.

The communal activities of the group were oppositional in other ways too. Making music in the home, for example, undermined an elite monopoly on culture by making it available to everyone. In 1819, when Hunt and Novello prepared a co-authored manual for democratic, domestic music making, they offered a model which was based on their own practice. In so doing, they wanted to show that music could be appropriated by anyone who cared to claim it. The political prize, Hunt believed, was the subversion of a cultural hegemony in which the voices of opposition and reform were silenced. In Hunt's parlour, the Hampstead fields and the Novellos' sitting room the communal practices of Surrey Gaol were repeated and extended until sociability – the self-conscious enactment of friendship – was transformed into a weapon in a battle for liberal survival.

Hunt's political philosophy soon had an impact on Shelley's work. In January and February, as he moved between Hunt and the Godwins, his discussions with Hunt and his experiences in Hampstead began to filter through into his writing. Week by week Shelley watched Hunt produce a political column for *The Examiner*. These columns demanded the reformation of politics through the constant invocation of the will of the people – a will thwarted by government, the Prince Regent, incompetent monetary policy and corruption. In response to this Shelley began work on his *Proposal for Putting Reform to the Vote*. Here, he put his faith in the collective good sense of the British people and advocated a referendum on reform. Through Crown and Anchor meetings (public gatherings in taverns) and a nationwide petition, the people would make their voices heard and the Government would submit to their will. In Shelley's proposal the entire population (or at least adult males who paid tax – this was not a call for universal suffrage) would come together to support reform, just as Hunt's friends joined together to resist repression. 'We the undersigned therefore declare . . . our firm and solemn conviction that the liberty, the happiness and the majesty of the great nation to which it is our boast to belong have been brought into danger and suffered to decay thro' the corrupt and inadequate manner in which members are chosen to sit in the Commons' House of Parliament.'⁸ Such an explicit demand from Shelley marked a departure from his earlier writing. The voice of Hunt – the reformer and crusading journalist – echoed throughout the pamphlet.

———

At the end of January, Mary left Claire, William and Alba in Bath and joined Shelley in London. She was warmly welcomed by both Hunt and Marianne, and, with Shelley, hosted dinner parties at Godwin's house and made friends with Horace Smith and other members of the Hunt circle. But the round of parties was disturbed by an event noted in typically brief fashion in Mary's diary: 'Miss K is ill.'⁹

On 15 February, Bess attempted to drown herself. Haydon dismissed her suicide attempt as attention-seeking silliness and was still giving comic accounts of the incident twenty-five years later. Elizabeth Barrett Browning was one of his recipients:

> Never shall I forget one day at Hampstead – Leigh Hunt had invited a large party to breakfast, I was lodging at Hampstead for bad health & was invited, as I knew the poetical irregularity of Hunt's domesticities I told Keats I should breakfast *before* I went & be over about 11 – saying I'll bet 5 to 1 by that time you will not have seen the breakfast Cloth.
>
> At 11 I walked over & found Keats and a party patrolling before the House on the grass, in doleful sarcasm, as they had been there two hours without a morsel – I laughed ready to drop & said What's the matter, for this is worse than usual – Oh said Keats his Wife's Sister, who is in love with Hunt, tried to drown herself this morning in one of the ponds, and it was so shallow, she only tumbled in the black mud, & has just gone in covered, being pulled out by *two labourers*!¹⁰

Bess's suicide attempt was far more serious than Haydon's account suggests. The Hampstead ponds were a series of reservoirs, and, as Nicholas Roe has shown, on the day Bess attempted to kill herself they were full from two nights of rain.¹¹ The pool behind the Vale of Health – just a few minutes' walk from Hunt's cottage – would have been quite deep enough to drown in.

What drove Bess to the Hampstead ponds in February 1817? It is certainly the case that she had been under a good deal of strain since the publication of *The Story of Rimini* the previous year. The poem inspired public speculation about her private life, exacerbating existing tensions between her and her sister. When Shelley arrived in Hampstead he increased that strain, since although his bodily needs were few – he ate and drank little, and only burdened the household with his laundry when Marianne, acting on a request from Mary, told him to do so – he was an exhausting guest, hyperactive, argumentative, eloquent, sometimes a little grandiose. More significantly, he displaced Bess as Hunt's soulmate. She had already watched as her brother-in-law lavished praise and affection on Keats, another frequent visitor at the crowded cottage. But with Shelley installed on the sofa in the parlour she became even more superfluous to Hunt's emotional and intellectual requirements. He did not need to talk to her about his *Examiner* columns when Shelley was on hand with praise and advice, and she had to stand by and watch as her brother-in-law lost his heart to his brilliant new friend. Since her relationship with Hunt was predicated on her ability to offer him the intellectual companionship absent from his relationship with Marianne, this was a bitter blow.

Mary's arrival made matters even worse. Mary had everything that Bess did not: a loving husband, striking good looks, a baby she adored, an intellectual pedigree, an impressive education and brains in abundance. She was writing a novel, was admired by Hunt, and was years younger than both Marianne and Bess. Her presence only made Bess feel her own inadequacy more bitterly. Why, she must have asked herself, would Hunt continue to value the company of a dame-school educated spinster when he now had such brilliant friends to entertain him?

There were other factors motivating Bess's suicide attempt, factors which were also linked to Shelley and Mary. As Shelley and Hunt discussed the progress of the court battle with the Westbrooks, Harriet's fate hung over their conversation. Bess knew that Harriet had drowned herself and that in so doing she had found an escape from her marginalised, twilight existence as a wife without a husband. And since

Shelley kept little from Hunt, Bess probably knew too about the death of Fanny, another sister who had grown tired of her nebulous, indebted existence. Whatever prompted her to try to drown herself – and the examples of Harriet and Fanny may well have played a significant part in her decision – it must have been appalling to find herself dragged out of the muddy water and carried home in full view of Hunt's waiting breakfast guests. For Haydon the incident represented ineptitude at its most ludicrous: Bess could not even commit suicide properly. For Hunt and Marianne (who frightened everyone a few days later by staying out on the heath late into the evening), Bess's attempt to drown herself was much more upsetting. It certainly reminded Shelley and Mary of their obligations towards another sister. Claire was sent for, and arrived in London three days later, with William and Alba in tow. She was installed in lodgings while Shelley made preparations to move his family into their new home: Albion House in Marlow.

By the last week in February, they had all formulated a plan. The Hunts agreed to a prolonged visit to Marlow which would take place in the spring, once the Shelleys were settled and after Godwin, who very much wanted to visit, had been and gone. The invitation provided Hunt with an ideal opportunity to retrench and he decided to give up his lease on the Hampstead cottage. Both he and Shelley attempted to persuade Keats to join the Marlow household, but he refused and instead embarked on a tour of southern England.

Keats was now a published poet, and his first volume of poetry, which came out in March, was a collection of short verses dedicated to Hunt. The dedication was appropriate, since many of the verses were directly influenced by their dedicatee, but Keats was anxious about his reliance on Hunt, and was already rather embarrassed by his own early work. He was keen to assert his poetic independence by moving away from the Hampstead circle, and from this point onwards he would play a lesser role in the intellectual and social life of the group. In a series of lonely boarding houses, he began work on a more ambitious project, entitled *Endymion*. At a little over 4,000 lines, this was his first long poem. It was a retelling of classical myth and was crucial to Keats's conception of himself as a poet. He described the poem as 'a test of invention', a 'task' which would take him closer to the 'Temple of Fame'.[12] It would both stretch and prove his imaginative powers and it would do so through an assertive rejection of the ideas of both the older Hunt and the aristocratic Shelley.

Writing in September to his friend Benjamin Bailey, Keats outlined the ways in which his work now differed from Hunt's. 'I have heard Hunt say', he reported, 'why endeavour after a long Poem? To which I should answer – Do not the Lovers of Poetry like to have a little Region to wander in where they may pick and choose, and in which the images are so numerous that many are forgotten and found new in a second Reading: which may be food for a Week's stroll in the Summer? . . . You see Bailey how independant my writing has been – Hunts dissuasion was of no avail – I refused to visit Shelley, that I might have my own unfettered scope.'[13] But despite his protestations, *Endymion* was deeply engaged with the ideas of both Hunt and Shelley. The poem displays the same lack of narrative impetus which characterises Hunt's *Story of Rimini*, and it incorporates Huntian effects throughout its four rambling books. Like *Rimini*, its tone is set by ornate and sensuous imagery (exemplified by the description of Endymion's eyes, which widen 'as when Zephyr bids/ A little breeze to creep between the fans/ Of careless butterflies') and its version of the pastoral is – like that envisaged by Hunt's poems about Hampstead – distinctly suburban. The bower in which Endymion pours out his troubles is domestic, with its 'couch, new made of flower leaves' and its arbour 'overwove/ By many a summer's silent fingering'. This is remarkably similar to the bower evoked by Hunt in a sonnet 'To Miss K' in which Bess is celebrated as a 'rural queen' sitting in state under a canopy of flowers.[14]

More generally, *Endymion* is a meditation on the consequences of isolation. It attempts to mediate between the sociability of Hunt's poetry and the intense solitude of Shelley's *Alastor*, and it finds both kinds of existence wanting. Its stylistic indebtedness to both poems (like *Alastor*, *Endymion* is a quest-romance) indicates how richly troubling Keats found the poetic models offered by Shelley and Hunt. His first long poem was an assertion of independence, but it remained rooted in the ideas and discussions of the spring of 1817. It may even have come about as a result of a challenge issued by Shelley. According to Shelley's cousin and biographer Thomas Medwin, Shelley and Keats 'mutually agreed in the same given time (six months each) to write a long poem, and . . . Endymion and [Shelley's] Revolt of Islam were the fruits of this rivalry.'[15] Medwin was never the most reliable of witnesses, but he seemed sure of his facts on this occasion, repeating the story several times in his various memoirs. It has also been suggested that Hunt's own long poem, 'The Nymphs', may have arisen from the same challenge.[16]

There is something arresting about the idea that Keats accepted such a challenge and then used it to prove himself as a poet; that a moment of co-operative rivalry should have given rise to the poem in which he both asserted his independence from and acknowledged his indebtedness to his contemporaries. Writing later to his publisher, he recalled his ambitions in writing the poem:

> In *Endymion*, I leaped headlong into the Sea, and thereby have become better acquainted with the Soundings, the quicksands, & the rocks, than if I had stayed upon the green shore, and piped a silly pipe, and took tea & comfortable advice.[17]

This image beautifully evokes the adventurous quality of *Endymion*, but the poem is as much a product of 'tea and comfortable advice' (or at least, of a reaction to this advice) as the result of independent exploration. Nevertheless, little was heard of Keats that summer. 'What has become of Junkets', Hunt wondered to Charles Cowden Clarke, using the diminutive nickname that Keats found so annoying. 'I suppose Queen Mab has eaten him.' When Keats did write to Hunt, however, it was to enquire rather wistfully after the activities of the circle he had left behind. 'Does Shelley go on telling strange Stories of the Death of kings? Tell him there are strange Stories of the death of Poets – some have died before they were conceived.'[18] This letter, written from the seaside at Margate, where Keats had been joined by his brother Tom ('I was too much in Solitude, and consequently was obliged to be in continual burning of thought as an only resource')[19] expresses Keats's anxiety about his fitness to fulfil his poetic vocation: an anxiety heightened by Shelley's visionary talent and confidence.

———

Albion House, the Shelleys' new home, was a sturdy, spacious building on one of the main coaching roads out of Marlow. It had comfortably proportioned rooms, a huge drawing room and an extensive garden, and it was near the Thames and Peacock's house. In many respects it was the home of Mary's dreams, 'a house with a lawn or river or lake [and] noble trees', although it was not near 'divine mountains' and neither was it in 'absentia Clariæ.' The Hunts arrived at the beginning of April, and Shelley set about transforming the drawing room into a library, ordering crate-loads of books from his new publisher and bookseller, Charles Ollier, while Marianne refurbished two mouldering sculptures found in the building to lend the books a whiff of classical grandeur. Shelley procured a boat big enough to transport several adults and a pile of laughing children up and down the river, while Hunt set about ordering a piano so that he could accompany Claire's singing in the evenings. Good-natured Vincent Novello organised delivery of the piano from London, and was still trying to arrange payment for his supplier years later. Other distractions were provided by Peacock, who spent much of his time at Albion House, and Hogg, who visited once the summer recess freed him from the demands of his legal profession.

In the upper reaches of Albion House Claire and Bess presided over the nursery, where William and Alba were joined by the little Hunts: Thornton, John, Mary and Swinburne. The presence of so many children helped to distract Shelley from the blow received in March when, to his surprise and dismay, he lost his custody battle with the Westbrooks. Charles and Ianthe were removed from their grandfather's house and placed in the care of neutral guardians, and Shelley was instructed to make regular maintenance payments. He never saw either of his children by Harriet again.[*]

———

[*] Charles Shelley died of tuberculosis in 1826, aged eleven. Ianthe married a banker, Edward Esdaile, in 1837, and died in 1876. In the late 1850s she became extremely distressed by the way in which her mother's name was being blackened by Shelley's other descendants, and she subsequently ceased contact with her father's family.

The Hunt children had little experience of spring out of London, and while they ran wild in the garden and by the river, a pattern of daily activities slowly emerged. Claire spent her days playing with baby Alba, with whom she remained happily besotted. Marianne was suffering from the effects of yet another pregnancy, and was relieved to be free from the responsibilities of housekeeping for the first time since Hunt's release from prison. Bess kept a watchful eye on her niece and nephews, but, when her services were not required by her sister, would slip away into the nearby countryside to study trees and flowers. Shelley, Hunt and Mary spent part of each day engaged in separate literary tasks. Hunt continued to write his *Examiner* editorials, sending them to London each week in time for publication. He drifted between house and garden, working either in Shelley's library, among the books and sculptures, or in an outdoor study, which he described in a letter to Vincent Novello: 'I am writing this letter, seated on a tufty mound in my friends' garden, a little place with a rustic seat in it, shrouded and covered with trees, with a delightful field of sheep on one side, a white cottage among the leaves in a set of fields on the other, and the haymakers mowing and singing in the fields behind me.'[20] Surrounded by scenes of English bucolic bliss, Hunt wrote a series of *Examiner* editorials on how the follies of an oligarchic ruling class impoverished 'our native soil' and offered only 'an abundant harvest of weeds'.[21]

Mary, meanwhile, established herself at a desk inside to correct the drafts of *Frankenstein*, a laborious, painstaking task which entailed transforming a two-volume draft into a three-volume novel, the incorporation of manuscript changes and the transcription of the entire corrected manuscript into fair copy. And Shelley embarked on a new poem: an allegorical, revolutionary epic entitled *Laon and Cythna*. He spent his working hours away from the house, drafting stanza after stanza in the garden, in a boat on the Thames, or in the woods around Marlow. Bess later recalled him returning from day-long rambles, pen and notebook in hand, 'with his hat wreathed with briony, or wild convolvulus; his hand filled with bunches of wild-flowers plucked from the hedges as he passed.'[22]

Once work was over, the Shelleys and the Hunts joined forces for massed family outings. Transcriptions, editorials, and fragments of new verse were laid aside in favour of picnics and boating expeditions. While the children dangled their feet in the water and Mary and Hunt argued about politics, Shelley lay at the bottom of the boat with a book, his face turned up to the sunshine. But he was quite capable of joining in the fun when required, and Thornton Hunt, who was seven in 1817, later recalled his childish admiration for his father's friend: a delightful, slightly frightening figure who was strong enough to tow a boat full of people up the Thames and who enjoyed sliding down steep banks as much as any child.[23] Their expeditions took them to what Peacock described as 'spots which were consecrated by the memories of Cromwell, Hampden and Milton'.[24] These were places associated with seventeenth-century English republicanism, and with a historical narrative in which a corrupt monarchy was overthrown by a combination of patriotic resistance (represented by Hampden) and soaring intellectual indictment (represented by the Milton of *Tenure of Kings and Magistrates* and *Eikonoklastes*). The contrast between the glorious history embedded in the Buckinghamshire countryside and the present suffering of the people who worked the land threw the need for a new moment of idealised political resistance into sharp relief. Mob rule had failed to do anything other than antagonise the government. Now, surrounded by the abject poverty of the Marlow villagers, discussion at Albion House turned to the form a new intellectual resistance, which took its inspiration from Hampden and Milton, might take.

These conversations were modulated into a long series of letters from Hunt 'to the English People', published in *The Examiner* between March and June 1817. In one such letter, Hunt wrote confidently that 'the Corruptionists are certainly in a bad way, notwithstanding their apparent victories now and then, military and civil. They find that they cannot make people forget the broken promises of the Allies, or give up their right to a Reform in Parliament, or turn traitors to the advancing cause of philosophy and justice; and all this seems to deprive them of the little wits they possess.'[25] The suffering of the rural poor provoked Shelley to organise schemes for their relief. Blankets were distributed from Albion House, and Shelley took upon himself the education of a village girl called Polly Rose, who remembered her eccentric tutor arriving back from rambles with foliage in his hair.

In the evenings, once poor relief had been distributed, children put to bed and the boat put away, Shelley, Mary, Hunt, Marianne, Bess, Claire and Peacock would gather in the library for music and conversation. Marianne cut silhouettes of the others, an intricate procedure involving the rigging up of candles to cast a shadow and concentrated stillness from the sitter. They took turns to read aloud, and discussed the progress of the day's work – Mary's *Frankenstein* corrections, the subject of Hunt's next *Examiner* column. They planned future expeditions and read and dissected the newspapers from London. The variety of indoor and outdoor spaces at Albion House served Shelley and Hunt well, and allowed them to replicate the separate habits of previous friendships. Hunt could remain ensconced in the house or in the intimate corners of the flowery garden, in spaces which allowed him to talk and write in stationary calm. Shelley, in contrast, could talk, read and battle out ideas with Mary and the others in woods and on water. In the evening the entire party could retire to the library, where they re-enacted the musical scenes of the Novellos' sitting room. Like Geneva, Hampstead and Bishopsgate before it, Marlow was transformed by Shelley, Hunt and Mary into a site of co-operative creativity.

The combination of people and place resulted in an intensely productive summer. Mary finished work on *Frankenstein* in May, a mere nine months after the novel's ghostly conception at the Villa Diodati. She immediately embarked on a new work, her *History of a Six Weeks' Tour*, a compilation of letters and poetry, written by both her and Shelley, describing their travels through Europe in 1814 and 1816. Hunt sent column after column to the *Examiner* offices and embarked on 'The Nymphs', a long poem of his own. Shelley and Peacock pursued a study of Greek poetry and philosophy which built on their conversations and shared reading in Bishopsgate in 1815. The effect of this study on Peacock's thinking was most evident in *Rhododaphne*, a poem in seven cantos (described by Shelley in an

unpublished review as 'Greek and Pagan') written during the spring
and summer of 1817 and subsequently transcribed by Mary.[26] Once
Rhododaphne was completed, Peacock began putting together ideas for
a new novel, which would synthesise the conversations and characters
of Albion House with a critique of the philosophy of Coleridge and
the Lake poets to glorious effect. This novel – published in the autumn
of 1818 as *Nightmare Abbey* – was a comic masterpiece, and it pleased
Shelley greatly, despite the fact that he was lampooned in the figure
of Scythrop, a melancholic dreamer hopelessly caught between two
women. Stella, one of *Nightmare Abbey*'s two heroines, is herself a
complicated amalgam of Mary and Claire, and the pronouncements of
the cheerful Mr Hilary, who is the living embodiment of his philosophy
that 'a happy disposition finds materials of enjoyment everywhere', are
benign pastiches of similar pronouncements by Hunt.[27]

Peacock later remembered the summer of 1817 with particular
affection and as one of the most companionable periods of the Shelleys'
residence in England. It brought with it its own disappointments
though: he fell in love with Claire, and wanted to marry her. She was
too absorbed in Alba and her hopes for a reconciliation with Byron to
be interested in Shelley's academic, cerebral friend.

While Mary turned *Frankenstein* into a printer's draft, Hunt wrote
political columns and Peacock produced *Rhododaphne*, Shelley turned
his attention to *Laon and Cythna*, his first major poem since *Alastor*.
Even in a highly productive household, in which two other writers
were working on long poems, the scale of *Laon and Cythna* was in itself
a significant achievement: Shelley wrote almost 5,000 lines of poetry
between March and October. The idea of writing a long poem on the
subject of revolution probably first occurred to him during conversations
with Byron in Geneva in 1816, although his original suggestion was that
Byron should be the one to write it.[28] Byron showed little interest in
doing so, however, and in the spring of 1817 Shelley embarked on the
ambitious project. The evening conversations at Albion House – about
parliamentary reform, political unrest and Cromwellian republicanism
– all found their way into *Laon and Cythna*'s complex revolutionary
allegory. As had happened to Hunt in Surrey Gaol, Mary in Geneva

and Shelley himself in Bishopsgate, the presence of friends inspired him to new heights of creativity. Like *Frankenstein* and *Alastor*, *Laon and Cythna* was proof that great literature did not have to be the work of isolated genius; that it could also be inspired by conversation and friendship.

Laon and Cythna tells the story of a brother and sister who rise up against the forces of oppression to lead a brief moment of revolutionary success. It draws on eighteenth-century narratives of secular and political progress, notably Volney's *Ruins of Empire*, but its brilliance lies in the multiplicity of its engagements: in it Classical and Renaissance epic combine with French and English history and politics in poetry of extraordinary allusive depth. It is also an autobiographical poem in which Shelley addresses his indebtedness to Godwin and his relationship with Mary, who, in the Dedication, is celebrated for her idealised ancestry ('They say that thou wert lovely from thy birth/ Of glorious parents', 'thou Child of love and light') and for her friendship and wisdom. Recalling her declaration of love for him, he hymned the effect on him of her companionship:

> No more alone through the world's wilderness,
> Although I trod the paths of high intent,
> I journeyed now: no more companionless[29]

Laon and Cythna is a celebration of the transformative power of companionship: just as Shelley in the dedication finds inspiration in the life he and Mary have built together ('friends' and 'two gentle babes' who 'fill our home with smiles' are the 'parents' of his poem), so do Laon and Cythna find an escape from tyranny in their love for each other. In his long Preface, which focused on the history of the French Revolution, Shelley was unambiguous about the sexual nature of the relationship between brother and sister:

> In the personal conduct of my Hero and Heroine, there is one circumstance which was intended to startle the reader from the trance of ordinary life. It was my object to break through the crust of outworn

opinions on which established institutions depend. I have appealed
therefore to the most universal of all feelings, and have endeavoured
to strengthen the moral sense, by forbidding it to waste its energies
in seeking to avoid actions which are only crimes of convention. It
is because there is so great a multitude of artificial vices, that there
are so few real virtues. Those feelings alone which are benevolent or
malevolent, are essentially good or bad. The circumstance of which I
speak, was introduced, however, merely to accustom men to that charity
and toleration which the exhibition of a practice widely differing from
their own, has a tendency to promote.[30]

This passage had a note appended: 'the sentiments connected with
and characteristic of this circumstance, have no personal reference to
the writer.' Given the nature of Shelley's household, with its motley
collection of children, friends, wives, and sisters, this sop to social
convention was highly necessary. And while there is no suggestion that
his relationship with Claire was anything other than fraternal in the
summer of 1817, it is certainly the case that he wrote his celebration
of incest in a community which included both Claire and Bess, two
sisters whose ambivalent position in their respective households was
intellectually tantalising and sexually suggestive.

The unconventional nature of the Albion House collective did
not go unnoticed, and by mid-summer Shelley was viewed by his
Marlow neighbours as thoroughly eccentric. Blankets and poor relief
might be welcomed; the lessons he taught the village girl Polly Rose
were more worrying. Horace Smith, who spent a few days at Albion
House, remembered him hurling the full force of his reason at urchins
throwing stones at a squirrel, until they 'threw down their missiles and
slunk away'. He also recalled how the Marlow woods excited Shelley
to great heights of oratory: 'becoming gradually excited as he gave way
to his sentiments, his eyes kindled, he strode forwards more rapidly,
swinging his arms to and fro, and spoke with a vehemence and a
rapidity which rendered it difficult to collect his opinions on particular
points.'[31] Smith's description is undoubtedly that of a man who might
have scandalised the Marlow locals, but it is also a portrait of Shelley

at his most alert to his surroundings and to the productive influence of his friends.

It is not quite clear at what point Horace Smith visited Marlow, but, for the peace of Albion House, one is inclined to hope that his arrival post-dated the Hunts' departure in June. Horace Smith was a peaceable, generous man, but his patience was badly tried by Hunt that spring. In an attempt to alleviate Hunt's permanent financial distress, Smith asked him to edit a manuscript he was preparing for publication. Smith was eager to draw on Hunt's experience and to present his work to a bookseller in as polished a form as possible, and he offered Hunt £100 for his services. Hunt took the manuscript and then promptly forgot about it. 'I need not remind you how many enquiries I made', Smith remonstrated: 'how many assurances I got that it was in hand and nearly completed, – how many *months* elapsed, (great part of which you were in perfect leisure at Marlow), and finally with what trouble I extracted it from your hands after being told that it was, you believed, left behind, or in a Table Drawer, or in short you knew not where.'³² Smith wrote this in response to a request from Hunt, made at the end of 1817, for a loan of £200 and his frustration with his friend spilled into a letter which nevertheless remained measured and fair. 'True friendship, you will perhaps again say, would overlook these offences; to which I reply that true friendship would not commit them. You have met more friends than any man I know or have even heard of, but you may depend on it Hunt that such a system of utter negligence will finally alienate them all.'

Smith was not the only one among Hunt's friends to feel that his prolonged stay with Shelley was making him neglect his duties. By June, John Hunt too had tired of his brother's prolonged absence, and he suspected that Shelley was a bad influence on his erratic sibling. He turned his attention to finding a house to which Leigh and Marianne could return and wrote with mounting irritation of the problems with *The Examiner*, and the 'continued depression' of its sales. John Hunt's prescription was clear. Leigh needed to return to London and resume his theatrical column ('that would be two guineas a week saved at once') and to cease writing inflammatory, Shelley-influenced columns about religion which alienated their readership.[33] Hunt and Marianne returned to London, leaving Bess and the children in Marlow while they established themselves in new lodgings.

By the end of August the peace and productivity of the first part of the summer had given way to renewed anxiety about the future. In September Mary gave birth to a baby girl, named Clara to please Claire. Despite this affectionate gesture, Clara's birth disrupted a temporary period of calm in Mary and Claire's relationship, as, each with a baby to care for, their visions of a happy future diverged sharply. Claire wanted little more than to stay with Alba, and was worried about the prospect of parting with her. It seemed inevitable that Alba would have to live with her father, and Claire's uncertainty about Byron's plans made her irritable and difficult to live with. Meanwhile, Mary's mood appears to have dipped after she gave birth, and she became concerned about the need to secure her family against gossip and innuendo. More than ever, she wanted a home which was free of interloping sisters.

For this reason, Clara's birth also complicated Mary's relationship with Shelley. The tensions between them were exposed, appropriately enough, by descriptions of the children. Shelley told Byron that 'Little Alba & William who are fast friends, & amuse themselves with talking a most unintelligible language together, are dreadfully puzzled by the stranger [Clara], whom they consider very stupid for not coming to play with them on the floor',[34] but Mary reported to Shelley (during one of his autumn absences in London) that William preferred his own sister to Alba. 'He will not go near Alba and if she approaches him he utters a fretful cry until she is removed – but he kisses Clara – strokes her arms & feet and laughs to find them so soft and pretty.'[35] Mary's remarks might appear to be rather childishly territorial, but as the autumn progressed and she was left in a chilly house with only Claire for company (and Claire was 'unhappy and consequently cross')[36] Alba came to represent much more than a focus for petty maternal jealousy. She became a symbol for all Mary's worries about an existence in England which seemed uncertain and provisional.

By October, Albion House bore little resemblance to the happy, productive place it had been in the spring. Damp set in, covering the books in the library with mildew. The Hunts, who had settled into new lodgings in Paddington, arrived back in Marlow in September and stayed for a few days while Shelley was in London, but this time they made Mary cross by staying in bed late and then slipping off for walks by themselves, leaving her to make her first expeditions since Clara's birth alone. Such a 'contrary fit' from the normally friendly Hunt suggests that both he and Marianne were finding their hostess rather difficult.[37] Peacock was a further source of irritation, arriving every day 'uninvited to drink his bottle'. Mary told Shelley that she did not see him, since 'he morally disgusts me and Marianne says that he is very ill tempered', and if, as this suggests, the Hunts were left to entertain Shelley's friends while Mary hid upstairs, it is quite understandable that their visit lasted only a few days.[38]

Shelley spent September and October shuttling between London and Marlow. He found a publisher for *Frankenstein*, Lackington and Co., a firm specialising in inexpensive novels, and he simultaneously oversaw the production of Mary's proofs and made plans for the printing of *Laon and Cythna* with his publisher, Charles Ollier. Like Mary he was concerned about Alba, and his concern was in no way lessened when a letter finally arrived from Byron, indicating that he would like his daughter to be brought to him at a convenient moment. Perhaps the child could be sent out under the care of a courier? Unlike Byron, both Shelley and Mary were alert to the difficulty of despatching a nine month old baby across Europe and to Claire's likely reaction to the suggestion that Alba should travel to her father in the care of strangers.

It seemed as if the best way to get Alba to Italy would be for the Shelleys and Claire to take her to Byron themselves. With Alba settled with her father it might be possible to address the question of Claire's future properly, and a journey to Italy would also provide a welcome escape from the dreariness of an English winter. Albion House could be given up, and Shelley felt his health would benefit from the Mediterranean climate. But throughout the autumn they vacillated between one plan and another. Byron's request was ignored and Mary's letters became petulant in their anxiety. 'Alba's departure ought certainly not to be delayed', she told Shelley at the end of September. 'You do not seem enough to feel the absolute necessity there is that she should join her father with every possible speed.'[39]

Mary sent many letters like this to Shelley during the autumn of 1817 and they make difficult reading for her admirers. She had much to say about the problem of Alba and Claire, but her letters were also full of domestic demands – for flannel for baby Clara, and a sealskin fur hat for William in 'a fashionable round shape <u>for a boy</u> . . . let it be rather too large than too small – but exactly the thing would be best.' Later in the same letter she changed her mind: 'perhaps you had better not get William's hat as it may not fit him or please me.'[40] She complained constantly about Claire, who was 'forever wearying with her idle & childish complaints'.[41] Such missives made Shelley uncommunicative, in part because of their tone and in part because he was much less interested than his wife in resolving the question of Claire's long-term living arrangements.

Mary's tone was attributable to several factors apart from her continued anxiety about Claire. She had only recently given birth, her house was becoming uninhabitable, and it was evident that another disruptive move would need to be arranged. Shelley's health was suffering from the damp autumn and from the strain of finishing *Laon and Cythna*. In the years following her elopement in 1814 Mary was forced to grow up very quickly and now, aged just twenty, she stood on the brink of professional authorship, was the mistress of a large house and several servants, and had two small children in her care. But even at her most irritable, she held fast to a vision of a life in which she and Shelley could live with their children in uncomplicated peace. Every letter she wrote to Shelley during that difficult autumn contained expressions of love and news of the children. 'Willy is just going to bed – When I ask him where you are he makes me a long speech that I do not understand' – 'Clara is well and gets very pretty. How happy I shall be when my own dear love comes again to kiss me and my babes' – 'Clara already replies to her nurse's caresses by smiles – and Willy kisses her with great tenderness.'[42] But with Shelley away and Claire too absorbed in Alba and her own worries to pay much attention to the pressures on her stepsister, it was almost impossible for Mary to remain optimistic about the likelihood of an undisturbed future.

There was further trouble in December when Charles Ollier was forced to withdraw the early editions of *Laon and Cythna* from sale. The first readers of the poem reacted angrily to its depiction of incest, and the threat of prosecution was real. As printer, it was Ollier rather than Shelley who was liable for the poem, and other publishers had been convicted of blasphemous libel that year. Shelley had already distributed copies of the poem among his friends, but in order to ensure its sale he was forced to agree to a series of alterations. Ollier arrived in Marlow with an annotated copy of the poem and laid out the changes which needed to be made in order to make it publishable. Peacock described how a 'literary committee' was formed, consisting of Ollier, Shelley, himself, Mary and Claire. Together they worked out changes which would make the poem acceptable and it was reissued at the beginning of 1818 as *The Revolt of Islam*, its explicit attacks on Christianity and its overt depictions of incest removed. It was a humiliating compromise. In the spring the inhabitants of Albion House had provided Shelley with his inspiration. Now a different configuration of friends was censoring his poetry; hemming and cutting his verses so that they conformed to the hypocritical taboos of the society Shelley had sought to transform.

Throughout the autumn Hunt continued to provide Shelley with practical, intellectual and emotional support. His house provided a London base, freeing Shelley from the necessity of staying too regularly with the Godwins. November saw the two friends engaged once more in a productive exchange of ideas, as they turned their attention to the melodramatic public grieving which followed the death of Princess Charlotte. Charlotte was the only daughter of the Prince Regent and his estranged wife, Caroline of Brunswick. She was very popular, and attracted much public sympathy after her refusal to marry Prince William of Orange led her father to confine her to her house and sack her ladies-in-waiting (*The Examiner* had been among many newspapers loud in its support of her). In May 1816 she married Prince Leopold of Saxe-Coburg and in November 1817 she died shortly after giving birth to a stillborn son.

Charlotte's death was greeted with an outpouring of public grief and a display of massed sentiment quite unlike anything the country had ever known. The bells of churches up and down the country tolled her passing, from St Paul's cathedral in the capital to tiny parish churches. In Liverpool the ships in harbour flew their flags at half-mast, and in London shops closed, theatrical performances were cancelled and all other public entertainments suspended. The opprobrium heaped on the doctor who attended the Princess in childbirth was so great that he committed suicide a few months later. Both Shelley and Hunt were saddened that a figure who seemed to offer hope for a more virtuous monarchy had died so prematurely, but they were disgusted by the behaviour of those who could watch the sufferings of the masses with equanimity, but not contain their grief when a rich girl shared the fate of thousands of neglected women.

Within days of Charlotte's death, both Hunt and Shelley settled down to work on essays on the politics of her demise. In a series of *Examiner* editorials Hunt articulated the hypocritical contradictions exposed by her death, focusing his ire on a popular press which used extravagant mourning for Charlotte as a way of avoiding discussion of the real issues of the day. *The Examiner* devoted one black-rimmed editorial to praise of Charlotte, before moving on to discuss other matters of foreign and domestic policy. Three weeks later Hunt launched a broadside against 'the uncharitable slavishness of the flatterers of *royalty*'. Their activities, he proclaimed, did a disservice both to Britain and to the memory of the young woman they purported to mourn: 'It is not in this way that royalty is to be upheld, and the community made to believe that it's sympathies are in common. It is not in this way; neither is sympathy of any kind to be expressed by perpetual and ostentatious talking.'[43] Shelley's pamphlet, *An Address to the People on the Death of Princess Charlotte*, was published on 15 November, and extended Hunt's arguments and his rhetoric until Charlotte's death was transformed into a pale imitation of the death of English liberty:

Mourn then People of England. Clothe yourselves in solemn black. Let the bells be tolled. Think of mortality and change. Shroud yourselves in solitude and the gloom of sacred sorrow. Spare no symbol of universal grief. Weep – mourn – lament. Fill the great City – fill the boundless fields, with lamentation and the echo of groans. A beautiful Princess is dead: – she who should have been the Queen of our beloved nation, and whose posterity should have ruled it for ever . . . LIBERTY is dead. Slave! I charge thee disturb not the depth and solemnity of our grief by any meaner sorrow. If One has died who was like her that should have ruled over this land, like Liberty, young, innocent, and lovely, know that the power through which that one perished was God, and that it was a private grief. But *man* has murdered Liberty, and whilst the life was ebbing from its wound, there descended on the heads and heart of every human thing, the sympathy of an universal blast and curse.[44]

This was not a welcome response to the death of a much-loved figure, and Shelley struggled to find a printer and readers for his pamphlet, while Hunt's editorials only served to widen the gap between *The Examiner* and popular patriotic feeling. But at stake for both Shelley and Hunt in these writings was a battle for emotional engagement. They watched as the press whipped the public up into a state of communal grief, which blinded them to their real grievances and allied them sympathetically to the royal family. Hunt's editorials and Shelley's pamphlet attempted to channel that emotion towards causes more deserving and more needful of public sympathy. Both showed an innate understanding of the role choreographed emotion could play in public life and felt that Charlotte's death was being used to manipulate a vulnerable populace into a state of political pliability. A private sorrow was being distorted by government papers to undermine the will of the public and it thus represented a complete aberration of the philosophy – demonstrated by Hunt in his personal, engaging *Examiner* columns and by Shelley in the autobiographical elements of *Laon and Cythna* – that one's private life should be lived as an example for the public good.

At the end of 1817 this philosophy rebounded on Hunt when *Blackwood's Edinburgh Magazine* published the first of its 'Cockney School' articles. (In this context 'Cockney' referred to suburban vulgarity, rather than to the East End of London.) The 'Cockney School' series was published under the pseudonym 'Z.', but the articles were actually written by *Blackwood's* chief rabble-rouser, John Lockhart, and were a series of attacks on Hunt and his circle. They underscored Hunt's alienation from the literary establishment more brutally than ever before, and they tarred all his friends in a similar manner, by highlighting their unorthodox religious views, their radical politics, and their unusual domestic arrangements with indiscriminate zeal. In the first article, the 'extreme moral depravity' of the Cockney School was explored and Hunt's poetry used to suggest his family were legitimate targets for rhetorical assault: 'His poetry resembles that of a man who has kept company with kept-mistresses. His muse talks indelicately like a tea-sipping milliner girl.' Lockhart was explicit about the relationship between the private man and the public figure and was uncompromising in his equation of the two: 'There can be no radical distinction between the private and public character of a poet. If a poet sympathises with and justifies wickedness in his poetry, he is a wicked man. It matters not that his private life may be free from wicked actions.'[45]

The *Blackwood's* articles were devastating because of their scope and their brilliant, virulent wit. The label 'Cockney School' stuck and is still used by literary commentators on the Hunt circle today. Hunt was represented in the articles as the 'King of the Cockneys', and Lockhart presented himself as the brave slayer of a corrupt monarch. 'I will not part with your Majesty till I have shewn your crown, which you imagine is formed of diamonds and pearls, to be wholly composed of paste and parchment.' Everything associated with Hunt was ridiculed – smug suburban tea-parties (poor Charles Lamb, Lockhart reported, had his brains sucked 'at tea-drinkings and select suppers'), sonnet-writing competitions ('this fashion of firing off sonnets at each other was prevalent in the metropolis a short time since among the bardlings, and was even more annoying than the detonating balls'), and Hunt's friends all attracted Lockhart's attention. Hazlitt was lampooned, Haydon mocked, and Keats's poetry destroyed by Lockhart's pen. When *Endymion* was published in the spring of 1818, *Blackwood's* pulled it apart before it had any chance of reaching a sympathetic readership. 'Endymion is not a Greek shepherd, loved by a Grecian goddess; he is merely a young Cockney rhymester, dreaming a phantastic dream at the full of the moon.' Keats was mocked for his Cockney incomprehension of the classics, and for his adherence to the 'Cockney School of Politics, as well as the Cockney School of Poetry.'[46]

These attacks were extremely damaging. Lockhart's anonymity made it hard for Hunt to fight back in the pages of *The Examiner*, which was itself the subject of ribald insults. Those members of the 'Cockney School' who were ambivalent about their connection with Hunt found themselves lampooned in print for their loyalty to him. By the end of 1817 Hunt found himself attacked from all sides. John Hunt criticised a series of *Examiner* editorials on 'seamen suffered to die in the streets' on the grounds that they were unfocused and unjust. Tensions with Haydon erupted into a furious quarrel about money and Marianne's failure to return some silver she had borrowed. Haydon ended the year by despatching a bitterly unkind letter to Hunt in which he described his former friend as 'a man totally absorbed in yourself, whose perceptions have actually been deadened by the pernicious flattery of humble advocates.' 'I was never more so thoroughly disgusted with your conduct', he continued. 'Nothing you can say or do will ever in my mind raise you to the state of affection I once had for you.'[47]

As old friendships disintegrated, Keats distanced himself from Hunt's coterie. 'I went to Hunt's and Haydon's who live now neighbours', he told his friend Benjamin Bailey. 'Shelley was there – I know nothing about any thing in this part of the world – every Body seems at Loggerheads – There's Hunt infatuated ... there's Horace Smith tired of Hunt. The web of our Life is of mingled Yarn.'[48] Members of Hunt's circle continued to meet in shifting formations: Shelley and Horace Smith held a sonnet-writing competition, during which Shelley wrote his greatest sonnet, 'Ozymandias', and at the end of the year Haydon held a dinner party to celebrate his progress on *Christ's Entry into Jerusalem*, a painting of which he was justifiably proud and which contained portraits of several of his friends. In an evening much described by both Haydon and his guests, Wordsworth, Keats,

Lamb and others joined together to celebrate Haydon's achievements and the delights of friendship. Hunt, however, was noticeable by his absence. It was as if he had lost control of his own circle – the poets and painters he championed and supported had abandoned him in his hour of need. Just as the 'Cockney School' came into being in the public consciousness, its 'mingled yarn' began to unravel, pulled apart from without by *Blackwood's* and from within by its *soi-disant* members.

———

By the beginning of January 1818 Shelley was back in Marlow. He was unwell; a bout of ophthalmia made it difficult for him to read and Albion House had become so cold it was almost uninhabitable. A quiet January was punctuated by visits from Godwin and Hogg and by the arrival of early copies of *Frankenstein* and *The Revolt of Islam*. The publication of *Frankenstein* was an exciting moment for Mary, establishing her as a startlingly original novelist. Shelley celebrated her achievement by sending a copy of her novel to Sir Walter Scott for review, and Claire was extremely impressed by her stepsister's work. She spent one evening writing a 'criticism' of *Frankenstein* and in one of the many unanswered letters she sent to Byron reported that it was a book full of genius, which made her 'delight in a lovely woman of strong & cultivated intellect'.

In the same letter she made a plea for his kindness to her and to Alba, now renamed Allegra on Byron's instructions. 'Suppose that in yielding her to your care I yield her to neglect & coldness', she worried. But she was in no position to bargain with him, and could only hope for his understanding. 'My affections are few & therefore strong – the extreme solitude in which I live has concentrated them to one point and that point is my lovely child.' Her description of their daughter bore out this sentiment and there is something timeless in her account of the bewildering emotions associated with the care of a small child: 'She can neither speak nor walk but whenever she dislikes any thing she calls out upon Papa. The violence of her disposition is discouraging but yet it is so mixed up with affection & her vivacity I scarcely know whether to laugh or to cry.' [49] She went on to tell Byron how much she envied the role he would play in Allegra's life, and noted hopefully that she had seen him be kind to children and servants – to the weak and defenceless – that it was only to his equals that he was cruel. Claire was reconciled to the prospect of entrusting her daughter to Byron's care (after all, she had received assurances she would be allowed frequent contact and she knew she had no choice in the matter) but she was afraid that his concern for Allegra's welfare might be less ardent than hers. Claire wrote little of herself in this letter. All her energies were focused on ensuring that Byron's dislike of her did not translate into neglect of their daughter.

At the end of January a buyer was found for the lease on Albion House and there was much rejoicing. Shelley, Mary and Claire were now able to turn their attention to the future, and to their journey to Byron in Italy. In the second week of February they arrived in London, accompanied by Elise Duvillard and Milly Shields, the servants who were to accompany them abroad, and took temporary lodgings while they finalised their plans for their departure. For a brief period they plunged once more into London social life and, as before, spent much of their time in the company of the Hunts. They visited the British Museum and went to the opera; Peacock and Hogg called frequently. Shelley joined in another sonnet-writing competition, this time with Hunt and Keats, during which all three wrote sonnets on the Nile. Shelley and Keats finished their poems within the allotted fifteen minutes, but Hunt became carried away and sat up late into the night working on his verse.[50] They dined at Horace Smith's, listened to Vincent Novello play the piano, and spent long days and evenings in the Hunts' new home in Paddington. Hazlitt was giving a series of lectures on the English poets at the Surrey Institution and his friends congregated to hear one of their own establish himself as the most incisive critical voice of their generation.

All this activity could not mask the fact that the Shelleys' imminent departure represented the loss of another strand of Keats's 'mingled yarn'. The group which had been so important to Hunt both intellectually and emotionally since his imprisonment in 1813 looked even more precarious with no Shelley and Mary to hold it together. The Shelleys were leaving their friends behind to take Claire's daughter to Byron, who was the only person they knew in Italy. The fertile months of 1817 had given rise to a rich variety of work, much of which owed its genesis or fruition to the company of others. Such stimulating companionship would prove increasingly hard to find, both for Hunt in England and for Mary, Shelley and Claire in Italy.

———————

On 10 March 1818, the Shelleys and Claire spent a last day in London. Bess had said her goodbyes the day before, but Hunt, Marianne and Godwin came to wish them well. Godwin made his way home after dinner, but Hunt and Marianne stayed on, talking late into the night. Eventually everybody fell asleep and when Shelley awoke it was to find that the Hunts had slipped away without waking him to say goodbye. From France he wrote to reproach them: 'Why did you not wake me that night before we left England, you & Marianne. I take this rather as a piece of unkindness in you.' Consoled by Hunt's newly published volume of poetry, presented to him as a parting gift, he decided to forgive them, 'in consideration of the 600 miles between us.'[51] Missing his friend badly, Shelley comforted himself with the thought that Hunt would be prevailed upon to leave London, and that they would all be reunited in Italy. But it would be four years before Hunt and Shelley met again.

PART TWO

Italy and England

Counts and Cockneys

As the Shelleys made their way by coach through France, Hunt marshalled his forces for a counter-charge against his critics. *Blackwood's* had depicted him as the corrupt king of the Cockneys, and ridiculed both his friends and his style of poetry. A lesser man might have kept quiet in the face of such an assault, but Hunt had a history of refusing to creep away, and spiteful persecution brought out his literary and rhetorical talents far more effectively than sycophantic praise. In March 1818, he responded to his detractors by publishing a new volume of poetry, *Foliage*, which celebrated everything that *Blackwood's* attacked.

In *Foliage* Hunt brought together many of the poems he had written in the years following his release from prison in 1815. Some of these poems had previously been published in *The Examiner*, and some circulated in manuscript among the members of his circle. All were linked by the theme of friendship. The volume opened with a long poem, 'The Nymphs', begun at Marlow in 1817, in a dialogue with *Endymion*, *Laon and Cythna* and *Rhododaphne*. This was followed by sonnets addressed to Shelley, Keats, Marianne, Bess, Haydon, Novello, Horace Smith and Reynolds, and by longer epistles to Byron, Lamb, Hazlitt and Thomas Moore. These poems created a public picture of Hunt's private life through the presentation of details – a fleeting glimpse of the books in his parlour, a sleeping Thornton, a laughing Mary Lamb shaking the snow from her coat. Bess was depicted in a floral garden bower; Marianne as an artist at work, modelling a bust of her husband as he wrote a poem in tribute to her, and Shelley as a questing knight in search of the 'spirit of beauty'.

Hunt prefaced his poems with an explicit statement of his philosophy of 'sociality'. 'I do not write, I confess, for the sake of a moral only, nor even for that purpose principally: – I write to enjoy myself; but I have learnt in the course of it to write for others also; and my poetical tendencies luckily fall in with my moral theories.' The 'main features of the book', he continued, 'are a love of sociality [and] of the country.'[1] This Preface established a collection of light-hearted, ephemeral poems as a serious philosophical project, in which friendship fulfilled a moral, aesthetic and political function.

Moral, aesthetic and political functions were linked in *Foliage* through the depiction of creative practice. Hunt's friends were idealised in the volume as admirable people in their own right, but also as sources of poetic inspiration. They were the impetus for his poetry, and were represented in *Foliage* as both subject and sustaining influence. Since the *Foliage* poems were passed between the group before their publication for comment, criticism and praise, this was an accurate reflection of the role Hunt's friends played in shaping his work. Furthermore, sonnets written in competition with Keats and Shelley recalled similar poems written by them, some of which were published in *The Examiner*, suggesting that they too derived inspiration from the company of their friends.

Creativity for the first generation of Romantic poets was inherently solitary, since it stemmed from, and idealised, the genius of the individual spirit. Hunt's poetry subverted this model of Romantic individualism, and suggested that inspiration was located in communality and in collaborative creative practice. He also located inspiration in tangible everyday things: firesides, tea parties and the Hampstead fields. *Foliage* thus represented an avowedly democratic project, since it suggested that anyone could be a poet, as long as he or she understood that poetic inspiration was present in the sights and relationships of ordinary life, and not just in the vistas of the Lake District, which were only accessible to those who could afford to travel. 'I need not inform any reader acquainted with real poetry',

Hunt wrote, 'that a delight in rural luxury has ever been a constituent part of the very business of poets as well as one of the very best things they have recommended . . . But I may as well insinuate that the luxuries which poets recommend, and which are thought so beautiful on paper, are much more within the reach of everyone, and much more beautiful in reality, than people's fondness for considering all poetry as fiction would imply.'[2]

In 1818, this was as radical as anything Hunt had written in *The Examiner*. In the words of the literary critic Jeffrey Cox, Hunt's poems sought 'to provoke the reader into new practice, to argue we should adopt what we might see as a counter-cultural lifestyle devoted to free nature, a liberated community and imaginative freedom.'[3] As Byron noted when he received his copy of *Foliage* in 1818, there was nothing particularly unified about the circle it represented: 'men of the most opposite habits, tastes and opinions in life and poetry (I believe), that ever had their names in the same volume.'[4] But for Hunt, this was an irrelevance. He viewed *Foliage* as a line in the sand: as a response to critical voices both from within and without his circle. In it he reasserted his central position in his network by proclaiming his affection and respect for its various members, and by codifying its activities as philosophically significant for English poetry. *Blackwood's* had sought to destroy Hunt by imposing a pejorative collective identity on his friends and now Hunt proclaimed that identity in his own writing, wearing his leadership of the 'Cockney School' as a badge of honour. The combination of *Blackwood's* and *Foliage* meant that in the public imagination figures such as Keats and Hazlitt now became indelibly associated with Hunt. As a result, his circle gained in significance as they came to represent a distinct 'counter-culture'.

Such cultural significance, however, came at a high cost for the various members of the group, and it did little to shore up some faltering personal relationships. Haydon, the addressee of one of *Foliage*'s sonnets, was particularly angry at the enforced association with Hunt. 'What affectation in Hunt's title – "*Foliage!*"' he wrote to Keats before adding, with seeming irrelevance, 'I met that horrid creature Miss Kent, looking like a fury and an old maid, mixed.'[5]

The consequences of being annexed to Hunt were particularly serious for Keats, and in April 1818, a month after the appearance of *Foliage*, the *Quarterly Review* published a vicious attack on *Endymion*. In it, John Croker, the *Quarterly's* reviewer, castigated Keats as a disciple of Hunt, and declared that his work was infected with silly ideas and uncouth language. Croker lampooned Keats as an even more appalling poet than his mentor: 'the author is a copyist of Mr Hunt, but he is more unintelligible, almost as rugged, twice as diffuse, and ten times more tiresome and absurd than his prototype.'[6] Keats was hurt by this review and his friends were outraged. They were convinced that his association with Hunt was damaging his career and that his reputation would only recover once he separated himself from the tainted Cockney School. Keats insisted that there was nothing Huntian about the Preface to *Endymion* while at the same time seeking to justify his debt to his friend, telling Reynolds that 'it is my natural way, and I have something in common with Hunt'.[7] He rejected Hunt's critique of the overlong first book of *Endymion*, but this was partly motivated by jealousy of Shelley. 'The fact is', he informed his brothers, 'he & Shelley are hurt & perhaps justly, at my not having showed them the affair officiously & from several hints I have had they appear much disposed to dissect & anatomize, any trip or slip I may have made.'[8] And he too attributed his treatment by the *Quarterly* to his association with Hunt, noting, rather ruefully, 'they have *smothered* me in "Foliage"'.[9] As his friends united around him in opposition to Hunt, Keats too turned away from him. He did not reject the creative model proposed by Hunt in *Foliage*, but he no longer wanted Hunt himself to be his source of inspiration. Instead, he embarked on a project to recast the stories of Boccaccio's *Decameron* into poetry with Reynolds and, in the summer of 1818, left London to undertake an extended tour of Scotland with his friend Charles Brown.

As Keats's admirers beyond Hunt's circle coalesced around him, the group celebrated in *Foliage* changed once again. By the time Keats and Brown arrived back from Scotland, Haydon and Reynolds had moved out of Hunt's orbit of influence, and Keats was himself more independent. He was also preoccupied by nursing his brother Tom, who was slowly dying from tuberculosis. By the beginning of 1819, Keats was bemoaning Hunt's mannerisms and his poetry. He described how he and Brown were taken by Hunt to Novello's house, only to be 'devastated and excruciated with bad and repeated puns'.[10] Musical evenings, which had once been the centrepiece of the group's social calendar, were now presented by Keats as a penance; as something to be avoided at all costs. But as the group began to splinter, Hunt's assertions of its strength and importance increased.

The reasons for this were twofold. First, Hunt still had a close group of supporters and acolytes who gathered around him. Even if Keats, Haydon and Reynolds no longer formed part of his immediate circle, and the Shelleys were abroad, Charles and Mary Lamb, the Novellos, Charles Cowden Clarke and Hazlitt continued to visit and to contribute material to his various publications. Second, *Foliage* altered the significance of the group for Hunt. It transformed it from a social network into an imaginative construct which had the potential to democratise English poetry. Throughout 1818 and 1819, Hunt's literary efforts centred on creating more examples of the 'counter-cultural' practice exemplified in *Foliage*. *The Examiner* carried reviews of work by Shelley and Charles Lamb, as well as occasional pieces by Keats and John Reynolds. Towards the end of 1818, Hunt was to be found working on a new project, the first of several *Literary Pocket-Books*. Part-diary, part-anthology, these books contained work by Hunt, Shelley, Keats, Cowden Clarke and other poets who once formed part of his Hampstead set. The irony was that the group was stronger in the realms of ink and the imagination than it was in reality. The Cockney School finally attained solidity and coherence through the ephemera of newsprint and anthologies. But even as it became a powerful literary ideal, the relationships of its founding members remained strained and difficult.

For Shelley, Mary and Claire, travelling through Europe for a third time, the ideal community represented in *Foliage* had to suffice for the absence of the real thing. Shelley was delighted with the volume, which he read as they made their way through France. 'It is truly *poetical*', he told Hunt, 'in the intense & emphatic sense of the word.'[11] Their journey towards Byron took them further and further away from the friends who had come to mean so much to them – Peacock and Hogg, and Hunt and his circle. They made their way slowly through northern Italy, with thoughts of their London acquaintances foremost in their minds. Mary noted in her diary how much the Italian scenery would please Hunt and wrote a long letter to him and Marianne from Milan in which she described the countryside through which they were passing. From Milan Mary and Shelley travelled onwards to Lake Como, leaving Claire in charge of the children. They hoped to find a house there for the summer, where Byron might be persuaded to join them. But no houses were available, and Byron showed no interest in leaving Venice. He refused to collect Allegra himself, and instead sent a messenger to escort her to her new home.

Shelley was taken aback by Byron's absolute refusal to enter into negotiations with Claire about Allegra's future. In Geneva, Byron had given undertakings that Claire would be allowed to see her daughter at reasonable intervals, but these now seemed to count for little. Honourably, Shelley told Claire that if she decided she was unable to surrender her daughter to Byron he would continue to support both of them. Mary was worried by this turn of events; for at first Claire held on to Allegra desperately, protesting that she was ill and could not be sent across Italy with a stranger. Letters went back and forth. Claire begged for a promise that Allegra would be well cared for; Byron wrote grudgingly to Shelley that every effort would be made to make her happy. Mary offered to send Elise, the nursemaid who had looked after the Shelley children since 1816, to Venice with Allegra, so that they would at least know that Claire's daughter was being cared for by a responsible adult.

Eventually Claire herself made the final decision. 'I have sent you my child because I love her too well to keep her', she told Byron bleakly.[12] She recognised that she could not provide Allegra with a secure future, and that Byron, whatever his faults, would be generous in his provision for her. The day after Claire's twentieth birthday, Elise and fifteen-month-old Allegra left for Venice, escorted by Byron's messenger. They took with them letters to Byron from Shelley and Claire, as well as copies of *Foliage* and *Frankenstein*. Claire's letter was a heartbreaking plea for understanding. 'My child was born in sorrow and after much suffering', she wrote. 'Then I love her with a passion that almost destroys my being she goes from me.'[13] Shelley's letter was more neutral, written with Byron's callous conduct still vivid in his memory. They were moving to Pisa, he reported, in the hope that a change of scenery might divert Claire's attention and relieve her suffering.

The Shelleys and Claire left Milan on 1 May 1818, and travelled slowly south, stopping at Parma, Modena and Bologna en route. They arrived in Pisa a week later, but left again almost immediately, having decided that the town was claustrophobic and unpleasant. Mary was particularly horrified by the sight of chained criminals labouring in the streets while their armed guards stood over them. So, rather than remain in an unfriendly town, they decided to make use of a letter of introduction provided by Godwin to his old friend, Maria Gisborne, who was living with her husband and son at the nearby seaside port of Livorno.

On 9 May Shelley, Mary and Claire made the short journey south to Livorno, where they sought out the Gisbornes. In the two months since their departure from England they had met few people and made no new friends. Yet again, they were flung together, although this time it was Claire's anxiety which made her a difficult companion. It was therefore a relief to meet an old acquaintance. Maria Gisborne had looked after Mary and Fanny in the weeks following Mary Wollstonecraft's death, and when her first husband died in 1799 Godwin asked her to marry him. She refused, and instead married John Gisborne, with whom she moved to Livorno in 1815.

The Gisbornes and the Shelleys warmed to each other immediately. There was a nice symmetry to the two parties, and Maria Gisborne's grown-up son, Henry Reveley, was rather taken with Claire. As had happened before when Shelley and Mary formed new friendships, a pattern of communal daily activities was quickly established. In the mornings Mary and Claire read and practised their Italian and in the evenings the Gisbornes and the Shelleys walked together, discussing the day's reading and Henry Reveley's plans to build a commercial steamboat. Mary's friendship with Maria Gisborne was one of the most important she would form in Italy. After the Shelleys left Livorno in mid-June she and Maria maintained a regular correspondence which provided twenty year old Mary with motherly support of a kind she had never known before.

After a pleasant month in Livorno, the Shelleys and Claire travelled northwards again, to the house Shelley had taken for the summer. Their new home was a day's journey away, in the Appenine spa town of Bagni di Lucca. The house Shelley found, the Casa Bertini, was a small, colourful building surrounded by chestnut woods and delightful walks. A river ran nearby, and the house was freshly painted and newly furnished. There was a shady laurel arbour in the garden and in the evenings Mary, Claire and Shelley sat outside watching the fireflies make strange patterns in the darkness. After an itinerant few months it was good to be settled for a while, and Mary wrote cheerful descriptions to Maria Gisborne of their 'quiet pleasant life'.[14]

She had reason to be contented that summer. Allegra was settled with her father (in whose house, she told the Hunts, she was dressed 'in little trousers trimmed with lace & treat[ed] like a little princess'),[15] Claire was more cheerful after a mild flirtation with Henry Reveley, they had a house they could call a home again, and Peacock wrote enclosing flattering reviews of *Frankenstein*. One such review was by Walter Scott, who, having received a copy from him upon its publication, attributed authorship of the novel to Shelley. Mary was quick to relieve him of this misapprehension. 'I am anxious to prevent your continuing in the mistake of supposing Mr Shelley guilty of a juvenile attempt of mine', she told him, rather coyly.[16] Moreover, Italy was a stimulating place to read, and she immersed herself in sustained study of English and Italian poetry and history.

Shelley was more ambivalent about the solitude of life at Bagni di Lucca. Surrounded by quiet and natural beauty, he found himself unable to write, and the productivity of the previous summer in Marlow proved frustratingly elusive. He retreated alone into the woods, and spent much of his time at a natural pool 'formed in the middle of the forests by a torrent'.[17] There he would sit on the sunny rocks reading Herodotus, before diving into the clear water to cool down. His great achievement of the previous year, *Laon and Cythna*, was written amongst friends and in their absence Shelley found it hard to sustain his creativity. He finished *Rosalind and Helen*, a poem begun some years earlier, and produced a translation of Plato's *Symposium*. This translation was highly accomplished and it built on the neo-Platonic philosophy developed two years before in 'Hymn to Intellectual Beauty' and 'Mont Blanc', but such activity was a poor substitute for the composition of original poetry. News from England served to increase Shelley's isolation. In the same letter which reported that *Frankenstein* was well received, Peacock informed Shelley that his name was linked (by implication) with Hunt's in a cutting review of *Foliage* in the *Quarterly Review*. Shelley found himself under attack as a direct result of Hunt's praise for him in *Foliage*, and his reputation was damaged by Hunt's public acknowledgement of their friendship.

As Shelley was dismissed by the critics as a Huntian disciple, he received further reminders of the way things had once been. Peacock wrote to tell him of his walks with Hogg through the Buckinghamshire countryside, walks which recalled the republican ramblings Shelley himself had enjoyed the year before. 'We think', Peacock reported, 'of walking to Chalgrove field, where Hampden was killed, and to Chequers, the seat of Cromwell in the Chiltern Hills.'[18] How delightful it would have been to be part of Peacock's party, Shelley replied. 'My thoughts for ever cling to Windsor Forest, and the copses of Marlow, like the clouds which hang upon the woods of the mountains, low trailing, and though they pass away, leave their best dew when they themselves have faded.'[19] Letters from the Hunts were equally evocative, as Marianne sent amused descriptions of Hogg ('you will hardly know him, he is grown such a beau')[20] and Hunt glowing accounts of his reading of Italian literature and his various literary projects.

Separated from his friends, Shelley turned to his imagination to compensate for their loss. Just as *Foliage* described a group of friends at the very point at which it began to fracture, so Shelley began to explore lost and damaged relationships in his writing. Indeed, some of the most moving and personal poetry he would write in Italy stemmed from this impulse. Among friends, Shelley had created his vision of the solitary poet in *Alastor*. Now he was parted from those friends, he turned his attention to the men and women who had inspired him.

Shelley's first poetic engagement with the ideas of his friends came about because of Claire. By August Claire was desperate to see her daughter, of whom little had been heard since her departure for Venice in April. Elise, who stayed on in Venice to act as Allegra's nanny, sent confused and partly illegible reports of her welfare, in which, Claire later recalled, she appeared to report that Byron had threatened to make Allegra his mistress as soon as she was old enough.[21] Elise would prove to have a flexible relationship with the truth, but Byron had given Claire little reason to trust him, and she reacted to Elise's allegations with horror. During the long, lonely summer at Bagni di Lucca, Shelley and Claire grew closer than they had been for some time, as with no Allegra to look after, Claire once more devoted her attention to Shelley's interests.

Mary, by contrast, was occupied by running a house and looking after her own small children. Moreover, the positive reviews *Frankenstein* received far eclipsed any attention paid to Shelley's poetry in the press. Shelley was proud of his wife's achievements but, given his frustration with his own creative inabilities during the summer of 1818, it is possible that her success acted as a barrier to communication between them. Certainly there is no suggestion that he discussed his failure to write original poetry with her in the same frank terms in which he described his lack of productivity to Peacock. There seems little doubt that he was growing restless, and that he did not share Mary's enjoyment at their quiet life. So when Claire insisted on going to Venice to reassure herself about Allegra's welfare, Shelley was only too happy to accompany her.

Shelley and Claire left for Venice on 17 August, leaving Mary behind at Bagni di Lucca. Although the ostensible reason for their journey was to see Allegra, Shelley also grasped the opportunity to renew his acquaintance with Byron. The prospect of seeing him again was intellectually bracing, even if his conduct towards Claire had revealed a crueller, darker side to his character than Shelley had previously observed. Mary, meanwhile, was told to put the time on her own to good use: 'If you love me you will keep up your spirits – & at all events tell me the truth about it, for I assure you I am not of a disposition to be flattered by your sorrow though I should be by your cheerfulness.'[22]

Shelley and Claire arrived in Venice on 22 August, after almost a week on the road. The following day, acting on information received from Elise, they made their way to the house of the British Consul and his wife, Richard and Isabelle Hoppner. There Claire was reunited with Allegra, who turned out to have been farmed out to the Hoppners shortly after her arrival in Venice. Byron had apparently decided, possibly with some justification, that his house was not a suitable place for a nursery. Shelley reported to Mary that Allegra was pale and less lively than she had been before her departure, but that she nevertheless seemed to be healthy. On the advice of the Hoppners, who were compulsive gossipmongers with much to say about Byron's hatred of Claire and his louche lifestyle, Shelley decided to conceal Claire's presence in Venice from Byron. He left her with Allegra and the Hoppners while he made his way to Byron's home on the Grand Canal.

Shelley arrived at Byron's grandly dilapidated *palazzo* in the middle of the afternoon, and received a warm welcome. He immediately tackled the issue of Claire and Allegra, and Byron was unexpectedly amenable to the suggestion that his estranged mistress should be allowed to spend some time with their daughter. Shelley gave him the spurious impression that Claire was with Mary and the children in nearby Padua, and Byron offered to house them all in his villa in the Euganean Hills for the remainder of the summer. It was an ideal solution. Claire and Allegra could be together, Byron could remain in Venice unbothered by either of them, and the Shelleys could leave their isolated retreat at Bagni di Lucca. Shelley accepted Byron's offer with alacrity. The one problem was that in order to cover the lie he told Byron, Mary and her children would have to be spirited over the Appenines from far off Bagni di Lucca almost instantaneously. But this was a minor detail, and could easily be surmounted by the efforts of other people.

With the troublesome question of Claire so easily settled, Shelley was free to enjoy himself in his old friend's company. Byron's gondola was summoned, and they were taken across to the desolate, empty beaches of the Lido, where Byron's horses were saddled and waiting. For the first time since leaving England, Shelley was able to talk freely about politics, literature and philosophy to someone other than Mary and Claire, and it had a powerful effect on his thinking. It was also a relief for both men to have an opportunity to talk about the personal difficulties of the last two years. 'We rode along the sands of the sea talking', Shelley told Mary. 'Our conversation consisted in histories of his wounded feelings, & questions as to my affairs, & great professions of friendship and regard for me ... We talked of literary matters, his fourth Canto which he says is very good, & indeed repeated some stanzas of great energy to me, & Foliage which he quizzes immoderately.'[23] Byron was a sympathetic listener and he was reassuringly indignant at the failure of the English courts to award Shelley custody of his children by Harriet. Shelley's ardently expressed admiration for *Foliage* – expressed in letters to Hunt – was conveniently forgotten in the face of Byron's disdain for the volume. Even if he privately disagreed with Byron, it was good to be talking about literature again, and it was equally pleasurable to hear a fellow poet talk frankly about his own compositions.

The day with Byron reignited Shelley's imagination. In the weeks following their ride along the Lido, Shelley began to transmute their conversation into poetry, in his first major poem since the completion of *Laon and Cythna* almost a year before. The poem in question was 'Julian and Maddalo: A Conversation' and in it Shelley attempted to address the difficulties of conversation with Byron, even while he drew inspiration from their renewed acquaintance. 'Julian and Maddalo' tells the story of a conversation between the titular characters, which starts as they ride on the 'ever-shifting sand' of the Lido and which takes them, via Count Maddalo's Venetian *palazzo*, to a madhouse where they visit an imprisoned poet, who has been driven mad by his cold-hearted lady.

Julian, who is based on Shelley, is 'an Englishman of good family, passionately attached to those philosophical notions which assert the power of man over his own mind, and the immense improvements of which, by the extinction of certain moral superstitions, human society may be yet susceptible.' Count Maddalo, based on Byron, 'is a person of the most consummate genius, and capable, if he would direct his energies to such an end, of becoming the redeemer of his degraded country.' But while Julian has an optimistic faith in the power of the human mind, Count Maddalo is an embittered cynic: 'it is his weakness to be proud: he derives, from a comparison of his own extraordinary mind with the dwarfish intellects that surround him, an intense apprehension of the nothingness of human life.'[24] Julian and Maddalo explore their philosophical differences through a discussion of the poem's Maniac, who reveals the problems with both Julian's faith in the human spirit and Maddalo's essential pessimism. Neither philosophy is able to explain the Maniac's plight, and their conversation founders when they are confronted with the reality of the Maniac's suffering. The Maniac himself is represented through speeches which, although they are disrupted by periods of silence (marked in Shelley's poem by ellipses and textual gaps), present a more coherent narrative of his own life and the reasons for his suffering than that offered by either Julian or Maddalo. The Maniac is in fact the poem's only poet, and several critics have argued that he, like Julian, is partly autobiographical.

'Julian and Maddalo' is, on the one hand, a celebration of conversation, of its philosophical and intellectual possibilities. But it also exposes problems with that which it celebrates. The final image of conversation in the poem is based, not on reality, but on an unobtainable ideal. 'If I had been an unconnected man', Julian announces, 'I, from this moment, should have formed some plan/ Never to leave sweet Venice.' He goes on to envisage the possibilities of a Venetian life:

> I might sit
> In Maddalo's great palace, and his wit
> And subtle talk would cheer the winter night
> And make me know myself, and the firelight
> Would flash upon our faces, till the day
> Might dawn and make me wonder at my stay:
> But I had friends in London too: the chief
> Attraction here, was that I sought relief
> From the deep tenderness that maniac wrought

> Within me – 'twas perhaps an idle thought,
> But I imagined that if day by day
> I watched him, and but seldom went away,
> And studied all the beatings of his heart
> With zeal, as men study some stubborn art
> For their own good, and could by patience find
> An entrance to the caverns of his mind,
> I might reclaim him from his dark estate.

Julian imagines conversation with Maddalo which will cheer him and lead him to greater self-knowledge. Talking the night away is presented as an affirmation of friendship; conversation as the physical manifestation of companionship. Yet the lines which precede this image show that Julian's vision has little basis in reality. Conversation with Maddalo has been neither cheering nor self-enlightening. Julian remains unaware of the flaws in both his argument and action. Briefly, he is entranced by the image of himself as the ideal friend, but he turns instead to the acquaintances he has been neglecting and the Maniac and Maddalo are forgotten. 'The following morning', Julian concludes, 'urged by my affairs,/ I left bright Venice.'

'Julian and Maddalo' represented Shelley's most sustained attempt to explore the philosophical ramifications of his friendship with Byron. In it he acknowledged how much he was influenced by Byron's conversation, but he also pointed to the limitations of this influence. *Alastor* – written among friends at Bishopsgate – explored whether the poet needed to act alone in order to achieve a state of transcendent genius. Now, in the sad and solitary months that followed his encounter with Byron, Shelley wrote a poem which presented a sceptical critique of friendship as a vehicle for philosophical enlightenment. But, despite such scepticism, the very existence of 'Julian and Maddalo' testified to the inspirational power of human interaction. Through Count Maddalo's speeches, Shelley incorporated Byron's views into the most moving and important poetry he had produced for over a year.

'Julian and Maddalo' was composed during a period of great personal tumult for the Shelleys. The root cause of this was the lie Shelley told Byron: that Mary and the children were in Padua with Claire. This lie made it possible for Shelley to spend time with Byron, since it sidestepped any discussion of Claire's whereabouts. But when Byron offered the Shelleys the use of his villa at Este, it became necessary to make the lie true with all possible speed. In the same letter in which Shelley related his conversation with Byron, he instructed Mary to pack up and bring the children to Este immediately. He enclosed detailed and demanding instructions for the journey: 'Pray come instantly to Este, where I shall be waiting with Claire & Elise in the utmost anxiety for your arrival. You can pack up directly you get this letter & employ the next day in that. The day after get up at four o'Clock, and go post to Lucca where you will arrive at 6. Then take Vetturino for Florence to arrive the same evening. From Florence to Este is three days vetturino journey, and you could not I think do it quicker by the Post.'[25] In Bagni di Lucca, Mary acceded to these demands. She spent her twenty-first birthday packing; kindly Maria Gisborne helped her close up the house; and on the evening of 31 August, three days after she received Shelley's letter, she arrived in Florence. But it was not a good moment for her to be making an arduous journey, and Shelley had given little thought to the impact it would have on both her and their children, William and Clara. His carelessness would have disastrous consequences.

Baby Clara, born in Marlow the previous year, was already suffering in the August heat. She was teething and feverish, and six days on dusty Italian roads had a terrible effect on her health. By the time they reached Este she had developed dysentery and Mary was beside herself with anxiety. But when they arrived at Byron's villa in the Euganean Hills they found that Claire was also ill with some mysterious ailment, and that Shelley, always prone to hypochondria, had made himself unwell by eating Italian cakes. Worse, Shelley appeared to think that Claire's illness was more important than Clara's. Claire was unwell; Clara could tag on to her aunt's doctor's appointments. After Mary's arrival he departed temporarily for Venice, from where he sent her a further set of demanding instructions: 'Claire says she is obliged to come to see the

Medico whom we missed this morning, and who has appointed as the
only hour at which he can be at leisure, half past eight in the morning
– You must therefore arrange matters so that you should come to the
Stella d'Oro a little before that hour – a thing only to be accomplished
by setting out at half past three in the morning.'[26] Mary duly made her
way with Clara to Padua, where they were met by Shelley. The baby's
condition deteriorated and Shelley, now realising the urgency of the
situation, rushed mother and child back into Venice, in search of more
expert medical advice. As they were taken into the city on a gondola,
Clara's health worsened and Shelley deposited her and Mary in an inn
while he went in search of a doctor. By the time he returned, the baby
was dying in Mary's arms. She was buried the following day.

On the day of the burial Shelley wrote to break the news to Claire,
who was in Este with Allegra, William and Elise. 'This unexpected
stroke', he told her, 'reduced Mary to a kind of despair.'[27] In the same
letter he reported that Mary was now 'better', but this underestimated
the devastating impact of her loss. Clara was the third child Mary had
borne and the second to die. She attributed Clara's death directly to
Shelley's actions and to the long journey she had made from Bagni
di Lucca: a journey undertaken at his insistence for the sake of Claire
and her illegitimate daughter. Moreover, Claire's concerns were still
paramount in Shelley's mind, and after spending ten days alone with
her at Este he was intensely focused on her and her problems. In a
letter written just two days after Clara's death, he assured her that
Mary would do all she could to persuade Byron to let Allegra remain
in their care. If Shelley did, as this suggests, ask Mary to champion
her stepsister's maternal needs just two days after the death of her own
daughter, it is not surprising that he found her distant and cold in the
months that followed.

Clara's death marked the start of a period of restless, unhappy
travelling for the Shelleys. From Venice, Shelley and Mary returned
to Este, where they occupied themselves quietly. Shelley worked
intermittently on 'Julian and Maddalo' and began a new project, a
recasting of Aeschylus's *Prometheus Bound*, and wrote complaining
letters to Peacock which dwelt on the degraded nature of the Italians,

borne down by Austrian and French rule, and on Hunt's failure to keep up a regular correspondence. Mary copied 'Mazeppa' and the early cantos of *Don Juan* for Byron, a task he had asked her to take on in the hope that its mechanical nature would distract her from her grief. She also sent a subdued letter to Maria Gisborne, informing her of Clara's death and of their plans for the winter. Since neither of the Shelleys wished to return to England, and Claire would not leave Italy while Allegra remained there, they decided to travel south, to Naples.

In November, Claire reluctantly relinquished Allegra for a second time and they began the long journey down through Italy. Their route took them to Bologna and Rome, from where Shelley sent vivid descriptions of the scenes through which they had passed to Peacock. They arrived in Naples at the beginning of December and found lodgings for the winter. Their new rooms had panoramic views over the Bay of Naples, but were nevertheless rather cramped after the Casa Bertini and Byron's Euganean villa. Their days, briefly chronicled in Mary's 'journal of misfortune', were spent reading, or on sightseeing trips to Herculaneum and Vesuvius. Claire was unwell, and was suffering after a second separation from Allegra. Elise, who travelled to Naples with them, embarked on a relationship with the Shelleys' manservant Paolo Foggi and became pregnant. Paolo and Elise subsequently married and left the Shelleys' service, and the manner of their parting does not appear to have been particularly friendly. Mary remained withdrawn and unhappy, and Shelley wrote a series of poems which expressed his own misery and isolation.

These verses – which included 'Lines written among the Euganean Hills' and 'Stanzas Written in Dejection' – arose in quite different circumstances to 'Julian and Maddalo' and *Laon and Cythna*. They were poems prompted by misery, emotional isolation from Mary and continued separation from his friends. 'I am one/ Whom men love not', he wrote in 'Stanzas Written in Dejection'. He later made plans to publish some of these poems together; all his 'saddest verses raked up into a heap'. 'Julian and Maddalo' was to be included in this collection. Had he done so, he would have produced a volume which encapsulated solitude and sociability as the twin sources of poetic inspiration. The short, sad poems of Este and Naples stand in striking contrast to 'Julian and Maddalo', shot through with memories of a day spent in the company of a friend.

Shelley's letters to Peacock and Hunt from this period give some indication of the depth of his loneliness. He wistfully imagined his friends meeting in London, and pleaded with them to join him in Italy. He told Hunt that if he wanted to come to Italy Byron would lend them the money to pay for the journey, and stressed that Hunt should not feel awkward about accepting such an offer, though it is interesting to note that Byron's offer of a loan of £400 or £500 was probably not enough to transport Hunt's entire family to Italy.[28] The reunion that he envisaged was to be a meeting of men, not of wives and children, an impression strengthened by his suggestion that Peacock and Hunt could travel out to Italy together.

Shelley sent Hogg fewer descriptions of Italian life than the others, but had an explanation for this seeming neglect: 'I consider the letters I address to Peacock as nearly the same thing as a letter addressed to you, as I know you see him at certain intervals.' Moreover, he continued, 'I hear of you from Hunt. Do you often go there?'[29] Shelley's pleas did not have their desired effect: both Peacock and Hunt wrote regretfully that it was quite impossible for them to leave London.

There was an additional reason for unhappiness that winter. On 27 February 1819 Shelley registered the birth of a child: Elena Adelaide Shelley, born on 27 December 1818. The history of Elena Adelaide Shelley is one of the most mysterious episodes in Shelley's biography. The facts are scarce. We know that at some point between December 1818 and February 1819 a female child was born in Naples, and that Shelley was either her father or felt in some way responsible for her welfare. We know that the child was not Mary's, although on the birth certificate Shelley stated that he was Elena's father and Mary was her mother. (Since Elena was left with foster parents in Naples this cannot be true.) We know that as a result of Elena's birth Shelley was later the victim of a blackmail attempt, probably because he lied on her birth certificate, a criminal offence. That he did so suggests that he felt it was imperative that the true facts of Elena's parentage be disguised. We also know that when Elena died aged eighteen months Shelley was deeply unhappy.* On 28 February, the day after Shelley had registered the birth, there was, according to Mary's elliptical diary entry, 'a most tremendous fuss'[30] and they packed up and left Naples immediately.

We know almost nothing else about Elena Adelaide, but theories abound about her parentage and her short life. It has been suggested that Claire was Elena's mother, and that her mysterious illness at Este was in fact the side effects of pregnancy. There is, however, no way of attesting to the accuracy of this supposition, and – unsurprisingly – there are no written records to support it. Richard Hoppner later insinuated that Claire attempted to procure an abortion during her visits to the Medico in Padua, and if this was the case, it would explain Shelley's overriding concern for her health when Mary, William and Clara arrived at Este. The letter in which Shelley told Claire of Clara's death had a scratched out final line among its expressions of grief and affection: 'All this is miserable enough – is it not? but must be borne. <Meanwhile forget me and relive not the other thing> – And above all, my dear girl, take care of yourself.'[31] There were doubtless undercurrents between Claire and Shelley which they did not wish to share with Mary.

However, if Claire did become pregnant in the course of 1818 then, in the words of Mary, she 'had no child'.[32] Mary emphatically denied that Claire had given birth to a second baby when the suggestion was put to her some years later, and she went as far as to swear the truth of her denial on the life of her sole surviving son. Since she and Claire were sharing cramped lodgings at the time of Elena's birth, it is impossible

---

* When Elena became dangerously ill in June 1820, Shelley wrote of his distress in a letter to the Gisbornes, who were among the few people to know of her existence. 'I suppose she will die, and leave another memory to those which already torture me', he told them. A week later, when news arrived of the death of the baby, he wrote to them again in a similar vein: 'My Neopolitan charge is dead. It seems as if the destruction that is consuming me were an atmosphere which wrapt & infected everything connected with me' (Shelley, Letters, II, 206, 211).

that Claire could have given birth without her stepsister's knowledge. In any case, it is entirely improbable that Claire would have given birth to an illegitimate child and then abandoned it to foster parents. She was a devoted mother to Allegra, and missed her desperately. She would not have left a second child to a life of Neapolitan poverty. Likewise, she would not have aborted a child by Shelley, and Shelley would not have asked it of her. In *The Pursuit*, Richard Holmes put forward an alternative theory: namely that Elena was the child of Shelley and the nursemaid Elise. He then retracted this suggestion in a subsequent essay on the Shelleys, in which he argued it was unthinkable that Shelley would have left a child of his alone in a strange city.[33] There is nothing in Shelley's papers, or in those of his contemporaries, to suggest that he had any kind of relationship with Elise.

It is possible – probable, even – that Elena was a foundling, adopted by Shelley to console Mary for the loss of Clara.[34] This theory is, in many ways, the most convincing. It has the merit of fitting with what we know of Shelley's impulsive behaviour, and of his desire for action. He had also attempted to acquire children before. In France in 1814 he tried to adopt a pretty little girl he saw on the side of the road, and in Marlow he turned the village girl Polly Rose into his pet and protégée. In Naples, Mary was bitterly unhappy and was mourning the loss of her daughter, a loss for which she held Shelley responsible. Shelley might have adopted Elena in the hope that doing so would ease Mary's pain and give her another child to love. This theory fits the pattern of Mary's pregnancies, which in two cases immediately followed the deaths of her children. William was born less than a year after Mary's first baby died prematurely, and by the spring of 1819, a few months after Clara's death, she was pregnant for a fourth time. There was clearly an element of planning in the timing of these pregnancies, as she and Shelley reacted to the loss of their children by conceiving new babies. Shelley may have wanted to speed up this process by adopting an unwanted infant. And we know that Elena's existence provoked a heated row between Shelley and Mary: 'fuss' in Mary's diary usually referred to an argument with Shelley, and the 'fuss' on the day after Shelley registered Elena's birth was, apparently, 'tremendous'.[35] If Shelley presented Mary with an adopted baby girl in compensation for the loss of her daughter, then it would not have been surprising if she reacted furiously to his well-meant insensitivity.

The foundling theory accords with Shelley's character, but it fits less well with the events as they unfolded. It is hard to see why the adoption of a foundling should have laid Shelley open to blackmail, or why it would have led him to lie on a birth certificate. It also seems unlikely that the death of an adopted baby would have caused Shelley the grief he felt when Elena died, aged eighteen months. In his 2005 biography of Shelley, James Bieri offered an alternative suggestion, based on the memoirs of Thomas Medwin.[36] Medwin claimed that Shelley was propositioned by an aristocratic lady before he left London. According to him, this lady fell in love with Shelley through reading his poetry (especially *Queen Mab*), and offered herself to him in the spirit of free love. This sounds far-fetched, and Medwin is an unreliable witness, but he was sure of this story and retold it in all his accounts of Shelley's life. It is possible that Medwin's mysterious lady became pregnant by Shelley shortly before his departure for Italy, and that she followed him to Naples to give birth to her child. The Shelleys planned to go to Naples at the end of 1818 in advance of the event, and this was out of character. Their Italian movements were generally more spontaneous than their Neapolitan winter. Perhaps Shelley had arranged to meet his mysterious lady (who, in the analysis presented by Bieri, may have been one of the daughters of Lady Charlotte Campbell Bury) in order to take responsibility for his illegitimate offspring. But Shelley would have had few opportunities to conduct a liaison in the spring of 1818 and none of the contemporary sources contains any hint that he embarked on such a relationship. There are also problems with making the lives of the various possible candidates for Shelley's 'mysterious lady' fit the evidence of the dates. The truth about the parentage of Elena Adelaide Shelley will probably never be known, but what is clear is that her birth and tragically short life was a cause of great heartache for all concerned.

The Shelleys left Naples on 28 February, the day of the 'tremendous fuss', and travelled back to Rome, where they took smart lodgings at the Palazzo Verospi on the Corso. After the misery of the winter, Rome appeared to offer everyone a new beginning. All three were entranced by its beauty and its history, evoked by Shelley in letters to Peacock which indicated that the city tested his powers of description to the limit. 'Come to Rome', he pleaded. 'It is a scene by which expression is overpowered: which words cannot convey [. . .] It is a city of palaces and temples more glorious than those which any other city contains, and that of ruins more glorious than they.'³⁷ From Naples Shelley had written to Peacock asking him to join them out of a sense of desperate isolation, just as he asked Hunt to come because he needed someone to whom he could talk about the emotional turbulence which had overcome him. Now, he issued the invitation in a different vein.

Shelley wanted Peacock's company so he could discuss his impressions of 'the capital of the World' with someone who would help him understand the intellectual and aesthetic implications of its beauties. He still sought companionship, and seemed to dread the thought of more lonely months with Mary and Claire. In April he wrote to the Gisbornes of his plan to return with Mary and Claire to Naples in June (due to an unspecified 'combination of circumstances')³⁸ where they would spend the remainder of the year. 'The object of this letter is to ask you to spend that period with us . . . What is a sail to Naples? it is the season of tranquil weather & prosperous winds. If I knew the magic that lay in any given form of words I would employ them to persuade; but I fear that all I can say is, as you know with truth – we desire that you would come – we wish to see you.'³⁹ Mary added her voice to this request, and told Hunt and Marianne how sorry she was that they would not join them in Italy. Like Shelley, she took pleasure in imagining their friends together in England. 'I suppose', she wrote to the Hunts, 'that Peacock shews you Shelley's letters so I need not describe those objects which delight us so much here.'⁴⁰ Rome and a new pregnancy lifted her mood, and she sent the Hunts happy descriptions of William's childish glee at the paintings of goats in the Vatican, and exchanged gossip about Hogg, whom Marianne was finding something of a trial.

Shelley spent his days wandering through Rome's ancient cityscapes, notebook and pencil permanently on his person. He also started a play, *The Cenci*, which was based on an Italian story of incest and patricide read in a manuscript borrowed from the Gisbornes. Hunt was delighted when he received *The Cenci*, not least because he was the subject of its dedication. The dedication repaid Hunt for the praise lavished on Shelley in *Foliage,* in reviews of his poetry in *The Examiner* and in his article on 'Young Poets'; and it was Shelley's first public proclamation of loyalty to his critically beleaguered friend. It was also a public proclamation of the value of friendship:

> Had I known a person more highly endowed than yourself with all that it becomes a man to possess, I had solicited for this work the ornament of his name. One more gentle, honourable, innocent and brave; one of more exalted toleration for all who do and think evil, and yet himself more free from evil; one who knows better how to receive, and how to confer a benefit though he must ever confer far more than he can receive; one of simpler, and, in the highest sense of the word, of purer life and manners I never knew: and I had already been fortunate in friendships when your name was added to the list.
>
> In that patient and irreconcilable enmity with domestic and political tyranny and imposture which the tenor of your life has illustrated and which, had I health and talents should illustrate mine, let us, comforting each other in our task, live and die.[41]

The dedication to *The Cenci* celebrated Hunt's good qualities, but it also praised his reaction to the personal attacks which had appeared continuously in the British press since the Shelleys' departure. If Peacock provided Shelley with a model for intellectual engagement with the sights of classical antiquity, then Hunt provided a lesson in patience, and the manner in which a principled man could rise above critical opprobrium in the service of his art. For Shelley, whose work had received so little praise and so little notice, this was a valuable lesson.

Inspired by the thoughts of his friends and by the splendour of Rome, Shelley was finally able to produce work of astonishing complexity and grandeur. Over the course of long days in the secluded, grassy ruins of the monumental Baths of Caracalla he wrote *Prometheus Unbound*, a work considered by many to be his masterpiece. *Prometheus Unbound* was the product of months of sustained thinking, reading and writing, and it cost Shelley more effort than any poem he had written since eloping with Mary. Unlike *Alastor*, *Laon and Cythna* and 'Julian and Maddalo', it was conceived and written in solitude. Shelley was no Hunt, needing his friends by his side in order to write, and nor was he Keats, who felt compelled to withdraw from Hunt's circle in order to discover an independent poetic voice. His poetry was inspired by both the company of friends and by isolation, as his circle faded in and out of his life and his poetic consciousness. By the end of 1819, he had begun to reach towards the answers to the questions asked in *Alastor*. Could a poet achieve greatness supported by others? Did the development of powers of intense perception necessarily involve a rejection of society? The answer, for Shelley at least, was for the poet to move between solitude and sociability, for the two opposing states to be suspended in productively balanced tension.

While Shelley wrote, Claire took singing lessons and Mary and three year old William toured the sights of Rome by carriage and sat in the gardens of the Villa Borghese, where Mary drew while William tumbled about on the grass. In the evenings they read and visited the Roman hostesses in whose salons the city's intellectuals gathered. They renewed their friendship with Amelia Curran, the artist daughter of John Curran, whom Shelley had met in Ireland in 1812. She painted their portraits and, although Claire disliked hers and Amelia Curran was dissatisfied with the image she produced of Shelley, everyone was delighted with her depiction of William, who appears in his portrait as a blue-eyed, chubby, and rather serious toddler. With such delightful company in Rome, the Shelleys decided to postpone their journey back to Naples, and instead moved to airy new lodgings on the Via Sistina. In mid-May they were still in Rome, and their plans for the summer had become uncertain. They made the acquaintance of an English doctor,

Dr Bell, who agreed to superintend the birth of Mary's fourth child, due in November. Since Dr Bell was planning to spend his summer in either Pisa or Florence, this meant travelling north, rather than south, in order to be near him. Meanwhile William was beginning to wilt in the Roman sun. He too, his parents decided, would benefit from the cooler climate of Lucca and the north of Italy. They had already stayed in Rome longer than they intended, and were a little frightened by the effect of its cruel heat on their only surviving child.

The precautions made to safeguard William's health came too late. At the end of May he developed malaria, and by the first week of June he was gravely ill. Mary and Shelley sat constantly by his bedside, Dr Bell called regularly, and Amelia Curran visited daily, hoping for more cheerful news. None came. On 7 June, Claire made a brief entry in her journal: 'at noon-day'.[42] Mary had lost two children in the space of a year. In 1815, after the death of her premature baby, she had written sorrowfully, 'I was a mother & am so no longer.'[43] Now she was a mother without children once again.

6

Exiles

The thought of remaining in Rome was unbearable. Three days after William's death, the Shelleys and Claire left the city for good and travelled northwards to Montenero, a woodland village just outside Livorno. There they rented the Villa Valsovano, and settled for the summer. The Villa Valsovano was idyllic: a light, airy house, surrounded by vines and olive trees. Throughout the summer the air was thick with the scents of ripening peaches and hedgerows full of myrtle, and Italian labourers sang Rossini while they worked the land, accompanied by a perpetual, rhythmic chorus of cicadas.

The beauty of the house and its surroundings did little to lift Mary's mood. On arrival at Montenero she collapsed into a deep and prolonged depression. Clara's death and the unhappiness of the Neapolitan winter had placed great strain on her, and she was still only twenty-one years old. Now, faced with the death of another child, she broke down completely. She wrote few letters, and those she did write were dominated by expressions of her own inadequacy. She tried to tell Marianne Hunt about their house and to avoid writing of her own feelings, since 'if I would write any thing else about myself it would only be a list of hours spent in tears and grief'. But she could not help expressing something of her anguish to Marianne, with whom she had discussed the joys and trials of pregnancy and motherhood in Marlow in 1817. 'Hunt used to call me serious what would he say to me now', she pondered. 'I feel that I am not fit for any thing & therefore not fit to live.'[1]

Hunt and Marianne, along with the rest of the Shelley's English circle, greeted the news of William's death with much sorrow, and in the weeks following their escape from Rome the bereaved parents were flooded with sympathetic letters. Some of their correspondents were better at expressing their condolences than others. Hogg wrote awkwardly and sincerely to Shelley, taking two pages to muster up the courage to address his friend's loss. 'I am truly sorry, both for the sake of Mary, and of yourself', he wrote, 'and I am myself much disappointed in the high expectations which I had indulged, of his proving the instrument of good to his own family and friends, and to the human race.'[2] Shelley was grateful to Hogg, who allowed him to rationalise his grief by representing William's death as a public loss. His letter also permitted Shelley to write affectionately and unselfconsciously of his lost son. 'Your little favourite had improved greatly both in mind and body before that fatal fever seized him', he replied. 'It was impossible to find a creature more gentle and intelligent. – His health and strength appeared to be perfect; and his beauty, the silken fineness of his hair, the transparence of his complexion, the animation and deep blue colour of his eyes were the astonishment of everyone.'[3]

Mary's devastating grief, meanwhile, provoked a panic-stricken response from Godwin. Her mother and half-sister had suffered from suicidal depression, and now her reaction to William's death suggested that she might too succumb to its annihilating lure. He was terrified that she would follow Fanny's example, and responded to her grief in the only way he knew, by seeking to reason her out of her misery. The result was a letter of condolence that can have done little to cheer its recipient. Godwin meant to be bracing, to remind her of the good that remained in her life, and of the good that she could do:

> You must however allow me the privilege of a father and a philosopher, in expostulating with you upon this depression. I cannot but consider it as lowering your character in a memorable degree, and putting you quite among the commonality and mob of your sex, when I had thought I saw in you symptoms, entitling you to be ranked among the noble spirits that do honour to our nature. Oh, what a falling off is here! How bitterly is so inglorious a change to be deplored!

What is it you want that you have not? You have the husband of your
choice, to whom you seem to be unalterably attached, a man of high
intellectual endowments . . . you have all the goods of fortune, all the
means of being useful to others, and shining in your proper sphere. But
you have lost a child: and all the rest of the world, all that is beautiful,
and all that has a claim upon your kindness, is nothing, because a child
of three years old is dead![4]

Godwin was right to be worried about his daughter, but his rhetorical
flourishes were unfortunate, and his advice was sent too soon. In any
case, Godwin had his own troubles that summer. His letters were full
of his financial woes, and were of little comfort to Mary.

Of all their correspondents, it was Hunt – a loving father himself –
who worked hardest to comfort Shelley and Mary; to find the words
which would express his sympathy without exacerbating their grief.
Like Hogg, he was full of praise for William, but he was able to express
more fluently than the lawyerly Hogg an acknowledgement that friends,
no matter how well-meaning, could do little in such circumstances. He
wrote lightly of his views on poetry and the soul, in the hope that his
fancies might lift his friends momentarily from their despair, and that
his letters might make them smile. But he was not afraid to confront
their grief. 'My dear friends, I affront your understanding & feelings
with none of the ordinary topics of consolation. We must all weep
on these occasions, & it is better for the kindly fountains within us
that we should.'[5] In 1813, Hunt's friends had rallied round to make
sure he knew he was not forgotten as he languished in his flower-filled
prison cell in Surrey Gaol. Now he did the same for Shelley and Mary,
immured not in prison but in a geographical and emotional exile. In
a series of long letters written between July and December 1819 he
attempted to bridge the distance between them through an imaginative
evocation of physical proximity. 'Whenever I write to you', he told them
in a letter written towards the end of August, 'I seem to be transported
to your presence. I dart out of the windows like a bird, dash into a
southwestern current of air, skim over the cool waters, hurry over the
basking lands, rise like a lark over the mountains, fling like a swallow

into the vallies, skim again, pant for breath.'[6] He suggested that they should all write letters to each other every Monday morning, so that they might have the satisfaction of knowing that despite the hundreds of miles which separated them they were thinking of each other at the same time. At the Shelleys' request, Hunt sent them a portrait of himself, along with letters which brimmed over with messages of love from Marianne and Bess, with news of friends and his work, and with descriptions of the English summer.

Hunt shared Godwin's concerns about Mary, although he expressed his anxiety more delicately. He was grieved, he told her, by accounts of her low spirits, and by her susceptibility to depression: 'you have a tendency, partly constitutional perhaps & partly owing to the turn of your philosophy, to look over-intensely at the dark side of human things; & they must present double dreariness through such tears as you are now shedding.'[7] He asked her to turn her attention back to her work and her friends, talking of *Frankenstein* and describing picnics in the fields with the Lambs, Hazlitt, the Novellos and Charles Cowden Clarke. He told her she and Shelley were much missed by their friends in London. At the opera, he reported, 'we look up to your box, almost hoping to see a thin patrician-looking young cosmopolite yearning out upon us, & a sedate-faced young lady, bending in a similar direction with her great tablet of a forehead, and her white shoulders unconscious of a crimson gown.'[8] But he recognised the limitations of such evocations, and that letters alone could not break through Mary's grief or relieve Shelley's isolation. 'I wish in truth I knew how to amuse you just now, & that I were in Italy to try', he confessed. 'I would walk about with Shelley, wherever he pleased, having resumed my old good habits that way; & I would be merry or quiet, chat, read, or impudently play and sing you Italian airs all the evening.'[9] But his obligations to *The Examiner* and his permanently precarious finances made it impossible for him to travel to Italy, so he had to content himself with laying bare the constituent parts of his life for his friends, in the hope that they might thus derive some vicarious comfort.

Hunt's life in the summer of 1819 was dominated by politics. On 16 August, a reform meeting in Manchester was broken up by mounted yeomanry. At least eleven people were killed and hundreds injured, among them many women and children. In the immediate aftermath of 'Peterloo',* newspapers such as the *Courier* condemned the crowd and offered their sympathy to the soldiers who perpetrated the violence, but such a response was rapidly drowned out by a groundswell of public anger. Supported on this occasion by several other commentators, Hunt elided the local militia who attacked the crowd with the government. 'A body of military dashed through them sword in hand, tramped down opposition, bruised and wounded many, and bore off the flags and speakers to the county jail . . . The sensation in the Metropolis is great and bitter.'[10] As the organisers of the meeting in St Peter's Field were tried for sedition and found guilty, Hunt reserved some rhetorical animus for a legal system, which was 'too quick to take a *side* in these questions'.[11] He was equally scathing about the Whigs, who failed to hold the government to account in either the Lords or the Commons. 'None of the Opposition in Parliament have come forward to second the voice of the people. Are they doubtful whether Ministers are right or wrong in this instance? Oh no! Is it because they do not like Radical Reform? But where is the necessity of identifying themselves with the Radical Reformers, because they join in reprobating a violence *done* to law, justice, and humanity?'[12]

Strident editorials in *The Examiner* proved of little use in the weeks and months following Peterloo. The government, horrified by an outbreak of seemingly revolutionary violence in Britain, rushed a package of repressive measures through parliament. The 'Six Acts' clamped down on the reform movement by banning meetings, increasing stamp duty (which made newspapers much more expensive) and by tightening up the laws against 'blasphemous and seditious libel' to make it easier to prosecute those who criticised the actions of the government. Local magistrates saw their powers increased, and the legal process was

---

* So called because the meeting took place in St Peter's Fields, in an ironic tribute to the British military victory at Waterloo.

streamlined so that bail could be denied and cases prosecuted more quickly. Such a legislative assault on freedom of speech and movement had not been seen in Britain since the mid-1790s.

Peterloo demonstrated two things to Hunt. It revealed the limits of language in the war between liberalism and repression; that language itself was fragile and vulnerable to attack. It also highlighted the limitations of the collegiate approach to reform represented by Hunt and his friends in *The Examiner*. Confronted by punitive new legal restrictions, Hunt was compelled to alter the focus of his writing. In 1809, after the first two triumphant years of *The Examiner*, he had proudly proclaimed 'that if with a good cause on our side, we summon up the wisdom and virtue of our forefathers, we shall have powers with us over which nothing can prevail.'[13] The events of 16 August 1819 proved that this was naïve, and that the sword was definitively mightier than the pen.

Hunt responded by turning to a new project, in which the discussion of politics was put aside in favour of a more imaginative kind of writing. In the autumn of 1819 he established a new journal, *The Indicator*, designed as an antidote to *The Examiner* for both Hunt and his readers. Its title – a reference to an African honey-hunting bird – was suggested by Mary Novello, and its focus was determinedly apolitical:

The Indicator will attend to no subject whatsoever of immediate or temporary interest. His business is with the honey in the old woods. The Editor has enough to agitate his spirits during the present eventful times, in another periodical work; and he is willing to be so agitated: but as he is accustomed to use his pen, as habitually as a bird his pinion, and to betake himself with it into the nests and bowers of more lasting speculations, when he has done with public ones, he is determined to keep those haunts of his recreation free from all noise and wrangling, both for his own pleasure and for those who may chuse to accompany him.[14]

The Indicator appeared every Wednesday morning 'at an hour early enough for the breakfast-table'.[15] It contained essays on country houses, autumnal firesides, toleration, famous Londoners, the weather, sleep, 'old gentlemen', hats and shops, as well as critical commentary on new and old literary works. Unlike *The Examiner*, its engagement with the business of everyday life was observational rather than political. It was dominated by Hunt's voice but was also collaborative: short stories by Mary Novello and Charles Cowden Clarke appeared in its pages, as did original poetry by Shelley and long discussions by Hunt of *The Cenci* and Keats's *Lamia*, published in 1820.

Hunt was sensitive to accusations that the appearance of *The Indicator* marked a decline in the fortunes of *The Examiner* and that the new periodical would lead to neglect of the paper which had made his name. He reassured his readers that *The Indicator* would be dropped should it threaten to injure *The Examiner*, but the analogy he used to support his argument was illuminating:

> The fact is, that as far as the Editor is concerned, the Examiner is to be regarded as the reflection of his public literature, and the Indicator of his private. In the one he has a sort of public meeting with his friends: in the other, a more retired one. The Examiner is his tavern-room for politics, for political pleasantry, for criticism upon the theatres and living writers. The Indicator is his private room, his study, his retreat from public care and criticism.[16]

The imaginative shift in the location of Hunt's engagement with the world from public tavern-room to private study was significant. He had always retreated to the comfort of his books and his fireside in times of strain, making his study, or his prison cell, a refuge from the cares of the world. Now, this physical haven had a rhetorical equivalent. *The Indicator* represented an intellectual withdrawal from the cut and thrust of political discussion – a discussion in which, for over a decade, Hunt played a key role. He was not the first to respond to a barrage of repressive legislation by retreating from the public stage, but his self-imposed exile from political debate worried his friends. Shelley liked *The Indicator* and promised to send material for it, but he did not like the change it represented in Hunt's writing. 'You . . . never write politics', he protested, towards the end of 1819:

I wish . . . that you would write a paper in the Examiner on the actual
state of the country; & what, under all the circumstances of the
conflicting passions & interests of men, we are to expect, – Not what
we ought to expect or what if so and so were to happen we might expect;
but what as things are there is reason to believe will come; & send it
me for my information. Every word a man has to say is valuable to the
public now, & thus you will at once gratify your friend, nay instruct
& either exhilarate him, or force him to be resigned, and awaken the
minds of the people.[17]

Shelley's reaction to the shift in Hunt's writing illustrated that the
ramifications of Peterloo were personal as well as political. In its aftermath
Shelley and Hunt differed sharply about how best to respond to its
violence and about how to contend with the clampdown on freedom
of speech which followed. This was the first serious disagreement
in their three-year friendship, and it was an important moment for
both of them, since it demonstrated that despite the closeness of their
relationship, and the outpouring of sympathy which followed William's
death, they were not immune to failures of understanding.

———

Shelley's stay in Italy placed him at a distance from the momentous
political events taking place in England that summer. News of Peterloo
reached the Villa Valsovano in early September, when Shelley received
a letter and a package of articles about the outrage from Thomas
Love Peacock. He responded with a poem, 'The Mask of Anarchy',
written in a white heat of rage in the two weeks following the arrival
of Peacock's parcel. The poem's 372 lines describe Anarchy, faithfully
accompanied by Murder ('He had a mask like Castlereagh')* and Fraud
('and he had on,/ Like Eldon, an ermined gown'),† wreaking havoc
through the towns and counties of England. Children have 'their
brains knocked out by them', and their followers 'With their trampling

---

* Robert Stewart, Viscount Castlereagh, Foreign Secretary.
† Lord Eldon, the Lord Chancellor, who had deprived Shelley of his children by Harriet.

shook the ground,/ Waving each a bloody sword,/ For the service of their Lord'. The violence of Peterloo is reproduced as Anarchy achieves dominion throughout the country. His forces are eventually banished by a maiden who represents both Hope and Despair. The poem ends with her commanding the masses to 'Rise like lions after slumber' against the forces of oppression, to shake off the chains of their own political lethargy. Shelley sent 'The Mask of Anarchy' to Hunt on 23 September, but Hunt, most unusually, remained silent on the subject in his letters, and he did not publish the poem. In mid-November Shelley wrote to Hunt again, reiterating that 'The Mask' was intended for the political *Examiner*, rather than for the light-hearted *Indicator*. But despite Shelley's urging 'The Mask of Anarchy' did not appear in either of Hunt's publications, nor did Hunt explain the reasons for this to Shelley.

Shelley and Hunt never had a frank exchange about Hunt's failure to publish 'The Mask of Anarchy', but it is easy to see why each man felt injured by the actions of the other. From Hunt's perspective, Shelley, safely beyond the reach of English law in Italy, had asked him to risk his livelihood and his liberty just when the laws on libel had been tightened considerably. Had 'The Mask of Anarchy' appeared in either *The Indicator* or *The Examiner*, it is likely that Hunt, as editor and proprietor, would have been found guilty of libel and sedition and would have had to serve a second custodial sentence. Moreover, he would have been tried by a legal system which was substantially more punitive than that which had sent him to prison in 1813. As far as he was concerned, it was simply not worth taking such a risk.

For Shelley, on the other hand, Hunt's failure to publish the poem represented an abnegation of political responsibility which began when he turned his attention away from *The Examiner* to write ephemeral froth for *The Indicator*. Hunt's own political silence was bad enough, but he was now silencing Shelley's voice as well. This was a far cry from the heady days of 1817, only two years previously, when they talked politics and produced heated political prose on reform and the death of Princess Charlotte. As far as Shelley was concerned, Hunt's failure was twofold: he denied Shelley the opportunity to contribute to political debate, and he refused to enter into conversation about his decision not to publish and the shift in his own writing. Hunt's silence on the subject – which represented a refusal of open communication – was almost more wounding than his decision to suppress Shelley's work in the first place. It was a personal, political and literary betrayal, and it caused Shelley's faith in Hunt to falter.

This loss of trust was distressing, but it did not mark the end of Hunt and Shelley's friendship. Indeed, in one of the more surprising twists in their story, Shelley discovered renewed creative impetus in the columns of *The Examiner* even as he reacted to the shock of Hunt's failure to publish. Earlier that summer, before news of Peterloo broke, he had received a bundle of old copies of *The Examiner*, in which were included two reviews of poems entitled *Peter Bell*. The original *Peter Bell* was by Wordsworth, and was reviewed by Hunt in *The Examiner* on 2 May. Hunt objected strongly to the pedagogic morality of Wordsworth's poem, in which Methodism, repentance and religious piety were presented as redemptive forces. Hunt castigated the poem as a 'didactic little horror . . . founded on the bewitching principles of fear, bigotry, and diseased impulse.'[18] He thought its vision of salvation was repugnant, and its self-satisfied piety abhorrent. This view was shared by John Hamilton Reynolds, the young poet whose work Hunt praised in his 'Young Poets' article of 1816. Reynolds produced a parody of *Peter Bell*, which was reviewed in *The Examiner* by Keats. Keats was rather embarrassed by Reynolds's denigration of Wordsworth, but he nevertheless praised the wit of his friend's poem and, in so doing, demonstrated his underlying loyalty to Hunt and to the circle of writers who had supported him at the start of his career.

The *Peter Bell* poems were important for Hunt, Keats and Reynolds, since they demonstrated that the conversation which once held them together could still flare back into life. But the belated discovery of the poems was equally significant for Shelley. With 'The Mask of Anarchy' completed, he embarked on his own Wordsworthian parody, entitled 'Peter Bell the Third'. His poem was inspired by *The Examiner* reviews and by the thought of Keats, Reynolds and Hunt united once more in productive conversation, and was indebted to Hunt's objections to

Wordsworth's didactic religious morality. It was of course also indebted to Wordsworth himself, although it is not clear whether Shelley actually saw Wordsworth's poem before he completed his parody, or whether he instead relied on the extracts printed by Hunt in *The Examiner*. Shelley's poem mocked Wordsworth's emphasis on hell-fire damnation, and it also poked fun at the abusers of Hunt, whom Shelley ventriloquised in a prefatory description of 'Mr Examiner Hunt' as a 'murderous and smiling villain', an 'odious thief, liar, scoundrel, coxcomb and monster'.[19] But 'Peter Bell the Third' was more than a straightforward comic parody. Shelley used Hunt's review as a cue to launch a poetic attack on the corrupt society of which Wordsworth had become both a symptom and a part. In his poem the Devil plans to build himself a mansion in fashionable Grosvenor Square, before 'aping fashion' by travelling to Wordsworth's Lake District, 'To see what was romantic there.'

'Hell is a city much like London', Shelley wrote, in one of the poem's most famous stanzas. The world of his poem is peopled with soulless spectres: the Poet Laureate Southey ('who has lost/ His wits, or sold them'); a thieving parliament; the corpses of Canning and Castlereagh. Together the ghosts of politicians, lawyers and fawning poets meet at 'Suppers of epic poets; – teas,/ Where small talk dies in agonies'; or at balls and in 'drawing rooms –/ Courts of law – committees – calls/ Of a morning – clubs – book stalls –/ Churches – masquerades and tombs'. These were the spaces where a corrupt elite met, and they stood in stark contrast to the private, domesticated havens created by Hunt for his friends. Like 'The Mask of Anarchy', 'Peter Bell the Third' formed part of Shelley's response to post-Peterloo Britain. It was an angry poem, but it balanced its anger with a celebration of Hunt's oppositional political and religious views. It remains one of Shelley's funniest and most enduring works.

From the summer of 1819 onwards, Shelley found it increasingly difficult to disseminate his writing. He became disenchanted with Charles Ollier, his publisher and bookseller, who, despite his protests, ignored 'Peter Bell the Third' just as Hunt had ignored 'The Mask of Anarchy'. Peacock tried and failed to arrange a production of *The Cenci* at Covent Garden, and the play remained unstaged. In July, Hunt sent an encouraging report of Shelley's reputation in England, but his analysis ('your reputation is certainly rising greatly in your native country')[20] was not supported by critical reaction to his friend's work. Nor did it acknowledge the battering Shelley's reputation received in the April edition of the *Quarterly Review*, which carried a long review of *The Revolt of Islam*. The review was by John Taylor Coleridge (nephew of the poet), who was at Eton at the same time as Shelley. This was the most negative review of his work to appear in Shelley's lifetime, and it was a vicious attack which hurt him deeply. It contained unpleasant insinuations about Mary (who, it suggested, was the model for Cythna); it brought up his expulsion from Oxford; and, in a clear reference to Harriet's death, dismissed him as a reprobate on a 'downward course of infidelity and immorality'. It ended with a condemnation of everything for which Shelley stood:

> If we might withdraw the veil of private life, and tell what we *now* know about him, it would be indeed a disgusting picture that we should exhibit, but it would be an unanswerable comment on our text; it is not easy for those who *read only*, to conceive how much low pride, how much selfishness, how much unmanly cruelty are consistent with the laws of this 'universal' and 'lawless love'. But we must only use our knowledge to check the groundless hopes which we were once prone to entertain of him.[21]

Nor did the *Quarterly Review* reserve its animus for Shelley alone. Yet again, he found himself publicly linked with Hunt in terms which were unfavourable to them both. *The Revolt of Islam*, John Coleridge told his readers, was the work of a Cockney songster, who shared the faults of his 'friend and leader Mr Hunt': 'Like him . . . Mr Shelley is a very vain man; and like most very vain men, he is but half instructed in knowledge, and less than half-disciplined in his reasoning powers'. John Coleridge magnanimously accepted that Shelley did not display Hunt's 'bustling vulgarity, the ludicrous affectation, the factious flippancy, or [his] selfish heartlessness', but this was hardly very comforting. The *Quarterly Review* insulted Shelley's work, his friends and his morals. It also dismissed *The Revolt of Islam* as a Cockney grace note, thus denying Shelley's intellectual significance and making it more difficult for Hunt to write in his defence.

Despite this, Hunt published a three-part rebuttal of the review in *The Examiner* between September and October. He was angry about both its substance and approach, and was particularly incensed by the way in which its anonymous author* dragged Shelley's private life into discussion of his work:

> The Reviewer talks of what he '*now*' knows of Mr Shelley. What does this pretended *judge* and actual male-gossip, this willing listener to scandal, this minister to the petty wants of excitement, now know more than he ever knew, of an absent man, whose own side of whatever stories have been told him he has never heard? ... If the use of private matters in public criticism is not to be incompatible with the decencies and charities of life, let it be proved so; and we know who would be the sufferers.[22]

John Coleridge's review of *The Revolt of Islam* was undeniably petty and vindictive, but Hunt's rebuttal of it was at its least convincing when he attacked its focus on Shelley's private life. After all, in the days and months following their elopement, Shelley, Mary and Claire had attempted to live out their private lives according to a set of public ideals, and they planned to reform the world by refusing to conform to its hypocritical conventions. *The Revolt of Islam* contained a long

---

* Reviews in the *Quarterly* were published anonymously, which made it difficult for defamed writers to defend themselves, since they had to mount counter-attacks against unknown assailants. Shelley believed the author of the *Quarterly*'s review of *The Revolt of Islam* to be Robert Southey, whom he had met in Keswick shortly after his marriage to Harriet. He believed that Southey had betrayed him by publishing details of their private conversations and wrote to him challenging him to deny his authorship. Southey duly did so, in a politely furious letter. 'I can think of you', this letter concluded, 'only as of an individual whom I have known, and of whom I had once entertained high hopes – admiring his talents – giving him credit for good feelings and virtuous desires – and whom I now regard not more with condemnation than with pity' (Shelley, *Letters*, II, 205).

dedication to Mary which told the story of their courtship, and Hunt himself pioneered the practice of using the personal and the private to public ends. 'Cockney' poetry stood out because of its proclamation of private pleasures: this was one of the ways in which it established its counter-cultural practices, and it was the element which its critics found most objectionable. It all meant that, as far as John Coleridge and the *Quarterly Review* were concerned, Shelley's private life was fair game.

———

The second half of 1819 was one of the bleakest periods either the Shelleys or Claire had yet experienced. Their children were dead or living far away, and Mary was trapped in a black depression from which Shelley was unable to lift her. His letters show that he was fiercely protective of her, and that he understood she was ill. He was determined not to let her depression suffocate their relationship, and recognising that he could do little to help her apart from provide stability and companionship, he concentrated on his own writing, producing an extraordinary rich variety of work in the months following William's death. In addition to 'The Mask of Anarchy' and 'Peter Bell the Third', he composed several sonnets, including the gloriously angry 'England in 1819'; completed *The Cenci* and, towards the end of the year, wrote the visionary fourth act of *Prometheus Unbound*. He spent his mornings alone in his study at the top of the house, and after lunch read Dante with Mary. He visited Mrs Gisborne in Livorno (with whom he was learning Spanish) and every evening returned with her to the Villa Valsovano to take Mary for a walk. He was lonely and missed his friends in London, complaining to Peacock that Claire did not get up early enough to walk with him. But he was patient, pinning his hopes for a restoration of normality on the fact that Mary was pregnant again, and expecting a baby in November. 'The birth of a child', he told Hunt, 'will probably relieve her from some part of her present melancholy depression.'[23]

The quiet, studious days and weeks at the Villa Valsovano and the peaceful agricultural rhythms of the surrounding countryside did slowly begin to have a beneficial effect on Mary's health. Prompted by Shelley's example she began writing again, although the work she produced that autumn, 'The Fields of Fancy', was more private and internalised than Shelley's politically engaged poetry. 'The Fields of Fancy' opens with a description of Rome, a city where the un-named narrator has 'suffered a misfortune that reduced me to misery and despair'.[24] The narrator is led through the Elysian Fields, where she hears the story of Matilda, who has been released by death from her grief for her dead father. In the novella which arose from 'The Fields of Fancy' – *Matilda* – Mary positioned the story of Matilda's tragic life at the centre of her narrative, allowing the grieving Roman narrator to fade away. *Matilda* remained unpublished during Mary's lifetime because its principle theme was the incestuous love Matilda's father feels for his daughter. It is this which leads him to commit suicide and which causes her subsequent isolation, since she cannot share the reason for her guilt-stricken grief with anyone. Nor, indeed, does she want to: *Matilda* contains a powerful description of the selfishness of grief, and of the absolute need of the bereaved to be alone:

> I was silent to all around me. I hardly replied to the slightest question, and was uneasy when I saw a human creature near me. I was surrounded by my female relations, but they were all of them nearly strangers to me: I did not listen to their consolations; and so little did they work their designed effect that they seemed to me to be spoken in an unknown tongue. I found if sorrow was dead within me, so was love and desire of sympathy. . . . the living were not fit companions for me, and I was ever meditating by what means I might shake them all off, and never be heard of again.[25]

It is tempting to read this as autobiographical, but *Matilda* is far more than a simple expression of Mary's disabling depression. Paradoxically, from the depths of her emotional exile, Mary produced a prolonged meditation on the key relationships of her life. In the novella she acknowledged how much Godwin's voice had shaped her writing while exploring the problems of her upbringing. *Matilda* thus confronts the dangers inherent in an excessive degree of fatherly love, but it is also intellectually indebted to Godwin. Like the novel he published in 1817, *Mandeville*, it is an exploration of an obsession, and it shares certain stylistic qualities with his earlier *Caleb Williams*.

In the character of Woodville – the young poet who comforts Matilda towards the end of her life – Mary also explored her relationship with Shelley. Woodville endows Matilda with a sense that her life might have some value, even if she herself is unable to feel joy or love. 'Indeed I dare not die', he tells her after she asks him to commit suicide with her:

> If you can never be happy, can you never bestow happiness. Oh! believe me, if you beheld on lips pale with grief one smile of joy and gratitude, and knew that you were parent of that smile, and that without you it had never been, you would feel so pure and warm a happiness that you would wish to live for ever again and again to enjoy the same pleasure.[26]

Through Woodville Mary expressed the importance of human interaction, of suppressing one's own sorrow in order to relieve the suffering of others. In part, he represented an acknowledgment of the value of the advice Shelley had given her in the past: to focus on keeping up her spirits, to direct her energy into her work and to remain, at all costs, open about her feelings with those who cared for her. But Mary also presented Woodville as naïve and overly optimistic and, in so doing, introduced a note of scepticism into the presentation of his arguments. Ultimately, *Matilda* acknowledged both the value of love and the bitter pain and suffering it could cause. It represented a brave attempt by Mary to rationalise her relationships with her father and her husband, as well as the emotional turmoil which overcame her in the months following William's death.

The Shelleys left the Villa Valsovano at the beginning of October and settled in lodgings in Florence, in time to prepare for the birth of Mary's fourth child. Percy Florence Shelley was born on 12 November, and was a robust and healthy baby. Mary sent happy descriptions of him to Maria Gisborne and Marianne Hunt. To Maria, in a letter written very soon after Percy Florence's birth, she related that her baby was lively, alert, and had a nose which promised to become as big as his grandfather's. To Marianne, who had recently given birth to a sixth little Hunt, she sent a more sober assessment of the last few months. In the period between Clara's death and Percy's birth Mary learnt to fear for her children, and she recognised that this changed the way she felt about them and her own existence. Even the joy of renewed motherhood could not rid her of the feeling that life was vengeful and capricious. Percy, she told Marianne, was her 'only one' and it was hard to know that her happiness depended so absolutely on a single fragile little life. Yet it was much better to fear for the life of a new baby than to be childless, as she had been for five hateful months. 'Do not let us talk of those five months: when I look back on all I suffered at Leghorn* I shudder with horror yet even now a sickening feeling steps in the way of every enjoyment when I think – of what I will not write about.'[27]

Shelley sent his own account of his new son to Hunt. He was relieved that the baby was healthy and feeding well, but more relieved that 'poor Mary begins (for the first time) to look a little consoled. For we have spent as you may imagine a miserable five months.'[28] Shelley believed that the birth of Percy Florence would mark the end of Mary's depression and that with a new baby to enjoy she would return to her old self. In some respects he was right: her mood and the tone of her letters lightened and superficially she seemed far removed from the grief-stricken woman who had shut herself away from human contact over the summer. But the events of 1818–1819 scarred her much more deeply than Shelley realised, and she remained emotionally withdrawn and fragile well into 1820. Her recovery was delayed by her anxiety about Godwin, who at the end of 1819 was found liable for years of unpaid rent on his Skinner Street house, a judgement which threatened to plunge him into bankruptcy.

Shelley became frustrated by Godwin's aggressive demands for money and by Mary's failure to rouse herself completely from her depression now that the cause of her misery was, in his word, 'obsolete'. A letter from him to the Gisbornes, dated March 1820, gives the lie to the superficial cheerfulness of Mary's own letters. The purpose of his letter was to ask Maria to stay with them while her husband and son travelled to England on business:

---

* The name given by the English to Livorno in the first part of the nineteenth century.

Mary has resigned herself, especially since the death of her child, to a train of thoughts, which if not cut off, cannot but conduct to some fatal end. Ill temper and irritation at the familiar events of life are among the external marks of this inward change, and by being freely yielded to, they exasperate the spirit, of which they are expressions. Unfortunately I, though not ill tempered, am irritable, and the effect produced on me, awakens the instinct of the power which annoys me in her, and which exists independently of her strong understanding, and of her better feelings, for Mary is certainly capable of the most exalted goodness – If she could be restrained from the expression of her inward sufferings, the sufferings themselves, the cause having become obsolete, would subside – A new habit of sentiment would take place – But all my attempts to restrain exasperate –

It needs a slight weight to turn the scale to good or evil. Mary considers me as a portion of herself, and feels no more remorse in torturing me than in torturing her own mind. [29]

Shelley did not just ask for Maria Gisborne's company for Mary's sake. He was 'tortured' by her mood: the presence of friends would at least spread the emotional burden he carried. But, despite his pleading, Maria accompanied her husband and son to England in the spring. Once again, Mary and Shelley needed the companionship of others, this time in order to escape from the growing distance between them. So in January 1820 they moved the short distance to Pisa to renew their acquaintance with 'Mrs Mason', an old friend of the Godwins whom they had met briefly during their journey to Florence.

'Mrs Mason' was Lady Mountcashell, the estranged wife of an Irish peer. She was born Margaret King and, as a girl, had received an unusually enlightened education from her beloved governess, Mary Wollstonecraft. Her marriage to Lord Mountcashell was unhappy and in 1804 she formed a connection with George Tighe, with whom she was living when the Shelleys met her in Pisa. She had two daughters with Tighe, Laurette and Nerina, in addition to eight Mountcashell children whom she was not permitted to see. She was unconventional in her dress, manner and politics. Shelley, Mary and Claire took to her instantly, and spent a good deal of time at her house, the Casa Silva. They developed a fondness for her quiet partner, George Tighe, whom they nicknamed 'Tatty' because of his interest in potatoes, and Claire befriended ten year old Laurette and played with four year old Nerina, who was only eighteen months older than Allegra. 'Mrs Mason' as they called her, was a source of much sage advice for all three. She advised Claire to live more independently, and took a robust approach to Shelley's health, which continued to be a source of anxiety for both him and Mary, introducing him to an eminently sensible physician, Andrea Vaccà Berlinghieri. Vaccà, as he was universally known, was one of the best-known doctors in Europe and he advised Shelley to relax, stop dosing himself with quack remedies and to make the most of Pisa's mild climate. Mrs Mason also helped Mary to establish her household, giving her much advice about the procurement of servants and suitable lodgings. With a supportive friend in residence, Mary, Shelley and Claire warmed to Pisa, and to the large, light, riverside apartments they took on the Lung'Arno. It was good to be out of their Florentine lodgings, and to have space to spread out again.

Mrs Mason's influence over her young friends extended beyond the way they ordered their lives. She was actively interested in the question of Irish independence and had written pamphlets on the subject which both Shelley and Mary read during their first Pisan winter. It had been a long time since they had had a friend with whom they could talk politics and it had an impact on their work and their thinking. Shelley immersed himself in histories of the revolutions in South America and spent hours with Mrs Mason, discussing his discoveries. Inspired by their new friend's talk, both Mary and Claire re-read Paine, while Mary described her reading and the lively conversation at Casa Silva in letters to the Hunts. She had no wish to be in England, she told Marianne. Life in Pisa was cheap, they were slowly accumulating a group of pleasant acquaintances, the climate suited Shelley's health and Claire wanted to remain in the same country as Allegra. There was no reason for them to return to London, Mary concluded, 'if I could but import a cargo of friends & books . . . here.'[30] After almost two years of restless travelling,

Mary felt they had finally found themselves in a place where they could make a permanent home.

———

At the end of December 1819 Byron left his Venetian *palazzo* and travelled to Ravenna, some seventy miles down the Adriatic coast. His journey was prompted by a woman, Teresa Guiccioli, whom he had first met earlier that year. Teresa was young, beautiful, and newly married to the elderly Count Guiccioli. She was an unhappy bride, and she and Byron embarked on an affair. In the autumn, Teresa went to join her cuckolded husband in Ravenna, leaving Byron unsure about his future in Italy. In England his work was once more back in the public eye. The first instalment of *Don Juan* was published in July 1819 and it did not take long for the secret of its authorship (the cantos were published anonymously) to leak out. *Don Juan* was Byron's masterpiece: a brutally funny critique of Regency culture and society which only increased his notoriety. Frustrated by his separation from Teresa, Byron toyed with the idea of taking Allegra back to England, to face his public for the first time in three years. But he dithered about his plans throughout the autumn and at the end of the year was prevented from leaving Italy by Allegra, who became worryingly unwell. The delay occasioned by Allegra's illness provided Teresa's father, who had forbidden the couple to meet, time to reconsider his opposition to their liaison. At the end of the year they had a passionate reunion in Ravenna, and by the spring Byron had established himself as Teresa's acknowledged consort.

Byron was soon drawn into the political intrigues of Teresa's father and brother, Ruggiero and Pietro Gamba. Through them he became involved with the Carbonari, a secret society who agitated for independence for Romagna. The year 1820 saw a resurgence of revolutionary activity in the Italian city states as their inhabitants sought to throw off the imperial rule imposed upon them following the partitioning of Europe at the Congress of Vienna. None of these movements was successful. A revolution in Naples was quickly crushed and Byron came to realise that the Carbonari were inefficient and unlikely to achieve their ambitions. Nevertheless, he was initiated into their ranks, stored arms for them and acted as the keeper of their records.³¹ The Carbonari provided him with his first experience of direct political action, for which he was to acquire a taste.

By the summer of 1820, Teresa was living in her father's country house outside Ravenna, waiting for the Pope to issue her with a decree of separation from her husband, and Allegra had been dispatched from Venice and installed in a villa near the Gambas' home. There she was visited occasionally by her father and more frequently by Teresa, who sent Byron encouraging reports of his daughter's improving health. Teresa was fond of 'Allegrina' and reported that the little girl was comically like her father. Allegra was depicted in Teresa's letters gleefully teasing Byron's manservant, and showing an unholy delight while watching Pietro Gamba kill birds: a delight Teresa sensibly attributed to 'that type of cruelty that one observes in all Children'.³² The brief glimpses of Allegra in the letters are of an imperious, funny little girl much petted by servants and her father's mistress, her every need catered for, denied only the love and attention of her mother and father.

Byron made elaborate arrangements for Allegra's comfort but he was deeply unsure about what to do with her. His disquiet was exacerbated by Claire, who started writing to him again on the subject of their daughter in 1820. Claire had not seen Allegra for well over a year, and she was determined to spend the summer with her. In March, she sent Byron a polite letter asking him to send Allegra to visit her in Pisa. Byron did not answer this letter and on 23 April Claire wrote again, informing him that in the absence of instructions from him she was planning to come to Ravenna to collect Allegra herself. Knowing that Byron would not wish to see her, she asked him to send Allegra as far as Bologna, where the Shelleys could collect her more easily. She assured Byron she did not wish to annoy him with her presence and reiterated that the hot Romagna summer would not be good for their daughter's health.

However, Byron's attitude to both Claire and the Shelleys had shifted since Claire's last meeting with her daughter in November 1818. By 1820 he was finding headstrong little Allegra increasingly troublesome, and he was quick to attribute all her negative characteristics to her mother. Richard and Isabelle Hoppner, who had briefly housed Allegra, Claire and the Shelleys, had passed on gossip about an affair between Shelley and Claire which, although he did not entirely believe it, provided Byron with grounds to dispute Claire's claims to moral authority. Claire was not to know that Byron had grown more conservative with age, or that he was increasingly sceptical about the Shelleys' unorthodox lifestyle. She learnt this in the cruellest possible way, when Isabelle Hoppner forwarded her a letter from Byron. 'About Allegra', he wrote, 'I can only say to Claire – that I so totally disapprove of the mode of Children's treatment in their family – that I should look upon the Child as going into a hospital. – Is it not so? Have they *reared* one? – Her health here has hitherto been excellent – and her temper not bad – she is sometimes vain and obstinate – but always clean and cheerful – and as in a year or two I shall either send her to England – or put her in a Convent for education – these defects will be remedied as far as they can in human nature. – But the child shall not quit me again – to perish of Starvation, and green fruit – or be taught to believe that there is no Deity.'[33]

Claire's response to this letter, with its cruel jibe at the double tragedy the Shelleys had suffered, was a model of restraint. She reminded Byron that he had given her a solemn promise that she should see Allegra at regular intervals, and that eighteen months had elapsed since their last meeting. She assured him that she respected his right to dictate the particulars of Allegra's diet and her religious upbringing but could not refrain from a reproof of his mean-spirited dismissal of Shelley's ideas, reminding him 'though my creed is different from Shelley's I must always feel grateful for his kindness.'[34] Byron's response was to write directly to the Shelleys reiterating his reasons for keeping Allegra with him. This letter, now lost, was evidently quite as cruel as that sent to Richard Hoppner, since it produced an anguished response from Claire in a letter which she drafted, but may never have sent.

Byron's lost letter must have reiterated his proposal to put three year old Allegra in a convent for her education, a suggestion which Claire understood as a threat; as an act of revenge against her. 'You answer my request by menacing if I do not . . . continue to suffer in silence, that you

will inflict the greatest of all evils on my child.' She reminded him of the
care she had lavished on Allegra before their parting: 'I injured my health
by my attentions to Allegra whom I nursed night & day the first year
of her infancy as your friend Hunt and also his wife well knew, for they
were the only people I saw & used to remonstrate with me.' And, in a
flash of sisterly loyalty, she reproached him for his cruelty towards Mary.
Having watched her stepsister's agony as her children died, she would
not allow Byron to treat such suffering casually. 'You are in the wrong',
she told him, 'when you impute neglect . . . as the cause of Mary's losing
her children.'[35] Shelley and Mary were also hurt by Byron's suggestion
of neglect. They were furious with the Hoppners, whom they suspected
of spreading gossip about them, but they knew that their position with
regard to Byron and Claire was fragile. Shelley wrote his own dignified
response to Byron, in which he tried to convey some sense of Claire's
anxiety without appearing to be too partisan, as well as his own concern
for Allegra's welfare. 'I smiled at your protest about what you considered
my creed', he wrote lightly.[36] Given the context of Byron's comments,
which used the deaths of William and Clara to reproach the Shelleys,
it is doubtful whether this was really true. In any case, Byron remained
unmoved, and Claire and Allegra remained apart.

Claire's preoccupation with Allegra now became a source of serious
vexation for Mary. Mary was sympathetic to her stepsister's plight,
but she had suffered great tragedy too and was entirely absorbed
in caring for her new baby, whose health caused her quite as much
obsessive anxiety as the absent Allegra's caused Claire. Claire may also
have found it difficult to see Mary occupied with an infant while she
remained separated from her own child. This did not make for peaceful
coexistence. 'Heigh-ho the Claire and the Ma/ Find something to fight
about every day', Claire wrote in her diary in July.[37] Shelley, caught
between a fractious pair of step-siblings, now felt himself to be the
chief victim of the tension between Mary and Claire. In a private
communication with Maria Gisborne he reported that 'Mary, who, you
know, is always wise, has been lately very good. I wish she were as wise
now as she will be at 45, or as misfortune has made me. She would then
live on very good terms with Claire.'[38]

Other sources of stress emerged in the summer of 1820 which taxed everybody's patience and fortitude. Mary, Shelley and Claire spent a quiet spring in Pisa, during which Mary and Shelley worked on a joint translation of Spinoza and two collaborative verse dramas, *Proserpine* and *Midas*. But their peace was shattered in mid-June when they discovered that Paolo Foggi, their former manservant, was attempting to blackmail them. Paolo had been in Naples in the winter of 1818 and had married the nursemaid Elise. Although the specifics of his blackmail attempt are not known, it is clear that it concerned Elena Adelaide, whom Shelley was still supporting financially. It may have related to the birth certificate that Shelley filed just before his departure from Naples, or to the mystery of Elena's parentage. On 12 June, Mary's diary entry read 'Paolo . . . dine and spend evening at Casa Silva – sleep there.'[39] 'Paulo' was followed by a half-moon symbol, which Mary periodically used in her diary to denote crises or serious problems. Claire's diary for the same day was only marginally more informative: 'Bother & Confusion with packing up – We sleep in Casa Silva. Oh Bother.'[40] Paolo's actions prompted the Shelleys and Claire first to take refuge with Mrs Mason, and then to leave Pisa altogether, and go to the Gisbornes' empty house in Livorno. There, Shelley consulted the lawyer through whom he was channelling funds for Elena, who helped rid them of Paolo's threats.

Once the fuss caused by Paolo subsided, Shelley, Mary and Claire found themselves alone once more, without the sustaining companionship of Mrs Mason. In the Gisbornes' deserted house they were surrounded by memories of their friends, who had recently departed on their visit to England. Seated at Henry Reveley's desk, which was covered by the detritus of his steamboat designs ('a dusty paint box, some odd hooks,/ A half-burnt match, an ivory block, three books'), Shelley wrote his 'Letter to Maria Gisborne', an elegiac evocation of the social circle she would meet in London. Like 'Julian and Maddalo', 'Letter to Maria Gisborne' took its inspiration from the thoughts of friends: Godwin ('greater none than he/ Though fallen – and fallen on evil times'); Hogg ('He is a pearl within an oyster shell/ One of the richest of the deep'); Peacock ('his fine wit/ Makes such a wound, the knife is lost in it'); Horace Smith (in whom 'wit and sense,/ Virtue and human knowledge' are combined) and, most importantly, Hunt, whom Shelley depicted in the cheerful chaos of his study, surrounded by his ever-faithful female companions:

> one of those happy souls
> Who are the salt of the Earth, and without whom
> This world would smell like what it is, a tomb –
> Who is, what others seem – his room no doubt
> Is still adorned with many a cast from Shout*
> With graceful flowers tastefully placed about,
> And coronals of bay from ribbons hung,
> And brighter wreaths in neat disorder flung,
> The gifts of the most learn'd among some dozens
> Of female friends, sisters-in-law and cousins.

The wistfulness of 'Letter to Maria Gisborne' was most apparent in its concluding stanza, which presented a dream of a future in which the bitterness of the past could be buried and forgotten:

> Next winter you must pass with me; I'll have
> My house by that time turned into a grave
> Of dead despondence and low-thoughted care
> And all the dreams which our tormentors are.
> Oh, that Hunt, Hogg, Peacock and Smith were there,
> With everything belonging to them fair!

'Letter to Maria Gisborne' imagined the gatherings of Marlow and London transported to Italy for a utopian summer. As in 'Julian and Maddalo', Shelley used the evocation of friends as a vehicle for discussion of a particular aspect of his philosophy. In the earlier poem he had presented Byron's nihilistic pessimism in order to interrogate the intellectual foundations of his own optimism; in the later, the memory of friends acted as a springboard for a meditation on the

---

* Robert Shout, who made plaster copies of well-known statues.

relationship between memory, knowledge and the poetic imagination. 'Letter to Maria Gisborne' illustrated that the act of imagining one's friends could be intellectually stimulating, but that, emotionally, doing so was no substitute for their physical presence. 'I send you some verses', Shelley told Maria in a letter accompanying his verse epistle, 'which will show you that I struggle with despondency.'[41] Mary was once more, in Shelley's words, in 'agony' about Godwin; and she and Claire were finding each other impossible.

In the autumn of 1820, Claire travelled back to Livorno to stay there by herself, officially because the sea bathing was good for her, but in reality because she and Mary could no longer bear to live under the same roof. Shelley and Mary thus found themselves alone for the first time since arriving in Italy, and were forced to confront the changes which had taken place in each other and in their relationship in the intervening years. The passionate couple who dodged bailiffs and spent Sundays together in bed had disappeared, to be replaced by two sadder, older individuals, both wary of acknowledging the distance which entered their relationship following the deaths – only nine months apart – of Clara and William. Shelley reacted by issuing invitations to Peacock, Hogg and Hunt, friends among whom he and Mary had once been happy. None of them was able to leave England.

––––––

As a result, Shelley and Mary had to content themselves with second-hand news of their friends passed on by the Gisbornes, who arrived in London at the beginning of the summer. There they visited Coleridge and Horace Smith, and spent time with the Godwins in Skinner Street, where they were taken aback by Godwin's animosity towards Shelley and Mrs Godwin's towards Mary. Godwin railed against Shelley's failure to keep his promises of financial support and continually betrayed 'his dislike of S in some shape or another'.[42] His dislike of Shelley was largely motivated by the fact that Shelley refused to hand over as much of his income as Godwin felt to be his due, but both he and Mrs Godwin were intensely worried about Claire. Both of them remained in ignorance about Claire's relationship with Byron, and for

a long time they were unaware of Allegra's existence. When they did
eventually discover that Claire had produced an illegitimate child they
assumed that Shelley was responsible. They also laid Fanny's death
at his door, an accusation duly recorded by Maria in her diary. 'He
supposes', she wrote of Godwin, 'that C[laire] had given herself up
entirely to melancholy and despondence . . . Mr G told me that the
three girls were all equally in love with —— and that the eldest put
an end to her existence owing to the preference given to her younger
sister.'[43] Godwin did not share his wife's bitterness against Mary (who,
Mrs Godwin believed, was equally culpable in Claire's downfall), but
he refused to arrange for the publication of *Matilda* on the grounds of
its 'disgusting and detestable' subject.[44]

The Gisbornes sought light relief from the bitterness of the Godwins
with the Hunts. They took tea together and Maria was pleasantly surprised
by Hunt's appearance and his conversation. 'He considers S[helley]',
she remembered, 'as the discoverer of a pure original spring of human
knowledge.' Hunt was in good spirits that summer, and was a more than
usually pleasant companion. The political columns of *The Examiner*,
neglected after the establishment of *The Indicator*, leapt back into life in
the middle of 1820 with a splutter of outrage at the treatment of Queen
Caroline by the new monarch and his cronies in the House of Lords.

In January 1820 George III died and the Prince Regent finally
became King. His estranged wife, Caroline of Brunswick, travelled
back to England from Italy, where she had been living in exile, to claim
her throne. In order to prevent her from becoming Queen, George IV
instigated divorce proceedings and brought an adultery charge against
her, in a protracted trial in the House of Lords. The treatment of the
Queen won her the sympathy of the British public, and reformers and
radicals alike were outraged at the way the full weight of the state was
being used to torment a woman whose husband had been unashamedly
adulterous himself. Hunt recognised that although Queen Caroline was
not a particularly impressive or attractive personage the invective directed
against her by the King and his government supporters symbolised all that
was corrupt and self-serving in the British political system. In a long series
of *Examiner* editorials on the subject of the Queen's trial, he poured scorn

on her detractors. When the case against the Queen collapsed into farce, Hunt was suitably jubilant, both at her private triumph and at the way in which the public had been mobilised to call for change. 'We congratulate her MAJESTY and her sex', he proclaimed. 'We congratulate her friends; which is another word for the whole country. We congratulate human nature. The QUEEN has triumphed.'[45]

Queen Caroline's triumph seemed to Hunt to harbour a new phase in the progress of reform, in which the forces of corruption and 'cant' could be defeated by sound argument, good sense and the overwhelming force of public opinion. After the dark days of the winter of 1819–20, during which freedom of speech was drastically curtailed, Hunt and his fellow reformers seized on any indication, however slight, that the tide might be turning in their favour. The *Examiner* editorials on Queen Caroline's trial were a rhetorical tour de force, but in the week following the trial's culmination their cost became apparent, when a brief editorial note announced that Hunt would be taking a rest from his duties. His health was, once again, precarious, and the effort of producing two weekly newspapers was telling badly on him. He was acutely short of money, much to the disgust of John Hunt, who continued to resent the strain that his brother and sister-in-law's haphazard impecuniousness placed on the resources of their extended family.

In the summer of 1820, in addition to the stresses of work and of providing for his ever-growing collection of offspring, Hunt accepted an additional claim on his time and money. On 23 June, John Keats moved into the Hunts' new house, 13 Mortimer Terrace, on the borders of Hampstead and Kentish Town. On the face of it, this was rather surprising. After the death of his brother Tom from tuberculosis at the end of 1818, Keats moved away from Hunt's orbit of influence and the two saw little of each other in the winter and spring of 1819–20. The *Peter Bell* interlude brought them briefly into contact, but thereafter Keats's poetry – *The Eve of St Agnes, Hyperion, Lamia,* the Odes – revealed a genius and an intellectual ambition which sat uneasily with Hunt's ephemeral work. For Keats, 1819 was characterised by periods of intense creativity and by his romance with Fanny Brawne, the daughter of his next door neighbour.

In January 1820, like his brother before him, Keats developed tuberculosis and became too ill to write. On 22 June, he suffered a massive haemorrhage, and his frantic landlady went to Hunt's nearby house in search of help. Hunt insisted that Keats should move to Mortimer Terrace to be properly cared for, and within twenty-four hours Keats was installed in the house and had been visited by Hunt's doctor. He remained there for several weeks, the old tensions about influence and discipleship swept away by Hunt and Marianne's kindness. Hunt distracted him with talk of the forthcoming *Indicator*; Marianne by cutting his silhouette as he lay propped up on two chairs. Even those of his friends who disliked his old association with Hunt conceded that he could not have received gentler or more considerate care. Meanwhile his doctors decided that his only hope for survival rested on travelling to Italy, away from the dampness of an English winter.

When Shelley heard of Keats's illness and projected voyage to Italy he wrote immediately urging him to join them in Pisa, where, he told Marianne, 'I shall take care to bestow every possible attention on him.'[46] Keats was touched by Shelley's offer, but knew too much from his medical training to believe he would be able to travel as far as Pisa. 'If I do not take advantage of your invitation', he replied, 'it will be prevented by a circumstance I have very much at heart to prophesy.'[47] On 17 September 1820, accompanied by his friend Joseph Severn, he boarded the *Maria Crowther*, and set sail for Italy.

Few outside Keats's immediate circle noticed his departure from England, but Hunt, faithful as ever to his friends, made sure that the readers of *The Indicator* knew of the loss he, and the world of English letters, was suffering. 'Ah dear friend', he wrote, in a direct address to Keats. 'We cannot, after all, find it in our hearts to be glad, now thou art gone away with the swallows to seek a kindlier clime.' But, he added hopefully, 'thou shalt return with thy friend the nightingale, and make all thy other friends as happy with thy voice as they are sorrowful to miss it. The little cage thou didst sometimes share with us, looks as deficient without thee, as thy present one may do without us.' 'Farewell for awhile', he concluded. 'Thy heart is in our fields: and thou will soon be back to rejoin it.'[48]

7

Travellers

By the time the *Maria Crowther* pushed out into the English Channel, Keats's strength was fading. The voyage was appalling for all concerned. Keats and another ill female passenger had to cope with the horrors of tuberculosis – fever, sweats, coughing blood – in cramped and airless quarters. They lacked privacy and fresh provisions, and the ship was rocked by storms. Severn thought it was a wonder that Keats survived the passage, since he was tormented not only by his illness but by thoughts of the friends he knew he would never see again.

After a miserable quarantine period in Naples, Keats and Severn moved on to Rome, where Severn found a set of lodgings above the Spanish Steps. In stuffy rooms from which Keats could hear the sounds of Rome but see little of its glory, he wrote letters to his friends, including one, dated 30 November 1820, to Charles Brown. ''Tis the most difficult thing in the world to me to write a letter', he confessed. 'I have a habitual feeling of my real life having past, and that I am now leading a posthumous existence.'[1] A month after writing this Keats was confined to his bed, and both he and Severn knew that there was little they could do except wait for the end.

As Keats lived out his 'posthumous existence' in a hinterland between the life left behind in England and the death he knew to be inevitable, his poetry was being read with renewed interest by his friends and acquaintances in both England and Italy. Hunt, with characteristic generosity, sent letters in praise of his work, which he

hoped would remind Keats of the richness of his life's achievements.
Hunt recognised that Keats had achieved a poetic greatness he could
never hope to equal, and was confident that the world would come
to realise the extent of his talent. 'Tell him', he implored Severn, 'that
we shall all bear his memory in the most precious part of our hearts,
and that the world shall bow their heads to it, as our loves do.'[2] Keats's
final volume of poetry, *Lamia, Isabella, The Eve of St Agnes and Other
Poems*, was published a few months before his death. In August 1820
he had sent a copy to Shelley, who was re-reading *Endymion*, and who
thought that the new volume showed great promise. He lent *Lamia*
to Claire, who read it attentively in the months that followed. She
was in no doubt about Keats's talent, describing him in her diary as
'the brightest promise of genius which England had seen for many
days'.[3]

In October 1820, Claire left Shelley and Mary in Pisa and moved to
Florence, where Mrs Mason had arranged for her to stay as a paying
guest in the house of Antonio Bojti, a distinguished Florentine doctor.
Mrs Mason had grown fond of Claire, and was convinced, with
justification, that she needed to separate herself from the Shelleys. Bojti
had a German wife who taught Claire to speak German, and a bevy of
small children, to whom Claire taught English in return. The Bojtis
moved in elevated social circles and were willing to introduce Claire
to their friends, thus allowing her to develop a group of acquaintances
who had no connection with either Shelley or Mary. Mrs Mason knew
how much Claire enjoyed playing with her own daughters, Laurette
and Nerina, and hoped that if Claire were installed in a house full of
children she would miss Allegra a little less. Even if this did not prove
to be the case, the Bojtis' young and lively household was a suitable
place for Claire to get used to the idea of living independently and
earning her own living. Although she was supported in Florence by
Shelley, Mrs Mason believed that life with the Bojtis would equip her
with experiences which would help her forge a career as a governess.

Claire knew that it made sense for her to try to live apart from

Shelley and Mary, but the transition was lonely and difficult. Apart from brief visits back to Pisa (during which she stayed with Mrs Mason rather than the Shelleys) she was alone for much of the winter, surrounded by strangers who knew nothing of her troubled past, and who therefore could offer her little sympathy. It was important that matters remained thus, since if Florentine society had discovered that Claire was the mother of Byron's illegitimate daughter she would not have been received in the grand houses frequented by the Bojtis. She was therefore compelled to turn to her diary for comfort, and spent her time writing long meditations on the direction of her life, the events of her past and the activities of her acquaintances. These meditations give a poignant insight into her state of mind during this period. 'Think of thyself as a stranger & traveller on the earth, to whom none of the many affairs of this world, belong and who has no permanent township on the globe', she wrote on 29 October, a few weeks after her arrival in Florence.[4] An entry from the following spring presents a bleak picture of an empty life. 'After dinner walk in Boboli – I mounted the hill & sat an hour at the foot of the statue of Ceres. Below the groves of evergreens were shaken by a high wind, and the noise resembled the dashing of waves on the sea-shore. Being alone there, with such a sound brought to my mind the many solitary hours of Lynmouth.'[5] Many of her musings focused on Byron, whom she presented in prose caricatures as a semi-demonic figure. In an entry entitled 'Hints for Don Juan' she recorded the words she wished to say to Byron himself. 'You are dead to everything beautiful, whether of shape or essence; you rot and are corrupted, while the light of Truth is upon you, as a Corpse which putrifies in the rays of the Sun.'[6]

Claire knew that her anger at Byron increased her unhappiness, recording rather guiltily that 'one of Madame M[ason]'s rules [is] to consider a prejudiced person as one labouring under a serious illness',[7] but Byron's actions made it impossible for her to moderate her dislike of him. In March 1821 he placed Allegra in the Capuchin Convent at Bagnacavallo in the north-east corner of Romagna, and sent word of his decision in a letter to Shelley. It was not unusual for Italian families to send their daughters to convents for their education, but at four years old Allegra was very young for such treatment. Indeed, she was the youngest resident at Bagnacavallo.

Byron had a variety of reasons for placing her there. Ravenna, where he was living, was no place for a child in 1821. It was unsettled politically and at one point it looked as if the Carbonari, inspired by the example of the Neapolitans, might be about to start a revolution. Allegra had not yet received any formal education and Byron thought it important that she should start to learn to read and write. Teresa Guiccioli had been granted a decree of separation from her husband and although she was fond of Allegra she had little interest in acting as stepmother to Claire's daughter. In any case, it seems that Byron initially intended Allegra's residence in Bagnacavallo to be temporary and that he planned to make more permanent arrangements for her once Ravenna calmed down. But Claire was not to know this, and she was horrified by his decision. Byron had promised her in Geneva that Allegra would always live with one or other of her parents, and he had broken his word. She wrote to warn him that his actions would be attacked by all who learnt of Allegra's fate:

> Allegra's misfortune in being condemned by her father to a life of ignorance & degradation, in being deprived . . . of the protection & friendship of her parents friends (so essential to the well-being of a child in her desolate situation) . . . will be received by the world as a perfect fulfilment on your part of all the censures passed upon you. How will Lady Byron never yet justified for her conduct towards you be soothed and rejoice in the honourable safety of herself & child, and all the world be bolder to praise her prudence, my unhappy Allegra furnishing the condemning evidence. I alone, misled by love to believe you good, trusted to you, & now I reap the fruits.[8]

This letter made Byron both furious and defensive, and he refused to consider Claire's suggestion that Allegra should be placed in an English boarding school at her (by which she meant Shelley's) expense. He sent a self-justifying letter to the Hoppners in which he blackened Claire's name, was rude about the Shelleys ('to allow the Child to be with her mother – & with *them* & their principles – would be absolute insanity') and denied making Claire promises at Geneva.[9]

Byron was angry about Claire's accusations of neglect, partly because he knew that they contained a grain of truth. Allegra had become an encumbrance and she threatened to restrict both his freedom of movement and his relationship with Teresa (who, Claire later claimed, was jealous of Allegra). Once Allegra was safely installed at Bagnacavallo he appears to have made little effort to visit her. Geographical distance and Byron's attitude combined to make it impossible for Claire to visit the convent either, and she was left with the knowledge that she exercised no influence over Byron, that he was deaf to her pleas for kindness, and that her daughter was now being cared for by strangers. Alone in Florence, she had only her diary for comfort, and she used it to record disturbing dreams in which she was reunited with Allegra.

Shelley and Mary's loyalties were divided on the subject of Allegra. Although they pitied Claire, they were anxious not to alienate Byron, who wrote to them complaining of the tone of Claire's letters. Neither of them had seen the letters, but they knew from experience that Claire could be intemperate and demanding. Nevertheless, given Claire's distress, Shelley's response to Byron does not reflect particularly well on either him or Mary. They were certainly not prepared to sacrifice their friendship with Byron for Claire's sake. A more charitable explanation of their response is that they knew Byron could not be won over by reproaches and demands, and that it was therefore important they maintained a cordial relationship. 'I never see any of Claire's letters to you', Shelley reminded him, rather passively. 'I can easily believe, however, that they are sufficiently provoking, and that her views respecting Allegra are unreasonable. Mary, no less than myself, is perfectly convinced of your conduct towards Allegra having been most irreproachable, and we entirely agree in the necessity, under existing circumstances, of the placing her in a convent near to yourself.'[10]

With Claire absent, Shelley and Mary spent a peaceful summer and autumn in San Giuliano, a tiny hamlet buried among the mountains outside Pisa. They took a spacious house in the village's single run of buildings, which looked out towards San Giuliano's one imposing building, the eighteenth-century bathhouse, and the lower reaches of Monte Pisano. There Shelley wrote 'The Witch of Atlas', a poem which revealed in its dedication a disagreement between him and Mary about the direction his work was taking. Mary felt that his work was at its best and most politically potent when – as in *The Cenci* – he focused on the experiences of humanity, rather than on abstraction and mythology. Shelley responded with a dedicatory poem in which he made her the following plea: 'Prithee, for this one time,/ Content thee with a visionary rhyme.'

They also eagerly followed the progress of the trial of Queen Caroline in the bundles of *The Examiner* sent out from England. Inspired by Hunt's *Examiner* accounts of events in London, and perhaps also by Mary's representations about the importance of focusing on reality, Shelley produced a dramatic satire on the trial, 'Swellfoot the Tyrant', in which a jury of pigs is arraigned to try Swellfoot's wife, Queen Iona. Shelley's friend Horace Smith subsequently arranged for the publication of 'Swellfoot', but was threatened with prosecution by the Society for the Suppression of Vice, and the drama remained unpublished until Mary's 1839 edition of Shelley's poems.

For her part, Mary embarked on her second novel, set in medieval Italy. She spent much of her summer absorbed in research, reading Sismondi's monumental *History of the Italian Republics*. When the Shelleys moved back to Pisa in the autumn she was able to make full use of the rich resources of Pisa's university libraries. The resulting novel, *Valperga*, drew its setting from a wide variety of historical sources, and presented its vividly realised characters against a carefully researched background.

Valperga was deeply engaged with Italy's past, but it was also a meditation on Italy's present and her future. Mary set her novel in fourteenth-century Lucca, an Italian city state in what is now Tuscany. Her subject was the defeat of Guelph Florence by the Ghibelline Castruccio Castracani, Duke of Lucca. Written in the period following the Neapolitan Revolution of 1820–1, Mary's novel deliberately avoided what the literary critic Tilottama Rajan has termed 'historical consolations'.[11] It ends with Castruccio's death and makes no attempt to describe the peace and prosperity of Renaissance Italy which followed the civil strife of the fourteenth century. The Italy of *Valperga* is in its inception, and reveals the intellectual and libertarian possibilities of the unformed nation state. The parallels between the past and the period in which Mary researched and wrote her novel pointed towards the possibilities of the fledgling nationalist revolutions taking place in Italy and elsewhere in the southern Mediterranean in 1820 and 1821. The failure of these revolutions, *Valperga* suggests, should not negate the fact that they took place. In a later biography of the Italian poet and nationalist hero, Vittorio Alfieri, Mary would claim that Italy needed to rise out of political lethargy in order to achieve its independence. The characters of *Valperga* do just that and their actions herald the unspoken possibility of political and cultural renaissance. Mary's second full-length novel was a significant work of fiction, but it was also an important engagement with the reality of the power struggles shaking Europe at the beginning of the 1820s. It represented a major development in her work since the introversion of *Matilda*, written the previous winter.

Valperga was influenced by Mary's reading, but it was also a response to changing social circumstances, as she and Shelley were drawn into a new circle of writers and intellectuals. Through Mrs Mason they met Francesco Pacchiani, a former Professor at the University of Pisa. He was witty, brilliant and socially unreliable, and although the Shelleys soon tired of him he introduced them to other Pisan intellectuals, with whom they formed more lasting friendships. These included John Taaffe, an earnest Irish writer working on a rather laborious translation of Dante, and Tommaso Sgricci, a minor celebrity and *Improvvisatore* – a theatrical declaimer of spontaneous poetry, of the type depicted by Madame de Staël in *Corinne*. A more important acquaintance made through Pacchiani was Alexander Mavrocordato, an exiled Greek nobleman who was preparing to lead the fight for Greek independence. Mavrocordato was rather enamoured of Mary, and the two became close allies. They came to an arrangement whereby she taught him English in return for lessons in Greek. He called frequently, and sent apologetic notes when he was unable to visit her. Together they walked and discussed Greek politics and when the Shelleys moved back to San Giuliano in the spring of 1821 he frequently made the journey out of Pisa to see her. He proved himself to be a steadfast and attentive companion, and was the first friend of her own generation Mary had made independently since her elopement. Shelley was less keen on him, confessing to Claire that 'I reproach my own savage disposition that so agreeable accomplished and amiable a person is not more agreeable to me.'[12]

One cannot help but wonder whether Shelley's feelings towards Mavrocordato were influenced more than he realised by the fact that, at twenty-three, Mary had acquired her first close male friend. Moreover, even though Mavrocordato was barely a year older than twenty-eight year old Shelley, he was glamorous, well-connected, and intimately involved with the political progress of Europe. Mavrocordato seems to have taken some pleasure in Shelley's discomfort. In May, as he was preparing to leave Italy, he wrote triumphantly to Mary of the transport which was to take him to war in Greece. His letter contained a dig at Shelley, who had recently acquired a small sailing boat to carry him up and down the Arno. 'My departure cannot be delayed much longer', he told Mary. 'I have a brigantine at my disposal, a ship was sent to me by my compatriots, who are inviting me to move close to them. If Mr Shelley was most proud to have a small boat . . . at his disposal, imagine what my pride must be now that I have a brigantine which carries eighteen at my disposal.'[13] Although Shelley subsequently dedicated his verse drama *Hellas* to Mavrocordato 'as an imperfect token of the admiration, sympathy, and friendship of the Author', his letters suggest he did not lament his departure for Greece as Mary did.

Shelley was in fact extremely lonely during the period that Mary developed her friendship with Mavrocordato. While both he and Mary were beginning to accept that their relationship had changed, and that the intimacy which marked their elopement and their lives together in 1815–16 could not easily be recaptured, they responded to this realisation differently. Mary made new friends, looked after Percy Florence (now a sturdy one year old) and concentrated on *Valperga*, about which Shelley was dismissive, perhaps because he felt that he was no longer influencing the intellectual direction of her work. Mary's novel, he told Peacock, was 'raked out of fifty old books',[14] hardly a flattering description of his wife's meticulous historical research.

Shelley responded by turning once more to the absent Claire. Claire had few of the distractions available to Mary, and was able, even at a distance, to focus much of her attention on Shelley. He spent a good deal of time writing long letters meant for her eyes alone. 'I wrote to you a kind of scrawl the other day merely to shew that I had not forgotten you,'[15] he explained at one point, '& as it was taxed with a postscript by Mary, it contained nothing that I wished it to contain.' Claire sent her responses care of Mrs Mason (or to 'Mr Jones' at the Pisa post office) in order to keep Mary in the dark about their correspondence. To Claire, Shelley expressed some of the frustration he felt at the quiet domestic life he was leading in Pisa, and even suggested he was meditating a change in his circumstances. He told her he had been asked to join an expedition to Greece, Eygpt and Syria, by a gentleman who admired his verses. 'How far all this is practicable, considering the state of my finances I know not yet. I know that if it were it would give me the greatest pleasure, & the pleasure might be either doubled or divided by your presence or absence.'[16] Was Shelley, as this hints, really contemplating fleeing Italy with Claire, leaving Mary and their baby behind? Probably not: even in the darkest days of their relationship, he never seems to have made serious plans to abandon Mary as he had Harriet. But this letter shows, at the very least, that the possibility of freedom – from domestic cares, from Mary, to act on his feelings for Claire – was enticing.

The letters to Claire suggest that Shelley did not treat Mary well during their second Pisan winter, but he was himself under a good deal of strain. Mary's depression was deep and long-lasting and when she emerged from the worst of its blackness she often seemed like a different woman, who had thrown up impenetrable defences against further emotional torment. Shelley was unwell again, and locked into a marriage which must sometimes have felt more isolating than a solitary bachelor existence. It was therefore almost inevitable that with Mary absorbed in other things and with Claire living separately, a man who had always needed female attention should find a new object for his affections. She was Teresa Viviani, the daughter of the governor of Pisa.

The Shelleys met Teresa through Claire, who was introduced to her by Pacchiani during one of her visits to Pisa. Teresa was living at the Convent of St Anna while her father conducted negotiations for her marriage. She was nineteen years old, extremely pretty, and more than capable of persuading Shelley, Mary and Claire that she was a victim of a tyrannical and patriarchal system which deprived her of her liberty while arrangements were made to sell her to the highest bidder. The Convent of St Anna, like Allegra's convent at Bagnacavallo, operated both as a nunnery and as an exclusive private boarding school for well-bred young ladies, and a less dramatic interpretation of the facts is that Teresa was kept at school until a suitable husband and home could be found for her. But her situation was unenviable, since one reason for her continued residence at the convent was the presence at her father's house of a young and jealous stepmother, even if the reality of her day to day existence was not as romantically awful as the Shelleys and Claire believed. They promptly christened her Emilia, a name which, with its Chaucerian connotations, seemed more suited to the romance of her plight. Mary and Claire felt sorry for her. They, after all, had made their own choices, and it was a shock to find that a young woman could be so constrained by the orders of her father. Mary may also have had additional sympathy, since she knew all too well the difficulties of living with one's stepmother. But although Mary was sufficiently interested in Emilia to include a portrait of her in *Valperga*, she came to realise that she was manipulative, had exaggerated her suffering, and was determined to catch Shelley's attention.

In this, she succeeded. Shelley's interest in Emilia's predicament was quickly succeeded by interest in her person. She was beautiful, unobtainable and had plenty of time to write him slightly melancholic but undeniably coquettish letters. She wrote to him as her 'dear brother' and deployed the language of sisterhood which Shelley himself had used in the past to rationalise his relationship with Claire. She knew exactly what she was doing, and how to respond most tantalisingly to Shelley's increasingly ardent letters. 'To show that your familiarity does not displease', she told him in mid-December, 'I write to you in your own tone of confidence and sweet friendship.' 'My Claire', she continued coyly, 'will say that she is *jealous*: but let her reflect that I do not write thus save to her good brother and to mine.'[17] Mary probably recognised the signs of infatuation in her husband, but knew enough of his character to realise she could do little about it. Perhaps she did not feel inclined to do so. She was too reserved and too proud to impose her affections where she felt they were not wanted. A year later she wrote dismissively of the episode to Maria Gisborne, in a letter which contained a wry reference to Shelley's 'Italian platonics'.[18] It was beneath her to compete for her husband's attention with the teenage martyr of the Convent of St Anna.

It was, however, one thing for Shelley to exchange letters with a beautiful prisoner, but quite another for him to write a poem about his enchantment. The poem in question was *Epipsychidion* ('On the Subject of the Soul').[19] Shelley attempted to keep knowledge of its existence from Mary, sending it to Charles Ollier for anonymous publication from Mrs Mason's house and including with the poem a fictional Preface which announced 'the writer of the following lines died at Florence'. Florence was the town in which baby Percy was born, and it was during the Shelleys' time there that Mary had (in Shelley's eyes) failed to lift herself from the depression caused by the death of William. The winter they spent there thus marked a turning point in their relationship, so this Preface cannot have offered Mary much comfort when she became aware of the poem's existence some time after its completion. Shelley told Ollier that the poem was 'a production of a portion of me already dead'[20] and later confessed to John Gisborne that 'it is an idealised history of my life and feelings'. He continued 'I think one is always in love with something or other; the error, and I confess it is not easy for spirits cased in flesh and blood to avoid it, consists in seeking in a mortal image the likeness of what is perhaps eternal.'[21]

Epipsychidion is Shelley's spiritual autobiography. In it Emilia is transformed from convent girl into a vision of ideal womanhood. She is a 'Seraph of Heaven! too gentle to be human' and 'Youth's vision thus made perfect', who leads him into 'light, life and peace'. She presents a striking contrast with Mary, who is presented in the poem as 'the cold chaste Moon', 'Who makes all beautiful on which she smiles,/ That wandering shrine of soft yet icy flame/ Which ever is transformed, yet still the same,/ And warms not but illumines.' Claire makes an appearance in the poem as a comet, 'beautiful and fierce,/ Who drew the heart of this frail Universe/ Towards thine own; till, wreckt in that convulsion,/ Alternating attraction and repulsion,/ Thine went astray and that was rent in twain.' But *Epipsychidion* is more than a straightforward exploration of Shelley's relationships with women. Like 'Julian and Maddalo' and 'Letter to Maria Gisborne' it is a meditation on the nature of human interaction. However, unlike 'Letter to Maria Gisborne' it has an ambivalence about the value of interaction, which is expressed through the stylised allegory and through Shelley's presentation of himself as a passive recipient of female companionship. The women of *Epipyschidion* are strange and disturbing figures who bear little relation to the male friends evoked so lovingly in 'Maria Gisborne'.

Shelley's interest in Emilia slowly waned over the course of 1821 and dissipated by the time of her marriage to an Italian nobleman in September of that year. But the interlude widened the developing rift between Shelley and Mary, and made her more cautious in both her emotional and her intellectual engagement with him. She moved steadily forward with *Valperga*, a novel in which elements of Shelley's character appear in the heroine, Euthanasia, but in which she nevertheless asserted her intellectual independence. For his part, Shelley was involved in a separate dialogue in the spring of 1821, with one of those friends celebrated in 'Letter to Maria Gisborne', Thomas Love Peacock. In February he received a copy of Charles Ollier's *Literary Miscellany*, a short-lived magazine which printed in its first issue an essay by Peacock on 'The Four Ages of Poetry'. Peacock's essay purported to be a history of poetry, but the main focus of its witty rhetoric was an attack on the preoccupations of contemporary writers.

'Mr Scott digs up the poachers and cattle-stealers of the ancient border. Lord Byron cruises for thieves and pirates on the shores of the Morea and among the Greek Islands ... Mr Wordsworth picks up village legends from old women and sextons.' From these examples Peacock produced a grand rhetorical flourish: an indictment of modern poetry:

> A poet in our times is a semi-barbarian in a civilised community. He lives in the days that are past. His ideas, thoughts, feelings, associations, are all with barbarous manners, obsolete customs, and exploded superstitions. The march of his intellect is like that of a crab, backward. The brighter the light diffused around him by the progress of reason, the thicker is the darkness of antiquated barbarism, in which he buries himself like a mole.[22]

Shelley was hurt by Peacock's sparkling denunciation of contemporary poetry and responded by writing his own essay in 'A Defence of Poetry'.

The 'Defence' is a magisterial assertion of the significance of the poetic vocation. It draws on a wide variety of philosophical and intellectual traditions to support its subtle and detailed argument and is a plea for the importance of poets and poetry in the regeneration of a corrupt and damaged universe. This is most apparent in the essay's famous conclusion. 'Poets', Shelley claimed, 'are the hierophants of an unapprehended inspiration, the mirrors of the gigantic shadows which futurity casts upon the present, the words which express what they understand not, the trumpets which sing to battle and feel not what they inspire: the influence which is moved not, but moves. Poets are the unacknowledged legislators of the World.'[23] This final phrase, which Shelley first wrote, in a modified form, in his 'Philosophical View of Reform', is one of his most enduring. But it is illuminating to remember that this powerful claim for the value of the poetic consciousness (a claim which has become indelibly associated with the idea of the Romantic genius) arose because of the gauntlet thrown down by Peacock, Shelley's brilliant, challenging friend.

———

In Rome, another 'unacknowledged legislator' was finally fading from the world he once hoped to enchant. Keats's last days were a nightmare of pain and grief, although narratives of his end were later sanitised to emphasise his heroism. His hagiographer in chief was Joseph Severn, who was at his side throughout his illness, but even Severn's determination to present Keats as a triumphant immortal spirit could not mask the despair of his friend's final weeks. In mid-January, despite the severity of Keats's illness, Severn considered bringing him back to England, since, as he told one correspondent, 'half the cause of his danger has arisen from the loss of England – from the dread of never seeing it more.'[24] But Keats was far too ill to be moved, and at the end of February Severn sent the following letter to Charles Brown:

> He is gone – he died with the most perfect ease – he seemed to go to sleep – on the 23rd (Friday) at ½ past 4, the approaches of death came on – "Severn – S – lift me up for I am dying – I shall die easy – dont be frightened – thank God it has come" – I lifted him up in my arms – and the phlegm seemed boiling in his throat – this increased until 11 at night, whe[n] he gradually sunk into death – so qui[e]t that I thought he slept – but I cannot say more now.[25]

Severn did his best to depict Keats on his deathbed as calm and resolute, but he could not hide from his correspondents the grim reality of the events which followed his friend's death: first an autopsy, then, at the insistence of the Roman authorities, the burning of the contents of their shared apartment in a bid to reduce the spread of infection. Keats was buried in the Protestant Cemetery, in a plot near William Shelley's small grave.

———

Back in England, Keats's friends immersed themselves in discussions about headstones and epitaphs, in an attempt to distract themselves from the tragedy of a young poet's untimely end. For Hunt such distractions offered few consolations, as the period following Keats's death brought with it further departures from his social circle. The ties of friendship which bound Hunt, Hogg and Peacock together were weakened by Shelley's continued absence, and they now met less often, particularly after Peacock's marriage in 1820. Hunt's longstanding friendship with William Hazlitt was badly strained when Hazlitt published disparaging remarks about Shelley in an essay 'On Paradox and Commonplace'. Although they patched up their quarrel through an exchange of courteous letters, Hunt could not easily forgive Hazlitt's attack on his friend. And in 1821, Horace Smith, a devoted companion of both Shelley and Hunt, decided to take his family to join the Shelleys in Italy, although his wife's illness meant that they only made it as far as Versailles, where they settled for a number of years. For Hunt, it must have seemed as if his centre of gravity was shifting inexorably east and south. His closest friends were no longer in England, and the independence movements in Spain and Italy suggested that Europe's best hope for political regeneration lay in the countries of the Mediterranean, rather than in post-Peterloo Britain.

The winter of 1820–1821 was blighted for the Hunts by a series of calamities, which weakened Hunt's health and strained his finances even further. In February, in the week that Keats died, John Hunt was found guilty of libel, fined £1,000 and given a year in Coldbath Fields, the prison in which he had spent his first gaol sentence. John Hunt had effectively retired from *The Examiner* by mid-1820, leaving its day to day running to his son Henry, but he nevertheless wrote a letter to the newspaper on the trial of Queen Caroline, in which he described the House of Commons as a body 'composed of venal boroughmongers, grasping placemen, greedy adventurers and aspiring title-hunters, – or the representatives of such worthies, – a body, in short, containing a far great portion of Public Criminals than Public Guardians'.[26] John Hunt was tried, not as the author of the offending letter, but as the owner and printer of *The Examiner*. Leigh was not named in the indictment because he had withdrawn from ownership of the newspaper, in part because of his own ill health and also to ensure that, should another libel action arise, *The Examiner* would survive. The Hunt brothers doubted the feasibility of keeping the newspaper going if they were both sent to prison, since the friends who had helped them in 1813–1815 had dispersed, and, in the wake of the Six Acts, *The Examiner*'s finances were in a precarious state. However the terms of Leigh's withdrawal were unclear and ownership of the paper would be a major bone of contention between the Hunt brothers in the years to come.

In the months after the culmination of the trial of Queen Caroline, Hunt wrote little for *The Examiner*, and *The Indicator* was filled with old essays, the work of friends, and short apologies from its editor, which cited his continuing ill health as the cause of the journal's lack of material. Both he and his children were unwell over the course of the winter, and Marianne was afraid for the life of her youngest child, who at the age of nine months suffered a terrifying series of convulsions. Marianne's troubles were compounded by a brutal letter from her nephew, Henry, who was himself under immense strain, as he tried to keep *The Examiner* going in spite of his father's impending imprisonment (itself a worry, since John Hunt was now forty-six and less able to withstand the hardships of Coldbath Fields) and his uncle's continuing ill health and financial mismanagement. Marianne wrote to Henry asking him for a loan, which she stipulated should be kept secret from Hunt. He responded furiously, citing the repeated warnings she had been given about the need to rein in her spending, the unhappiness her mismanagement was causing the entire family, and the damage her financial incompetence was doing to John Hunt's health. He concluded with a warning: 'The consequence of your continuing to encroach on my father's share of *The Examiner* is obvious: the concern would be suddenly stopt by an execution for debts which my advances to you would prevent me from meeting; – & we should all be ruined.'[27]

Marianne's inability to hold on to money was infuriating to all those who tried to help the Hunts, but there is no doubting the extent of her desperation that winter. She became convinced that their only hope for financial and physical survival was to sell their furniture and travel to the Shelleys in Italy, preferably by water, which would be cheaper than travelling over land. 'Oh! how much I wish we could come to you!' she told Mary. 'I cannot – I dare not – unburden my heart, but read the numbers of the 'Indicators' and you will comprehend me.'[28] There were only a few numbers of *The Indicator* left in which Mary

and Shelley could judge the state of Hunt's mood and health, since
he was forced to give the journal up at the end of March. Spurred by
Marianne's desperation, in August Shelley reissued his invitation to the
Hunts to join them in Italy. This time, however, the invitation offered
more than companionship. It contained a proposal for a literary project
which Shelley believed would secure Hunt's future and his political and
literary reputation.

———

By the spring of 1821, the Shelleys were settled once more at San
Giuliano. It was there that Shelley wrote the bulk of the poem which
formed his own response to Keats's death, *Adonais*, in which Shelley,
Byron, Hunt and others appear in stylised form as mourners in a
funeral procession for Adonais, a youthful poetic spirit proclaimed by
Shelley as a descendant of Milton. Again, Shelley's friends peopled his
verses, but this time they did so to mark the passing of a fellow poet.
In the eerie final stanza Shelley envisaged himself following Adonais,
whose soul, 'like a star,/ Beacons from the abode where the Eternal
are'. This was both a comment on his own mortality and a defiant
assertion of the value of his poetry, which, he claimed, would one day
bring him the kind of immortality won by Adonais. Shelley told Claire
that *Adonais* was 'better than any thing I have yet written, & worthy
both of him & me'.[29] He was proud enough of the poem to have it
printed in Pisa, thus protecting his manuscript from the vagaries of
international postage, as well as from the maulings of Charles Ollier
and his typesetters. Yet again, it was through the imaginative evocation
of friends that Shelley discovered new confidence in his poetic voice.

Perhaps the experience of writing *Adonais* spurred Shelley's actions
in the months that followed. With Claire in Florence, Shelley and
Mary were able to develop a new kind of friendship, with a couple their
own age. Their new acquaintances were Jane and Edward Williams,
and they had arrived in Pisa – at the suggestion of their friend and
Shelley's cousin Thomas Medwin – in January 1821. Despite the fact
that Jane was universally known as Jane Williams she and Edward
were not actually married, since her abusive husband refused to grant

her a divorce. She met Edward in India, where he and her husband were serving in the army. At the time of their arrival in Pisa Jane and Edward had lived together for two years, had a one year old son, named Medwin, and were expecting a second baby. They were, as their letters testify, very much in love.

Both Shelley and Mary were initially unimpressed by Jane, who was pretty, amiable and rather dim, but they were charmed by Edward's cheerfulness and his enthusiasm for life. He was an eager reader and writer, a devoted father and partner, and both he and Jane joined in with the Shelleys' daily pursuits with high-spirited energy. They took a house in the village of Pugnano, which was linked to San Giuliano by the canal joining the Arno to the river Serchio. Mary later described the canal as 'a full and picturesque stream, making its way under verdant banks sheltered by trees that dipped their boughs into the murmuring waters'[30] and here, and in the houses at Pugnano and San Giuliano, the Shelleys and the Williamses established their daily routine of reading, writing, walking and talking. Together the two couples explored mountain paths and river walks, meandered along the canal in Shelley's boat, and in the evenings would sit amongst the cypress trees talking about the play Edward was writing. Mary rediscovered her love of the countryside and Shelley was so entranced by the beauty of their surroundings that he considered buying a farmhouse on the hills outside Pisa, so that they might always have a rural home. But he was also restless and shuttled back and forth to Pisa, where he visited Mrs Mason, sent letters to Claire not meant for Mary's eyes, and organised the publication of *Adonais*. With Mrs Mason's assistance he made arrangements for Claire to lodge in Livorno for the summer, and escorted her there himself in mid-June. Meanwhile Mary followed Greek politics and the progress of Mavrocordato's battle for his country's independence with much interest. She was thrilled that yet another Mediterranean country had thrown off the yoke of imperial rule, as her letters to Claire, Maria Gisborne and Hunt testify.

Byron was also watching the independence movements of southern Europe with a keen personal interest that summer. By the middle of 1821 it was clear that the efforts of the Carbonari to secure independence for

Romagna had failed, and Teresa Guiccioli's family, the Gambas, were exiled from the city-state. Since Teresa's decree of separation from her husband was conditional upon her residence in her father's house, Byron's future was closely linked with the Gambas. If they had to leave Romagna then he had to go with them, in order to be with Teresa. By the summer he was therefore in a state of considerable uncertainty about his future. Shelley had proved himself to be a sympathetic listener in Geneva and in Venice, and, as Byron knew, felt a keen interest in his plans for Allegra, whose sequestered existence at Bagnacavallo was continuing to cause Claire much distress. In April Byron sent a long letter to Shelley, in which he expressed his thanks for Shelley's support for his treatment of Allegra and discussed Keats's death and *The Cenci*, as well as Shelley's desire that Byron should stir himself to write a great poem. This he declined to do, on the grounds that 'I have not the inclination nor the power', and because 'this late failure of the Italians has latterly disappointed me for many reasons, – some public, some personal.' But the crux of his letter came at its very end, in a postscript: 'Could not you and I contrive to meet this summer? Could you not take a run *alone*?'[31]

At the beginning of August, Shelley took a 'run' over to Ravenna, as Byron had suggested. Claire was kept in ignorance of the fact he was going to visit Byron, and Mary in equal ignorance of the night he spent with Claire in Livorno on the way from Pisa to Florence – the night of his twenty-ninth birthday. He arrived in Ravenna on 6 August, two-and-a-half years after his last meeting with Byron. Since their parting in Venice in 1818, friction over Claire and Allegra had introduced a renewed formality to their relationship, but Shelley was nevertheless pleasantly surprised by the changes he discovered in Byron's lifestyle, and by the improvements in his friend's health, which he attributed to the calming effect of Teresa. Shelley was impressed too by Byron's actions on behalf of the Carbonari, which, he told Mary, 'will delight & surprise you'.[32] He rapidly accommodated himself to Byron's timetable, rising at twelve (two hours before his host), talking and reading in the afternoon; riding through the pine forests to the sea in the early evening; dining, and then talking the night away, before retiring to bed at four or five in the morning.

After an interval of more than two years, Byron and Shelley had much to talk about. Since their previous meeting Byron had written more of his masterpiece, *Don Juan*, and Shelley had produced a rich body of work, which instilled in him a new confidence about his poetic abilities. They renewed their conversation about poetry, although, perhaps as a result of Shelley's increased confidence, they differed 'more than ever', since Byron affected 'to patronise a system of criticism fit only for the production of mediocrity'.[33] They discussed Allegra (now four-and-a-half), who, Byron reported, was growing very beautiful. Shelley had an opportunity to see this for himself when he visited Allegra at the Convent of Bagnacavallo. He observed that she was treated with kindness by the nuns, even after 'she made me run all over the convent like a mad thing . . . and began ringing the bell, which calls the nuns to assemble.' Asked whether she had any messages for her father, she replied that she wanted both Papa and '*mammina*' to visit her. Allegra's '*mammina*' was probably Teresa – the pretty lady who occasionally brought her presents and dresses – rather than Claire, whom she had not seen since before her second birthday. Shelley was nevertheless reassured to learn that Byron had no intention of leaving Allegra in her convent indefinitely, since he, like Claire, was convinced the nuns would only give her a poor and prejudiced education.

There were, however, pressing matters apart from Allegra's future to be discussed. Byron reported a claim by Elise Foggi, passed on by the Hoppners, that Shelley had fathered a child with Claire at Naples, and that both Shelley and Claire had treated Mary brutally. When Shelley related this in a letter to Mary, she responded, as he requested, with a horrified denial. Her letter was directed to Isabelle Hoppner but was written for Byron's eyes. Byron sensibly doubted Elise's veracity, but he did not care sufficiently about clearing his friend's name to confess to the Hoppners that he had told Shelley about the rumours, and nor did he ever forward Mary's letter to them. In any case, he had more immediate concerns to discuss with Shelley, and many of their afternoons and evenings were taken up with talking about Byron's plans for the future. He could not stay in Ravenna, and the Gambas were talking of relocating (with Teresa) to Geneva, in order to escape the political anger directed towards them after the failure of the Carbonari.

With Shelley's help, Teresa and her father were persuaded to stay in Italy. He proposed that both they and Byron should move to Pisa, to join the colony of sympathetic individuals gathering there. The Williamses and Mrs Mason were *in situ*, and Shelley believed that Horace Smith and his family were on their way to join them. Claire was based in Florence, so would not be present to bother Byron. And, over the course of his Ravenna visit, Shelley made a suggestion which would allow the Hunts to join them in Italy as well. For some time, Byron had been toying with the idea of starting a literary journal, at one point asking Thomas Moore to join him as a fellow editor in Italy. Now Shelley reshaped and broadened that idea into a project which could provide gainful employment for Hunt. Hunt would come to Italy to edit a new journal, which he would produce in partnership with Byron. Shelley volunteered to act as facilitator, to bring Hunt to Italy and to organise Byron's accommodation in Pisa. He secured a loan from Byron to fund the Hunts' journey, and wrote eagerly to Hunt of the benefits of the project: 'there can be no doubt that the *profits* of any scheme in which you and Lord Byron engage, must, from various yet co-operating reasons, be very great.'[34] After some vacillation, both Byron and Hunt agreed to his proposal. The Gambas prepared to move to Pisa, and Hunt and Marianne packed up their belongings and made arrangements to transport their family to Italy by boat.

Writing to Mary of his plans, Shelley outlined the benefits of remaining in Pisa and of gathering their friends around them. In the company of the Williamses, the Hunts, Byron and the Masons, they could put down permanent roots in Italy, celebrated in 'Julian and Maddalo' as a 'paradise of exiles'. He also outlined the dilemma which was central to his emotional and intellectual existence, about how best one should live one's life. 'My greatest content', he confessed, 'would be utterly to desert all human society. I would retire with you & our child to a solitary island in the sea, would build a boat, & shut upon my retreat the floodgates of the world.' Recognising this to be an impossible dream, he suggested 'the other side of the alternative (for a medium ought not to be adopted)': 'to form for ourselves a society of our own class, as much as possible, in intellect or in feelings; & to connect ourselves with the interests of that society.'[35] This was a mature reworking of the meeting of 'unprejudiced members of the community' which Shelley had proposed to Hunt back in 1811. The Pisan version of this community would be comprised of individuals buffeted by the blows of a cruel world: by the deaths of children and friends, by political repression, and by the vitriol of critics. In companionship they would take refuge from all that hurt them. From the safety of Italy, unhampered by the vicious libel laws of England, Hunt, Byron and Shelley would produce a journal which might still have the power to change the world.

———

Shelley returned to Mary at the end of August, and together they made preparations to receive their community of exiles, now slowly making its way toward them across land and sea. They returned to Pisa in the autumn and settled themselves in large unfurnished apartments on the Lung'Arno. Shelley rented a *palazzo* for Byron opposite their own home, on the other side of the river. The ground floor of Byron's house was set aside for the Hunts, who were expected to sail from England before Christmas. Claire was fetched from Livorno, where she had been all summer, and spent a short holiday with the Shelleys before returning to Florence.

On 1 November 1821 Byron's cavalcade rolled into Pisa, complete with travelling carriage, mountains of baggage, over a dozen horses and a menagerie of exotic household pets. Allegra remained in her convent, far away now from both her mother and her father. Claire left Pisa to return to Florence on the day of Byron's arrival and passed his 'travelling train'[36] on the road. Her last encounter with the man who had changed her life was a fleeting glimpse of his carriage from the window of a public coach.

8

Corsairs

Byron's new home was the Palazzo Lanfranchi, a cavernous Renaissance building overlooking the Arno. Three days after his arrival Edward and Jane Williams moved back to Pisa from Pugnano, and took rooms in the same building as the Shelleys. Edward was introduced to Byron by Shelley, and was rather dazzled by his celebrity. He was surprised that Byron bore so little resemblance to the brooding figure of popular imagination: 'so far from being . . . wrapt in a melancholy gloom he is all sunshine, and good humour with which the elegance of his language and the brilliancy of his wit cannot fail to inspire those who are near him.'[1] Shelley's cousin Thomas Medwin arrived in Pisa for the winter and was equally entranced by its newest and most famous resident. He spent long evenings drinking at the Palazzo Lanfranchi, during which he assiduously wrote down Byron's pronouncements on his life, his work, and his acquaintances. Medwin saw himself as the Boswell to Byron's Johnson, recording the words of the great man for posterity (and, of course, to ensure a posthumous reputation for himself, just as Boswell had). Everyone – Byron included – found Medwin's incessant scribbling rather comical, and Byron, knowing that his every word was being recorded, ensured that his conversation was suitably outrageous. Byron's friends were less amused when Medwin rushed his *Conversations of Lord Byron* into print in 1824, particularly since the volume was full of inaccuracies and shredded the reputations of men and women who had known Byron for much longer than Medwin himself. But in

1821, Medwin was accepted into the fold of the Pisa group. Like John
Taaffe, who frequently joined Byron's parties, he was a figure of fun and
nobody guessed he would go on to refashion his new friends in print
so unscrupulously.

Byron's position at the centre of the Pisan group was unassailable.
He was rich, famous, brilliant, had a large house and the resources
with which to entertain his friends, not to mention a glamorous Italian
mistress. He rose late, breakfasted, and then rode out from Pisa with
Shelley, Pietro Gamba (Teresa's brother), Medwin, Taaffe and Edward
to a farm where they practised shooting. It was Byron who provided
the horses and who negotiated shooting rights outside the city walls,
since the governor of Pisa would not allow him to fire his pistols in his
own garden at the Palazzo Lanfranchi. They used silver coins wedged
atop split canes for targets, and Shelley and Byron vied to prove their
prowess, competing with each other for the title of best shot. Sometimes
Mary and Jane rode out with Teresa in her carriage to watch the fun;
sometimes Jane and Edward (who found the permanent presence of
others a little wearing) would hide away, and walk out to meet the
group on their return. Usually Byron dined alone, called on Teresa, and
then returned to his *palazzo*, where he worked late into the night by
candlelight, with a bottle of wine at his elbow – first on a tragedy, *Werner*,
and subsequently on new cantos of *Don Juan*. Every Wednesday he put
aside his work to host a dinner party for his new acquaintances. These
were heavy drinking, heavy eating affairs, and they could be something
of a penance for Shelley, who usually ate and drank little, rose much
earlier in the morning, and was overawed by Byron's productivity. On
rainy days Shelley and Edward played billiards in Byron's *palazzo* and
Shelley and Byron discussed the progress of the latter's poetry, just as
they had done in Venice. Edward and Shelley also made occasional
expeditions down the Arno in Shelley's boat, sometimes taking Mary
and Jane with them.

It was an exceptionally well-documented winter. All its participants,
but particularly those, like Edward and Medwin, who knew themselves
to be in the company of more talented men, recognised that the
confluence of personalities in Pisa was extraordinary; that they were

living through (in the words of a youthful Keats, anticipating his meeting with Hunt) 'an Era in [their] existence'.[2] While Medwin wrote down Byron's conversations, Edward kept a diary, in which he recorded discussions with Byron about women, politics, and poetry. Edward's diary recorded a strange incident which took place in mid-December, when Medwin reported rumours that a man was to be burnt alive for sacrilege in the nearby province of Lucca. These rumours turned out to be incorrect, but not before Shelley and Byron had dispatched John Taaffe to Lucca to investigate, and Byron had been prevailed upon to use his influence to stop the punishment taking place. On other occasions Edward recorded Byron reading his poetry aloud in draft, and the admiration with which his recently published works were read by his friends.

Mary was particularly delighted by Byron's work, as her letters to Maria Gisborne testify. *Cain*, she wrote, was 'a revelation', and quite unlike anything she had read before. 'Of some works one says – one has thought of things though one could not have expressed it so well – It is not thus with Cain.'[3] Mary's enthusiasm for Byron's work can only have exacerbated Shelley's renewed feeling of poetic inferiority. He wrote little that winter, directing most of his energy into an abortive drama based on the life of Charles I. Nor did it improve her relationship with Claire, who reacted badly from Florence to news of Mary's cordial friendship with Teresa Guiccioli.[4]

Byron was an amusing and invigorating companion, but his arrival in Pisa marked a shift in both the daily patterns of the group's activities and its delicate, complicated relationships. Mary quickly realised that she would not again occupy the central position she had enjoyed during the Swiss summer of 1816. The group which now coalesced around Byron divided along gender lines. The men rode and shot, and gathered for dinner parties at Byron's *palazzo*. Mary, Teresa and Jane were not invited to these gatherings, and instead had to content themselves with riding out to watch the shooting from a carriage, with paying calls on each other, and with receiving their male friends at home on the nights when Byron did not require their company at the Palazzo Lanfranchi (Byron himself rarely called on Mary that winter). For the

most part Mary kept her thoughts on her exclusion from dinner parties
and literary conversation to herself, but she could not resist conveying
a mild complaint to Marianne Hunt, at whose Hampstead house she
had enjoyed the company of a group notable for its equitable inclusion
of men and women. 'How I wish you were with us in our rambles!'
she wrote, while Marianne was still in England, waiting to sail to Italy.
'Our good cavaliers flock together, and as they do not like <u>fetching a
walk with the absurd womankind</u>, Jane . . . and I are off together, and
talk morality and pluck violets by the way.'⁵ By this point Mary was
genuinely fond of Jane and enjoyed her company, but it was something
of a disappointment for the author of *Frankenstein* to be reduced to
flower picking with a female companion while the men talked politics
and poetry.

The separation of male and female activities also introduced further
distance into Mary and Shelley's relationship. They were not like
Edward and Jane, stealing away from the group to be alone together,
although Shelley did occasionally walk with Mary and Jane rather
than ride out with Byron and his attendants. Denied entry to Byron's
parties, Mary made other friends in Pisa, and began to show an interest
in attending balls and the kind of functions that made Shelley recoil
in horror. He sought and valued the company of intimates, but the
idea of venturing out into Pisan society – of acting the part of a society
husband and talking to inconsequential strangers – was appalling to
him. At one point Mary suggested they host a party of their own, but
Shelley reacted to the suggestion with such disgust that the idea was
dropped.

With *Valperga* finished and sent to Godwin for publication, Mary
amused herself by preparing the empty rooms on the ground floor of
the Palazzo Lanfranchi for the Hunts, making mince pies for Christmas,
and playing with Percy, now an active toddler. She also copied some
of Byron's poems from manuscript for him, just as she had done in
Geneva in 1816 and, in her desolation after Clara's death, in Este in
1818. This meant that it was Edward, rather than Mary, who acted
as Shelley's literary companion: transcribing his poems, reading with
him, and taking over Mary's role as amanuensis in the translation of

Spinoza. Edward had literary ambitions too, and received much advice (not all of it welcome) from Shelley about the play he was writing. One effect of this was that Shelley spent more time in Edward and Jane's apartments than he did in his own. He quickly came to appreciate the charms of their cheerful, affectionate home, and of his pretty hostess. As the winter progressed, his attraction to Jane grew stronger. Jane was musical, and he asked Horace Smith to send a harp for her from Paris. Smith declined to spend his money on Shelley's behalf, so Shelley had to content himself with giving Jane a guitar, and with writing admiring lyrics about her.

At the end of January, Shelley sent his poem, 'The Serpent is Shut Out from Paradise', down to Edward and Jane's apartment. In it he lamented his own 'cold home', and, in the final stanza, Mary's unsympathetic scorn:

> I asked her yesterday if she believed
>> That I had resolution. One who *had*
>>> Would ne'er have thus relieved
>>> His heart with words, but what his judgement bade
>> Would do, and leave the scorner unrelieved. —
>>> These verses were too sad
>> To send to you, but that I know
>> Happy yourself, you feel another's woe.

Edward recorded receipt of Shelley's 'beautiful but too melancholy lines' in his journal,[6] but not the fact that the note accompanying the poem stipulated that it should be seen by no one but him and Jane. Edward seems to have been flattered that his beautiful partner was so admired by Shelley, but at the beginning of March he called on Mary 'by appointment'[7] which suggests that they may have had a private conversation about Shelley's latest infatuation, and about the best way to deal with it. Mary knew from experience that unobtainable women were always more attractive to Shelley (as the Emilia Viviani episode demonstrated) and neither she nor Edward made any effort to keep Shelley and Jane apart. Edward was convinced of Jane's loyalty to him, and – perhaps correctly – interpreted Shelley's interest in her as a sign of admiration for them both, as well as a desire for the companionable romance they personified. And, as Mary realised, Shelley's interest in another woman in no way precluded his continued fascination with her. Unlike any other woman he had met, she was his intellectual equal. It was for this reason that it mattered so much when she lavished praise on Byron's poetry. In her old age, Claire claimed that Mary was the only person Shelley had ever truly loved, and that this was 'because of her intellect'.[8] Mary and Claire spent a lifetime competing over Shelley, so this comment, made many years after Mary's death, must carry some weight. In any case, the events of the winter of 1821–22 testify to the complexity of Shelley and Mary's relationship. At the point that Shelley found a new object for infatuation in Jane, Mary became pregnant for a fifth time.

Christmas was celebrated by the 'Pistol Club' (named thus by Edward in tribute to their shooting expeditions) at a grand dinner hosted by Byron. Edward sent a glowing account of this 'splendid feast' to a friend, Edward John Trelawny, whom he and Medwin had met in Geneva two years previously.[9] In the same letter he urged Trelawny to come to Pisa, holding out the prospect of Lord Byron's company as an inducement.

Edward was eager that Trelawny should join them in Pisa because in January 1822 the Pistol Club discovered a new hobby: boating. Shelley already owned the small vessel which he and Edward used to meander up and down the Arno, but by January they had exhausted the possibilities offered by so modest a craft. Edward decided that Trelawny was the ideal person to advise them on the design and construction of a grander, seafaring boat. 'I shall reserve all that I have to say about the boat until we meet at the select committee, which is intended to be held on that subject when you arrive here', he told his friend. 'Have a boat we must.'[10]

Edward's letter also presented an alluring picture of a Byron who had revealed his hidden self to a select group of contemporaries. Trelawny was not the man to pass up the opportunity to find out the truth of Byron's character for himself. He arrived in Pisa on 14 January, tempted too by the prospect of friendship with Shelley, whose *Queen Mab* he admired. Within days of his arrival, this rugged, bearded creature had the entire Pisan group mesmerised by his charisma and by the extraordinary stories he related of his past adventures.

However, few of these stories were true. Edward Trelawny was the younger son of an MP and minor landowner, and he had in fact achieved remarkably little in the twenty-nine years of his existence. He was expelled from school for attacking a master who flogged him; joined the navy in 1805 (shortly *after* the battle of Trafalgar); and left it in 1812 without gaining an officer's commission. He married in 1813 but his marriage ended in a messy and public divorce after his wife had an affair and Trelawny sued her lover for 'Criminal Conversation'. In 1819 he left England and embarked on a restless progress around Europe.

No one who met Trelawny after his departure from England in 1819 would have guessed that his history consisted of an inglorious naval career and an unhappy marriage. Instead he constructed a fantastical history for himself, in which he deserted the navy, took up with a dashing privateer called de Ruyter and sailed the seas, acquiring an alluring teenage bride called Zela in the process. This was the story Trelawny recorded in his 'autobiography', *Adventures of a Younger Son*, summarised thus by Peter Cochran: 'There are cruel pranks, sea fights, land raids, a shipboard orgy, and a tiger hunt from which only the elephants emerge with credit . . . Scotsmen, surgeons, and other human annoyances exist only to be beaten up or dropped into pits of offal, buildings exist only to be burnt or pulled down, and animals only to be hamstrung, shot, or eaten.'[11] It is one of the more abiding mysteries to biographers of Shelley and Byron that a semi-literate Cornishman managed not only to convince both them and their friends of the veracity of his history (to the extent at least that they never openly questioned the stories he told them) but also that he inserted himself so seamlessly into the daily rituals of their circle. Byron eventually came to doubt Trelawny, but there is no suggestion that anyone present in Pisa in 1822 realised the extent of his deception. This may well be because Trelawny was such an able fantasist that by the time he arrived in Pisa he had half-convinced himself of the truth of his own tall tales.

There was an additional reason why Byron – the most sceptical and experienced member of the group – did not examine Trelawny's history too closely. Trelawny was himself a Byronic creation. He modelled himself on the hero of *The Corsair*, Byron's tale of eastern adventure which had taken London by storm in 1814. Trelawny was more Byronic than Byron himself, and it was flattering – if a little odd – for a poet to meet a man who had taken on the identity of one of his creations. For the others, the combination of Byron and the personification of his hero was irresistible.

Mary was entranced by Trelawny, and her diary provides one of the best descriptions we have of him:

> Trelawny is extravagant . . . if his abrupt, but not unpolished manners be assumed, they are nevertheless in unison with his Moorish face (for he looks oriental yet not Asiatic) his dark hair his herculean form. And then there is an air of extreme good nature which pervades his whole countenance, especially when he smiles, which assures me that his heart is good. He tells strange stories of himself – horrific ones – so that they harrow one up, while with his emphatic but unmodulated Voice – his simple yet strong language – he portrays the most frightful situations – then all these adventures took place between the ages of 13 & 20 – I believe them now I see the man – & tired with the everyday sleepiness of human intercourse I am glad to meet with one whom among other valuable qualities has the rare merit of arresting my imagination.[12]

Now that the Pisan circle had both Byron and a Byronic hero in their midst they ceased to be the 'Pistol Club' and became the 'Corsair Crew'.[13] Mary's diary makes frequent references to the 'Corsair' and also to visits from the 'Crew', although, as had been the case before Trelawny's arrival, these visits did not include the Crew's erstwhile leader, Byron. A year later, when Joseph Severn met Trelawny in Rome, he christened him the 'Cockney Corsair',[14] which suggests that he detected a Huntian vulgarity underlying the persona of Byronic adventurer. But there were no such detractors in Pisa.

Trelawny's arrival marked a new phase of theatricality in the lives of the Corsair Crew. 'Trelawny dine[s]', Edward recorded in his diary on 10 April. 'We talk of a play of his singular life, and a plot to give it the air of Romance.'[15] This theatricality was given a focus when, at Trelawny's instigation, the group decided to stage a performance of *Othello* at Byron's *palazzo*. Trelawny was to play the Moor, and Byron – a great admirer of Edmund Kean – took the part of Iago. According to Teresa, Byron's performance in the handkerchief scene in *Othello* was deeply moving, but she nevertheless put a stop to rehearsals because there was no suitable part for her. Thwarted in their theatrical ambitions, Trelawny escorted Mary and Jane to the public theatre of the Pisan carnival, for which they donned extravagant carnival outfits: Jane a 'Hindoostani dress' and Mary a 'Turkish costume'.[16] He also took total command of the boat building project. Shelley ordered a thirty-foot sailing boat for himself and Edward; while Byron, not to be outdone, decided that he required a larger schooner, complete with cabins and guns. Lord Byron 'intend[s] to enter into a competition with us in sailing', Edward recorded somewhat ambivalently in his diary.[17] Trelawny placed the orders with his friend Daniel Roberts and made himself indispensable as plans for the summer were discussed. Meanwhile, the shooting and dinner parties continued. It was as if Trelawny had always been one of the 'Corsair Crew', rather than an interloper who had so recently imposed his imagined, plagiarised identity on the group.

By the beginning of 1822 Shelley's long-imagined community of exiles had finally come into being. The only absentees were the Hunts, who were still in England several months after deciding to travel to Italy. Hunt 'is hoped for in the Spring', Byron told a correspondent. 'I suppose', he continued, 'we shall see him by Xmas next.'[18] Hogg was ruder about the Hunts' slow progress. 'I would have written by Hunt', he told Shelley at the end of January, 'but I was unable to muster up sufficient gravity to address a grey-headed, deaf, double, tottering, spectacled old man, for such I was persuaded you would be before he reached Pisa'.[19] It was certainly the case that the Hunts did not have a great deal of luck as they attempted to leave their old life in England behind them. Their journey started on 14 November 1821 and their departure from Hampstead was witnessed by Charles Brown. It was, he told a friend, a 'melancholy sight to see the whole of the family stuffed into a Hackney Coach, in search of a more favourable climate and more favourable friends.'[20] The occupants of the Hackney Coach were Hunt, Marianne, an unnamed servant and the six Hunt children: Thornton (aged eleven), John (nine), Mary (eight), Swinburne (five), Percy (four) and Henry (two). It was a significant logistical undertaking to transport this number of children across the sea to Italy, but despite the fact that Marianne was dangerously ill – her main symptom, coughing blood, was thought to be an early sign of tuberculosis – Bess was not included in the party.

The letters Hunt wrote to his sister-in-law after his arrival in Italy suggest that her exclusion from the expedition caused both of them much pain. But the same letters make reference to the malice of scandalmongers, and to the circulation of persistent rumours about the exact nature of Hunt and Bess's relationship. Bess was left behind in order that her reputation – and Hunt's – might be salvaged, but also because Marianne was utterly opposed to the idea that she should accompany them. Like Claire, marooned in Florence, Bess was to be left out of Shelley's community of exiles.

The Hunts' hackney coach took them to Blackwall, where they boarded the vessel which was to take them to Italy. The Novellos accompanied them on board and presented them with a goat, in order that the children could have fresh milk for breakfast during their journey. Their transport, the *Jane*, was a cargo ship, and its official cargo sugar. Also on board were fifty barrels of gunpowder, which were being illicitly transported to Greece. These barrels rightly caused Hunt and Marianne a good deal of concern, especially when the ship's drunken cook staggered down into the hold with his candle alight. The Hunts were the only passengers, and had the boat's main cabin to themselves. Even so, there were not enough berths available for everyone, so the children shared the bunks lining the walls while Hunt and Marianne made themselves a bed on the floor. Their servant slept in a tiny closet adjoining the main cabin, and the captain in a similar cubby hole. The rest of the crew occupied cramped quarters at the other end of the ship, which were permanently soaked by waves crashing overhead. The goat was tethered on deck, along with some equally unfortunate caged ducks. Eventually Hunt took pity on the goat and carried it into the cabin, where it slid around as the ship pitched from side to side.

Hunt never forgot the start of their journey in the *Jane*. The conditions were so bad that the captain was forced to make for port at Ramsgate, where they stayed for three weeks, waiting for an improvement in the weather. The Hunts took lodgings in the town (thus incurring more expense) and by the time they set sail again, on 11 December, Marianne was so ill she had to be carried aboard. For ten days, the *Jane* battled down the English Channel towards the Atlantic, fighting against the worst weather in seafaring memory. Storm after storm pitched the boat and its passengers all over the place, one gale lasting fifty-six hours without pause. It was bitterly cold and wet: water dripped through the cabin roof, making it impossible to keep anything dry. The constant motion made a mockery of meal times. Hunt later described how he was compelled to throw food from the table in the middle of the cabin to the inhabitants of the bunks at its side, since neither Marianne nor the children were able to stand. Everyone was seasick, and Marianne continued to spit blood, and to spend her waking hours frantic with worry about her children.

It was no better for the other inhabitants of the *Jane*. The goat was so terrified that her milk supplies dried up, and the waves which battered the boat broke the wings and legs of the ducks, spraying bones and bird carcases everywhere. Hunt devoted his energies to playing elaborate games to distract the children, telling them, on one occasion, that the squawking of the tortured ducks was in fact the sound of a friend laughing, but he was horrified by the danger to which he had exposed his family, and tormented by thoughts of the friends they had left at home. 'I used to think of them', Hunt confessed in his memoirs, 'reading, chatting, and laughing, playing music . . . then retiring to easy beds amidst happy families; and perhaps, as the wind howled, thinking of us.'[21] Once, when despondency overcame him, and the rocks off

the Scilly Isles looked dangerously close, he asked the ship's mate to
throw open the lid to the cabin stairs if the worst should happen, so
that his children should not know the agony of a prolonged death. The
ship's crew appear to have been very kind to the terrified family, telling
the children stories of sea adventures and reassuring Marianne that the
conditions they were experiencing were not dangerous. But in actual
fact they were worse than anybody on board had ever known. On 22
December, after an abortive attempt to reach the safety of Falmouth
harbour, the *Jane* turned back and put into port at Dartmouth.

At the beginning of January the *Jane* set sail for Italy once more,
but this time it left its passengers behind. The torments of their battles
down the English Channel had been too much for Marianne, who
flatly refused to be carried on board again. Her health had deteriorated
to the extent that Hunt doubted whether she would even survive the
journey. So they forfeited their passages and travelled to Plymouth,
where they waited for the spring. 'Oh Novello!' Hunt wrote at the
beginning of February, 'what a disappointing, wearisome, vexatious,
billowy, up-and-downy, unbearable, beautiful world it is!'[22] But Hunt
had more than disappointment to contend with. His expenses were,
once again, escalating out of control. The delay was not his fault, but
new passages had to be bought, and Plymouth lodgings had to be paid
for. In November, John Hunt had written to Shelley from his prison cell
in Coldbath Fields, to thank him for his generosity towards his brother.
But his letter also contained some serious words of advice. 'You will,
above all, advise him to be more mindful of his domestic expenses, a
negligence of which has been the chief cause of his embarrassments.'[23]

It was now Shelley's turn to learn something of the strain Hunt's
impecuniousness placed on his friends. His own resources were not
sufficient to permit him to fund Hunt's delayed journey, so he was
forced to ask Byron for more money on Hunt's behalf. This placed him
in an invidious position. It turned him from an equal of Byron's into
yet another supplicant, and Byron was at his least generous when he
was required to provide financial support. Byron agreed to lend Hunt
money (a loan guaranteed by Shelley since, as he told Byron, 'I do
not think poor Hunt's promise to pay in a given time is worth very

much'),[24] but the request did not dispose him more favourably towards the plan for the journal, in which he was beginning to lose interest. To make matters worse, both Shelley and Byron believed that Hunt was coming to Italy supported by income from *The Examiner*, in which they supposed him still to have a share. In fact, he was bringing his family across the sea without any means of support at all, and had all hopes of economic survival pinned on the new journal.

Hunt himself did not help the delicate financial negotiations conducted on his behalf by Shelley. Once Byron had agreed to lend him money to complete his journey he wrote a letter of thanks which both illustrated his streak of vanity and which might have been calculated to annoy his benefactor. It started badly: 'My dear Byron (For I will not abate a jot of my democracy, at least on occasions of letter-writing).' This mode of address might have pleased Byron when it came from an imprisoned radical but it did not endear him to a man who had importuned him for money. Hunt did not improve matters by electing to patronise his patron. He confessed his unease at accepting Byron's money since 'from the first hour I knew you, I had got a romantic notion in my head, perhaps a coxcombical one . . . of awakening your school-day ideas of friendship again, & shewing you that a man could cultivate your regard, merely from a disinterested love of your intellectual qualities and of that very generosity.'[25] Byron was rewarded for lending money to Hunt not with gratitude but a lecture on his flaws, and by the news that he would be further reformed once Hunt arrived in Italy.

Shelley did warn Hunt to treat Byron with respect and caution, but, despite this, Hunt remained unaware of the strain his demands placed on Shelley and Byron's relationship, and on the whole journal scheme. He wrote enthusiastically to both of them of his plans for their periodical; his desk, he told them, was 'teeming' with ideas. The first number could open, he suggested, with an account of Byron's journey to Italy, 'which I might follow in the next number with that of a sea-one, and then we might have essays, stories, poetry, poetical translation, especially from the Italian, – in short, any thing we chose to blurt out or to be inspired with.' One can only imagine Byron's reaction when he

discovered he had been co-opted into funding and co-writing a Pisan
version of the thoroughly bourgeois *Indicator*. But Hunt's enthusiasm
was boundless. A vision of literary collaboration in Italy sustained him
through the winter in Plymouth. 'I fancy', he told Byron, eagerly, 'the
delight of sitting with you & Shelley round a green table with some
Italian wine & fruit upon it, settling what is to be done.'[26]

Others in England were equally enthusiastic about the projected
journal, and about the colony gathered in Pisa. Hogg, tied to England by
the legal circuit, wrote offering to contribute articles to the periodical, as
did William Hazlitt, while Joseph Severn, who remained in Rome after
Keats's death, received a friendly invitation from Shelley offering him
hospitality in Pisa. Charles Brown now seriously began to contemplate
following Severn and Hunt to Italy. Keats, his closest friend, had died
there and Severn showed no signs of returning to England. Shelley and
Byron were there, gathering interesting friends around them, and the
Hunts had talked of Italy as the place where one could start a new life.

Brown had plenty of reasons for wanting to follow his friends abroad,
and his own life in England was not free from complications. These
complications centred around his illegitimate son, Charles (known as
Carlino), who was born to Brown's housekeeper in July 1820, and was
given into his sole care in the spring of 1822. Brown cut an unusual
figure in London, as a single father with responsibility for the welfare
of a toddler. 'What think you of my playing the nurse? – washing,
combing, dressing &c a marmoset of 2 years old' he asked Severn
shortly after he and Carlino arrived in Pisa in September 1822.[27]
Although a servant was eventually hired to attend to Carlino, Brown's
son was never to know the pampered loneliness of Allegra's aristocratic
childhood in Byron's houses and at the Convent of Bagnacavallo.

The Hunts spent the winter quietly in Plymouth, waiting until spring
to resume their journey. Marianne was confined to her bed for much
of the time, although her health did improve a little as a result of the
enforced peace and quiet. The children grew strong in the sea air, and
Hunt found that their suspended seaside existence restored his own
health. He walked a great deal, and even felt strong enough to write the
occasional column for *The Examiner*, after an absence from its pages of

many months. His spirits were buoyed when some *Examiner* readers in Plymouth presented him with a silver cup in token of his efforts 'for freedom, truth and humanity' and invited him into their houses for tea and conversation. Bess wrote to him of the kindness of the Novellos, who were doing their best to cheer her up and to relieve the pain of separation from her brother-in-law. 'It delights me to see the intimacy there is between you and Miss K.', Hunt told Novello. 'She speaks in the most affectionate terms of you and your wife, and receives all the solace from your intercourse which I expected.'[28] He begged the Novellos to visit him in Plymouth, noting that the road from London was excellent, and the journey could be easily accomplished. 'You must not talk of your music, till Novello is here to inspire a pianoforte which I have just hired for a month. It is the only pleasure to which I have treated myself, and without him find it but a pain.'[29] It was probably a good thing that neither Shelley, who was scraping together all the money he could spare for Hunt, nor Byron, who lent the remainder so reluctantly, got to hear of the piano. It was a relief to all concerned when the Hunts secured new passages aboard the *David Walter* and finally set sail once more, on 13 May 1822.

Shelley and Byron's relationship, already complicated by negotiations over Hunt's expenses, was put under further strain by Claire's affairs. Claire was bitterly unhappy in Florence, especially after a meeting with Elise Foggi exposed her to the rumours circulated by the Hoppners about her relationship with Shelley. In the spring of 1822, her actions became impetuous and desperate, and she wrote a series of letters to the Pisan colony announcing her intention of leaving Italy for good. The only one of these letters which survives is that which she wrote to Byron, in which she begged to be allowed to see Allegra for a final time. 'I leave my friends with regret', she told him, 'but indeed I cannot go without having first seen and embraced Allegra.' The same letter expressed the fear at the forefront of Claire's mind: 'I can no longer resist the internal inexplicable feeling which haunts me that I shall never see her any more.'[30] Byron ignored this letter, but the Shelleys took Claire's plans seriously. She was immediately collected from Florence and taken back to Pisa, where she succumbed to Mary, Shelley and Mrs Mason's arguments that she should not act precipitately, before returning to her isolated life in Florence.

A month later Byron was as unrelenting as ever. Claire, convinced that she would never be allowed to see her daughter again, now asked Mary and Shelley to help her kidnap Allegra from the convent. They were horrified by the suggestion and by the danger to which Claire's request exposed them. Their response, which was clearly co-ordinated in such a way as to compel Claire to recognise the folly of her idea, illustrates the extent to which the issue of Allegra's future had begun to damage their relationship with Byron. Mary's letter focused on the practical difficulties of taking Allegra from the convent without her father's permission. High walls, she wrote, made it impossible to remove her without alerting the nuns, and Byron's fortune made him a dangerous enemy:

> What then would you do having A. on the outside of the convent walls? Would you go to America? the money we have not, nor does this seem to be your idea. You probably wish to secrete yourself. But LB would use any means to find you out – and the story he might make up . . . with money at command – above all on the spot to put energy into every pursuit, would he not find you? If he did not he comes upon Shelley – he taxes him; Shelley must either own it or tell a lie. In either case he is open to be called on by LB to answer for his conduct – and a duel – I need not enter upon that topic, your own imagination may fill up the picture.[31]

Mary's depiction of Byron as a vengeful pursuer trampling on his enemies with whom Shelley would be compelled to duel was in marked contrast to the glowing accounts of *Cain* sent to Maria Gisborne before Christmas. Shelley shared his wife's horror of the 'thoughtless violence' of Claire's plans[32] and insisted in a postscript to Mary's letter that Byron's virulent dislike of Claire hampered his ability to negotiate on her behalf. 'Lord Byron is obstinate and *awake* about Allegra' he reported. 'The idea of contending with him in Italy, and defended by his enormous fortune, is vain.'[33] By the end of March, Shelley and Mary were feeling suffocated by Byron's presence in Pisa. His wealth, his implacable resentment of Claire, his cynical, brilliant poetry and his dominance of the group they had created combined to make his company thoroughly oppressive. But the knowledge that the dependent Hunts were now inching their way towards Italy gave the Shelleys little room for manoeuvre. It was unthinkable that Hunt should arrive to find that the journal he had come to Italy to edit had already collapsed in a welter of acrimony over a five year old child.

Byron's attitude to the Shelleys during this period is harder to divine. His surviving letters do not suggest he viewed them as negatively as their correspondence indicates, although Trelawny recalled that Byron felt a degree of ambivalence about their influence over their mutual friends. 'I am for making a man of the world of you', Byron is reported to have told him, adding, 'they will mould you into a Frankenstein monster.'[34] Trelawny recounted this conversation in his *Recollections of the Last Days of Shelley and Byron*, the memoir he published in 1858. In some respects, *Recollections* is as unreliable a testimony as his fictional *Adventures of a Younger Son*, and its long accounts of conversations need to be treated with a good deal of caution. Nevertheless, Trelawny was skilled at evoking time and place, and his memoir gives some idea of the tensions which dominated the activities of the 'Crew' during the spring of 1822. He recalled, for example, looking for Shelley at Mary's behest, and finding him in the woods, scribbling away under a tree with volumes of Shakespeare and Sophocles by his side:

> He started up, snatched up his scattered books and papers, thrust them into his hat and jacket pockets, sighing, 'Poor Mary! her's is a sad fate . . . she can't bear solitude, nor I society – the quick coupled with the dead.'

Trelawny's description then shifts to Mary, 'her clear grey eyes and thoughtful brow expressing the love she could not speak. To stop Shelley's self-reproaches, or to hide her own emotions, she began in a bantering tone, chiding and coaxing him.'[35]

Recollections of the Last Days of Shelley and Byron paints a picture of an unfocused group, unsure of its future and its purpose. The Shelleys and the Williamses decided to spend the summer by the sea, in order to use the boat being built for Shelley in Livorno. Byron also had thoughts of retreating to the countryside for the summer, but it gradually became apparent that neither he nor Shelley wished to put themselves in the same place for a prolonged period. Shelley, Mary, Edward and Jane made various trips to the Bay of Lerici to look for suitable houses, but could find none that they liked. Meanwhile, the Corsair Crew continued in the routine established the winter before, riding out with Byron to shoot outside the city walls, and dining once a week at the Palazzo Lanfranchi. At one dinner Shelley and Byron made a bet that whoever came into their inheritance first would pay the other £1,000. A few weeks later, Byron's mother-in-law, Lady Noel, died, leaving him a substantial portion of her vast estate. But Byron did not pay Shelley the money he owed him, a failure which contributed to a further deterioration in Shelley's opinion of his friend.

On 24 March the first of two events took place which would shake the seemingly calm co-existence of the group. Byron, Shelley, Pietro Gamba, Trelawny and John Taaffe rode out as usual to practise shooting at the farm. They were joined by Captain Hay, a Byronic acolyte who had arrived in Pisa earlier in the year. Mary and Teresa Guiccioli had watched the shooting from Teresa's carriage, and were following the horsemen back into Pisa. When they were just outside the city walls an Italian dragoon by the name of Masi came up behind them at a gallop, and in his haste disrupted the English party, knocking Taaffe to the ground. Affronted by this, Shelley and the others gave chase, and there was an angry confrontation. In the ensuing confusion, Shelley's face was cut by Masi's sword and he was thrown from his horse, as was Captain Hay. Masi then disappeared back into the city, but was confronted shortly afterwards by Byron and his servants. Byron apparently intended to challenge him to a duel but, as a crowd gathered, one of his servants stabbed the dragoon in the back. Masi was carried away, believed by all who had seen his inert form to be at death's door.

Edward's diary contains a vivid description of the return of the Corsair Crew to the building in which he and the Shelleys had apartments. Trelawny raced ahead to tell him and Jane of the day's events, so the Williamses knew something of the background when 'Lord B. came in – the Countess [Teresa] fainting on his arm – S. sick from the blow – Lord B. and the young Count [Pietro Gamba] foaming with rage – Mrs S. looking philosophically upon this interesting scene – and Jane and I wondering what the Devil was to come next.'[36] Teresa had hysterics, but luckily she had been taken home by the time Taaffe arrived with 'a long face saying that the Dragoon could not live out the night'.[37]

The severity of Masi's injuries put paid to any hope the group had that the fuss caused by their fracas would subside. The Pisan authorities were already unhappy with the presence of such prominent exiles as the Gambas in their midst: it was partly for this reason that Byron was refused permission to practise shooting within the city walls. Over the next few weeks the police took long statements from Mary, Teresa, Edward and the others, and Byron's servants were arrested. Pisa hummed with gossip about the incident, and the group found themselves pointed at every time they stirred from their houses. In the end Masi recovered, but the episode transformed Pisa into an uncomfortable place for Byron, the Gambas and their friends. They were questioned continually and fell out over differences in their accounts. Particular animus was directed towards John Taaffe, whom the others felt had made cowardly reports to the police. The authorities took their revenge for the trouble caused by banishing Byron's servant, Tita, from the city.

On 9 April, three weeks after the fight with Masi, Claire wrote once more to Mary about Allegra. Her wild kidnap plans had now given way to straightforward anxiety: 'I fear she is sick,'[38] she insisted. Four days after Claire wrote this letter Byron received news that Allegra was unwell. The information came from his banker in Ravenna, Pellegrino Ghigi, who was in charge of the little girl's expenses and who, on hearing of her illness, travelled to the convent at Bagnacavallo to find her tucked up in a tiny bed, attended by three doctors and all the nuns. She had suffered multiple attacks of 'little slow fevers', and had been bled three times by a doctor who feared she was exhibiting the symptoms of tuberculosis. In fact, Allegra had contracted typhus, and on 20 April she died, 'after a convulsive catarrhal attack'.[39] She was five years old. At no stage during her brief illness do Byron and Teresa appear to have considered travelling to Ravenna to see her, and nor did they inform either Claire or Shelley of her condition.

It was Teresa who first heard the news from Bagnacavallo, and it was she who had to tell Byron of his daughter's death. In her memoir of Byron she was defensive about his treatment of Allegra: 'undoubtedly Lord Byron's behaviour towards this little girl had always been that of an affectionate father; but owing to his abhorrence of undue sentimentality, his paternal love would not have been thought to be so profound.'[40] Byron was similarly defensive in his communications with Shelley. 'I do not know that I have anything to reproach in my conduct', he wrote, 'and certainly nothing in my feelings and intentions towards the dead.' But, he continued, the memory of Shelley's representations about the unsuitability of leaving Allegra in Romagna vivid in his mind, 'it is a moment when we are apt to think that, if this or that had been done, such event might have been prevented.'[41]

———

Claire was the last person to be told of Allegra's death. Quite by chance, she was in Pisa when news reached the Shelleys of the catastrophe. They were frightened that she would hear what had happened by accident, and felt it was imperative that she should be far away from Byron before they broke the news. Plans for the summer therefore took on a new urgency. On 23 April – the same day that Teresa told Shelley what had happened – Mary and Claire departed for the Bay of Lerici in the company of Edward and Jane. In their haste to get Claire away from Pisa they left before securing lodgings and had to settle for a bleak house – the Casa Magni – perched right on the coast, at the foot of dark wooded hills. The Casa Magni did not have extensive living quarters and the Shelleys were obliged to share it with Edward and Jane, who could find no lodgings of their own. Mary later wrote that she hated the villa and the strange, desolate beauty of its surroundings. It was a difficult house to run: provisions were hard to find in the poverty-stricken villages nearby, and the Shelley and Williams servants occupied themselves in a never-ending turf war. The ground floor of the house was uninhabitable, so the Shelleys and the Williamses lived in cramped conditions on the first floor, which had a balcony overlooking the sea. Claire was unimpressed with the whole arrangement. She did not want to travel to the coast, and was put out that Shelley and Mary, having exiled her from their Pisan circle, now insisted that she accompany Mary to Lerici rather than return to the life she had made for herself in Florence. On 2 May, almost two weeks after Allegra's death, the household at Casa Magni was settling into 'a kind of disorderly order',[42] when Claire walked into a hushed conference in Jane's room, convened to discuss how best to break the news to her. The same instincts which had led her to write to Mary of her fears for Allegra's health led her to guess the purpose of their meeting.

Allegra's death proved Claire right. Byron was an inattentive father; the convent's marshy environment a disastrously unsafe place for a small child. But this was of little consolation. In the first agony of her grief she wrote one last letter to Byron, a murderous indictment of his negligence, in which she reminded him of her constant warnings about the dangers posed to Allegra's health by the Romagna climate, and accused him of culpability in their daughter's death. Byron was a great hoarder of correspondence, but he was sufficiently shocked by Claire's accusations to send her letter to Shelley, and to deny the responsibility she attributed to him. Neither Claire nor Byron's letters have survived, so we have to construct their contents from the drafts of earlier letters Claire planned to send to Byron, from her subsequent conviction that he killed her daughter, from diary entries she made before Allegra's death, and from Shelley's response to Byron's protestations of his innocence. Claire wrote her letter, Shelley assured Byron, immediately after the first shock of the news. 'I had no idea that her letter was written in that temper', he continued, apologetically. 'I think I need not assure you, that whatever mine or Mary's ideas might have been respecting the system of education you intended to adopt, we sympathise too much in your loss, & appreciate too well your feelings, to have allowed such a letter to be sent to you had we suspected its contents.'[43]

Claire's letter did have certain positive effects. Byron had ignored her pleas regarding Allegra for years, but her indictment of him – as well as the guilt he felt for disregarding her concerns about Allegra's health – caused him to accede to her final requests. He sent her a miniature of Allegra and a lock of her hair, and offered to implement her instructions about the funeral. At first, Claire wanted to go to Livorno to view Allegra's coffin, but to Shelley's relief, she later decided against it. Eventually, exhausted by her suffering, she permitted Byron to organise matters as he desired. Allegra's small form was transported to England, where John Murray organised a burial in Harrow Church. The parishioners there refused to allow any memorial to the illegitimate daughter of a notorious peer, so Allegra was buried in an unmarked tomb.

After Claire's first, desperate grief, Mary and Shelley were relieved and surprised to find her calmer than she had been for a long time. The certainty that she would never see Allegra again was easier to deal with than the limbo she had been in for four years. Forthright Mrs Mason shared the Shelleys' relief at Claire's reaction, which she saw for herself when Claire arrived unannounced in Pisa on 21 May. Now that nothing bound Claire to Italy, Mrs Mason hoped she would be able to live an independent life, which would separate her permanently from the Shelleys. She was therefore disappointed to learn that Claire planned to go back to Lerici. Allegra's death released Claire from her connection with Byron, but it did not resolve the uncertainty over her future. She returned to Casa Magni on 7 June, apparently a member of Shelley's community of exiles once more.

Claire's assistance was in fact much needed at Lerici. Mary's fifth pregnancy, still in its early stages, was progressing badly, and, possibly as a result of this, she was slipping once more into a terrible, disabling depression. 'I was not well in body or mind', she later told Maria Gisborne. 'No words can tell you how I hated our house & the country about it. Shelley reproached me for this – his health was good & the place was quite after his own heart.'[44] She found peace only on Shelley's new boat, 'when lying down with my head on his knee I shut my eyes & felt the wind & our swift motion alone.' There are many images of Mary and Shelley on boats together: buffeted across the English Channel in an open boat in 1814; reading Wollstonecraft and winding up monarchists on ponderous Rhine barges; skimming across Lake Geneva with Byron. But this image – of Mary, ill and depressed, taking comfort from Shelley's physical presence but unable to explain her emotional torments to him – is unique in its desolation.

Shelley was entranced by the Bay of Lerici. He pitied Mary (who, he told Claire, suffered 'terribly from languor and hysterical affections')[45] but he could not understand her antipathy to the area. His boat arrived in mid-May, and both he and Edward were delighted with it, although they insisted on adding additional topmasts, a false stern, and on refitting a sail which had been marked with the words 'Don Juan'. Shelley planned to call his craft *Ariel*, and he was put out to find that Daniel Roberts, acting on instructions from Byron, had named the boat on his behalf. But once the necessary alterations had been made, the *Don Juan* (the name stuck, even if the sail was changed) provided him with matchless joy. 'It is swift and beautiful', he told John Gisborne. 'Williams is captain, and we drive along this delightful bay in the evening wind, under the summer moon, until earth appears another world. Jane brings her guitar, and if the past and the future could be obliterated, the present would content me so well that I could say with Faust to the passing moment, "Remain, thou, thou art so beautiful."'[46]

Despite Shelley's delight at his surroundings, it was a strange, unsettling period for all the inhabitants of Casa Magni. Shelley experienced visions and hallucinations – of a child rising from the sea; of Edward and Jane – bloodstained and lacerated – telling him the sea was flooding the house; of strangling Mary. Jane had visions, too, of Shelley appearing on the terrace when he was known to be miles away. Edward immersed himself in *Queen Mab* ('an astonishing work'),[47] while Shelley wrote his haunting 'Triumph of Life' in which a ghostly Rousseau guides the poet through a pageant of human history. He also wrote more poems in praise of Jane – 'To Jane' ('Sing again, with your dear voice revealing/ A tone/ Of some world far from ours') and 'Lines written in the Bay of Lerici', in which Jane is as fair as the moon (the symbol used for Mary in *Epipyschidion*) but 'far more true'. Jane was by this point firmly established as Shelley's muse, but he had not simply transferred his affections from Mary and Claire to her. At the end of May he told Claire that 'Jane . . . pines after her own house and saucepans to which no one can have a claim except herself. – It is a pity that any one so pretty and amicable should be so selfish.'[48] And although Jane was flattered by Shelley's attention she showed no sign of wavering in her affection for Edward. Indeed, she found Shelley's behaviour rather alarming, particularly when he discussed the delights of drowning while taking her and her children out for a sail in his boat.

On 16 June Mary suffered a miscarriage which nearly killed her. She haemorrhaged blood and slipped in and out of consciousness while Claire and Jane, frantic with worry, sent for a doctor and ice to stop her from bleeding to death. The ice arrived before the doctor and Shelley (who later congratulated himself on his 'decisive resolutions') forced Mary into an ice-filled bath, which at length stemmed the frightening flow of blood. By the time the doctor arrived, Shelley reported, 'all danger was over, and he had nothing to do but to applaud me for my boldness. [Mary] is now doing well, and the sea-baths will soon restore her.'[49]

Mary was, however, far from well. She had lost a great deal of blood, had been convinced she was going to die, and for days afterwards was too weak to do more than crawl from her bed to the balcony overlooking the sea. She had also lost another baby, and with it the prospect of a repaired family, still diminished by the deaths of her unnamed daughter, Clara and William. The episode added to the depression which overcame her after her arrival in Lerici, and it exposed further the gulf which now separated her from Shelley.

In the same letter in which he told John Gisborne of Mary's dangerous miscarriage, Shelley made the following complaint:

> I only feel the want of those who can feel, and understand me. Whether from proximity and the continuity of domestic intercourse, Mary does not. The necessity of concealing from her thoughts that would pain her, necessitates this, perhaps. It is the curse of Tantalus, that a person

possessing such excellent powers and so pure a mind as hers, should not excite the sympathy indispensable to their application to domestic life.[50]

It is difficult to read this letter now and not to find Shelley's failure to understand the extent of Mary's suffering – or the effect of a near-fatal miscarriage on her mood and her ability to be affectionate – extraordinarily heartless. It is also strikingly unselfconscious, in its placing of the blame for the breakdown of 'sympathy indispensable . . . to domestic life' entirely on Mary's shoulders. As his 1814 letters to Harriet illustrate, throughout his life Shelley remained unaware of his ability to hurt and damage the women with whom he came into contact. But, in some respects, this interpretation of Shelley's conduct is anachronistic, and it does not pay sufficient attention to the subtlety of his lament to John Gisborne. This was no ordinary complaint of a husband against a withdrawn wife, but a plea for the kind of understanding Shelley believed to be central to his emotional and intellectual experience. Moreover, even in a paragraph which now appears supremely self-centred, Shelley reiterated his determination to protect Mary and to shelter her from distress and harm. The tragedy of Shelley and Mary's marriage lay in her inability to convey to him the depths of her emotional attachments, and in his failure to understand how much pain his actions caused her.

As the residents of Casa Magni lived out their strange existence on the Bay of Lerici, the Hunts finally arrived in port at Genoa. From Genoa they travelled by sea to Livorno, and it was to Livorno that Shelley and Edward sailed to meet them. Mary was acutely unhappy at Shelley's departure, which, she told Maria Gisborne, added 'insufferably to my misery. I could not endure that he should go – I called him back two or three times, & told him that if I did not see him soon I would go to Pisa with the child – I cried bitterly when he went away.'[51] In her despair, she sent a heart-rending note to Hunt, begging him not to agree to Shelley's suggestion that he should bring his family to Casa

Magni. 'I am too ill to write the reasonings only let me entreat you let no persuasions induce you to come, selfish feelings you may be sure do not dictate me – but it would be complete madness to come – I wish I could write more – I wish I were there to assist you – I wish I could break my chains & leave this dungeon.'[52] By this point Mary was desperately asking Shelley to find them somewhere else to live for the rest of the summer, and she knew that the Hunts' presence in Lerici would make moving impossible.

While his family waited for Shelley in Livorno and the *David Walter* was disembarked, Hunt took a carriage to Byron's country villa outside Pisa. He was much surprised at the changes wrought by the passage of years in Byron, who had grown fat and lethargic – 'altogether presenting a very different aspect from the compact, energetic and curly-headed person, whom I had known in England'.[53] Hunt was introduced to Teresa Guiccioli, and was immediately plunged into a Byronic drama when Pietro Gamba interfered in a quarrel between Byron's servants and was stabbed. The offending servant was dismissed, but not before the entire household worked themselves up into a state of hysteria at the thought of him pacing outside the house, waiting to fight the first person who emerged. (In fact, when they did venture forth, the servant threw himself at Byron's feet, weeping and wailing and asking for forgiveness.) The whole episode, Hunt later recalled, was reminiscent of *The Mysteries of Udolpho*.

Hunt returned to Livorno, and there he and Shelley had a joyous reunion. They had not seen each other for four years, and their meeting was recalled many years later by Thornton Hunt. He remembered the 'shrill sound' of Shelley's voice, 'as he rushed into my father's arms, which he did with an impetuousness and a fervour scarcely to be imagined by any who did not know the intensity of his feelings and the deep nature of his affection for that friend. I remember his crying out that he was "so *inexpressibly* delighted! – you cannot think how *inexpressibly* happy it makes me!"'[54] But the euphoria of Hunt and Shelley's meeting was short-lived. After a night in a hotel in Livorno they travelled to Pisa, and the Hunts were installed in the apartments prepared for them on the ground floor of the Palazzo Lanfranchi. On their arrival, Marianne was seen by Vaccà, the doctor who had offered Shelley much sensible advice. He announced that she was in a decline and was unlikely to live out the year, a piece of news which devastated Hunt. Moreover, the Hunts had no money. Both Shelley and Byron were taken aback to find they had a destitute family on their hands. This was particularly problematic since Byron was now bored with the journal plan and, after the various affrays in which he and the Gambas had been involved, was contemplating leaving Tuscany for good.

Shelley threw himself into rescuing the journal, and, with it, Hunt's means of survival in Italy. He convinced Byron to stay in Pisa for the time being, and Byron agreed to give Hunt the copyright of 'The Vision of Judgment': a brilliant, witty satire (written shortly before Byron's arrival in Pisa) which had both Southey and George III as its targets. A title for the journal – *The Liberal* – was agreed. It looked as if Shelley had managed to yoke Hunt and Byron together. But he was dubious about the strength of their bond. 'Between ourselves', he told Horace Smith, who was marooned in Paris with his ill wife and family, 'I greatly fear that this alliance will not succeed . . . and how long the alliance between the wren and the eagle may continue I will not prophesy.'[55]

Despite his doubts about the future of *The Liberal*, its foundation was a huge achievement for Shelley. At last Hunt and Byron, the twin poles of his intellectual existence, were united in a creative partnership of his making. Hunt's problems, however, meant that it took longer to settle him and his family in Pisa than Shelley had anticipated, and Edward was waiting for him anxiously at Livorno, impatient at the delays which prevented him from returning to Jane and their children. Mary continued to send Shelley distraught letters, and Edward was painfully aware that at Casa Magni, Jane was bearing the brunt of her unhappiness. 'I am tired to death of waiting', he told her. 'This is our longest separation, and seems a year to me.'[56] Shelley wrote to Jane too, three days before his departure from Pisa. 'I fear you are solitary & melancholy at Villa Magni – & in the intervals of the greater & more serious distress in which I am compelled to sympathize here, I figure to myself the countenance which has been the source of such consolation to me, shadowed by a veil of sorrow.'[57] He wrote to Mary too, but in a different vein. 'How are you my best Mary?' he asked. 'Write especially how is your health & how your spirits are, & whether you are not more reconciled to staying at Lerici at least during the summer.'[58]

On 7 July Shelley returned to Livorno. The following day he and Edward met Trelawny and his boat builder Daniel Roberts at the *Don Juan* to prepare for their journey back to Lerici, a few hours' sail away. It was a swelteringly hot afternoon, and both Shelley and Edward were anxious to be home before the weather broke. They intended to race the sun across the bay, and to return in triumph to the waiting women at the Casa Magni. Just after 2 p.m. they set sail, accompanied by their boat boy, an English eighteen year old named Charles Vivian. Roberts remained on the shore, his sailor's eye trained on some clouds forming on the horizon. An hour after their departure he saw a storm come up and, through his telescope, spotted the *Don Juan* in the distance, taking in its topsails. Then the clouds hid it from view. Out at sea, waves engulfed the boat, filling its open hull with water and ripping off its false stern and masts. Shelley, Edward and Charles Vivian were drowned.

PART THREE

After the Storm

9

The Future

Violent storms battered the Bay of Lerici too. Edward had written to Jane that he expected to sail by Monday (8 July) but initially Mary and Jane assumed that their husbands had not appeared back at the Casa Magni because of the weather. When a boat from Livorno sent word that Shelley and Edward had set sail at the beginning of the week, the two women dismissed the news as ill-informed rumour. But by Wednesday, when the storm had calmed and there was still no sign of the *Don Juan*, serious anxiety began to mount. By Friday lunchtime Jane was so worried that she decided to travel to Livorno to find out what had happened, but was then prevented from carrying out her plan by the return of rough seas and high winds. This meant she was at the house later that day when a letter from Hunt arrived. It was addressed to Shelley, and contained the worst possible news. 'Shelley Mio', Hunt had written, 'pray let us know how you got home the other day with Williams, for I fear you must have been out in the bad weather, and we are anxious.'[1]

Horrified by the discovery that Shelley and Edward had sailed at the beginning of the week, Mary and Jane set out immediately for Pisa, in the hope that Hunt could tell them more. Claire, who had remained at the Casa Magni after Mary's miscarriage, stayed behind to look after Percy and Jane's children, two year old Medwin and baby Dina, aged sixteen months. Mary was still ill and weak, but she and Jane were rowed across to the town of Lerici, from where they travelled post to the Palazzo Lanfranchi. Though Hunt was asleep when they arrived, Byron was up late working, and a smiling Teresa emerged from his apartments to greet them. Both she and Byron were shocked by Mary's state: deathly white, half-fainting, and barely coherent. But they could not comfort her, since all they knew was that Shelley had left Pisa the previous Sunday, and it was clear to both of them from Mary's account that something had gone hideously wrong. They made strenuous efforts to persuade Mary and Jane to rest for a few hours in Pisa before continuing to Livorno, but their pleas were ignored and the two women travelled on through the night to find Trelawny, who had seen the *Don Juan* set sail. It was 2 a.m. by the time they arrived in Livorno and neither Trelawny nor his friend Daniel Roberts could be located. They slept for a few hours in their clothes at an inn, waiting for daylight. The following morning they went in search of Roberts, who confirmed that Shelley and Edward had indeed left the previous Monday. He described their impatience to be gone, and recalled that Shelley was in 'one of those extravagant fits of good spirits in which you have sometimes seen him'. Roberts also described how he had stood on the shore waiting for the storm to clear, and how, as the clouds lifted, he trained his telescope on the horizon, expecting to see the *Don Juan* returning to harbour in Livorno. But, he told Mary, in words she later reported to Maria Gisborne, 'there was no boat on the sea'.[2]

Even as the horrible truth began to emerge, Mary and Jane refused to despair. Perhaps the *Don Juan* had been blown off course to Corsica, or perhaps – and rumours circulated to this effect – they had been run ashore further up the coast. Accompanied by Trelawny, Mary and Jane left Livorno to return to Lerici, to see if letters or news awaited them there. Their journey took them past the town of Viareggio, where they learnt that the *Don Juan*'s dinghy had been washed to shore, along with one of its water casks. By the time they reached Lerici Mary was close to delirium. 'Looking down the river', she later recalled, 'I saw the two great lights burning – A voice from within me seemed to cry aloud that is his grave.'[3]

They arrived home on Saturday, 13 July, five days after Shelley and Edward set sail. Mary later remembered the week which followed as 'a universe of pain'. Strong winds blew, the sea remained stormy, and the villagers, who were celebrating a fiesta, spent their nights dancing on the sands, running in and out of the sea in front of Casa Magni, and singing – or, as Mary said, 'screaming', 'all the time one perpetual air'.[4] For six days there was no further news. Then, on 19 July, Claire intercepted a letter to Trelawny (who was searching for information in Livorno) from Roberts, informing him that two bodies had been discovered on the beach at Viareggio. Claire could not bear to confront either Mary or Jane with this latest rumour which, Roberts stressed, he had not yet had time to confirm. Instead, she wrote desperately to Hunt, asking for his advice. 'I cannot break it to them', she confessed. 'Nor is my spirit, weakened as it is from constant suffering capable of giving them consolation, or protecting them from the first burst of their despair.'[5]

In fact, Claire was not required to tell Mary and Jane of Roberts's fears. Later that evening Trelawny arrived at Casa Magni. He had seen the bodies. Edward's was badly mutilated, but Trelawny was able to identify him by his boots. Shelley's corpse had also suffered, after over a week in which it was attacked by rough seas and hungry fish. The flesh from his face and hands had been stripped away, but Trelawny recognised him from the books on his person: a volume of Sophocles in one pocket, and Keats's *Lamia* – bent backwards, as if it had been stowed away in a hurry – in the other. Charles Vivian's corpse was the last to surface, and only his skeleton had survived the sea's ravages. All three bodies were immediately buried in quicklime graves on the beach, in accordance with Tuscany's strict quarantine laws.

Trelawny broke the news to Mary, Jane and Claire and then escorted them back to Pisa, where they took refuge in the Shelleys' old apartment. On 15 August, Trelawny, Hunt and Byron returned to the coast without the two widows to cremate their friends. The ceremonies were orchestrated by Trelawny, and the strange rituals he designed have entered Romantic mythology. He requested official permission to disinter Shelley and Edward from their temporary graves, and was permitted to do so on condition that both bodies were cremated next to their original burial plots. He brought with him a portable furnace

– a peculiar iron contraption on a stand – and collected fuel of the type
'used by Shelley's much loved Hellenes on their funeral pyres'.[6]

They began with Edward. Then, on 16 August, almost a month
after the bodies had surfaced, Trelawny, Byron and Hunt met at
Shelley's grave on the beach at Viareggio. Byron, who had seen plenty
of burning flesh at Edward's ceremony the day before, absented himself
from Shelley's cremation, and swam far out to sea, giving himself bad
sunburn in the process. Hunt remained in the carriage, not, he later
claimed, because he was unable to bear the sight of Shelley's mangled
flesh, but because he was overcome with emotion. So Trelawny was left
to fulfil the role of high priest in a pagan rite of his own design. The
scene he orchestrated on the beach at Viareggio was quite as theatrical
as any of his fantastic stories. He later claimed that Byron wanted to
take possession of Shelley's skull, but that he refused this request, on
the grounds that Byron 'had formerly used [a skull] as a drinking-cup'
and 'I was determined Shelley's should not be so profaned.'[7] Trelawny
rewrote his account of Shelley's cremation many times during his long
life, rendering it more mystical with each iteration. But the description
he produced in his first memoir of his poet friends, *Recollections of the
Last Days of Shelley and Byron*, was dramatically graphic:

> After the fire was well kindled we repeated the ceremony of the previous
> day; and more wine was poured over Shelley's dead body than he had
> consumed during his life. This with the oil and salt made the yellow
> flames glisten and quiver. The heat from the sun and fire was so intense
> that the atmosphere was tremulous and wavy. The corpse fell open and
> the heart was laid bare. The frontal bone of the skull, where it had been
> struck with the mattock, fell off; and, as the back of the head rested
> on the red-hot bottom bars of the furnace, the brains literally seethed,
> bubbled, and boiled as in a cauldron, for a very long time.[8]

Byron, observing events from the sea, was overwhelmed by the tragic
grandeur of the scene. 'You can have no idea', he wrote to Thomas
Moore, 'what an extraordinary effect such a funeral pile has, on a
desolate shore, with mountains in the back-ground and the sea before,

and the singular appearance the salt and frankincense gave to the flame.'[9]

Richard Holmes has written that the story of Shelley's life remains caught 'in the glamorous headlights of [his] death'.[10] In the years following his cremation at Viareggio, Shelley would be transformed from an ordinary mortal into a visionary being. This process of transformation reached its pinnacle in 1889, when Louis Fournier painted a highly romanticised version of the ceremony, complete with a kneeling Mary and a 'miraculously undamaged' corpse.[11] In fact, there was nothing very romantic about either Shelley's death or his funeral. Trelawny and Daniel Roberts later sought to avoid the suggestion that their faulty boat design caused Shelley's death, by claiming that the *Don Juan* was rammed by pirates, but Shelley died because he and Edward were inexperienced sailors who ignored weather warnings and were unable to handle their unwieldy craft. Shelley's cremation – imagined by Fournier as a scene of holy solemnity – was dominated by the stink of burning flesh, a crowd of gawking villagers, and the soldiers drafted in to maintain quarantine regulations. After Trelawny's ceremony was over, an undignified quarrel broke out between Mary and Hunt about who should keep Shelley's heart, which somehow miraculously escaped the flames. In fact, the cherished relic was probably Shelley's liver, but Hunt was only persuaded to relinquish it to Mary when Jane Williams persuaded him that Shelley would have been horrified at the idea of his friends quarrelling over one of his organs.

Otherwise, however, Jane did not behave well in the aftermath of Shelley and Edward's death. Bereft of her husband, her friend, and her position as Shelley's muse, she responded by lashing out at Mary behind her back. She told Hunt that Mary had made Shelley unhappy in the last months of his life; that she failed to provide him with the emotional and intellectual support he needed. She continued to spread malicious gossip about the Shelleys' relationship after she returned to England. There was nothing in Jane's behaviour before Shelley's death to suggest that she disliked Mary, although their relationship was complicated by

Shelley's fascination with Jane. She may genuinely have felt that Mary had not made Shelley happy and that, during their difficult residence at Casa Magni, she did not make a sufficient effort to be a pleasant companion. Jane was not clever or intuitive, and she struggled to understand Mary's antipathy towards the house and its surroundings. She also struggled to understand Mary's response to Shelley's death, which contrasted sharply with her own reaction to the loss of Edward. Mary hid her emotions beneath a frozen façade throughout the summer of 1822, and, as a result, several of her friends quite unfairly thought that she was insufficiently distressed by the loss of her husband. Jane probably found her apparent coolness both baffling and alienating, and she may also have resented the way that Edward's untimely death was eclipsed by the tragedy of Shelley's demise.

There are, however, less charitable explanations for Jane's conduct. Once she returned to London she discovered that her friendship with Shelley made her an important personage, and that his admirers were eager to learn of his final months from someone who presented herself as his chief companion. In denigrating Mary, she was able to exaggerate the role she had played in Shelley's emotional and intellectual life and to suggest that it was she, rather than Mary, who had access to Shelley's most private feelings. Her determination to present herself as the central figure in the final part of Shelley's story may have been in part due to the fact that she was jealous of Mary, the daughter of a famous father, the author of a successful book, with the prospect of an income from Sir Timothy Shelley. (Shelley's executors, Byron and Peacock, were both initially confident that Sir Timothy would agree to support his daughter-in-law and grandson.) Jane, in contrast, had no right to grieve publicly for Shelley, and no way of supporting herself. So she convinced herself that in blackening Mary's reputation she was correcting the record of Shelley's final months. After all, he had written her poems which encouraged her to think that she and Edward had provided him with support and companionship he no longer received from Mary, poems in which her own talent and beauty was celebrated.

Matters were made worse by the fact that Jane masked her resentment with sweet affection, which made her behaviour all the more devastating when Mary eventually became aware of the truth several years later. None of Mary's friendships with women was straightforward, and the closest female relationship of her life – that with Claire – was fraught with tension from the moment that they condemned themselves to a shared future by running off to Europe with Shelley. Nevertheless, Mary thought of Jane as her closest friend in the world, and it took her several years to recover from the realisation that Jane did not return her devotion.

Perhaps more surprisingly, Hunt also behaved badly towards Mary after Shelley's death, treating her with outright hostility well into the spring of 1823. He chose to believe Jane's accusations, despite the fact that he had known Mary for years and Jane for only a few weeks. Hunt was a kind man; and the reasons for such uncharacteristically cruel behaviour towards Mary appear to stem from the depth of his devotion to Shelley, which became more obsessive as the months passed. He regarded Shelley as his greatest, most brilliant and closest friend. Wrapped up in his own loss, he seems to have convinced himself that he was more dedicated to Shelley's memory than Shelley's widow. Like Jane, he appears to have believed that he was Shelley's greatest confidant, and, again like Jane, he resisted the suggestion that Mary had the greater claim to sympathy. He believed himself to be the rightful custodian of Shelley's reputation and he saw in Jane's version of events an excuse to assert himself as mourner in chief. Shelley had probably told Hunt something of Mary's depression during their brief meeting in Pisa, and he now elected to interpret Mary's air of reserve as proof that she did not feel Shelley's loss as deeply as he. Mary was distressed and mystified by Hunt's coldness towards her. She had no idea that Jane was casting aspersions on her relationship with Shelley, nor that Hunt and Jane thought her unfeeling. None of them understood that the disputes about Shelley's memory and the quarrel over his heart were really about who should assume responsibility for enshrining his image for future generations; in short, about who should be keeper of the flame.

Mary later wrote that the events of the summer of 1822 transformed her circle from Keats's 'web . . . of mingled yarn' into 'a broken chain'.[12] By the end of September, Shelley's Pisan community had disintegrated. Jane and Claire left Italy; Mary, Byron and the Hunts left Pisa. Jane returned to England with her two children, armed with the tiny amount of money raised by the sale of her furniture and letters of introduction to the Novellos (provided by Hunt) and to Hogg (from Mary). In London she took particular comfort from the presence of Hogg, who proved to be an assiduous companion. Hogg, like the rest of Shelley's London friends, heard of his death via letters sent by Hunt to Bess, John Gisborne and John Hunt. Peacock received a 'dreadful' letter from Mary,[13] and it was he who conveyed the news to Sir Timothy Shelley that his son and heir was dead. Godwin received the news from an employee at the *Examiner* office. His response was to write angrily to Mary that no one – not even Claire – had thought to inform him of Shelley's death. He could not bring himself to write eulogies for the son-in-law with whom he had fought about money so bitterly, but he exhorted his daughter to keep her spirits up and to remember that she was a woman of talent and resource. But most of Shelley's friends were unanimous in their praise of him, and letters passed back and forth which lamented his passing as an unparalleled calamity. One dissenting voice was that of Benjamin Haydon, who recorded the news in his diary. Haydon never forgave Shelley for taunting him about Christianity. 'There certainly is something in Shelley's death!' he wrote, smugly. 'When one considers his early writings, his rash unbelief, and his writing αθεος* on Mont Blanc, there is something in his being whirled off in that way into eternity, awful & mysterious.'[14] The same sentiment was expressed, rather more bluntly, by the *Courier*, which reported Shelley's death in an article which proclaimed 'Shelley, the writer of some infidel poetry has been drowned; *now* he knows whether there is a God or no.'[15] Other similarly self-righteous notices of Shelley's death appeared elsewhere in the Tory press. Some of these notices

---

* Atheist.

conceded that Shelley was a poet of some promise, but their tone was overwhelmingly unfavourable.

Claire remained with Mary until the end of the summer, but with Shelley dead it was not possible for the stepsisters to stay together, even if they had wished to do so. Mary had no independent means of support, and for some time it looked as if Sir Timothy Shelley would refuse even to pay her Shelley's allowance for the quarter in which he died. Although Byron tried hard to get Sir Timothy to help Mary, it was clear that, in the meantime, she was going to have to earn her own living and live as cheaply as possible in order to survive. Supporting Claire as Shelley had done was out of the question. In one way, therefore, Shelley's death freed Mary and Claire from one another.

Before Claire left Pisa, she and Trelawny had one perfect day together, in which he appears to have declared his love for her. Neither of them ever wrote about this day, but they both remembered it in years thereafter and Claire marked it with a blank entry in her diary. Trelawny sent Claire many passionate letters in the months that followed, but she never seems to have seriously considered his offer of protection. Perhaps she realised that Trelawny was too absorbed in the constructed drama of his own life to provide any real shelter from the emotional storms she had endured; perhaps she recognised, quite sensibly, that Trelawny's passionate declarations of love were largely predicated on her unavailability. Still, this was yet another proposal Claire refused. She had declined Peacock's offer of marriage – an offer made even though he knew the truth about Allegra's parentage – and she was similarly uninterested in the attentions of Maria Gisborne's son Henry Reveley, who also knew something of her past. Claire's refusal to accept the support of men whom she could not love was a further sign of her independent streak. When she turned down Trelawny's rather vague proposals she had no funds of her own, Byron having refused to pay for a translation of Goethe she had done for him at Shelley's instigation. Mrs Mason was of the opinion that Byron, the original cause of Claire's troubles, should assume responsibility for her support, and wrote to him accordingly. But Byron disagreed, so Claire was left

with no option but to begin work as a governess. She decided to do so
in Vienna, where her brother Charles was teaching English.

Despite the prospect of a reunion with Charles, it was hard for Claire
to leave Pisa. She was only twenty-four at the time of Shelley's death,
and Italy was not only the country where Allegra had died, but the
place where she had lived for most of her adult life. During the journey
to Austria she 'remembered how hopelessly I had lingered on the Italian
soil for five years, waiting ever for a favourable change instead of which
I was now leaving it, having buried there everything I loved'.[16] She tried
to focus her attention on the scenery, but was unable to prevent herself
dwelling on memories of Allegra. As a result, she later told Mrs Mason,
'it was all in vain – I saw not mountains or vallies, woods or rushing
streams . . . I only saw my lost darling.'[17] Although she could write of
her pain to her friends, she would not accept any further assistance
from them. Both Mrs Mason and Mary tried to give her money, but
their offers were refused.

In Vienna Claire moved into lodgings found by Charles, and began
the difficult process of making an independent life for herself. She
wanted to find work as a governess, but fell ill and was forced to rely
on the charity of others. Just as she began to recover, she and Charles
discovered that further obstacles lay between them and gainful
employment. When officers of Austria's police state discovered the
presence of two members of Godwin's family in their midst, they
made their lives as uncomfortable as possible. Charles 'Claremont',
Viennese police records stated, was a subversive who had come to
Vienna to incite revolution, rather than to teach English. In February
1823 Charles wrote to Mary of their 'Police adventures', and of the
'perpetual state of uncertainty' which characterised their residence in
Vienna.[18] Secret files reported that he was the 'son of the authoress of
the "rights of Women" – his father was prosecuted in England some
years ago for sedition – his sister married Shelly – the author of Queen
Mab Shelly was a deist – was deprived of his rights of a father by the
Lord Chancellor of England – was the intimate of . . . Lord Byron'.[19]
As Marion Kingston Stocking has noted, Charles and Claire had
unwittingly made powerful enemies. Metternich, Austria's Imperial

Chancellor, was deeply opposed to the revolutionary movements sweeping Mediterranean Europe (observed by Claire in Italy and by Charles in Spain) since these movements threatened the power base established by the allied powers at the end of the Napoleonic wars. Austria was a key beneficiary of the distribution of Napoleonic territory which took place at the Congress of Vienna and Metternich was determined that the revolutions which were destabilising other European nations should not be allowed to infect his country. To this end, he imposed stringent controls on foreigners, oversaw widespread press censorship and ran 'an administration marked by arbitrariness and secrecy'.[20] The case against the Clairmonts was built entirely on rumour and innuendo, but this did not stop the Viennese authorities temporarily withdrawing Charles Clairmont's residency permit. Although the permit was eventually reinstated, the whole episode left both Claire and Charles disenchanted with Vienna and Austrian society. 'I believe it is the only civilized country in the world where foreigners have no legal protector', Charles told Mary. 'I am sick of this place and of the manner of living.'[21]

Claire shared her brother's low opinion of Vienna. She was deeply unhappy during the months she spent in Austria, her low spirits brought about by a combination of illness, the unwelcome attention of the authorities, memories of the past and separation from her friends. So, in early 1823, with the same bravado which originally led her to offer herself to Byron, she took drastic action to improve her situation. She accepted a position as governess to the children of the Countess Zotoff, a Russian aristocrat who was returning to St Petersburg. Claire's friends were horrified when they heard she was planning to go to Russia. Trelawny wrote several letters in which he begged her to return to her old life in Florence and declared that her refusal to do so made him deeply miserable. 'I would give up every other hope in life to have you near me, – you say it would not ultimately tend to our happiness – I know not that – nothing can be more outcast and wretched than we are now.'[22] Claire remained impervious to Trelawny's pleas. On 22 March 1823 she began what he termed her 'compulsive emigration to the north'.[23] Nothing more was heard from her for over a year. She seemed simply to disappear into a snowbound Russian wilderness.

––––––––

Back in Pisa, the community of exiles dwindled still further. By the end of September only Charles Brown, recently arrived from England, remained in the city. Mary's departure came about because of a decision by the authorities to exile Teresa Guiccioli's father and brother from Tuscany. The Gambas were allowed into Tuscany on sufferance after their exile from Romagna, on condition that they lived quietly, without disturbing the authorities or inciting public disorder. Both the Masi affair and the brawl between Byron's servants and Pietro Gamba contravened this condition and the Gambas were instructed to leave the state. In order for Byron to remain close to Teresa he had to go too. This forced the Hunts to leave Pisa in his wake, because they were entirely dependent on him and *The Liberal* for their survival. Byron decided to move his household to Genoa, and the Hunts had little option but to follow him there.

Mary had no wish to be left behind alone in Pisa. In spite of all the tension between herself and Hunt she hoped that by remaining with the others she would be able to live more cheaply than if she returned to England. Accordingly, she packed up her apartment and made the long journey north ahead of the Hunts to find a house she could share with them. She rented the Casa Negroto in Albaro, a suburb of Genoa, which was about a mile from Byron's new home. Casa Negroto was a large, imposing building, with a grand hall and dozens of barely furnished rooms which were cheap to rent but prohibitively expensive to heat. For several weeks Mary lived alone in the empty house, with only Percy (now almost three years old) and her memories of Shelley for company. In some ways, it was a relief to be alone for a while, but Mary recognised that such isolation was not healthy. 'There are moments', she told Maria Gisborne, 'when . . . quite alone . . . it is with difficulty I prevent myself from flying . . . in to that vast grave (the sea).'[24] Percy provided her with a reason to stay alive, and she hoped that by immersing herself in his well-being, her writing, and the education and care of the Hunt children she would be able to regain a degree of equilibrium. In any case, she wrote in her diary, she did not expect to live very long. Her mother only lived until the age of thirty-six, and Mary decided that she would die at the same age. In the years which remained to her she planned to memorialise the past and to ensure that, in death, Shelley gained the recognition denied him during his lifetime. Accordingly, she wrote to Peacock requesting a writing desk left at Marlow, which was full of letters and manuscripts, and began the difficult task of pulling Shelley's unpublished verse together from his many draft notebooks.

The Hunts, meanwhile, prepared to embark on their own progress north. They broke their journey at Lerici, where they paid a melancholy visit to Casa Magni and joined forces with Byron's party. Travelling part of the way in Byron's lengthy entourage may have saved the Hunts a little money but it also highlighted problems which had been brewing since the beginning of the summer. In the months following Shelley's death, Byron tired of living in close quarters with the Hunts. He found Hunt over-sensitive, Marianne censorious, and their children out of control. Byron had kindly offered to buy Mary's furniture in order to supply her with funds without hurting her pride but by the time he arrived in Genoa he had found an additional reason for this gesture. 'I have a particular dislike to any thing of S's being within the same walls with Mr Hunt's children', he told her. 'They are dirtier and more mischievous than Yahoos what they can['t] destroy with their filth they will with their fingers.'[25]

Hunt's unfortunate children were indeed wild and unruly. Their father was preoccupied by trying to scrape together a living through the establishment of *The Liberal*, and their mother was often ill and depressed, spending long hours in her bed, where she imagined being visited by the ghost of Shelley. But the children were not the main reason for Byron's disenchantment with his new living companions. Shelley's death threw the Hunts entirely on Byron's mercy, and committed him to participation in a project in which he had lost interest. Even more sympathetic members of Hunt's coterie were irritated by his neediness and Byron found his endless demands for money particularly annoying. To make matters worse, Byron's more conservative friends disapproved of his connection with Hunt, and he was forced to defend his decision to support him. 'I am afraid the Journal *is* a *bad* business', he confessed to John Murray, 'but in it I am sacrificing *myself* for others – *I* can have no advantage in it':

> I believe the *brothers* H to be honest men – I am sure they are poor ones.
> – They have not a rap – they pressed me to engage in this work – and
> in an evil hour I consented . . . The death of Shelley left them totally
> aground – and I could not see them in such a state without using the
> common feelings of humanity – & what means were in my power to set
> them afloat again.[26]

Byron's desire to help Hunt was genuine but, as others had found out before, he was not an easy man to help and this was made worse by Shelley's death, which was a huge loss for a man so sensitive to the literary and political implications of friendship. As a result, Shelley quickly became an icon of perfection in Hunt's eyes, while Byron was riddled with faults. The relationship between Byron and Hunt also snagged on Hunt's vanity and on the way Hunt reacted to his financial dependence on Byron by adopting a superior tone. Hunt's memoirs suggest he and Marianne made little effort to conceal their disgust with their patron's habits and style of life. Byron, Hunt reported, was unimpressed when he realised that Marianne 'was destitute, to a remarkable degree, of all care about rank and titles'. Hunt refused to laugh at Byron's 'worldly common-places' and his 'bad jokes on women', and found himself labelled a 'proser' by his host. After his arrival in Pisa, Hunt, this time heeding Shelley's warning, insisted on addressing Byron by his full title. Byron attempted to 'banter' Hunt back into his old habits, one day addressing a letter to him beginning 'Dear Lord Hunt'. But Hunt remained adamant because, he wrote, 'neither of us could afford a change back again to the old entire familiarity'.[27]

This was a key problem for both Byron and Hunt. They had based their plans for *The Liberal* on the way life had been six years earlier, in 1816: Byron, glad of Hunt's congenial friendship during his separation from Annabella, and proud of his acquaintance with the martyr of

Surrey Gaol; Hunt, convinced that Byron saw him as an equal, both as a poet and a friend, whom he could address as 'my dear Byron' without a thought for etiquette. But both men had changed a good deal between 1816 and 1822, and they were bitterly disappointed by the disjunction between memory and reality. Hunt learned that being Byron's pensioner was very different from being his friend, and Byron discovered that Hunt was no longer the brave, independent figure he so much admired, but rather a man diminished by poverty, illness and misfortune, who masked his decline with infuriating conceit. Without Shelley there was little to hold the two men together. It was not a good basis for a collaborative enterprise.

Despite this, plans for *The Liberal* moved steadily forward through the summer and autumn of 1822. By the time everyone was settled in Genoa, Hunt was putting the finishing touches to the first issue. Even though he was compelled to write a substantial proportion of the issue himself, it nevertheless looked as if the journal might succeed. John Hunt was in the process of extricating Byron's 'The Vision of Judgment' from John Murray's clutches for publication in the first number, and Mary supplied a manuscript of Shelley's translation of *Faust*. Charles Brown, Hogg, Hazlitt and Mary promised to contribute to future issues, and Hunt busied himself with the composition of a long Preface, which was to set out the new journal's aims and philosophy. He identified its contributors with the 'large bodies of men who are called LIBERALS' and promised that although the journal was not explicitly political, it would expose cant and hypocrisy wherever it found it. 'The force of our answers', Hunt announced, 'will always be proportioned to the want of liberality in the assailant.' Hunt envisaged *The Liberal* as a collaborative endeavour, in which he and his fellow contributors would 'do our work quietly' and 'contribute our liberalities in the shape of Poetry, Essays, Tales, Translations, and other amenities, of which kings themselves may read and profit.'[28]

Like *The Examiner*, *The Liberal* celebrated the allegiances of its contributing members, but it also announced a much wider allegiance, with all those who wanted to see the cause of liberalism furthered throughout Europe. Its focus was highlighted in its subtitle: 'Verse and

Prose from the South'. Translations of Italian poetry; stories set, like Mary Shelley's *Valperga*, in medieval Italy; and essays on Rousseau and on the Greeks' discussions of love set the tone for a journal which allied itself with the independence movements of southern Europe, rather than with the Germanic Romanticism of the Lake Poets and their northern contemporaries. *The Liberal's* principal villain was Southey, who had labelled Byron's friends 'the Satanic School' and expressed his horror at the Swiss 'league of incest'. In 'The Vision of Judgment', poems by Hunt and essays by Hazlitt, Southey was denounced as an apostate traitor of the liberal cause.

The first number of *The Liberal* met with disdain from Tory reviewers, who were particularly displeased that Byron was involving himself with a vulgar Cockney like Hunt. 'What, in the name of Katterfelto', *Blackwood's* screeched, 'can Byron mean by patronising a Cockney? A Bear at College was all very well; – but, my lord, think on it, a Cockney at Pisa! – Fie, my lord! This is by far the greatest outrage you have ever yet committed on manners, and morals, and intellectuals.'[29] The reviews were full of thinly veiled references to the incestuous practices of the 'Pisan Alliance'. Such innuendo was directed at all the participants in the endeavour: Byron (whose liaison with Augusta was still the subject of society whispers), Hunt (whose relationship with Bess had been discussed in reviews of *The Story of Rimini*) and Shelley, who had eloped with two sisters and was rumoured to be the author of *Epipyschidion*, a poem which, *Blackwood's* noted, made references to both 'sister' and 'spouse'.[30]

Bad reviews of the first issue of *The Liberal* were compounded by a piece of mischief-making by John Murray, who had been told by Byron to hand over 'The Vision of Judgment' to John Hunt, the journal's printer. Murray did so, but he handed over the wrong version of the poem, and kept back the placatory Preface Byron wrote to minimise the chances of libel charges. Since the poem depicted mad King George III attempting to gain entry into heaven, the threat of libel action was real. John Hunt published the poem without its Preface, and found himself faced with a libel writ and the prospect of yet another court case, fine, and prison sentence. Byron broke with John Murray after this, but not before Murray spread rumours that Byron was regretting his alliance with the Hunts and had written him a letter to that effect. When news of this got back first to John Hunt, and then to Leigh, both were very hurt. Byron was apologetic, defensive, and angry with Murray, but the affair nevertheless contributed to a further cooling of his relationship with the brothers. He was also angry with John Hunt, who had freely advertised Byron's connection with the journal. 'That d——d advertisement of Mr J. Hunt is out of the limits', he raged to Murray before their break. 'I did not lend him my name to be hawked about in this way.'[31]

Although four issues of *The Liberal* appeared before the journal's eventual collapse, Hunt never managed to overcome the difficulties which it faced from its inception. He was in no doubt as to the cause of *The Liberal*'s failure, placing the blame squarely on Byron and his narrow-minded friends. 'Enemies', he wrote in 1828, in his *Lord Byron and some of His Contemporaries*, 'had been already at work. Lord Byron was alarmed for his credit with his fashionable friends; among whom, although on the liberal side, patriotism was less in favour, than the talk about it.'[32] Hunt bitterly resented the failure of *The Liberal*, which left him stranded in Italy without any means of supporting his family, and made him even more dependent on Byron's largesse. As the inevitability of the journal's collapse became apparent, communication between Byron and the inhabitants of Casa Negroto became less frequent. Hunt visited Byron periodically, and Byron remained a loyal friend to Mary, dealing with Timothy Shelley on her behalf and asking her to accept money in return for copying *Don Juan*. But his interest in Shelley's widow did not extend to paying frequent visits to a house dominated by Hunt's objectionable offspring.

Despite its premature failure, *The Liberal* occupies an important place in the history of British Romanticism. It was the final statement from a group of writers who had known and influenced each other for ten years. By the time the Hunts had dealt with the remaindered copies of *The Liberal*, the network celebrated in *The Examiner*, Keats's *Poems* (1817), *Foliage* and *Frankenstein* had dispersed. *The Liberal* was a celebration of this network, but it was also its elegy: a monument to both the exiles and the paradise Shelley envisaged in 'Julian and Maddalo'. The shattered group who united to piece *The Liberal* together – Hunt, Byron and Mary in Genoa; Charles Brown in Pisa; Hogg, Hazlitt and John Hunt in London – was held together only by fragile and unstable allegiances, and by memories of a shared past.

———

The winter of 1822–1823 tested Mary's fortitude to its limits. Isolated and depressed, she started a new diary, which was quite different in tone and scope from anything she had kept before. Her previous diary entries were brief and to the point: lists of books read, letters written, places visited, or calls made and received. Now, in the bleak privacy of her unheated rooms at Casa Negroto, she poured out her private agony in a journal which still makes painful reading. More than any other document, this journal gives the lie to the accusation – levelled by both those who knew her and by posterity – that Mary was a cold, unfeeling woman. Mary felt this accusation deeply. 'Oh my beloved Shelley', she wrote, in her first entry, 'it is not true that this heart was cold to thee . . . did I not in the deepest solitude of thought repeat to myself my good fortune in possessing you?'[33]

The contrast between the life she had known and the future to which she was condemned dominated her private writing, alongside imaginary conversations with Shelley in which she poured out her heart to him. These conversations seemed more real than those which punctuated her isolated life in Genoa. They were certainly more emotionally fulfilling than the conversations she had with the living. 'My own Heart', she wrote on 2 October, 'I would fain know what you think of my desolate state – what you think I ought to do – what to think.' Shelley, she decided, would answer thus: 'seek to know your own heart & learning what it best loves – try to enjoy that.' But she was unable to take much comfort from this imagined advice. 'When I meditate or dream on my future life, one idea alone animates me – I think of friends & human intercourse . . . [and] I weep to think how unstable all that is.'[34] She had been deserted by her 'Father, Mother, friend [Edward], husband, children'³⁵ and had little hope that the Hunts' presence would relieve her loneliness.

In this, she was quite correct. Marianne continued to be unwell and lethargic, and Hunt barricaded himself in his study, where, according to Byron, he 'sweated' articles for *The Liberal*.³⁶ In the evenings Mary was compelled by intense cold to sit with the Hunts in the only room where a fire burned, but Hunt's attitude towards her made these evenings a penance to be endured rather than a bright spot in her day. She knew that Hunt considered her to be unfeeling and therefore unworthy of Shelley, but – since she did not know that Jane had spread gossip about her – she was unable to understand why. 'No one seems to understand or to sympathize with me', read one bewildered diary entry. 'They all seem to look on me as one without affections – without any sensibility – my sufferings are thought a cipher – & I feel myself degraded before them; knowing that in their hearts they degrade me from the rank which I deserve to possess. – I feel dejected & cowed before them, feeling as if I might be the senseless person they appear to consider me.'³⁷ As Mary wrote desperate, deeply private meditations on her grief and her loneliness, Hunt poured out his troubles to his friends, writing to the Novellos and to his nephew Henry about how much he missed Shelley.

Hunt's behaviour exacerbated Mary's guilt about the depression leading up to her miscarriage which had blighted her final weeks with Shelley. As she slowly began to gather his poems and manuscripts together, she was made aware that, at times, she had not been the companion he desired. In the second week of October her writing desk arrived from Peacock, as she had requested. It was full of letters written by her to Shelley during the autumn of 1817, letters which recalled scenes dominated by William, Clara and Allegra – three children who died before their sixth birthdays. This was painful enough, but her Marlow letters were also full of demands about petty domestic issues: linen, houses, and the need to reunite Allegra with her father. They were written at a time of great anxiety for both Mary and Shelley, when their future looked uncertain and precarious. But stripped of their extenuating context they presented Mary with a picture of her younger self as a less than ideal wife, who bore little resemblance to the idealistic girl with whom Shelley had fallen in love.

It was equally difficult to read the verses to Jane Williams Shelley had written at the end of his life, which were scattered throughout his papers. 'Dearest Shelley', Mary pleaded, 'raise me from self depression – fill me, my chosen one, with a part of your energy.' 'I am not mean or base', she protested, 'yet I feel at times as if I were – I am not unfeeling – my hourly agonies prove that, yet the presence of those who do not love me, makes me feel as if I were of marble.'[38] Hunt would have been horrified had he read this. Even without knowledge of Mary's suffering, his behaviour during this period does not do him much credit. Mary was punished for not acting as others expected her to act. It was a cruel way to treat a woman who, at twenty-five, had lost her husband and three of her children, and for whom the future promised so little.

Despite Hunt's coldness, Mary remained loyal to both him and Marianne throughout the winter. She mediated between him and Byron when they fell out over the gossip spread by John Murray, and did her best to make Byron understand the difficulty of Hunt's position by appealing both to his good nature and his business sense. After all, she argued, if *The Liberal* was characterised as a work of charity, designed only to help the Hunts, then few people would bother to buy it. 'Hunt is a very good man', she reminded him. 'Shelley was greatly attached to him on account of his integrity.'[39] She tried not to dwell on the contrast between evenings spent in gloomy silence with Hunt and Marianne and those she had enjoyed with Shelley, Edward and Jane in Pugnano, where, she wrote wistfully to Jane, 'we used, like children, to play in the great hall or your garden & then sit under the cypresses & hear [Edward] read his play.'[40] But memories of the past constantly recurred to make the present painful and the future frightening. Conversations with Byron were particularly upsetting, since his voice was indelibly associated in her memory with Shelley's. Talking to him reminded her of evenings at the Villa Diodati, and of the 'other sounds and objects from which it can never disunite itself . . . When Albe speaks & Shelley does not answer it is as thunder without rain, The form of the sun without heat or light, as any familiar object might be shorn of its dearest & best attribute.'[41]

Trelawny, who based himself in Genoa during the winter of 1822, provided welcome relief from Hunt's disapproval and the memories awakened by Byron's presence. He visited Mary regularly and she was grateful for his company, particularly since he was happy to sit and talk of Shelley's greatness for hours on end. However, a degree of constraint entered their relationship when she realised that Trelawny was writing passionate love letters to Claire while simultaneously enjoying an intrigue with the wife of one of his Genoan acquaintances. Still, Mary missed his company badly when, in April 1823, he travelled to Rome to take on a starring role as Shelley's ashes were interred in the Protestant cemetery. Trelawny commissioned a headstone for Shelley, and bought the plot next to his grave, so that he could eventually be buried there himself. Mary had wanted Shelley's remains to be buried in William's small grave, but when the grave was opened it was found to contain the skeleton of an adult rather than that of a child. News that William's bones had disappeared represented yet another loss for his mother.

Life at Casa Negroto was complicated by Marianne's seventh pregnancy. The Hunts could ill afford another child, but Vaccà (Mrs Mason's Pisan doctor) had suggested that a pregnancy might, in the long term, benefit Marianne's health. It is hard now to see how any doctor could have thought that another baby would help a woman worn out by childbearing, and throughout Marianne's pregnancy those closest to her felt that childbirth was more likely to kill than to cure her. Mary was determined not to abandon Marianne or her children until the outcome of her pregnancy was known. Throughout her stay in Genoa, she only publicly expressed real anger towards Hunt when he disturbed Marianne's peace by suggesting that Bess should be allowed to join them in Italy. 'Poor Marianne', Mary wrote to Jane. 'I hope life will afford her some of the pleasures that she is capable of enjoying as long as Hunt continues well and kind. You may guess to whom I allude in the last word – Her arrival would be a death blow to poor Marianne – but if it be delayed, yet some time or other I fear it will occur.'[42] Thankfully, Mary was later able to report, Hunt saw the wisdom of allowing Marianne to have her way. He 'has had the humanity to permit her to decide concerning the coming of Miss K.', she reported to Jane in April. 'So it will not be for the present. H. could not at so terrible a moment have acted against her wishes – and I think it would have killed her if that most selfish of human beings had arrived to disturb by her self will & violence the comparative peace she enjoys.'[43]

Mary's disapproval of Bess, whom she had not seen since 1818, was informed by Marianne's view of her sister. Despite their difference in age, Mary and Marianne had maintained a quiet and affectionate friendship since their first meeting in 1816. Each had a good deal of sympathy for the plight of the other, although Marianne was too absorbed in her family and her own ill health to offer Mary much comfort during the winter they spent together in Genoa, and Mary found Marianne's perpetual pregnancies exasperating. 'A woman is not a field to be continually employed either in bringing forth or enlarging grain', she told her rather sharply in March 1820, before adding a pointed instruction: 'take care of yourself.'[44]

There is little doubt that Hunt's separation from Bess contributed much to his unhappiness and that after Shelley's death he felt her absence badly. He seems, however, to have made little effort to hide this from his wife. He acquiesced to Marianne's demand that her sister should remain in England, and conveyed the news of this stipulation himself, writing to Bess that Marianne 'fears, though I do not, that some troubles might arise to us from the less considerate parts of your temper'. Moreover, he wrote, as if to soften the blow of Marianne's disapproval, there were other reasons for them to remain apart. 'Rumours have been industriously circulated that you are with us', he reported. 'Hobhouse, when he was in Italy, affected astonishment at not finding you; and Ld. B. is not a man to prevent the unpleasant effects of gossiping of any kind, or to make your neighbourhood to him the more comfortable.' All this was perfectly reasonable, and demonstrated a degree of loyalty to his wife, as well as his concern for his sister-in-law's reputation. But, in an extraordinary aside, he comforted Bess with the thought that her presence should certainly be required in Italy should Marianne die. 'Should anything happen to your sister meanwhile, of course I should want your support as instantly as I could obtain it', he told her. There was something thoroughly strange about the second half of Hunt's letter. 'Let the allusion which I have made to an event that has never before been alluded to between us, be the proof I wish it to be; or I shall have gone through the anguish of it to no purpose. I think circumstances altogether warranted it; and you know with what heart-felt sincerity I say all that I do, of everybody, – how truly upon my heart and upon my honour.'[45]

In the spring of 1823, as the Casa Negroto household watched and waited for the birth of Marianne's baby, Mary was forced to confront the problem of her own future. At first, it seemed unimaginable that a new year should begin without Shelley. 'When Spring arrives', she wrote in her diary, 'leaves you never saw will shadow the ground – flowers you never beheld will star it – the grass will be of another growth.'[46] She knew, however, that she could not remain indefinitely with the Hunts, and it was clear that, wherever she lived, she would need to earn her own living. Sir Timothy Shelley grudgingly offered to support Percy if Mary would relinquish all claim to her son, but he had no intention of aiding the woman with whom his own son had lived in sin, and at whose behest he had deserted his first wife. Mary was appalled by the idea that she should part with Percy, the only reason for her continued existence. She was thus deeply hurt when Byron advised her to accept Sir Timothy's offer to raise the little boy. It was a disagreement which introduced an unwelcome formality into their relationship.

Mary did however receive more valuable advice from Byron, who, along with Godwin, encouraged her to return to England. Both men believed that surrounded by her family and her old social circle she would be able to negotiate more effectively with both Sir Timothy's solicitor and her publishers. Their advice gathered strength early in the year when *Valperga* was published to moderately friendly reviews. Mary had sent the novel to Godwin in January 1822 and he had seen it through the press on her behalf, but if she intended to earn a living by her pen then it made sense for her to live in the country in which her books were printed. Byron even offered to fund her journey home, thus allowing her to travel in tolerable comfort.

Hogg and Jane Williams, by contrast, enthusiastically advised her from London to remain in Italy. However, their advice was self-interested, and had more to do with their developing friendship than with concern for Mary's welfare. Hogg grew extremely attentive to Jane after her return to London, and did not want a promising new relationship disrupted by Mary, who knew from experience that Jane was not the first woman connected with Shelley to attract his attention. Jane herself was most insistent that Mary should remain where she was. Although her advice was cloaked with solicitous concern, there was no mistaking the strength of her opposition to Mary's presence in England. Mary had no idea that Jane had blackened her name with both Hunt and Hogg, and was mystified and a little hurt by her friend's reluctance to welcome her back to London.

In the end, the counsels of Godwin and Byron prevailed over those of Hogg and Jane, largely because, by the middle of the year, there was nothing to keep Mary in Genoa. Byron was actively trying to withdraw from *The Liberal*, and when the London Greek Committee asked him to travel to Greece as their representative in the fight for independence, he was provided with an ideal excuse to end his involvement with the Hunt brothers. Teresa Guiccioli was most distressed by his plans, and expended considerable effort in attempting to persuade him to allow her to travel to Greece with him. Byron thought this nonsensical, and was immensely relieved when Teresa reluctantly agreed to accompany her father back to Ravenna, to where he had been recalled from exile. In June, Marianne confounded expectations by surviving the birth of her seventh child – a boy, named Vincent after Vincent Novello. Mary knew that without *The Liberal* her ability to earn money in Italy was limited, and felt that Marianne's safe delivery freed her from responsibility for the Hunts. She began to make arrangements for her journey home soon after Vincent's birth.

In the final weeks of Mary's time in Italy, Hunt and Mary finally confronted each other about the breakdown of their friendship, and the misunderstandings of the winter were swept away. Mary revealed something of her suffering to Hunt, and he realised how mistaken he had been to listen to Jane's gossip. Although he did not tell Mary that Jane had spread rumours about her, he did inform Jane that her malice had been exposed, and that he no longer believed in her reports of Mary's unfeeling coldness. By way of recompense, he wrote kindly of Mary to Vincent Novello, asking him to extend his friendship to her when she arrived in England, and warning him not to be put off by her calm exterior. 'She is a torrent of fire under a Hecla snow', he told his friend.[47] He wrote in a similar vein to Bess, in a letter which expressed a degree of embarrassment about how easily he had believed Jane's version of events, and guilt about his behaviour towards Mary. 'How sorry was I', he admitted, 'when I found that during all my cold and almost cruel treatment of her, on her first residing here, she had been recording her remorse in private!' Jane, he decided, did not have 'intellect enough to see very far into a case where great thoughts, passions, etc, are concerned.'[48]

Hunt failed to mention that he too had demonstrated the lack of intellect he detected in Jane, and that, even after a prolonged period of co-habitation with Mary, he had failed to understand the depth of her feelings. Instead he focused on Mary's 'repentance' for her failure to demonstrate her remorse publicly. He did not display much self-awareness as he cleared Mary of cruelty towards Shelley, but at least the breach was healed. As Mary made her preparations for her journey home, she did so secure in the knowledge that she had regained Hunt's support and affection. She wrote more cheerfully to Jane that 'Hunt is all kindness, consideration, and friendship' and noted happily that 'all feeling of alienation towards me has disappeared even to its last dreg – He perfectly approves of what I have done.'[49] This can not have made very satisfactory reading for Jane, who knew that Hunt's renewed regard for Mary could only have come about because he had started to disbelieve her stories about the state of the Shelleys' marriage.

Hunt's friendship was particularly valuable to Mary when her last weeks in Genoa were marred by a serious quarrel with Byron, which developed when Hunt tactlessly reminded Byron of his promise to pay for Mary's journey home, and of a debt of £1,000 – the sum of the old bet between Shelley and Byron – he owed to the Shelley estate. Byron was irritated at being reprimanded about his debts by Hunt, who, in assuming the role of Byron's conscience, seemed to forget that he was heavily indebted to Byron himself. He responded to Hunt's demands in a series of letters which, according to Mary, were 'so full of contempt against me & my lost Shelley that I could stand it no longer'.[50] Mary was too principled to take money from a man who made slighting remarks about her husband, and was compelled to borrow from Mrs Mason and Trelawny in order to pay for transport back to England.

What Mary did not know was that, despite their quarrel, Byron wanted to pay for her journey without her knowledge, in order to allow her to travel in comfort without denting her pride. He secretly advanced the money to Hunt, and asked him to hand it over to Mary. 'Thus', he told Hunt, 'she will be spared any fancied humiliation' and enabled to travel 'handsomely and conveniently in all respects.'[51] Mary never received this money but it seems Hunt did, and, as Miranda Seymour has argued (on the strength of evidence presented by John Cam Hobhouse, who was later shown a receipt signed by Hunt), 'shockingly, kept it'.[52] Such fraudulent deception seems out of character for Hunt, but it is equally unlikely that Hobhouse would have lied in his private diary. It is possible that Hunt was so short of money that the temptation to keep Byron's gift, while convincing himself that this was what Mary would have wanted, was irresistible. Whatever the truth of the matter, Mary left Genoa convinced of Byron's rudeness and Hunt and Trelawny's kindness. However, through the good offices of Teresa Guiccioli, Mary and Byron did part on a friendly note. 'I am too poor', Mary confessed to Teresa, 'to lose my friends as well – and if I lost the friendship of LB the rest would not be worth much.'[53] But neither Mary nor Hunt could easily forgive Byron's slights on Shelley's reputation. Byron acknowledged that Mary had a right to be indignant, but he did not accept that Hunt had a similar right to feel angry. '*I* knew you long before Mr. S knew either you or me', he reminded him.[54] Despite all that had passed between them, Byron was not prepared to leave Italy on bad terms with Hunt. They had known each other for too long, he suggested, for their relationship to crumble over a fancied spat about a dead friend. In a final act of generosity, Byron provided Hunt with funds to move his family to Florence, where they could enjoy the friendship and support of a lively English expatriate community.

Byron left Genoa first, on 13 July. He was accompanied by Trelawny, who sailed as factotum and self-appointed stage manager of Byron's Greek adventure. Mary's departure was fixed for 25 July and a *vetturino* (rather than a comfortable post-chaise, as Byron had intended) was engaged to take her as far as Lyon. She was sorry to leave the Hunts, particularly since, she told Jane, 'Hunt's kindness is now as active & warm as it was dormant before.'[55] She half-wished she could give up her journey to England and settle with the Hunts in Florence, thus remaining cushioned from the reality of a future without Shelley. But she knew that to do so was an unrealistic dream. Both she and Hunt had to find ways of starting their lives again, of facing the reality of the present. Five years earlier Mary had arrived in Italy accompanied by Shelley, Claire, William, Clara, Allegra and two servants. When she left Genoa to return to England, with only three year old Percy for company, she was still six weeks short of her twenty-sixth birthday.

The Present

Mary's journey across Europe was not easy, but she was glad to be travelling again. From Genoa she made her way north to Asti, where she started an affectionate journal letter to the Hunts, and then to Turin, where she and Percy spent their second night on the road. They passed through 'pretty scenery' and Percy behaved immaculately. Nevertheless by the time they arrived in Turin they were tired and Mary was moved to bless 'the man who first invented baths'. She was determined to be cheerful even though, as she told the Hunts, 'tomorrow . . . is the anniversary when nine years ago I quitted England with Shelley.' 'Never mind', she continued briskly. 'Sufferance is the badge of all our tribe – I will make an order of the badge & so it may feel lighter.'[1]

The following day, she and Percy travelled onwards to Susa, on a road which took them through the Alps. Now she was among the mountains Shelley had loved, it was harder to avoid melancholic thoughts of the past. They arrived in Lyon on 2 August, nine days after leaving Genoa. Once again, Mary found herself passing under the shadow of Mont Blanc, and she wrote wistfully to Hunt that the mountain was 'associated to me with many delightful hours'.[2] Memories of those delightful hours underlined how much her life had changed, and made her feel much older than her twenty-five years and certainly much older than thirty-five-year-old Marianne. Percy, meanwhile, missed the Hunt children, and babbled to his mother about sending Marianne's babies toys and kisses.

Ten days later they arrived in Paris. There they were visited by Horace Smith, who was taken aback by how tired Mary looked and swept her and Percy off to Versailles, where he had settled with his family. It was, Mary told Hunt, a pleasure to be among friends again, and to let someone else make the arrangements for their travel. She spent three days at Versailles, catching up on gossip about Hazlitt, the Lambs, Wordsworth and Coleridge, and rebuilding her strength for the rest of her journey.

On 25 August, a month after their departure from Genoa, the boat carrying Mary and Percy crossed the Channel and docked in the Thames. The crossing was easy, no one was seasick, and Percy rampaged about the deck in 'high glee'. The boat was met by Godwin and Mary's younger half-brother William, and any awkwardness which might have been felt after a separation of five years was swept away by Percy, who enchanted his serious grandfather by chattering enthusiastically in his own peculiar mix of Italian and English. Mary and her stepmother also had a reasonably civil reunion. She was resolved, she told Hunt, 'not to think of certain things, to take all as a matter of course and thus . . . to keep myself out of the gulph of melancholy, on the edge of which I was & am continually peeping.'[3]

In the weeks and months which followed her return to England, Mary would battle hard to keep away from the inviting edge of the 'gulph of melancholy'. Leaving Italy marked the beginning of a new life for her and Percy, one which she was determined they would survive. Stripped of the protection of Shelley's aristocratic mantle, she could not allow herself to fall into the lethargic depression that claimed her after the deaths of Clara, William and Shelley himself. Lodgings had to be found; money had to be made. She embarked on a long-running dispute with Shelley's father about an allowance, and, aided by Godwin and Peacock, eventually managed to persuade him to loan her £200 a year, to be paid back to the Shelley estate on Sir Timothy's death. This was Mary's first experience of financial negotiation, and it gave her confidence in her ability to live independently. With no husband to protect her, she had to learn quickly how to deal with solicitors and publishers. Godwin helped her as much as he could, but it was nevertheless her own resilience which enabled her to negotiate a new life as a single woman. She rediscovered some of the stubborn self-belief which had led her, at the tender age of sixteen, to declare her love for Shelley, as she embarked on a battle for her professional, emotional and physical survival. Mary understood that these three kinds of survival were intimately linked. She had to earn enough money to supplement her allowance so that she could put a roof over her head, feed and clothe herself and Percy, and pay the servant girl whose presence would allow her to concentrate on writing. Her letters indicate that she also knew that she stood a better chance of escaping depression if she was busy, and could see her work received with some degree of success.

It was therefore fortunate that she arrived back in England to be greeted by an astonishing piece of news. Almost overnight, she had become famous. The Lyceum Theatre was staging a production of *Frankenstein* which 'caused the ladies to faint away & a hubbub to ensue'.[4] Mary went to see the new incarnation of her novel with Godwin, William and Jane a few days after her arrival in London. Her unnamed Creature was represented by a long dash in the playbill, setting the tone for a delightfully silly production, described fully by Mary for the benefit of the absent Hunts:

> At the end of the Ist Act. the stage represents a room with a staircase leading to F̲ workshop – he goes to it and you see his light at a small window, through which a frightened servant peeps, who runs off in terror when F. exclaims 'It lives!' – Presently F himself rushes in horror & trepidation from the room and while still expressing his agony & terror —— throws down the door of the laboratory, leaps the staircase and presents his unearthly and monstrous person on the stage . . . I was much amused, and it appeared to excite a breathless eagerness in the audience.[5]

Godwin had cannily arranged for a new edition of *Frankenstein* to be published to coincide with the stage play, so Mary found that her book was both making her a little money and was enjoyed by the reading public once more. It meant that she attracted a certain amount of attention as she re-entered the literary world. Henry Crabb Robinson, the prolific diarist who met her one evening at a supper party, found it difficult to square her person with her reputation. 'She looks elegant and sickly and young', he recorded. 'One would not suppose she was the author of "Frankenstein."'[6]

Mary was gratified to find that her novel was once more in the public eye, but the celebrity it brought her was not entirely welcome. The association between *Frankenstein*, Shelley, and the Swiss 'league of incest' was still vivid in the public mind, and the drawback of her fame became apparent when the Lyceum production was placed under scrutiny by some self-appointed guardians of public morality. The *Theatrical Observer* for 9 August 1823 carried reports of placards 'posted widely throughout the Metropolis'. They carried a stark warning for 'The Play-Going Public':

> Do not go to the Lyceum to see the monstrous Drama, founded on the improper work called 'Frankenstein' – Do not take your wives and families . . . This subject is pregnant with mischief.[7]

This was hardly the kind of attention Mary wished to attract as she attempted to establish herself in London as a respectable literary widow. Nevertheless, the placards had the effect of drawing the crowds to the Lyceum, and *Frankenstein* appeared in many stage versions throughout 1823 and 1824. It all helped to build Mary's professional reputation, even if the methods by which her name was made were not of her choosing.

Mary was not, however, content merely to focus on her own career. Nor would her battle for emotional survival allow her to do so. Her diary demonstrates that she felt that she could only grieve for Shelley properly once she had made reparation to him for her coldness by devoting herself to the promotion of his work and reputation. Accordingly, she prepared an edition of Shelley's poems, many of which remained in manuscript at his death. Mary believed she had a sacred duty to present these poems to the world, in order to convince an ignorant public of his genius.

The resulting volume, *Posthumous Poems*, eventually appeared in June 1824, and in it Mary presented Shelley's major unpublished works (including 'Julian and Maddalo', 'Letter to Maria Gisborne' and the unfinished 'Triumph of Life') alongside translations and a large number of miscellaneous verses, many of which she carefully reconstructed from near-illegible fragments. She also reprinted *Alastor*, which was no longer in print. Shelley did not write his poems neatly, and Mary had to contend with a vast array of manuscripts – some loose, some bound in notebooks – where scraps of verse competed for space with doodles of boats, trees, letters and other ephemera.

Despite – or perhaps because of – the difficulty involved, working on Shelley's manuscripts brought Mary much solace in the months following her return to England. She was determined to enshrine his reputation and to reveal to an unappreciative world the full extent of his talent and goodness. To that end, she wrote a biographical Preface for her volume in which she portrayed Shelley as a transcendent, brilliant spirit, and as a man adored by his friends, with an immense capacity for love and affection. Creating such a portrait of her husband might have been comforting to Mary, but it necessitated some drastic rewriting of the past. Shelley had not always been as kind as Mary suggested, and she had not always been alert to the manifold virtues she attributed to him after his death. And while it was possible for her to forget the periods of unhappiness which occurred throughout their relationship, it was harder to ignore the evidence of his poetry. Her fair-copy manuscript of *Posthumous Poems* shows that she seriously considered publishing some poems which made direct reference to periods in which both she and Shelley experienced mutual alienation. The most notable example of this was the stanza 'To Mary', written during the dreadful summer of 1819, in the weeks after William's death:

> My dearest Mary, wherefore hast thou gone
> > And left me in this dreary world alone?
> > Thy form is here indeed, a lovely one;
> > But thou art fled, gone down the dreary road

Which leads to sorrows most obscure abode;
Thou sittest on the heath of pale despair;
         where
For thine own sake I cannot follow thee.[8]

This brief verse laid bare Shelley's compassionate response to Mary's despair, and cannot have been easy to read. Shelley's lines beautifully articulated his loneliness, even as they accepted that Mary could not control her emotions. Mary presented herself in *Posthumous Poems* as the grieving spouse of a great writer, and it was brave of her to consider revealing Shelley's response to one of the darkest periods in their marriage. She copied the poem into her fair-copy book in preparation for publication, but in the end she felt unable to publish such a private work. Other poems 'To Mary' appeared instead, but this one remained unpublished until 1840.

Even without the most painfully private of Shelley's poems, there was plenty in *Posthumous Poems* which was upsetting to print. The volume included the depiction of the cold lady of 'Julian and Maddalo'; the nostalgic final stanzas of 'Letter to Maria Gisborne'; poems which revealed Shelley's fascination with Claire and Emilia Viviani; and verses mourning William Shelley. These works demonstrated Shelley's talent, just as Mary intended they should, but they also highlighted the emotional strains of his life. *Posthumous Poems* was thus characterised by a disjunction between the beloved genius of its Preface and the troubled, introspective voice of its poetry.

John Hunt published 400 copies of *Posthumous Poems* and the volume was warmly received by the slowly increasing circle of Shelley's admirers. But before the edition could sell out Sir Timothy Shelley intervened, furious that his renegade son's name was once again in the public eye. Mary's allowance was stopped, and she had to agree both to recall all unsold copies of *Posthumous Poems* and to refrain from publishing or using Shelley's name during Sir Timothy's life. Her intended prose companion to *Poems* had to be abandoned, as did any thought of a biography or memoir. Mary was not unduly concerned by Sir Timothy's prohibition. She did not expect the old man to live very long, over 300 copies of the volume had already been sold, and she had no real wish to put herself through the emotional strain of writing Shelley's life. It was one thing to print Shelley's poems, but quite another to expose Shelley, herself or their friends and family to the glare of biography and public scrutiny.

Editing Shelley's manuscripts was a cathartic experience for Mary. It allowed her to compensate for the failures of understanding which had at times marred her marriage, and, in the process, to rediscover her own creativity. 'I feel my powers again', she wrote in her diary in the summer of 1824, shortly before the publication of *Posthumous Poems*. 'The eclipse of winter is passing from my mind – I shall again feel the enthusiastic glow of composition – again as I pour forth my soul upon paper, feel the winged ideas arise, & enjoy the delight of expressing them.'[9] Preparing the volume played an important part in Mary's efforts to rebuild her life, and it allowed her to reassert herself, not just as the author of a scandalous novel, but as a professional woman of letters, and as one half of a powerful literary couple.

———

In June 1824, Claire made contact, after a silence of more than a year. 'We have had a letter from her', Mary told Trelawny, 'but it details no particulars about her situation, while she complains of its extreme discomfort and the bad effect a Russian winter had on her.'[10] It was clear that Claire's battle for survival had been a good deal rougher than Mary's. A month before she wrote to Mary, Claire left St Petersburg and made the 400 mile journey to Moscow. There she built up a small group of pupils whose parents wanted to acquire the social cachet offered by an English governess, and subsequently gained a permanent position in a professional family with a five year old daughter, Dunia. She was determined to remain independent after Shelley's death and never again to rely upon another for survival. In her quest for self-sufficiency she battled bedbugs, brutal cold and barbarous Russian manners, all of which made life miserable and uncomfortable. She survived by holding herself apart from her employers and their acquaintances. 'With the Russians I never associate', she told Jane Williams, 'and am reckoned by them to be incurably proud.' At least their ignorance meant that 'I may say what I please, while, in England, I should be obliged to follow their opinion, and not my own.'[11]

Although she must have appeared stand-offish to Moscow society, Claire was a good and kind governess, and she daringly incorporated Wollstonecraft's educational theories into her lessons with her rote-bound Russian pupils. She was devastated when, a few months after becoming her governess, little Dunia died of diphtheria, a tragedy which threw Claire back into the Moscow governess market. She became increasingly worried that her scandalous family, as well as her Byronic entanglement, would prevent her from securing employment, and was careful to avoid sending letters directly to either 'Mrs Shelley' or 'Mrs Godwin'. 'How often do people here touch upon the brink of all my history' she told Jane. 'I do not wish, in any degree, to become an object of curiosity.'[12]

The dangers of becoming an 'object of curiosity' increased dramatically when news arrived in Moscow that Byron was dead. Byron's Greek adventure ended at Missolonghi, where Mavrocordato, now the leader of the Greek forces, had based his headquarters. At the beginning of April 1824 Byron developed a fever, which was then made fatal by over-zealous doctors who bled him and dosed him with purgatives and laudanum. He died on 19 April, watched over by his servants, Fletcher and Tita. It was not the heroic ending for which he might have hoped, but his death was quickly mythologised by the many admirers of his poetry drawn to the glamour of his presence in Greece, and his body was shipped back to England amid much pomp and circumstance. Claire was scathing about the reverential solemnity with which his ornate funeral procession was greeted in London. 'Pray think of the modest funeral of our Shelley', she wrote to Jane, 'and then of the one given to Lord Byron, and ask yourself, if anyone with a soul can condescend to interest themselves in human affairs.'[13] Claire was afraid that renewed interest in Byron's life would expose her, and she wrote frantically to Mary to ask about the glut of memoirs and biographies which quickly followed his death. When gossip about her connection with Shelley, Byron and the Godwins did eventually reach Moscow she found herself the subject of unwelcome interest, and a university professor who was on the point of employing her to teach his daughter abruptly terminated their agreement. 'You may imagine this man's horror when he heard who I was', she wrote bitterly, '[that] the charming Miss Clairmont, the model of good sense, accomplishments, and good taste was brought up, issued from the very den of freethinkers.'[14] As news of her exotic heritage spread, she was forced to endure snubs and listen to disparaging remarks about her former friends. One evening, two Russian aristocrats deliberately provoked her by discussing Shelley and Byron in her presence, and succeeded in tricking her into an admission of acquaintance with both poets. They 'praised Albè up to the skies and reviled our dearest Shelley', she wrote in her diary. 'I would not bear this and defended him. – Among other things he said that this paragon of generosity had pensioned Shelley's widow. Oh my God, the lies there are in the world.'[15]

Claire was a good hater, and she never ceased to detest Byron. Mary felt rather differently about him, and his death was a blow to her. Yet another of her circle had died, leaving her behind. 'What do I do here?' she wondered in her diary. 'Why am I doomed to live on seeing all expire before me? ... A new race is springing about me – At the age of twenty-six I am in the condition of an aged person – all my old friends are gone.'[16] Byron's death caused a sensation in London, but for those who had known him, or had been on the fringes of his world, it was an occasion for introspection and discussion of the past. For Trelawny, who parted company from Byron soon after their arrival in Greece, news of his old friend's death prompted powerful memories of the Pisan group. 'Our Pisa circle is not one to be forgotten', he wrote to Jane Williams. 'There was no other such in the wide world – such hearts as ours united under the sunny clime of Italy – such scenes and events no time can fade.'[17] But the privilege of happy nostalgia was not afforded to Claire as she fought her way through a succession of vicious Russian winters. She remained in Moscow until 1826, in isolation and poverty. It was a high price to pay for the independence she craved.

Claire and Mary were not the only women to be thrown into a battle for survival by the events of 1822. Back in England Bess, who had been left behind when the Hunts sailed for Italy, was forced to confront the impact of the life she had lived with her brother-in-law. All three women had learnt of the reality of free love back in the 1810s, when their unorthodox living arrangements, and the ideals of Shelley and Hunt, had variously exposed their lives to public scrutiny and, in the case of Mary and Claire, their bodies to illegitimate pregnancy. This was also true for Jane Williams, whose children were born outside of wedlock and who had lost her male protector. Now that the men of the group were dead, or living abroad, the women were left behind to count the cost of youthful idealism: damaged reputations, limited earning capacity, and exclusion from polite society.

After several years in which Bess had been superfluous to Hunt's requirements, supplanted in his affections by such figures as Shelley and Keats, she found that he once again required her support. Long, passionate letters passed between them and, in the summer of 1824, Hunt finally convinced Marianne to readmit her sister into their household. He wrote to Bess telling her to leave England for Italy but Bess, most unexpectedly, refused to accede to his demands. She believed she would be the subject of 'calumny' in Florence, and, she wrote frankly, had no wish to move to Italy merely to attend to the children's sewing and act as Marianne's unpaid housekeeper. Both Hunts were offended by this, and although Hunt attempted to mask his displeasure in affectionate remonstrance, his reply dripped with unspoken reproaches about Bess's self-confessed inability to control her 'fancies' (by which she meant her temper):

> As you still think yourself liable to those fancies . . . so, I on my part, in consequence of the progress of years . . . am certainly not a whit stronger, if so strong, to meet them without exhibiting anything angry. I should be so vexed at their appearance, especially after the patient and tranquil manner in which you have borne yourself so long, that I should infallibly be most agitated; and a series of these agitations would have the worst possible effect both on myself and your sister.[18]

Hunt did his best to counter Bess's refusal by implying that her presence was not necessarily desirable or welcome, but his tangled, grammatically tortured response gave the lie to this suggestion. He also noted that Marianne was particularly displeased by Bess's stated disinclination to resume responsibility for the family's needlework. Marianne did not like needlework either, Hunt reminded his sister-in-law, 'though she is still forced to attend to it'. And, he added, 'she is quite persuaded, as well as myself, that you could have been of pleasanter service to us than in that manner.'[19] Unsurprisingly, this missive, and others like it, did not change Bess's mind.

Bess's decision to remain in England rested – like the decisions made by Claire and Mary – on the issue of independence. Exclusion from the Hunts' Italian adventure kept her apart from her brother-in-law, but this experience had not been entirely negative. It had enabled her to achieve a degree of emotional stability which she knew would be compromised if she joined Hunt and Marianne. She therefore no longer wished to reclaim the position – usurped by Shelley in 1817 – of Hunt's intellectual soulmate. Distance appears to have revealed to Bess that, however much she loved Hunt, living in close proximity to him was simply too destructive. That she did love Hunt is clear from a rare surviving letter to him, written in September 1823. The letter centred on a message to 'the dear fugitive friend with whom I parted at Ramsgate'. 'Should you meet this other, warmer friend', she wrote, in a complicated third-person address to Hunt, 'tell him I have a painful pleasure in thinking of old times, some particular days, walks &c – more especially; – tell him I know how long and how sensibly, grasps may be felt . . . tell him, too, that I long most ardently, again, to return grasp for grasp, to see that dearest of dear faces, and you may add – in a whisper – that I should not be sorry to give him an opportunity of setting his conscience at rest.' 'God Bless you', she continued, 'my dear, dear, dear, dear, dear, dear dear Friend "One kind kiss before we part!" – again God Bless you.'[20]

Given the strength of her feelings, Bess's refusal to join Hunt was remarkable. But her decision was in part the result of a dramatic change which took place in the period following Shelley's death, when she too became a writer. In 1823, just over a year after she and Hunt parted, Bess published her first botanical book, *Flora Domestica*. It was no coincidence that she finally found the freedom to write after Hunt and Marianne left England. *Flora Domestica* was an exceptional achievement, especially for a woman who had received only a rudimentary education. Its full title gave some indication of the range of subjects it covered: *Flora Domestica; or, The Portable Flower-Garden; with Directions for the Treatment of Plants in Pots; and Illustrations from the Work of the Poets*. It was ostensibly a book about how to look after pot-plants written for those who, like the author, were 'lover[s] of the country' but 'reside[d] in town' and who might therefore wish to rear and preserve 'a *portable garden* in pots'.[21] Despite its seemingly contained purpose, its descriptions of plants ranged far beyond plant care, encompassing folk traditions, the genesis of plant names, Linnaean categorisations and discussions of the literary and historical significance of flowers. It was also an anthology, densely packed with quotations from English and Italian poets, from the Greeks and from living writers.

Most of all, *Flora Domestica* was a proclamation of Cockney ideals and the value of Cockney poetry. It quoted more from Keats and Hunt than from Shakespeare and Milton, and Keats was represented by excerpts from his early, Hunt-inspired poems, such as *Endymion*. It thus presented an alternative canon, in which the work of Horace Smith and Cockney acolytes like Bryan Procter overshadowed that of Wordsworth and Dryden. The Preface contained a long passage in praise of Shelley and Prince Mavrocordato, which allied *Flora Domestica* with the politics of European independence movements and, therefore, with the politics of *The Liberal*. *Flora Domestica* also extended and championed the democratic manifesto of *Foliage*. In it Bess showed that the beauties of nature were available to all. One did not need to be rich enough to travel to experience the pleasures of nature, since nature could be domesticated in a portable garden. Bess's insistence on the availability of such pleasures was implicitly oppositional. In his fourth essay on the 'Cockney School', John Lockhart had attacked Hunt's circle for presuming 'to talk with contempt of some of the most exquisite spirits the world ever produced, merely because they did not happen to exert their faculties in laborious affected descriptions of flowers seen in window-pots, or cascades heard at Vauxhall.'²² *Blackwood's* stereotyped the Cockneys as suburban gardeners, and attacked them for their limited knowledge of the beauties of nature untamed. Bess took this stereotype and subverted it, proclaiming a message of democratic luxury and suburban pleasure in the process.

Although Bess wrote *Flora Domestica* after Hunt's departure for Italy, he played a significant role in the volume's composition, sending her extracts of poetry and suggestions for quotation in long letters from Italy. The volume thus illustrated a curious tension in Hunt and Bess's relationship. She was able to produce her first major work only in Hunt's absence, but this work acknowledged his writing as an important influence. And though it arose from an enforced separation, *Flora Domestica* allowed Hunt and Bess to keep their relationship alive through letters in which discussion of her work was interspersed with ardent declarations of friendship and love.

But even as Hunt's voice permeated Bess's manuscript, her book allowed her to move away from his orbit of influence, and away from the circle in which her reputation had been tarnished. Although *Flora Domestica* was published anonymously, it established her as an author in her own right, who developed a professional working relationship with her publishers, Taylor and Hessey (who had also published Keats's poems), and with the writers who subsequently discovered and enjoyed her work. Coleridge wrote approvingly of *Flora Domestica* to Taylor and Hessey, and suggested that they should commission her to write a second volume – a suggestion both they and Bess accepted immediately. Her second botanical book, *Sylvan Sketches*, was published two years later, and, in a conciliatory gesture, was dedicated to Marianne. And through Taylor and Hessey Bess formed an enduring epistolary friendship with the 'peasant-poet' John Clare, whose work *Flora Domestica* praised. Although Bess and Clare never met, they embarked on a long correspondence, and planned to collaborate on a book about British birds. Clare provided Bess with something she had never had before: a male friend who accepted her on her own merits, rather than as a member of Hunt's circle. His poetic sensibility was also very different from Hunt's, and his work captured the transient beauty of nature as Hunt's had never been able to do. This was a revelation for a woman whose aesthetic and emotional existence was bound up with her response to the natural world. 'I earnestly wished for your descriptive pen', she wrote to Clare from the Isle of Wight, every part of which, she reported, was 'cloaked with trees'. But, she continued, 'I could command neither pen nor pencil that could do them justice, and could only bring away with me a pleasing recollection, which is not transferable.'[23]

Unlike *Foliage* and *Endymion*, *Flora Domestica* enjoyed some success. It went into a second edition within two years of publication, and met with approving notices in the London newspapers. This is perhaps surprising given Bess's defence of Cockney ideals. However, these ideals were more subtly stated than in Hunt's work, and Bess wrote her celebration of Hunt's circle only after the group celebrated in *Foliage* had dissolved in the wake of the deaths of Keats and Shelley. *Flora Domestica* was a Cockney retrospective, an attempt to reshape the literary canon in favour of the writers Bess met in Hampstead in the 1810s. The volume was a riposte to *Blackwood's*, but it was a riposte in defence of a memory. It was ironic that, in elegising the group in whose shadows she stood, Bess reinvented herself, in the short term at least, as a successful, independent woman. *Flora Domestica* freed her from overbearing personal associations with the men whose work she celebrated.

With Hunt abroad, Bess was also able to carve out a place in the group he had previously dominated. She became friendly with Mary, who warmed to her after her return to England, and saw a good deal of the Novellos, whose house acted as a magnetic focus for the surviving members of Hunt's circle. Mary drew real comfort from evenings spent at the Novellos' rambling, comfortable, musical house in Shacklewell, a village now completely assimilated into the London boroughs of Hackney and Islington. Hunt gave both Mary and Jane Williams letters of introduction to the Novellos, and they were warmly welcomed into a chaotic and friendly household. Mary found herself the unlikely object of an adolescent crush when she won the undying admiration of thirteen year old Mary Victoria Novello (afterwards Mary Cowden Clarke) by presenting her with an autographed copy of *Frankenstein* and a necklace of coral beads from Italy.

Mary Victoria later wrote a pen-portrait of Mary as she was in 1823, which presents a more vivid impression of its subject than any of the mournful extant pictures of her. It also demonstrates that sorrow and pain had had little impact on Mary's beauty. Mary Victoria recalled a slightly bowed golden-haired head, marble-white shoulders 'statuesquely' rising from a low-cut black velvet dress, thoughtful eyes and a surprisingly decisive expression, as well as 'exquisitely-formed, white, dimpled, small hands, with rosy palms, and plumply commencing fingers, that tapered into tips as slender and delicate as those in a Vandyk portrait.'[24] Mary could do extraordinary things with her hands, and good-naturedly amused Mary Victoria and her younger sister Clara by bending her fingers back so far that they almost touched her arm. Five year old Clara, who would became one of the most famous singers of her generation, divided her adoration between Mary and Percy. In later life she conceded that her devotion to Mary's son had been misplaced since he tyrannised her mercilessly, hitting her with his little wooden cart when the two of them were sent out to play with the elder Novello children in the overgrown Shacklewell garden.

Clara and Mary Victoria were not the only Novellos to adore Mary. Their father was equally entranced. 'I am absolutely in love with her', he told Hunt, 'and shall have you to answer for whatever mischievous consequence may occur, for not having purposely cautioned me beforehand . . . I can scarcely believe that the cordial, warm-hearted and kind creature I now see, can be the same Mrs Shelley I recollect formerly, so silent and reserved.'[25]

Mary had learnt a bitter lesson during the winter of 1823, when the experience of being ostracised by Hunt made her realise that her natural reserve alienated people, and that keeping her feelings buried away damaged her ability to establish a new life for herself. She made great efforts to demonstrate her affection after her return to England, self-consciously expressing emotions she had previously kept private. However, the fact that she was so relaxed and unreserved during her acquaintance with the Novellos testifies not just to her determination but also to how much she enjoyed spending time in their welcoming home. Indeed, Mary was at least as fond of Novello as he was of her. She called him Vincenzo – especially, Mary Victoria later recalled, when she wanted him to sing for her. In fact, she came dangerously close to falling in love with him. He was talented, creative and kind, and reminded her of all that was good in Shelley. 'I could talk to him', she wrote in her diary. For someone as private as Mary, this meant a great deal. Novello, however, was devoted to his wife, and to Mary, elliptical on the subject even in her private journal, it seemed typical of her misfortune that she should have lost her heart to someone 'attached to another'.[26]

Yet, in spite of the sadness which tinged Mary's affection for Novello, she was still able to draw inspiration from time spent in his company. 'I shall begin a Novel', she told Hunt in 1823. 'Novello will help it greatly – as I listen to music (especially instrumental) new ideas rise and develop themselves, with greater energy and truth than at any other time.'[27] The resulting work, *The Last Man*, was prompted both by evenings round the piano in Shacklewell and by memories of Shelley and Byron, whose characters provided the basis for the novel's two heroes. Byron appears in *The Last Man* as Raymond, a flawed, charismatic leader of men, and Shelley as Adrian, a selfless visionary, not quite of this world, who inspires his companions with hope and courage. *The Last Man* was Mary's first sustained creative work since *Valperga*, and thus marked a further stage in her transition from dependent widow to professional writer, able to earn her own living.

As Mary allowed herself to be inspired by musical evenings in the Novello household, so too did other members of Hunt's old circle. The Novellos held several such evenings in 1823–4, which in many respects were like those organised by Hunt and Novello in 1817. One particularly elaborate evening, which doubled as a celebration of the absent Hunt's birthday, took place at Shacklewell on 19

October 1823. Novello selected and arranged music to be sung by
the assembled company – who included Jane Williams, Charles
Cowden Clarke, Henry Charles Robertson (an old friend of Hunt's
from the Surrey Gaol days) and Novello's brother, Frank. Mary was
accompanied by her brother William, who was rather overawed by
his elder sister's starry friends. Hunt's health was drunk, songs were
sung, and Mary had so much fun, she shame-facedly confessed to
Hunt, she 'gave way a little to the "giddy school girl."'[28] Mary Novello
filled the house with flowers in homage to Hunt's luxurious study-
bowers. 'Your name', she later told him, 'ran through the room like
a charm . . . an universal spirit of enjoyment broke loose; puns, good
and bad – badinage, raillery, compliments; but, above all, music was
triumphant.' But despite all this, it was a poignant evening as well.
'So closely allied', she concluded, 'are pleasure and pain, that several
times . . . many tears were shed by friendly eyes . . . I was haunted
so constantly with your image during the evening, that I was almost
tempted to believe in the theory, that what we earnestly and intently
desire becomes realized.'[29] The Shacklewell party was a celebration
of friendship, but it was also a reminder of how much had changed
since the formation of the bonds which had originally knitted Hunt's
friends together. Its avowed purpose was to celebrate Hunt, but it
was more nostalgic than celebratory. Despite the apparently familiar
combination of music, puns, flowers and laughter, the Novellos' party
was a fantasy, a bringing together of people who had little more than
memories to unite them.

————

In his exile in Italy, however, Hunt remained unaware that the
community he had created was dissolving. He was delighted by letters
describing the festivities held in his honour, and he made repeated
attempts to convince his friends to join him in Italy. 'Cannot you as
well as C[owden] C[larke] come with Novello?' he asked Mary Novello
in January 1824. 'Bring some of the children with you. Why cannot
you all come . . . Mrs Williams, and Mary S., and Miss Kent . . . and
every other possible and impossible body'.[30] From a distance, Hunt

failed to realise that the ties holding his friends together were stronger
in his imagination than they were in reality. The Novellos made Mary
and Jane Williams welcome on their return to England, and they were
consistently kind and hospitable to Bess, but all led independent lives
in different parts of London and none of them had the means for the
kind of massed holiday proposed by Hunt.

Hunt's suggestions, however, were borne out of loneliness of the
kind he had never known before and which, at the beginning of 1824,
showed no signs of abating. The bleak farmhouse at Maiano outside
Florence in which he established his family had panoramic views of
rolling Italian countryside, and, like Casa Negroto in Genoa, was cheap
to rent. This was just as well, since inside it was shabbily furnished,
uncomfortable and – again like Casa Negroto – freezing cold in winter.
Hunt divided his time between his study, where he hung a portrait
of Keats and lined the walls with books sent out by Bess, and the
subscription libraries in Florence, where he read English periodicals
and made the acquaintance of a small group of sympathetic expatriates.
Chief among these was Charles Brown, who had moved from Pisa to
Florence with his son, Carlino. Brown was a loyal friend to the Hunts,
advising Marianne on the details of household economy, and providing
companionship and moral support to Hunt.

Such support was highly necessary, as the Hunts' residence at Maiano
was disrupted by a series of personal and professional crises. Marianne
had a miscarriage, and her relationship with Hunt suffered from the
financial strain they were both under. Previously, adversity brought
Marianne and Hunt closer together, but now it had the opposite effect.
Marianne would not join Hunt on his walks – the one part of his
day which consistently gave him pleasure. He wrote crossly to Bess
that her sister would be improved by exercise, and that her refusal to
take any was a character failing. Marianne was equally miserable and in
the autumn of 1823 had begun to spit blood again, which mistakenly
convinced both her and her doctors that she was consumptive. 'No
one seems to think I am long for this world', she told Mary. 'Indeed',
she continued dolefully, 'you have in all probability seen your friend
for the last time.'[31] The children continued to run wild and little John,

who was eleven in 1823, became so unhappy and badly behaved that Charles Brown, who was seriously worried for his welfare, took him off to Rome for the winter. Marianne felt guilty about sending the child away, and wrote apologetically to Mary of the treats he would enjoy in Rome. Hunt, in contrast, decided that his son was incapable of reform, and packed him off to stay with Brown with a sigh of relief.

Domestic problems were compounded by a serious argument with John Hunt about the ownership of *The Examiner*. The dispute was long and bitter, and it was a major blow to Hunt, since it threatened financial disaster and sparked the disintegration of the fraternal relationship which had underpinned the whole of his career. At John Hunt's suggestion, Leigh had withdrawn as co-proprietor of *The Examiner* in 1819. He did so in order to ensure the paper's survival after the government strengthened censorship and libel laws in the wake of Peterloo, and he continued to think of himself as a sleeping partner in the enterprise, still entitled to half *The Examiner*'s profits.

John Hunt saw things differently. His brother no longer bore the legal burden of proprietorship, and John viewed his decision to go to Italy at a time when the newspaper was in trouble and John himself was serving a prison sentence as an abandonment of his editorial responsibilities. After John's release from Coldbath Fields increasingly tense letters flew back and forth between the brothers until John, galled by Leigh's tone, informed him that he had no claim on *The Examiner*, and would in future be paid no more than the standard piece-rate of two guineas per article for his contributions. John also offered his younger brother an annuity of £100 a year in recognition of his years of service at the paper. He was not, however, inclined to be more generous. Over the years Leigh had borrowed vast amounts of money from him – by some accounts, as much as £18,000. (This was far more, for example, than Shelley, on an allowance of £1,000 per annum, had received from his father.) Given John's imprisonment and the scale of Leigh's debts, the fact that the relationship faltered is perhaps less surprising than the fact that John supported his brother for so long.

For Leigh, however, the dispute was financially calamitous and a devastating personal betrayal. He took advice from Charles Brown, who made a detailed study of the various accounts of *The Examiner*'s history and ownership. John, who was also distressed to find himself at odds with the sibling with whom he had worked for many years, suggested that they submit their dispute to a binding arbitration, to be conducted by their friends. Prompted by Mary, Novello agreed to act as an arbitrator, and one of his first actions was to convince Leigh to accept the annuity of £100 a year on a temporary basis, in order to allow him to feed his family. But with such limited resources available, it was impossible for the Hunts to come home, even though they had no way of supporting themselves in Italy. It appeared that they were doomed to perpetual exile, separated for ever from their friends and family by Hunt's inability to earn money.

In the spring of 1825, however, John Hunt did a remarkably selfless thing, when, in spite of the ongoing dispute, he persuaded Henry Colburn, a sympathetic fellow publisher and periodical proprietor, to print articles by Leigh in the *New Monthly Magazine*. As a result of these articles, Colburn, who had watched with interest as the reading public devoured rapidly produced memoirs of Byron, wrote to Hunt offering him an advance of £200 for his account of the poet. Even as the quarrel about *The Examiner* descended into open rancour, John's instinctive kindness and his sense of familial responsibility would not permit him to abandon the careless, talented younger brother whose career he had nurtured and whose character he had tried to reform. Leigh was ecstatic at the thought of an advance that would allow him to end his Italian exile. 'This is excellent!' he told Novello joyfully. 'I shall, then, see you all shortly! I shall drink tea in the garden! . . . I shall have dear Wilful* shaking her head, but not her heart at me, and giving infinite little laughs!' Colburn, he concluded, was 'the most *engaging* of publishers.'³² He never made the connection between Colburn's offer and his brother's influence.

The Hunts left Italy in September, and travelled back overland across Europe. They were sorry to leave Charles Brown, who organised the packing up and sending on of the many objects they left behind, but

---

* 'Wilful' was the nickname Hunt bestowed on strong-minded Mary Novello.

they had few other causes for regret. Although the journey was difficult, and the children became tetchy and cross after long hours cooped up in a carriage, Hunt wrote a series of happy letters to Bess charting their passage across Italy, Switzerland and France. Bess's brother Tom Kent had sent Hunt a pair of spectacles, causing him to 'profanely bless the Author of my eyesight'. 'Through his means', he told Bess, 'I had the pleasure of discerning the remotest beauties of the Alps, and of being frightened with the divers beautiful precipices in Savoy.'[33] Even being jolted along bad French roads and the fact that they had no home to go to in England could not diminish Hunt's delight.

They finally arrived back in London a month after their departure from Florence, and had a series of ecstatic reunions with Bess, the Novellos, Mary and the Lambs. Despite the disasters that had befallen him, Hunt still retained his belief in the essential power of friendship. Finding himself among his friends once more only served to confirm that sociability was not merely an intellectual conceit, but an article of faith.

But while Hunt's faith had not faltered during the years of his Italian exile, the same was not true for his friends. He arrived home expecting to find his network unaltered, and its members ready to resume their positions as satellites circling his sun. Instead he found them scattered and too busy with their own lives to do much more than welcome him home. Charles and Mary Lamb were preoccupied with worries about Mary's health, which was disrupted by severe periods of insanity throughout the 1820s. Hazlitt, who had recently remarried, was travelling abroad with his new wife for much of 1825, and Hogg was in Italy, indulging in reminiscences of Shelley with Mrs Mason and Teresa Guiccioli. Haydon had long since ceased to consider Hunt his friend and Charles Brown, Horace Smith and Joseph Severn remained dispersed throughout Europe. Bess was busy with her own work and with her correspondence with John Clare, and Mary, like the Novellos, had moved out of London and was living in Kentish Town near Jane Williams.[34] She was too poor to travel into town for frequent social calls and there was in any case a renewed *froideur* between her and Hunt, which stemmed from a dispute about a profile of Shelley Hunt planned to publish in the *Westminster Review*. Mary and Peacock acted in concert to prevent the profile from appearing, largely because it was inaccurate about Harriet and indiscreet about Claire. Hunt, however, was convinced that they had interfered in order to keep Shelley for themselves, and to prevent him from telling the world of the crucial role he had played in Shelley's life.

Hunt's homecoming was thus, in many ways, disappointing. The network which sustained his imagination during his absence turned out now to be a chimera. As far as Hunt's friends were concerned this was a natural progression, in which the demands of work and family took precedence over youthful ideals of communal living. They recognised that their intense, claustrophobic, clubbable circle of the 1810s belonged to a different era. Its public and private significance had faded as British politics entered the calmer waters of the 1820s and their individual responsibilities towards parents, husbands, wives and children increased. Hunt, in contrast, would cling to an ideal of sociability even when it no longer bore any resemblance to the reality of his life. Indeed, his vision of a community of gregarious spirits marching together against oppression and corruption had, if anything, become more strident in the decade since he had gone to prison a martyr for the causes of free speech and reform. This much was evident from a letter written in March 1825, when his Italian exile seemed never-ending. The letter's recipient was a young Shelley devotee called John Claris:

> What is wanted, to secure victory, is a regular supply of unchanging and strait-forward spirits, inflexible alike either to misfortune or worldly interest; and as long as the life in me will hold me up, I, for my part, am determined to be one. We ought to look upon ourselves as soldiers, and make it a point of honour to do for the greatest of all causes what any decent gentleman can do for the honour of his regiment. We will love deeply; we will not refuse any lighter solace of sociality, that comes; we will have our sprightly songs, as well as our war-songs & our marches; but for the honour of our *profession*, – of our intellectual and moral soldiership, – & above all, for the good of the world, & the deliverances we are to effect for it, let us never give in.[35]

The imagery of this letter suggested that the reverses suffered by Hunt's company of campaigners – the deaths of Keats and Shelley, betrayal by Byron and Haydon, the skirmishes with *Blackwood's* – could not dim their determination to unite in friendship to reform the world. What Hunt did not know when he wrote this letter was that his company had disbanded in his absence. The battles over sociability that would take place after 1825 would not be fought between Hunt's circle and the rest of the world, but between the members of that circle. At stake were competing visions of a shared past.

The Past

In 1836, eleven years after the Hunts returned to England, Charles Brown gave a lecture at the Plymouth Literary Institution. His subject was the 'Life of Keats', and he approached the evening with a certain amount of trepidation. 'Many a resolution and many an attempt have I made to write a life of our Keats, but the pain as often made me defer it', he told Hunt, a week before the lecture. 'Still', he continued, 'I felt it a duty . . . so, to-morrow week, in the evening, from seven to ten o'Clock, you may imagine me reading my paper to about a hundred gentlemen, explaining any question I may be asked, or discussing his merits as a poet, or reading his posthumous poems.'[1]

Brown made several attempts to write about Keats in the years following the poet's death. Indeed his 1836 lecture stemmed from a memoir begun in 1830, which he worked and reworked in the intervening years. Although he never managed to produce a full-scale biography of his friend, he did make repeated efforts to have his lecture published, in the hope that it would stand as a permanent record of the Keats he had known. But he met with little success, and in 1841 he emigrated to New Zealand with his son Carlino, leaving the unpublished manuscript of the lecture behind. He died a year later, and was buried in the settlement of New Plymouth, on New Zealand's North Island. In 1921, his descendants organised a headstone for his grave. The inscription they chose was one of which Brown would have approved. It read as follows: 'Charles Armitage Brown. The Friend of

Keats.' Brown knew that posterity would view his relationship with
Keats as his greatest achievement, and he understood that his own
history had been shaped by his friendships with famous men. On 27
December 1836, in the dimly lit rooms of the Plymouth Institution,
he acknowledged that he would always stand in Keats's shadow. 'His
fame', he told his audience, 'is part of my life.'[2]

In the years following the deaths of Keats, Shelley and Byron, their
old circle discovered the accuracy of this statement, as individual lives
were shaped by other people's fame. Some, such as Haydon and Hogg,
found this difficult, while others – chiefly Mary and Hunt – came to
realise that the stature of their friends offered them the chance to reshape
their own lives according to a particular set of ideals, and that they
could use the past to reinvent themselves. What they failed to realise
was that, in the process, the memories of friends would be transformed
from sources of consolation into sources of conflict, and that separate
versions of a shared history would test the allegiances of the remaining
members of Keats's 'web . . . of mingled yarn' to the limit.

———

Hunt fired the opening salvo in the battle for ownership of the past
in 1828 when he published the memoir of Byron commissioned by
Colburn in 1825. *Lord Byron and Some of His Contemporaries* was
Hunt's first serious attempt at autobiography, and in it he placed
himself at the centre of a vividly realised intellectual world. Its cast of
characters were united by their friendship with him, and he presented
himself as the axis around which the great figures of the Romantic era
revolved. It contained a detailed narrative of the Surrey Gaol years and
the journey to Italy, as well as pen-portraits of individual members of
his circle: Horace Smith, Charles Lamb, Keats and Shelley. In these
pen-portraits the group was recreated in print once more, just as it had
been over the years in *The Examiner*, *Foliage* and *The Liberal*.

Hunt was full of praise for his friends, highlighting Shelley's strong
sense of natural justice and Keats's prodigious talent. Nevertheless,
his appropriation of the legacies of the dead in support of his version
of the past was not well received by his contemporaries. Keats's

supporters were enraged that *their* poet was once again being tainted by association with Leigh Hunt. 'I should be extremely sorry', wrote Keats's brother George, 'that poor John's name should go down to posterity associated with the littleness of L. H., an association of which he was so impatient in his Lifetime.'[3] Byron's friends were equally horrified by Hunt's portrait of their poet, and they had good reason to feel affronted, since Hunt presented Byron as the villain of *Lord Byron and Some of His Contemporaries*, accusing him of miserliness, gluttony, indolence and capriciousness. He criticised Byron's treatment of those in need ('the first time Lord Byron discovered I was in want, was the first time he treated me with disrespect'),[4] his relationship with Teresa Guiccioli ('there was no real love on either side'),[5] and his disloyalty: 'he would do the most humiliating things, insinuate the bitterest, both of me and my friends, and then affect to do all away with a soft word, protesting that nothing he ever said was meant to apply to myself.'[6] All this made Byron's friends justifiably angry, and even the more temperate literary reviewers felt that Hunt's character assassination of a dead man was distasteful. For those who disliked Hunt and admired Byron his book was the quintessence of Cockney vulgarity. John Gibson Lockhart summarised many of the reviews when he condemned *Lord Byron and Some of His Contemporaries* as 'the miserable book of a miserable man'.[7]

Hunt was appalled by the reaction to his book and he attempted to make amends to Byron when he came to publish his *Autobiography* almost a quarter of a century later. There he sought to excuse the uncharacteristic vitriol of his earlier work by describing the unhappy circumstances of its composition. It had been written, after all, when he was at his lowest ebb, destroyed by Shelley's unexpected demise and by Byron's unaccountable unfriendliness. 'I can say . . . that I was then a young man, and that I am now advanced in years. I can say, that I was agitated by grief and anger, and that I am now free from anger. I can say, that I was far more alive to other people's defects than to my own, and that I am now sufficiently sensible of my own to show to others the charity which I need myself.'[8] But these admissions came too late, and Hunt's reputation never recovered from the critical onslaught that followed the publication of *Lord Byron and Some of His Contemporaries*. The book destroyed Hunt's credibility, and undermined his claim to be the chief custodian of his friends' posthumous reputations. With its publication Hunt, once the figure around whom others revolved, who had done so much to foster friendships and to celebrate the work of his friends, was categorised as a literary parasite. Journals that once bemoaned his influence on Shelley, Keats and Byron were able to position him as an isolated figure of fun, who inspired disdain rather than respect.* As a result, a work designed to celebrate the idea of the group actually hastened its ideological disintegration.

———

Lord Byron and Some of His Contemporaries also had a negative effect on Hunt's relationship with Mary. Although she never officially disavowed Hunt's account of the past, she was convinced that it was thoroughly misguided, and she made repeated attempts to disentangle Shelley's legacy from Hunt's damaged reputation. With Hunt's vision of a shared past irrevocably tainted by his mean-spirited attack on Byron, Mary was able to tap into a developing public preoccupation with the figure of the creative genius – a preoccupation which stemmed in part from Romantic poetry and from the phenomenon of Byron's unprecedented celebrity – in order to recreate Shelley as the voice of Romantic isolation.

Mary developed this version of Shelley, as well as a similar portrait of Byron, in the novels she wrote in the 1830s, in which she drew on memories of both of them to describe characters who are separated from the world in which they live, isolated by the strength of their visions and their personality. *Lodore* and *Falkner* (published in 1835 and 1837 respectively) both centred on the figure of the Byronic hero – charismatic, embittered and lonely. In these novels Mary replaced Hunt's vision of sociable creativity with a depiction of greatness that removed its subjects to the realm of tortured, brilliant individualism.

---

* Hunt's final humiliation came in 1852, when his weaknesses were cruelly immortalised by Charles Dickens in the figure of *Bleak House*'s Harold Skimpole.

And in 1839, Mary enshrined Shelley's solitary genius once and for all, in her four volume *Poetical Works of Percy Bysshe Shelley*.

Poetical Works was the first authorised edition of Shelley's work to appear since *Posthumous Poems* in 1824, and it represented the culmination of Mary's efforts to transform her husband's reputation. In the period between the publication of the two editions, pirated texts of Shelley's work began to appear in London and Paris and his reputation rose steadily. His poetry was discovered by idealistic young poets like Robert Browning and Alfred Tennyson, and the taint of political radicalism was gradually erased from his public image.* By the late 1830s even Sir Timothy Shelley (on whom Mary and her son depended financially) was forced to acknowledge the depth of public interest in his son's work, and grudgingly allowed Mary to bring out a new edition of his poetry. Hunt wrote to offer a biographical Preface for the edition but Mary was determined not to let him interfere. 'The edition', she replied, 'will be mine'.⁹

The Shelley of the *Poetical Works* was both a genius and a model man, but he was entirely disassociated from the world in which he lived. In a long series of biographical notes Mary idealised him as a uniquely creative individual, whose poetry was the product of 'genuine and unforced inspiration' of the kind envisaged by Wordsworth in the Preface to *Lyrical Ballads*. Mary transformed Shelley into the poet of *Alastor*, and endowed him with an intensity of perception which allowed him to understand the world anew and distanced him from its petty concerns. She described him taking refuge from society by delivering 'up his soul to poetry' and sheltering 'from the influence of human sympathies, in the wildest regions of his fancy'.¹⁰ This set the tone for a volume in which Shelley was far removed from the realm of his friends. 'Shelley never liked society in numbers', Mary wrote, in her note on the poems of 1818. 'But neither did he like loneliness, and

---

* Even as Shelley's reputation became more respectable, he still continued to attract the admiration of working-class writers and radicals. Pirated editions of *Queen Mab* circulated in London from the 1820s onwards, and the poem eventually became a key text of the Chartist movement. But this underground, subversive Shelley never attained the cultural significance of his ethereal, sentimental counterpart.

usually when alone sheltered himself against memory and reflection, in a book'.[11] As the literary critic Susan Wolfson has noted, the effect of Mary's argument was to divest Shelley 'of engagement with the political and historical world within which he wrote.'[12] As Mary stripped Shelley of his political philosophy, she also wrote his social and intellectual context out of his life story. *Poetical Works* presented Shelley afresh for a new age, and transformed him from radical thinker into the 'blithe spirit' – an image from his much anthologised 'Ode to a Skylark' – so beloved by the Victorians.

─────────

This was the vision of Shelley which would acquire cultural significance in the second half of the nineteenth century. It was also a vision which acquired a new champion in 1849 when Mary's son, Sir Percy Florence Shelley (he inherited the title directly from his grandfather) married Jane Gibson St John, a widow of independent means. The marriage of Percy and Jane brought Mary much happiness, even though she was seriously ill by the time of their wedding. Jane Shelley was devoted to her mother-in-law, and she was passionately interested in her husband's Romantic parentage. She was in fact far more engaged with the Shelley family's literary legacy than Percy, who, slightly to Mary's disappointment, did not inherit the intellect of his brilliant parents and Godwin grandparents. Instead he happily filled his days with the management of his estates, boating and amateur theatricals, slotting easily into the role of Victorian country gentleman. But he was a loyal and attentive son, and he amply repaid his mother's lifelong devotion.

Mary died of a brain tumour in 1851 at the age of fifty-three. Given the significance of her literary achievements, public reaction to her death was muted – just as it had been when Keats and Shelley died thirty years earlier. Sir Percy, however, was devastated by her early demise, and he willingly agreed to his energetic wife's plans to canonise his parents for posterity. Jane Shelley transformed the reputations of Shelley and Mary through the sheer force of her personality. She had admired *Frankenstein* and Shelley's poetry long before she met Percy, and after her marriage she came to view Mary as the embodiment of maligned virtue. After Mary died she appointed herself chief keeper of the Shelley flame, and created a shrine to her parents-in-law at Boscombe Manor, the house outside Bournemouth Percy bought shortly before Mary's death. Jane even arranged to have the bodies of William Godwin and Mary Wollstonecraft disinterred from the graveyard at St Pancras and reburied with Mary's in the churchyard at Boscombe. This episode demonstrated both Jane's forcefulness and her ruthlessness, since she left the body of the second Mrs Godwin to moulder alone at St Pancras. In addition, when the vicar of Boscombe refused to accept the bodies of Godwin and Wollstonecraft for burial, on the grounds of their dubious religious and political opinions, she waited with their coffins outside the churchyard until he relented. Above all, Jane collected Shelley papers. She jealously guarded Mary's letters from the eyes of prying individuals, and, with her husband's support, systematically added to the documents in the Boscombe collection by buying Shelley manuscripts whenever they were advertised for sale. She commissioned hagiographic biographies and ornate statues,* and dealt ruthlessly with anyone who threatened to disrupt her vision of the past.

As Jane presented her sentimental re-creation of Shelley to the world as historical fact, his contemporaries underwent a similar transformation. Keats was sanctified as 'the youthful poet', first by his biographer Lord Houghton and then by successive generations of admirers, few of whom had any interest in his connection with Leigh Hunt. Byron was also removed far from Hunt's orbit of influence, first by his friends and then by readers who wanted to remember him as a heroic freedom fighter, who died battling for the glory of Greece.

Hunt died eight years after Mary, and two years after his wife Marianne, whose final years were blighted by a descent into alcoholism. Those of his friends who outlived him had little investment in promoting his vision of a shared history. Like Claire, Bess Kent eventually became a governess, and died in 1861, worn down by poverty and ill health. She

* Among other memorials, Jane commissioned the statue of Shelley by Edward Onslow Ford which now sits in be-domed glory at University College, Oxford. It depicts the body of the drowned Shelley washed ashore at Viareggio. Ford's Shelley, like Louis Fournier's before him, appears remarkably unscathed by a week under water.

wrote a good deal about the past in her old age, but all in the form of letters to the Royal Literary Fund, who made her a series of hardship grants in recognition of the significance of her botanical works. Hogg died a year later, in 1862, having disgraced himself in the eyes of Hunt and Sir Percy by publishing an inaccurate, self-serving account of Shelley's time at Oxford, in which he shamelessly manipulated documents from the Shelley family archive. Peacock did make various attempts to set the record straight about Shelley's life, but his main concern was to rescue Harriet from any suggestion that she had behaved improperly. He died in 1866, one of the last witnesses to the early days of Shelley and Mary's romance. Haydon continued to praise Keats and attack Hunt and Shelley in his private diary until the end of his life, but he never published an account of his time among poets. On 22 June 1846 he purchased a pistol and a razor, locked himself in his studio, cut his throat and shot himself, having never achieved the public recognition he believed he deserved.

By the end of the 1860s, almost all of the individuals who had once gathered around Shelley and Hunt were dead, and the battles over how a shared history should be narrated subsided. Only two custodians of the past remained, and they had different ideas about the way in which their life stories should be written. The first was Edward Trelawny, who outlived all the friends of his youth. The second was Claire Clairmont. Unlike other members of the circle, Claire never published a memoir, but she did write about her life and, in recent years, thanks to the efforts of skilled editors and archivists, her account of the experience of living according to a set of philosophical principles has come to light. This is important because Claire idealised neither the individual nor the group, but instead presented a more complicated version of a shared history; and because when one looks afresh at the story of the network's turbulent communal existence, Claire's history takes on a particular significance.

After all, without Claire, the story of the intertwined lives of Shelley, Hunt and Byron would have been very different. It was because of Claire that Shelley and Byron met on the shores of Lake Geneva, and because of Claire's daughter that Shelley travelled in 1818 to Italy where he wrote the great poems of his maturity. Shelley's friendship with Byron had an immeasurable impact on both poets, on the history of Romantic poetry, and on the lives of those around them, Hunt's above all. Shelley's summer with Byron propelled him towards Hunt on his return to England in 1816, and towards a meeting which was certainly the most important of Hunt's life.

Claire had a profound effect on Mary's life too. Their upbringing, their closeness in age and their complex feelings for Shelley bound them together from the moment that Claire stepped into the Dover-bound post-chaise in 1814. Mary's marriage was shaped by Claire, and her character was altered by the difficulties of life with her stepsister. Claire's own life was also shaped by her relationship with Mary, who was the catalyst for a series of events – such as the expulsion from Skinner Street and exile in Lynmouth – which irrevocably altered Claire's history. Mary also provided Claire with an unusual example of female freedom. Claire's relationship with Byron was partly the result of Shelley's philosophy of free love, but it was also one element of a wider attempt on her part to establish her physical, emotional and intellectual independence. Claire, however, suffered the consequences of free love more acutely than any one else in the group. It is therefore intriguing to discover what she thought about it when, in her old age, she turned her attention once more to the events of her youth.

———

Claire's life after her departure from Russia in 1826 was unremittingly difficult. She worked as a governess for two decades, but she was never reconciled to her profession. She was finally able to stop working in 1844, when Sir Timothy Shelley died and she received a legacy of £12,000 under the terms of the will Shelley made in Geneva in 1816. She converted to Catholicism and spent her final years in Florence, the city in which she had lived as a young woman, cared for by her brother Charles's daughter Pauline. Although she was glad to be abroad, securely protected from the burgeoning English Shelley/ Byron industry, she nevertheless scoured books and articles about both poets for inaccuracies and, as she watched other people tell the story of which she had been a part, became determined to leave her own version of that story for posterity. She wrote long letters to Trelawny, in which she rehearsed the key events of her life and made a series of accusations against Byron. The wildest of these was that Allegra had not died in 1822 but that Byron, in the spirit of absolute villainy, decided to convince Claire of her demise by sending a goat in a child's coffin to England. Trelawny robustly contradicted this and other similarly far-fetched suggestions, but he was alive to the narrative power of her letters, and encouraged her to record her memories systematically. 'There is time for you to do it but not time to shilly shally', he told her in 1875, when Claire was seventy-six. 'Get some one to write and dictate – hitherto you have [done] nothing but prate: string the divers letters together by a simple narration – the unwilling have many excuses – they are always composed of lies!!!'[13]

Claire did not take Trelawny's advice, but she did leave behind strands of the memoir she never wrote. In sections of letters drafted and redrafted for Trelawny she presented herself as a victim, as a gentle creature who succumbed to Shelley's dominant personality, and as the innocent dupe of an unscrupulous Byron. And in conversations which took place when she was in her seventies she was markedly less coy about her past. We know this because one of her interlocutors, a retired Massachusetts sea captain named Edward Silsbee, wrote down her stories in a series of notebooks, which were discovered by the Romantic scholar Marion Kingston Stocking in 1991. Silsbee, an ardent Shelley devotee, was fascinated by Claire and made repeated efforts to buy her papers. When he failed to do so it was rumoured in Florence that the price demanded – marriage to Claire's niece Pauline – entailed too much of a sacrifice. Henry James heard this story a decade after Claire's death and used it as the basis for *The Aspern Papers*. Silsbee's notebooks capture Claire's voice in a remarkably vivid way, and they also give us an insight into her feelings. 'Shelley was <u>devoted in manner</u> to women like myself when young', she told him in one of her more confessional moments. 'He was moreover so handsome and attentive and attractive and very dangerous'. 'She loved him', Silsbee's note continued, 'and thus she has often described him.'[14]

If the Silsbee notebooks show something of the emotional reality of living one's life in accordance with Shelley's philosophy of free love, then a recently discovered additional strand of Claire's unwritten memoir reveals her anger about the experiments in living in which she participated. In a manuscript fragment buried amongst other papers, Claire did make one attempt at autobiography. This fragment lay undisturbed for many years, hidden in a cache of privately owned letters. In 1998 it was purchased by the Pforzheimer Collection of Shelley and his Circle, alongside the collection of manuscript letters in which it was filed. It is now held at the New York Public Library, and is published here for the first time. 'Reader of these pages', the fragment began, 'before you pursue them it is well that you should know they are written by a person, who knows nothing of composition much less of the art of Authorship.' 'I have to relate', Claire continued, 'my recollections of two great Poets, and . . . on their account I hope this recital will awaken many profound reflections.'

The text which followed this modest beginning was extremely surprising. It presented a viscerally angry perspective on the philosophy of Claire's contemporaries, and contradicted much of the surviving historical record. Nothing else quite like it survives, although it is reminiscent of the sixteen year old Claire sitting on a beach in Lynmouth, burning with resentment at the way she had been treated. In the fragment Claire demolished the reputations of both Shelley and Byron, and attacked both their behaviour and their principles:

> If I commit this sad tale to paper and finally to the public, it is with the intention of demonstrating from actual facts, what evil passion free love assured, what tenderness it dissolves; how it abused affections that should be the solace and balm of life, into a destroying scourge what . . . bitter tears [it] caused to flow, and what victims it immolated [the reader] will behold how the worshippers of free love not only preyed upon one another, but preyed equally upon their own individual selves turning their existence into a perfect hell.

Having set out the parameters of her attack, Claire turned her attention
to the effect of free love on the characters of Shelley and Byron:

> Such will be the picture my recollections of two great poets S & B –
> will present; they were the fondest and most obstinate advocates and
> partisans and followers of free love . . . it appears to me that in the
> eternal interest of religion and morality of truth and right require a plain
> straightforward description of their opinions and conduct.
>
> Under the influence of the doctrine and belief of free love I saw the
> two first poets of England . . . become monsters of lying, meanness
> cruelty and treachery – under the influence of free love Lord B became
> a human tyger slaking his thirst for inflicting pain upon defenceless
> women who under the influence of free love . . . loved him.

The savagery of Claire's language in these passages was not replicated
anywhere else in her papers. Free love, in her account, prompts
'evil passion', 'abuses' affections and is a 'destroying scourge' which
'immolates' its victims and causes 'bitter tears' to flow. It transforms
Shelley and Byron into 'monsters of lying, meanness cruelty and
treachery'. One might expect Claire to write about Byron in this
manner, but despite her late conversion to Catholicism, her attack on
Shelley is more unexpected. And it was in fact Shelley – according
to Silsbee, the love of Claire's life – who was the main target of her
offensive. In the second part of the fragment, Claire parodied the
marriage note in *Queen Mab* in order to demonstrate the hollow falsity
of Shelley's philosophy:

> The opponents of the institution of Marriage assert that it is a practical
> code of misery and servitude – that it is a despotism which inculcates
> falsehood and meanness and turns the body and mind of its followers
> into hideous wrecks of humanity . . . These pages are a record of the
> effects and workings of the free love system such as the writer of these
> pages beheld with her own eyes – this is no hearsay record – it is derived
> from the life of persons who had devoted themselves to the worship of
> free love and from their own account the reader must inevitably draw the

following conclusions that the selfishness, the treachery & meanness, & the cruelty practised by the opponents of marriage and the misery these same opponents induced . . . exceeded any amount of the same results produced by marriage.[15]

Here, Claire turned Shelley's own words against him, lifting phrases such as 'practical code of misery and servitude' directly from *Queen Mab*, along with a linguistic register that described marriage in terms of bigotry, disease and selfishness. Nowhere else did Claire explicitly accuse Shelley of cruelty, or reveal so minutely the dark underside of Romantic living.

When the disparate strands of Claire's unwritten memoir are assembled, a complicated picture of the group's communal history emerges. Finally it was Claire, rather than Mary or Hunt, who stood back to explore the practical, emotional and intellectual consequences of living as part of a politically and philosophically radical network. It was also Claire who produced a version of history that celebrated neither a particular individual nor a particular coterie. Instead, she presented posterity with an account of lived experience. This account was incomplete and, at times, contradictory, but it attempted to describe the reality underlying the idealism of her youth. And it presented a bleak indictment of that idealism. Claire's case appears to show that the visions of her Romantic contemporaries were illusory, naïve and damaging.

There is, however, a more nuanced way to read Claire's memoirs. Her papers suggest that, although her relationships with Shelley and Byron caused her much suffering, her character was shaped and strengthened by the relationships of her youth. The Claire who has fascinated generations of writers and biographers – from Peacock's celebration of her in *Nightmare Abbey*, or *The Aspern Papers*, to Richard Holmes's admission that he fell 'in love with Claire Clairmont'[16] – developed her extraordinary resilience and independence of spirit during her years with Shelley, Mary, Hunt and Byron. She was the great Romantic survivor, who continued to re-examine and reinterpret her story until the end of her life.

————

Claire died in 1879, almost sixty years after Shelley drowned in the sea off Viareggio. With her passing, only one other contemporary chronicler of the group remained. This was Trelawny. Trelawny only ever played a peripheral part in the stories of his famous friends, but this was not how he wished to be remembered. In 1881, at the age of eighty-eight, he accordingly orchestrated one final dramatic tableau, in which he would figure for ever as Shelley's chief companion. He left a complicated series of instructions about his burial wishes which, after his death on 13 August, were carried out to the letter. His body was shipped to Germany for cremation, and his ashes were taken on to Rome by Emma Taylor, the last in his long line of mistresses. Emma arranged for his ashes to be buried next to Shelley's in the Protestant Cemetery, in the plot he had purchased in 1823.

There the remains of Trelawny still lie, along with those of Shelley, Keats, and Joseph Severn. Keats's gravestone, designed by Severn and Charles Brown, is defiant both in its castigation of his enemies and in its claim, dictated by him, for the transience and the permanence of his reputation. 'This Grave contains all that was Mortal of a YOUNG ENGLISH POET, Who on his Death Bed, in the Bitterness of his Heart at the Malicious Power of his Enemies, Desired these Words to be engraven on his Tomb Stone. Here lies One Whose Name was writ in Water'. Shelley's epitaph, chosen by Trelawny, is more enigmatic, but it makes an equally bold claim for immortality, in the form of a quotation from *The Tempest*: 'Nothing of him that doth fade/ But doth suffer a sea-change/ Into something rich and strange'.

The graves of Severn and Trelawny themselves could not hold more of a contrast, either with their poet-companions or with each other. Severn's headstone acknowledges his talent with a short inscription and an engraving of an artist's palette, but celebrates him primarily as the 'Devoted friend and death-bed companion of John Keats'. Trelawny's – in accordance with his own instructions – is inscribed with four lines of Shelley's poetry:

These are two friends whose lives were undivided.
So let their memory be now they have glided
Under the grave: let not their bones be parted
For their two hearts in life were single-hearted.[17]

If Severn's epitaph symbolises loyalty and self-effacement, then Trelawny's represents the complicated undertow of friendship with the famous. No one, not even Trelawny himself, could claim that Shelley's lines were an accurate description of their relationship, which lasted for less than a year. But by 1881, to be a friend of Shelley was a significant claim to fame, and Trelawny died entirely convinced by his own fantasy of friendship.

Although Trelawny's gravestone celebrates a friendship which was always, at one level, inauthentic and mythical, the qualities embedded in the Protestant Cemetery remain the qualities which make the stories of the Shelleys, the Hunts and their friends important. The graves represent an ideal of intertwined lives and testify to the significance of a shared history. That history shaped all the figures who coalesced around Shelley and Hunt, and had an inestimable impact on their writing. Some of the greatest works in the English canon – *Frankenstein*, *Alastor*, 'Julian and Maddalo', *Childe Harold's Pilgrimage* – owed their genesis and their development to conversation and sociability. The lives of Shelley, Mary, Claire, Hunt, Bess, Keats, Byron and many others were transformed as their worlds intersected, and as, in complex and ever-shifting configurations, they talked to each other, fought with each other, hated each other, and fell in love. Their stories demonstrate that friendship is not always easy: that relationships with other people can simultaneously be a source of great strength and unknowable pain. But they also show that friendship can be the making of the man. This is an idea which lies at the heart of a story about a web of exceptional men and women, who were made by their relationships with one another.

Notes

Preface

1 William Shakespeare, *All's Well that Ends Well*, IV.iii.71–2.
2 Jeffrey Cox, *Poetry and Politics in the Cockney School*, p.6.
3 In academic circles this myth has been exploded in the work of such pioneering critics as Marilyn Butler (in *Romantics, Rebels and Reactionaries*) and Jack Stillinger (in *Multiple Authorship and the Myth of Solitary Genius*). Other significant recent academic studies of the creative Romantic group include Jeffrey Cox's *Poetry and Politics in the Cockney School* and *Romantic Sociability*, a collection of essays edited by Gillian Russell and Clara Tuite.
4 Wordsworth, Preface to *Lyrical Ballads* (1802), in William Wordsworth, *The Major Works*, p.611.
5 Percy Shelley, 'A Defence of Poetry', in *Poetry and Prose*, p.531.
6 John Milton, *Paradise Lost*, I, 13.
7 The history of biography is explored in detail by Hermione Lee in *Biography: A Very Short Introduction*.
8 John Worthen, *The Gang: Coleridge, the Hutchinsons and the Wordsworths in 1802*, p.6.

Chapter One: Husbands

1 *The Examiner*, 267 (07/02/1813), 83.
2 *Lord Byron and Some of His Contemporaries*, p.429.
3 *Lord Byron and Some of His Contemporaries*, p.422.
4 *Lord Byron and Some of His Contemporaries*, p.430.
5 *Lord Byron and Some of His Contemporaries*, p.424.

6   Academic interest in Hunt has, however, reawakened in recent years, and in 2005 he was the subject of a fine biography by Nicholas Roe: *Fiery Heart: The First Life of Leigh Hunt.*

7   *The Examiner*, 164 (17/02/1811), 104.

8   *The Examiner*, 221 (22/03/1812), 179.

9   *The Diary of Benjamin Robert Haydon*, ed. Willard Bissell Pope, I, 288.

10 Lord Byron to Thomas Moore, 19/05/1813. *Byron's Letters and Journals*, ed. Leslie Marchand, III, 49.

11 Thomas Moore, *Letters and Journals of Lord Byron*, I, 13.

12 Leigh Hunt to Marianne Hunt, 20/05/1813. *A Life in Letters*, ed. Eleanor Gates, p.40.

13 Lord Byron to Thomas Moore, 01/06/1818. *Byron's Letters and Journals*, VI, 45.

14 *Byron's Letters and Journals*, III, 228.

15 Nancy Hunter to Marianne Hunt, n.d. *My Leigh Hunt Library*, ed. Luther Brewer, p.101.

16 Nancy Hunter to Marianne Hunt, n.d. *My Leigh Hunt Library*, p.101.

17 *The Diary of Benjamin Robert Haydon*, II, 83.

18 Marianne Hunt to Leigh Hunt, 07/05/1813. *My Leigh Hunt Library*, p.65

19 Marianne Hunt to Leigh Hunt, 16/05/1813. *My Leigh Hunt Library*, p.69.

20 Leigh Hunt to Marianne Hunt, 18/05/1813. *My Leigh Hunt Library*, p.71.

21 *Lord Byron and Some of His Contemporaries*, p.426.

22 Percy Shelley to Thomas Hookham, 15/02/1813. *Letters of Percy Bysshe Shelley*, ed. Frederick Jones, I, 353.

23 Percy Shelley to Leigh Hunt, 02/03/1811. *PBS Letters*, I, 54–5.

24 Samuel Taylor Coleridge to Robert Southey, 24/12/1799. *The Collected Letters of Samuel Taylor Coleridge*, ed. Earl Leslie Griggs, I, 305.

25 See Kegan Paul, *William Godwin*, II, 214.

26 Charles Lamb to William Wordsworth, 29/01/1807. *The Letters of Charles and Mary Lamb*, ed. Edwin Marrs, II, 256.

27 William St Clair, *The Godwins and the Shelleys*, pp.353–4.

28 Percy Shelley to Thomas Hogg, 04/10/1814. *PBS Letters*, I, 402.

29 Godwin's Journal. Bodleian [Abinger] Dep. e. 196–277.

30 *The Journals of Mary Shelley*, ed. Paula Feldman and Diana Scott-Kilvert, I, 6.

31 Mary Shelley, *History of a Six Weeks Tour*, in *Travel Writing*, ed. Jeanne Moskal, p.21.

32 *The Journals of Mary Shelley*, I, 18.

33 Percy Shelley to Harriet Shelley. 13/08/1814. *PBS Letters*, I, 392.

34 *The Journals of Claire Clairmont*, ed. Marion Kingston Stocking, p.31.

35 *The Journals of Mary Shelley*, I, 23.

36 William Godwin, *Political Justice*, in *Political and Philosophical Writings*, ed. Mark Philip, IV, 338–9.

37 Percy Shelley to Harriet Shelley, 14/09/1814. *PBS Letters*, I, 394–5.

38 Percy Shelley to Harriet Shelley, 26/09/1814. *PBS Letters*, I, 397.

39 As told to Edward Silsbee. Silsbee Collection, Peabody Essex Museum. Box 7, file 2.

40 *The Journals of Mary Shelley*, I, 37.

41 *The Journals of Mary Shelley*, I, 35.

42 *The Journals of Claire Clairmont*, p.52.

43 Percy Shelley to Mary Shelley, 27/10/1814. *PBS Letters*, I, 413–4.

44 *The Journals of Claire Clairmont*, p.58.

45 *The Journals of Claire Clairmont*, p.58.

46 *British Lady's Magazine*, I (April 1815), in *The Romantics Reviewed: Part C*, ed. Donald Reiman, I, 235.

47 Henry Robertson, William Havell and Charles Ollier to Leigh Hunt, 22/01/1815. British Library. MS Add. 38108, ff 128–9.

48 *The Examiner*, 328 (10/10/14), 228.

49 Thomas Mitchell to Leigh Hunt, 23/09/1813. British Library. MS Add. 38108, ff. 83–4.

Chapter Two: Wives and Mistresses

1 *The Journals of Mary Shelley*, I, 56–7.

2 *The Journals of Claire Clairmont*, p.48.

3 Shelley, *Queen Mab* in *The Poems of Shelley*, ed. Geoffrey Matthews and Kelvin Everest, I, 370.

4 Percy Shelley to Thomas Hogg, 01/01/1815. *PBS Letters*, I, 423.

5 Mary Shelley to Thomas Hogg, 01/01/1815. *Letters of Mary Wollstonecraft Shelley*, ed. Betty T. Bennett, I, 6.

6 Mary Shelley to Thomas Hogg, 04/01/1815. *MWS Letters*, I, 7.

7 Mary Shelley to Thomas Hogg, 07/01/1815. *MWS Letters*, I, 8.

8 Mary Shelley to Thomas Hogg, 24/01/1815. *MWS Letters*, I, 9.

9 Silsbee Collection. Box 7, File 2. Quoted in Marion Kingston Stocking, ed., *The Clairmont Correspondence*, I, 11.

10 *The Journals of Mary Shelley*, I, 65.

11 *The Journals of Mary Shelley*, I, 68.

12 *The Journals of Mary Shelley*, I, 69.

13 Mary Shelley to Thomas Hogg, 25/04/1815 and 26/04/1815. *MWS Letters*, I, 13, 14.

14 Godwin's assumption that Shelley would continue to provide him with funds even while he was refused entry to his house was based on his doctrine of 'stewardship', summarised thus by William St Clair: 'If by the operation of an absurd economic system a teacher lacks the modest resources necessary to do his duty, then it becomes the duty of others to divert some of their surplus towards him' (*The Godwins and the Shelleys*, p.344). Godwin did not view Shelley's assistance as a favour, or as a symptom of the younger man's generosity, but as the proper fulfilment of his duty. Shelley initially accepted this argument, and, for the first few years of their

acquaintance, continued to fund Godwin even as he disputed his treatment of his daughters.

15   *The Journals of Mary Shelley*, I, 78.

16   *The Journals of Mary Shelley*, I, 79.

17   *The Examiner*, 371 (05/02/1815), 81.

18   All quotations from Keats's poetry are taken from John Keats, *Complete Poems*, ed. Jack Stillinger.

19   *The Diary of Benjamin Robert Haydon*, I, 451.

20   Leigh Hunt to Henry Brougham, 26/09/1815. *A Life in Letters*, pp.65–6.

21   Quoted in Malcolm Elwin, *Lord Byron's Wife*, p.250.

22   *Lord Byron's Wife*, p.250.

23   See Ethel Colburn Mayne, *The Life and Letters of Anna Isabella, Lady Noel Byron*, pp.159–61.

24   Ernest J. Lovell, ed., *Medwin's Conversations of Lord Byron*, p.36.

25   Lord Byron to Leigh Hunt, 15/10/1815. *Byron's Letters and Journals*, IV, 209.

26   Annabella Milbanke to Emily Milner, 23/09/1814. New York Public Library. MS Berg Collection.

27   Lord Byron to Thomas Moore, 02/02/1815. *Byron's Letters and Journals*, IV, 263.

28   See Mayne, *The Life and Letters of Lady Byron*, p.161.

29   Mayne, *Life and Letters of Lady Byron*, p.181.

30   British Library. MS Ashley 906.

31   Leigh Hunt to Lord Byron, 30/10/1815. Rowland E. Prothero, ed., *The Works of Lord Byron: Letters and Journals*, III, 418.

32   Leigh Hunt, *The Story of Rimini*, p.47.

33   Mary Shelley, ed., *Poetical Works of Percy Bysshe Shelley* (1839), I, 141.

34   Thomas Love Peacock, *Memoirs of Shelley*, p.59.

35   *Memoirs of Shelley*, p.57.

36   The literary critic Marilyn Butler, whose studies of both Peacock and Shelley revolutionised critical approaches to their work, has written that 'it was the live debate with Shelley that brought home to Peacock the literary potential of disputation. Each was just what the other had so far lacked: a really intelligent companion, another writer of the same generation, someone to sympathise and argue with.' See Marilyn Butler, *Peacock Displayed: A Satirist in his Context*, pp.37–8.

37   Thomas Love Peacock, *The Genius of the Thames*, p.29.

38   Charles Clairmont to Claire Clairmont, 13–20/09/1815. *The Clairmont Correspondence*, I, 14–15.

39   Charles Clairmont to Claire Clairmont, 13/20/09/1815. *The Clairmont Correspondence*, I, 15.

40   Percy Shelley, *Poetry and Prose*, ed. Donald Reiman and Neil Fraistat. Unless otherwise stated, all quotations from Shelley's poetry are taken from this edition.

41   *The Journals of Mary Shelley*, I, 25.

Chapter Three: Sisters

1   Claire Clairmont to Fanny Imlay, 28/05/1815. *The Clairmont Correspondence*, I, 9.

2   Claire Clairmont to Mary Shelley, 02/06/1835. *The Clairmont Correspondence*, II, 319.

3   *The Story of Rimini*, pp.77–8.

4   William Hazlitt to Leigh Hunt, 15/02/1816. *The Letters of William Hazlitt*, ed. Herschel Sykes, p.153.

5   Benjamin Haydon to Leigh Hunt, 21/02/1816. British Library. MS Add. 37219, ff. 155–6.

6   Charles Lamb to Leigh Hunt, 24/02/1816. Luther Brewer Leigh Hunt Collection, University of Iowa Libraries. MSLL21h.no.3.

7   *British Lady's Magazine* (April 1816) and *Eclectic Review* (April 1816) in *The Romantics Reviewed, Part C*, I, 240–2 and 324.

8   Charles Cowden Clarke, *An Address to that Quarterly Reviewer who touched upon Mr Leigh Hunt's* Story of Rimini. For Clarke's authorship of the pamphlet see John Barnard, 'Leigh Hunt and Charles Cowden Clarke, 1812–1818'.

9   *Blackwood's Edinburgh Magazine* (July 1818) in *The Romantics Reviewed*, Part C, I, 87.

10 *The Examiner*, 548 (28/06/1818), 411.

11 At some point Bess appears also to have published a book of stories for children, entitled *New Tales for Young Readers*. This work, like many children's books of the period, does not appear in library catalogues, and is unlikely to have survived. Bess told the Royal Literary Fund she thought her first work was published by the firm of 'Broadway and Kirby' in 1818, although she was not entirely sure, and in 1822 *The Monthly Review* published a brief notice of a volume entitled *New Tales for Young Readers, by a Lady*, published by 'Bowdery and Kirby'. Bess may have mistaken the original publication date when she put together her submission to the Royal Literary Fund (which formed part of a request for financial assistance, made in the late 1850s), or *The Monthly Review's* notice may refer to a subsequent edition of her book. *The Monthly Review* professed itself mildly amused by the volume, although it took issue with the morals of some of its stories: 'The story of the "Lovely Child," who always looked pretty when she was good, may perhaps encourage juvenile vanity; and, in "The Fairy Tale," the plan to deceive an old grandmother, even "with just cause," should not have been commended' (*The Monthly Review, or Literary Journal*, 1822, 216). *New Tales for Young Readers* was, by this account, fairly insignificant hack work, but it did pave the way for Bess to become a writer, and for the publication of her first major work, *Flora Domestica*, in 1823.

12 Mary Cowden Clarke, *The Life and Labours of Vincent Novello*, p.10.

13 *The Examiner* 434 (21/04/1816), 247–50.

14 Thomas Medwin, *Conversations of Lord Byron*, pp.253–4.

15 Claire Clairmont to Lord Byron, March/April 1816. *The Clairmont Correspondence*, I, 25.

16   Claire Clairmont to Lord Byron, ?16/04/1816. *The Clairmont Correspondence*, I, 36.

17   Claire Clairmont to Lord Byron, 21/04/1816. *The Clairmont Correspondence*, I, 39.

18   Claire Clairmont to Lord Byron, 22/04/1816. *The Clairmont Correspondence*, I, 42.

19   Percy Shelley to Thomas Peacock, 15/05/1816. *PBS Letters*, I, 474.

20   Mary Shelley to Fanny Imlay, 17/05/1816. *MWS Letters*, I, 16.

21   Lord Byron to John Cam Hobhouse, 16/05/1816. *Byron's Letters and Journals*, V, 76–7.

22   Claire Clairmont to Lord Byron, 25/05/1816. *The Clairmont Correspondence*, I, 46.

23   Claire Clairmont to Lord Byron, 27/05/1816. *The Clairmont Correspondence*, I, 47.

24   *The Diary of Dr John William Polidori*, ed. William Rosetti, p.101.

25   Thomas Moore, *Letters and Journals of Lord Byron*, II, 24.

26   Lord Byron to Douglas Kinnaird, 20/01/1817. *Byron's Letters and Journals*, V, 162.

27   Mary Shelley to Fanny Imlay, 17/05/1816. *MWS Letters*, I, 18.

28   Mary Shelley to Fanny Imlay, 01/06/1816. *MWS Letters*, I, 20.

29   *The Diary of Dr John William Polidori*, pp.123, 121.

30   Mary Shelley, *Frankenstein* (1831), pp.8–10.

31   Claire Clairmont to Lord Byron, March/ April, 1816. *The Clairmont Correspondence*, I, 24.

32   See Charles Robinson, ed., *The Frankenstein Notebooks*, I, 59.

33   *The Frankenstein Notebooks*, I, 75.

34   James Rieger is among those who think that Shelley should be accorded the status of *Frankenstein*'s secondary author, whereas both Anne Mellor and Johanna Smith have characterised his alterations as patriarchal. See James Rieger, 'Introduction' in Mary Wollstonecraft Shelley, *Frankenstein*, pp.xi-xxvii; Anne K. Mellor, *Mary Shelley: Her Life, Her Fiction, Her Monsters* and Johanna M. Smith, ' "Hideous Progenies": Texts of *Frankenstein*', in *Texts and Textuality: Textual Instability, Theory and Interpretation*, ed. Philip Cohen, pp.121–40. Shelley's annotations are visible in both *The Frankenstein Notebooks* and in Charles Robinson's new edition of the novel: *The Original Frankenstein*.

35   *Conversations of Lord Byron*, p.194.

36   Quoted by David Erdman in *Childe Harold's Pilgrimage: A Critical, Composite Edition*, p.164.

37   Ernest J. Lovell, ed., *Lady Blessington's Conversations of Lord Byron*, p.53.

38   S. C. Djabri and J. Knight, eds., *The Letters of Bysshe and Timothy Shelley and other documents*, p.121.

39   Fanny Imlay to Mary Shelley, 29/07/1816. *The Clairmont Correspondence*, I, 55.

40   Percy Shelley to Lord Byron, 20/11/1816. *Shelley and his Circle*, ed. Donald Reiman et al, V, 16–17.

41   *The Examiner*, 453 (01/09/1816), 545.

42   John Keats to Charles Cowden Clarke, 09/10/1816. *Keats Letters*, ed. Hyder Rollins, I, 113.

43   Andrew Motion, *Keats*, p.98.

44   Charles and Mary Cowden Clarke, *Recollections of Writers* p.135.

45   *The Diary of Benjamin Robert Haydon*, II, 46, 57, 63, 68.

46   Benjamin Haydon to Leigh Hunt, 31/12/1817. Luther Brewer Leigh Hunt Collection. MsLH416h7.

47   *The Diary of Benjamin Robert Haydon*, II, 83.

48   See Alan Lang Strout, 'Knights of the Burning Epistle', pp.93–5.

49   Haydon, annotations in Medwin's *Conversations with Lord Byron*, the Roe-Byron Collection, Newstead Abbey, quoted by Duncan Gray and Violet W. Walker in 'Benjamin Robert Haydon on Byron and Others', pp. 24–5.

50   John Reynolds to Benjamin Haydon, 22/11/1816. *Keats Letters*, I, 119.

51   *The Examiner*, 466 (01/12/1816), 761–2.

52   Claire Clairmont to Mary Shelley, 20/09/1816. *The Clairmont Correspondence*, I, 73.

53   *The Journals of Mary Shelley*, I, 138.

54   Fanny Imlay to Mary Shelley, 03/10/1816. *The Clairmont Correspondence*, I, 80–3.

55   Fanny Imlay suicide note, 09/10/1816. *The Clairmont Correspondence*, I, 86.

56   Fanny's death has been the cause of much speculation, most recently by Janet Todd, who has suggested that Fanny may have met Shelley on her way to Swansea. See Janet Todd, *Death and the Maidens* pp.223–6.

57   Fanny Imlay to Mary Shelley, 29/07/1816. *The Clairmont Correspondence*, I, 56.

58   Fanny Imlay to Mary Shelley, 26/09/1816. *The Clairmont Correspondence*, I, 74.

59   Fanny Imlay to William Godwin, 08/10/1816. *The Clairmont Correspondence*, I, 85.

60   *The Journals of Mary Shelley*, I, 141.

61   Silsbee Collection. Box 7, file 2.

62   Mary Shelley to Percy Shelley, 05/12/1816. *MWS Letters*, I, 22.

63   Claire Clairmont to Lord Byron, 06/10/1816. *The Clairmont Correspondence*, I, 84.

64   Claire Clairmont to Lord Byron, 19/11/1816. *The Clairmont Correspondence*, I, 92.

65   Percy Shelley to Leigh Hunt, 08/12/1816. *PBS Letters*, I, 517–8.

66   *The Journals of Mary Shelley*, I, 150.

67   Shelley made enquiries on this subject and told Mary that Harriet had taken up with a groom named 'Mr Smith', although Claire later claimed that Harriet's lover was a 'Colonel Ryan'. Two recent studies of the group have however suggested that Shelley himself may have been the father of Harriet's child (see Nicholas Roe, *Fiery Heart*, p.281 and Janet Todd, *Death and the Maidens*, pp.244–5). Both arguments are based on a diary entry by Henry Crabb Robinson: 'It is singular that it was not suggested to Basil Montagu by Shelley that he was not the father of his wife's child. Mrs Godwin had stated this to be as a fact. Basil Montagu thinks it improbable' (*Henry Crabb Robinson on Books and their Writers*, I, 211). As Nicholas Roe notes, Mrs Godwin had 'reason to cast Harriet in a bad light' (p.394) and, although it is the case that Shelley made some attempt to see Harriet in the months before her

death, there is little other evidence to support Robinson's insinuation. None of the primary sources gives any indication that a meeting between Shelley and Harriet took place in the spring of 1816 (the approximate time of the unborn baby's conception); the Westbrooks never attempted to suggest that Shelley was the father of Harriet's child, even though doing so would have strengthened their court case significantly; and Harriet's suicide increases the likelihood that her pregnancy was illegitimate. Claire refuted the suggestion that Harriet was pregnant with Shelley's child in conversations with Edward Silsbee, at a time when she was being indiscreet on a number of related topics. Silsbee Collection. Box 7, file 4.

68   Harriet Shelley suicide note, ?07/12/1816. *Shelley and his Circle*, IV, 805–6.
69   Percy Shelley to Mary Shelley, 16/12/1816. *PBS Letters*, I, 520.
70   Percy Shelley to Claire Clairmont, 30/12/1816. *Shelley and his Circle*, V, 31.

Chapter Four: Children

1   Mary Shelley to Lord Byron, 13/01/1817. *MWS Letters*, I, 26.
2   Percy Shelley to Lord Byron, 17/01/1817. *Shelley and his Circle*, V, 82.
3   Byron to Douglas Kinnaird, 20/01/1817. *Byron's Letters and Journals*, V, 162.
4   Haydon, annotations in Medwin's *Conversations with Lord Byron*, quoted in 'Benjamin Robert Haydon on Byron and Others', p.23.
5   For Haydon's account of this evening see *The Diary of Benjamin Robert Haydon*, II, 80–9.
6   *The Life and Labours of Vincent Novello*, pp.13–14.
7   Charles Lamb, 'A Chapter on Ears', in *Elia and the Last Essays of Elia*, p.48.
8   Shelley, *Prose*, ed. E.B. Murray, pp.173–4.
9   *The Journals of Mary Shelley*, I, 164.
10   Benjamin Haydon to Elizabeth Barrett Browning, 29/12/1842. Willard Bissell Pope, ed., *Invisible Friends: The Correspondence of Elizabeth Barrett Browning and Benjamin Robert Haydon, 1842–1845*, p.16.
11   Nicholas Roe, *Fiery Heart*, p.292.
12   John Keats to Benjamin Bailey, 08/10/1817. *Keats Letters*, I, 169–70.
13   John Keats to Benjamin Bailey, 08/10/1817. *Keats Letters*, I, 170.
14   Leigh Hunt, *Foliage*, p.cxxi.
15   Thomas Medwin, *The Life of Percy Bysshe Shelley*, I, 298.
16   Edmund Blunden, 'The Keats-Shelley Poetry Contests', p.546.
17   John Keats to J. A. Hessey, 08/10/1818. *Keats Letters*, I, 374.
18   John Keats to Leigh Hunt, 10/05/1817. *Keats Letters*, I, 139–40.
19   Leigh Hunt to Charles Cowden Clarke, 01/07/1817. David Cheney Collection, University of Toledo. Box 16, file 5.
20   Leigh Hunt to Vincent Novello, 24/06/1817. *Recollections of Writers*, p.198.
21   *The Examiner*, 486 (20/04/17), 241.
22   Elizabeth Kent, *Flora Domestica*, p.xix.
23   Thornton Hunt, 'Shelley', *Atlantic Monthly*, XI (1863), 188–9.

24   *Memoirs of Shelley*, p.66.

252 *The Examiner*, 493 (09/06/1817), 353.

26   Shelley, *Prose*, p.285.

27   Peacock, *Nightmare Abbey*, p.79.

28   See Jack Donovan, Headnote to *Laon and Cythna*, in *The Poems of Shelley*, ed. Kelvin Everest II, 20.

29   *The Poems of Shelley*, II, 53. All quotations from *Laon and Cythna* are taken from this edition.

30   *The Poems of Shelley*, II, 47.

31   Horace Smith, 'A Greybeard's Recollections', quoted in A. H. Beavan, *James and Horace Smith*, pp.171–2.

32   Horace Smith to Leigh Hunt, 03/01/1818. *My Leigh Hunt Library*, p.118.

33   John Hunt to Leigh Hunt, June 1817. Bodleian MS Shelley adds. d. 4, ff. 36–7.

34   Percy Shelley to Lord Byron, 24/09/1817. *Shelley and his Circle*, V, 291.

35   Mary Shelley to Percy Shelley, 07/10/1817. *MWS Letters*, I, 53.

36   Mary Shelley to Leigh and Marianne Hunt, 30/06/1817. *MWS Letters*, I, 38.

37   Mary Shelley to Percy Shelley, 24/09/1817. *MWS Letters*, I, 41.

38   Mary Shelley to Percy Shelley, 24/09/1817. *MWS Letters*, I, 41.

39   Mary Shelley to Percy Shelley, 28/09/1817. *MWS Letters*, I, 45.

40   Mary Shelley to Percy Shelley, 28/09/1817. *MWS Letters*, I, 45, 47.

41   Mary Shelley to Percy Shelley, 18/10/1817. *MWS Letters*, I, 57.

42   Mary Shelley to Percy Shelley, 28/09/1817, 26/09/1817, 16/10/817. *MWS Letters*, I, 47, 44, 56.

43   *The Examiner*, 517 (23/11/1817), 738.

44   Shelley, *Prose*, pp.238–9.

45   *Blackwood's* (1817–1818), in *Romantics Reviewed*, Part C, I, 51, 87.

46   *Blackwood's* (1818–1819), in *Romantics Reviewed*, Part C, I, 51, 87.

47   Benjamin Haydon to Leigh Hunt, 31/12/1817. Luther Brewer Leigh Hunt Collection. MsLH416h7.

48   John Keats to Benjamin Bailey, 08/10/1817. *Keats Letters*, I, 169.

49   Claire Clairmont to Lord Byron, 12/01/1818. *The Clairmont Correspondence*, I, 109–11.

50   This is how the occasion was remembered by Keats's friend, Richard Woodhouse. See Walter Jackson Bate, *John Keats*, p.300 and E. Pereira, 'Sonnet contests and verse compliments in the Keats-Hunt Circle', p.19.

51   Percy Shelley to Leigh Hunt, 22/03/1818. *Shelley and his Circle*, VI, 523.

Chapter Five: Counts and Cockneys

1   *Foliage*, p.18.

2   *Foliage*, p.18.

3   Jeffrey Cox, 'Leigh Hunt's *Foliage*: A Cockney Manifesto', in *Leigh Hunt: Life, Poetics, Politics*, p.63.

4 Byron to John Murray, 24/11/1818. *Byron's Letters and Journals*, VI, 83.
5 Benjamin Haydon to John Keats, 25/03/1818. *Keats Letters*, I, 259.
6 *The Quarterly Review* (April 1818) in *The Romantics Reviewed: Part C*, II, 768.
7 John Keats to John Reynolds, 09/04/1818. *Keats Letters*, I, 266.
8 John Keats to George and Tom Keats, 23/01/1818. *Keats Letters*, I, 214.
9 John Keats to Benjamin Bailey, 10/06/1818. *Keats Letters*, I, 294.
10 John Keats to George and Georgina Keats, 16/12/1818. *Keats Letters*, II, 8.
11 Percy Shelley to Leigh Hunt 22/03/1818. *Shelley and his Circle*, VI, 523.
12 Claire Clairmont to Lord Byron, 27/04/1818. *The Clairmont Correspondence*, I, 115.
13 Claire Clairmont to Lord Byron, 27/04/1818. *The Clairmont Correspondence*, I, 115.
14 Mary Shelley to Maria Gisborne, 15/06/1818. *MWS Letters*, I, 72.
15 Mary Shelley to Leigh and Marianne Hunt, 13/05/1818. *MWS Letters*, I, 68.
16 Mary Shelley to Walter Scott, 14/06/1818. *MWS Letters*, I, 71.
17 Percy Shelley to Thomas Love Peacock, 25/07/1818. *PBS Letters*, II, 25.
18 Thomas Love Peacock to Percy Shelley, 14/06/1818. *Peacock Letters*, I, 126.
19 Percy Shelley to Thomas Love Peacock, 25/07/1818. *PBS Letters*, II, 26–7.
20 Leigh and Marianne Hunt to Percy and Mary Shelley, 14/07/1818–04/08/1818. *Shelley and His Circle*, VI, 606.
21 Silsbee Collection. Box 7, file 3.
22 Percy Shelley to Mary Shelley, 18/08/1818. *PBS Letters*, II, 33.
23 Percy Shelley to Mary Shelley, 23/08/1818. *PBS Letters*, II, 36–7.
24 Shelley, 'Preface' to 'Julian and Maddalo', in *Poetry and Prose*, pp.120–1.
25 Percy Shelley to Mary Shelley, 23/08/1818. *PBS Letters*, II, 37.
26 Percy Shelley to Mary Shelley, 22/09/1818. *PBS Letters*, II, 39.
27 Percy Shelley to Claire Clairmont, 25/09/1818. *Shelley and his Circle*, VI, 692.
28 See James Bieri, *Percy Bysshe Shelley*, I, 101.
29 Percy Shelley to Thomas Hogg, 21/12/1818. *Shelley and his Circle*, VI, 763–4.
30 *The Journals of Mary Shelley*, I, 249.
31 Percy Shelley to Claire Clairmont, 25/09/1819. *Shelley and his Circle*, VI, 692–3. The scratched out line - <'Meanwhile forget me and relive [*or* revive] not the other thing'> has 'been heavily cancelled with the intention to obliterate completely in an ink at least very similar to that in which the sentence was originally written. The words were probably cancelled by either Shelley or Claire' (*Shelley and his Circle* editorial note, VI, 693).
32 Mary Shelley to Isabelle Hoppner, 10/08/1821. *MWS Letters*, I, 207.
33 Richard Holmes, *Footsteps*, pp.173–5.
34 This argument is made convincingly by Miranda Seymour in *Mary Shelley*, p.227.
35 *The Journals of Mary Shelley*, I, 249. For the implications of 'fuss' in Mary's diary, see James Bieri, *Percy Bysshe Shelley*, I, 349.
36 See James Bieri, *Percy Bysshe Shelley*, II, 107–113.
37 Percy Shelley to Thomas Love Peacock, 23/03/1819. *PBS Letters*, II, 85–7.

38   Percy Shelley to John and Maria Gisborne, 06/04/1819. *PBS Letters*, II, 90.
39   Percy Shelley to John and Maria Gisborne, 06/04/1819. *PBS Letters*, II, 90–1.
40   Mary Shelley to Leigh Hunt, 06/04/1819. *MWS Letters*, I, 90.
41   Shelley, *Poetry and Prose*, p.140.
42   *The Journals of Claire Clairmont*, p.113.
43   *The Journals of Mary Shelley*, I, 69.

Chapter Six: Exiles

1   Mary Shelley to Marianne Hunt, 29/06/1819. *MWS Letters*, I, 101–2.
2   Thomas Hogg to Percy Shelley, 02/07/1819. Bodleian [Abinger] Dep. b. 211/3 (a).
3   Percy Shelley to Thomas Hogg, 25/07/1819. *PBS Letters*, II, 104.
4   William Godwin to Mary Shelley, 09/09/1819. Bodleian [Abinger] Dep. c. 524.
5   Leigh Hunt to Percy Shelley, ?08/07/1819. *Shelley and his Circle*, VI, 839–41.
6   Leigh Hunt to Percy and Mary Shelley, 23/08/1819. *Shelley and his Circle*, VI, 879–80.
7   Leigh Hunt to Mary Shelley, 25–7/07/1819. *Shelley and his Circle*, VI, 845.
8   Leigh Hunt to Mary Shelley, 25–7/07/1819. *Shelley and his Circle*, VI, 846.
9   Leigh Hunt to Mary Shelley, 25–7/07/1819. *Shelley and His Circle*, VI, 846.
10   *The Examiner*, 608 (22/08/1819), 529.
11   *The Examiner*, 612 (19/09/1819), 593.
12   *The Examiner*, 613 (26/09/1819), 618.
13   *The Examiner*, 'Preface' to Volume II (1809), n.p.
14   *The Indicator*, 1 (13/10/1819), Preface.
15   *The Indicator*, 1 (13/10/1819), Preface.
16   *The Indicator*, 2 (20/10/1819), 9.
17   Percy Shelley to Leigh Hunt, 23/12/1819. *Shelley and his Circle*, VI, 1107.
18   *The Examiner*, 592 (02/05/1819), 282.
19   Percy Shelley, *Poetry and Prose*, p.339.
20   Leigh Hunt to Percy Shelley, ?08/07/1819. *Shelley and His Circle*, VI, 841.
21   John Taylor Coleridge, Review of *The Revolt of Islam* and *Laon and Cythna*, *Quarterly Review* (April 1819), *Romantics Reviewed: Part C*, II, 776.
22   *The Examiner*, 615 (10/10/1819), 652.
23   Percy Shelley to Leigh Hunt, 27/09/1819. *PBS Letters*, II, 122.
24   Mary Shelley, 'The Fields of Fancy', Appendix I to *The Novels and Selected Works of Mary Shelley*, Volume II (*Matilda*), ed. Pamela Clemit, p.351.
25   Mary Shelley, *Matilda*, ed. Pamela Clemit, p.40.
26   *Matilda*, p.60.
27   Mary Shelley to Marianne Hunt, 24/5/11/1819. *MWS Letters*, I, 114.
28   Percy Shelley to Leigh Hunt, 13/11/1819. *PBS Letters*, II, 151.
29   Shelley to Maria Gisborne, 11/03/1820. Marion Kingston Stocking and David M. Stocking, 'New Shelley Letters in a John Gisborne Notebook', pp.2–3.
30   Mary Shelley to Marianne Hunt, 24/03/1819. *MWS Letters*, I, 137.

31 See Peter Cochran, 'Introduction' to Teresa Guiccioli, *Lord Byron's Life in Italy*, pp.12–13.
32 Teresa Guiccioli to Lord Byron, 20/08/1820. *Shelley and His Circle*, X, 681.
33 Lord Byron to Richard Hoppner, 22/04/1820. *Byron's Letters and Journals*, VII, 80.
34 Claire Clairmont to Lord Byron, 01/05/1820. *The Clairmont Correspondence*, I, 145.
35 Claire Clairmont to Lord Byron, 04/05/1820. *The Clairmont Correspondence*, I, 146–7.
36 Percy Shelley to Lord Byron, 26/05/1820. *Shelley and his Circle*, VIII, 1050.
37 *The Journals of Claire Clairmont*, p.153.
38 Percy Shelley to Maria Gisborne, 19/07/1820. *PBS Letters*, II, 218.
39 *The Journals of Mary Shelley*, I, 321.
40 *The Journals of Claire Clairmont* , p.150.
41 Percy Shelley to Maria Gisborne, 30/06/1820. *PBS Letters*, II, 207.
42 *Maria Gisborne and Edward E. Williams,* ed. Frederick Jones, p.45.
43 *Maria Gisborne and Edward E. Wiliams*, p.39.
44 *Maria Gisborne and Edward Williams*, p.44.
45 *The Examiner*, 672 (12/11/1820), 721.
46 Percy Shelley to Marianne Hunt, 29/10/1820. *PBS Letters*, II, 240.
47 John Keats to Percy Shelley, 16/08/1820. *Keats Letters*, II, 322.
48 *The Indicator*, 50 (20/09/1820), 399–400.

Chapter Seven: Travellers

1 John Keats to Charles Brown, 30/11/1820. *Keats Letters*, II, 359.
2 Leigh Hunt to Joseph Severn, 08/03/1821. *Correspondence of Leigh Hunt*, ed. Thornton Hunt, I, 108.
3 *The Journals of Claire Clairmont*, p.228.
4 *The Journals of Claire Clairmont*, p.180.
5 *The Journals of Claire Clairmont*, p.223.
6 *The Journals of Claire Clairmont*, p.202.
7 *The Journals of Claire Clairmont*, p.195.
8 Claire Clairmont to Lord Byron, 24/03/1821. *The Clairmont Correspondence*, I, 163.
9 Lord Byron to Richard and Isabelle Hoppner, 03/04/1821. *Byron's Letters and Journals*, VIII, 98.
10 Percy Shelley to Lord Byron, 17/04/1821. *PBS Letters*, II, 283.
11 Tilottoma Rajan, 'Introduction', *Valperga*, p. 27.
12 Percy Shelley to Claire Clairmont, ?14/05/1821. *PBS Letters*, II, 292.
13 Alexander Mavrocordato to Mary Shelley, 27/05/1821. Bodleian [Abinger] Dep. c. 516. Translated by Paul Howard.
14 Percy Shelley to Thomas Love Peacock, 08/11/1820. *Shelley and his Circle*, X, 1037.
15 Percy Shelley to Claire Clairmont, 29/10/1820. *Shelley and his Circle*, X, 962.
16 Percy Shelley to Claire Clairmont, 29/10/1820. *Shelley and his Circle*, X, 963.

17 Emilia Viviani to Percy Shelley, 12/12/1820. Quoted in N.I. White, *Shelley*, II, 472.
18 Mary Shelley to Maria Gisborne, 07/03/1822. *MWS Letters*, I, 223.
19 For an explanation of the title and its etymology see *Shelley's Poetry and Prose*, p.392.
20 Percy Shelley to Charles Ollier, 16/02/1821. *PBS Letters*, II, 262–3.
21 Percy Shelley to John Gisborne, 18/06/1822. *PBS Letters*, II, 434.
22 Thomas Love Peacock, 'The Four Ages of Poetry', in *Peacock's Four Ages of Poetry*, ed. H. F. B. Brett-Smith, pp.15–16.
23 Shelley, *Poetry and Prose*, p.535.
24 Joseph Severn to Charles Brown, 27/02/1821. *Joseph Severn: Letters and Memoirs*, ed. Grant Scott, pp.136–7.
25 Joseph Severn to Charles Brown, 27/02/1821. *Joseph Severn: Letters and Memoirs*, pp.136–7.
26 *The Examiner*, 656 (23/07/1820), 467.
27 Henry L. Hunt to Marianne Hunt, 21/12/1820. *Shelley and His Circle*, X, 1097.
28 Marianne Hunt to Mary Shelley, 24/01/1821. *Shelley and Mary*, ed. Jane Shelley, III, 578–80.
29 Percy Shelley to Claire Clairmont, 08/06/1821. *PBS Letters*, II, 296.
30 *Poetical Works of Percy Bysshe Shelley* (1839), IV, 152.
31 Lord Byron to Percy Shelley, 26/04/1821. *Byron's Letters and Journals*, VIII, 104.
32 Percy Shelley to Mary Shelley, 10/08/1821. *PBS Letters*, II, 322.
33 Percy Shelley to Mary Shelley, 07/08/1821. *PBS Letters*, II, 317.
34 Percy Shelley to Leigh Hunt, 26/08/1821. *PBS Letters*, II, 344.
35 Percy Shelley to Mary Shelley, 15/08/1821.*PBS Letters*, II, 339.
36 *The Journals of Claire Clairmont*, p.253.

Chapter Eight: Corsairs

1 *Maria Gisborne and Edward E. Williams*, p.109.
2 John Keats to Charles Cowden Clarke, 09/10/1816. *Keats Letters*, I, 113.
3 Mary Shelley to Maria Gisborne, 21/12/1821. *MWS Letters*, I, 212.
4 See Claire Clairmont to Mary Shelley, 09/04/1822. *The Clairmont Correspondence*, I, 172.
5 Mary Shelley to Marianne Hunt, 05/03/1822. *MWS Letters*, I, 220–1.
6 *Maria Gisborne and Edward E. Williams*, p.127.
7 *Maria Gisborne and Edward E. Williams*, p.132.
8 Silsbee Collection. Box 7, file 4.
9 Edward Williams to Edward John Trelawny, 26/12/1821. *Maria Gisborne and Edward E. Williams*, pp.159–60.
10 Edward Williams to Edward Trelawny, 26/12/1821. *Maria Gisborne and Edward E. Williams*, p.159.
11 Peter Cochran, 'Trelawny, Edward John (1792–1881)'.

12   *The Journals of Mary Shelley*, I, 390–1.

13   *The Journals of Mary Shelley*, I, 392.

14   Joseph Severn to Charles Brown, 09/04/1823. *Joseph Severn: Letters and Memoirs*, p.238.

15   *Maria Gisborne and Edward E. Williams*, p.142.

16   *Maria Gisborne and Edward E. Williams*, p.131.

17   *Maria Gisborne and Edward E. Williams*, p.126.

18   Lord Byron to Bryan Waller Procter, ?Feb 1822. *Byron's Letters and Journals*, IX, 95.

19   Thomas Hogg to Percy Shelley, 29/01/1822. Bodleian [Abinger] Dep. c. 533.

20   Charles Brown to Thomas Richards, 15/11/1821. *The Letters of Charles Armitage Brown*, ed. Jack Stillinger, p.93.

21   *Lord Byron and Some of His Contemporaries*, p.453.

22   Leigh Hunt to Vincent Novello, 11/02/1822. *Recollections of Writers*, p.208.

23   John Hunt to Shelley, 16/11/1821. *Shelley and Mary*, III, 706–8.

24   Percy Shelley to Lord Byron, 15/02/1822. *PBS Letters*, II, 389.

25   Leigh Hunt to Lord Byron, 27/01/1822. *A Life in Letters*, pp.111–12.

26   Leigh Hunt to Lord Byron, 27/01/1822. *A Life in letters*, pp.113–14.

27   Charles Brown to Joseph Severn, 05/09/1822. *The Letters of Charles Brown*, p.104.

28   Leigh Hunt to Vincent Novello, 11/02/1822. *Recollections of Writers*, p.212

29   Leigh Hunt to Mary Novello, 02/03/1822. *Recollections of Writers*, p.213.

30   Claire Clairmont to Lord Byron, 18/02/1822. *The Clairmont Correspondence*, I, 169.

31   Mary Shelley to Claire Clairmont, 20/03/1822. *MWS Letters*, I, 226.

32   Percy Shelley to Claire Clairmont, 24/03/1822. *PBS Letters*, II, 400.

33   Percy Shelley to Claire Clairmont, 20/03/1822. *PBS Letters*, II, 399.

34   Edward Trelawny, *Recollections of the Last Days of Shelley and Byron*, p.36.

35   *Recollections of the Last Days of Shelley and Byron*, p.50.

36   *Maria Gisborne and Edward E. Williams*, pp.136–7.

37   *Maria Gisborne and Edward E. Williams*, p.137.

38   Claire Clairmont to Mary Shelley, 09/04/1822. *The Clairmont Correspondence*, I, 171.

39   Allegra's symptoms were described by Pellegrino Ghigi in letters quoted in Iris Origo, *The Last Attachment*, pp.310–11.

40   Teresa Guiccioli, *Lord Byron's Life in Italy*, ed. Peter Cochran, pp.439–40.

41   Lord Byron to Percy Shelley, 23/04/1822. *Byron's Letters and Journals*, IX, 147.

42   Mary Shelley to Maria Gisborne, 02/06/1822. *MWS Letters*, I, 236.

43   Percy Shelley to Lord Byron, 09/05/1822. *PBS Letters*, I, 416.

44   Mary Shelley to Maria Gisborne, 15/08/1822. *MWS Letters*, I, 244.

45   Percy Shelley to Claire Clairmont, 28/05/1822. *PBS Letters*, I, 427.

46   Percy Shelley to John Gisborne, 18/06/1822. *PBS Letters*, II, 435–6. Shelley quotes *Faust*, Part II, Act V, scene vi.

47   *Maria Gisborne and Edward E. Williams*, p.156.

48   Percy Shelley to Claire Clairmont, 28/05/1822. *PBS Letters*, II, 427.
49   Percy Shelley to John Gisborne, 18/06/1822. *PBS Letters*, II, 434.
50   Percy Shelley to John Gisborne, 18/06/1822. *PBS Letters*, II, 435.
51   Mary Shelley to Maria Gisborne, 15/08/1822. *MWS Letters*, I, 246.
52   Mary Shelley to Leigh Hunt, c.30/06/1822. *MWS Letters*, I, 238.
53   *Lord Byron and Some of His Contemporaries*, p.9.
54   Thornton Hunt, 'Shelley', *Atlantic Monthly*, pp.189–90.
55   Percy Shelley to Horace Smith, 29/06/1822. *PBS Letters*, II, 442.
56   Edward Williams to Jane Williams, 06/07/1822. *Maria Gisborne and Edward E. Williams*, p.162.
57   Percy Shelley to Jane Williams, 04/07/1822. *PBS Letters*, I, 445.
58   Percy Shelley to Mary Shelley, 04/07/1822. *PBS Letters*, I, 444.

Chapter Nine: The Future

1   Leigh Hunt to Percy Shelley, 09/07/1822. David Cheney Collection. Box 16, file 10.
2   Mary Shelley to Maria Gisborne, 15/08/1822. *MWS Letters*, I, 248.
3   Mary Shelley to Maria Gisborne, 15/08/1822. *MWS Letters*, I, 249.
4   Mary Shelley to Maria Gisborne, 15/08/1822. *MWS Letters*, I, 249.
5   Claire Clairmont to Leigh Hunt, 19/07/1822. *The Clairmont Correspondence*, I, 176.
6   *Recollections of the Last Days of Shelley and Byron*, p.87.
7   *Recollections of the Last Days of Shelley and Byron*, p.91.
8   *Recollections of the Last Days of Shelley and Byron*, pp.91–2.
9   Lord Byron to Thomas Moore, 27/08/1822. *Byron's Letters and Journals*, IX, 197.
10   Richard Holmes, 'Death and Destiny', the *Guardian*, 24 January 2004.
11   Richard Holmes, 'Death and Destiny'.
12   Mary Shelley to Maria Gisborne, 22/11/1822. *MWS Letters*, I, 290.
13   See John Gisborne to Thomas Hogg, 12/08/1822. *New Shelley Letters*, pp.136–7.
14   *The Diary of Benjamin Robert Haydon*, II, 372.
15   *The Courier*, 5 August 1822.
16   *The Journals of Claire Clairmont*, p.285.
17   Claire Clairmont to Mrs Mason, ?24/09/1822. *The Clairmont Correspondence*, I, 199.
18   Charles Clairmont to Mary Shelley, 22/02/1823. *The Clairmont Correspondence*, I, 202.
19   Quoted in *The Clairmont Correspondence*, I, 209.
20   Marion Kingston Stocking, *The Clairmont Correspondence*, I, 210.
21   Charles Clairmont to Mary Shelley, 22/02/1823. *The Clairmont Correspondence*, I, 208.
22   Edward Trelawny to Claire Clairmont, 11/04/1823. *The Letters of Edward John Trelawny*, ed. H. Buxton Forman, p.46.

23   Edward Trelawny to Claire Clairmont, 11/04/1823. *The Letters of Edward John Trelawny*, p.44.

24   Mary Shelley to Maria Gisborne, 17/09/1822. *MWS Letters*, I, 261.

25   Lord Byron to Mary Shelley, 04/10/1822. *Byron's Letters and Journals*, X, 11.

26   Lord Byron to John Murray, 09/10/1822. *Byron's Letters and Journals*, X, 13.

27   Hunt, *Lord Byron and Some of His Contemporaries*, pp.27, 27–8, 36.

28   Leigh Hunt, 'Preface', *The Liberal*, I, (1822), ix, xii, vii.

29   *Blackwood's*, XII (1822), p.781.

30   *Blackwood's*, XI (1822), p.238.

31   Lord Byron to John Murray, 09/10/1823. *Byron's Letters and Journals*, X, 13.

32   *Lord Byron and Some of His Contemporaries*, p.47.

33   *The Journals of Mary Shelley*, II, 429–30.

34   *The Journals of Mary Shelley*, II, 430.

35   *The Journals of Mary Shelley*, II, 432.

36   Lord Byron to Thomas Moore, 27/08/1822. *Byron's Letters and Journals*, IX, 197.

37   *The Journals of Mary Shelley*, II, 440–1.

38   *The Journals of Mary Shelley*, II, 441.

39   Mary Shelley to Lord Byron, 16/11/1822. *MWS Letters*, I, 288.

40   Mary Shelley to Jane Williams, 15/10/1822. *MWS Letters*, I, 280.

41   *The Journals of Mary Shelley*, II, 439.

42   Mary Shelley to Jane Williams, 19/02/1822. *MWS Letters*, I, 313.

43   Mary Shelley to Jane Williams, 10/04/1823. *MWS Letters*, I, 330.

44   Mary Shelley to Marianne Hunt, 24/03/1820. *MWS Letters*, I, 136.

45   Leigh Hunt to Elizabeth Kent, 07/04/1823. *My Leigh Hunt Library*, pp.126–7.

46   *The Journals of Mary Shelley*, II, 449.

47   Leigh Hunt to Vincent Novello, July 1823. David Cheney Collection. Box 16, file 11.

48   Leigh Hunt to Bess Kent, August 1823. David Cheney Collection. Box 16, file 11.

49   Mary Shelley to Jane Williams, c.2/07/1823. *MWS Letters*, I, 344.

50   Mary Shelley to Jane Williams, c.2/07/1823. *MWS Letters*, I, 344.

51   Lord Byron to Leigh Hunt, 28/06/1823. *Byron's Letters and Journals*, X, 205.

52   Miranda Seymour, *Mary Shelley*, p.324.

53   Mary Shelley to Teresa Guiccioli, 2–10/07/1823. *MWS Letters*, I, 348.

54   Lord Byron to Leigh Hunt, 28/06/1823. *Byron's Letters and Journals*, X, 205.

55   Mary Shelley to Jane Williams, 23/07/1823. *MWS Letters*, I, 349.

Chapter Ten: The Present

1   Mary Shelley to Leigh and Marianne Hunt, 26/07/1823. *MWS Letters*, I, 352.

2   Mary Shelley to Leigh Hunt, 03/08/1823. *MWS Letters*, I, 359.

3   Mary Shelley to Leigh Hunt, 09/09/1823. *MWS Letters*, I, 378.

4   Mary Shelley to Leigh and Marianne Hunt, 14/08/1823. *MWS Letters*, I, 369.

5 Mary Shelley to Leigh Hunt, 09/09/1823. *MWS Letters*, I, 378.

6 *Diary, Reminiscences and Correspondence of Henry Crabb Robinson*, II, 260.

7 *Theatrical Observer*, 9 August 1823. Miranda Seymour suggests that the placards may in fact have been a publicity stunt by the Lyceum management (*Mary Shelley*, p.334).

8 *Posthumous Poems of Shelley: Mary Shelley's Fair Copy Book*, ed. Irving Massey, p.88.

9 *The Journals of Mary Shelley*, II, 479.

10 Mary Shelley to Edward Trelawny, 28/07/1824. *MWS Letters*, I, 438.

11 Claire Clairmont to Jane Williams, 11/09/1824 (O.S.). *The Clairmont Correspondence*, p.212. Marion Kingston Stocking notes that 'since Russia had not yet adopted the Gregorian calendar, the O.S. (Old Style) date was twelve days behind the English'.

12 Claire Clairmont to Jane Williams, 29/04/1825. *The Clairmont Correspondence*, I, 222.

13 Claire Clairmont to Jane Williams, 11/09/1824. *The Clairmont Correspondence*, I, 213.

14 Claire Clairmont to Jane Williams, December 1826. *The Clairmont Correspondence*, I, 240.

15 *The Journals of Claire Clairmont*, p.403.

16 *The Journals of Mary Shelley*, II, 478.

17 Edward Trelawny to Jane Williams, 20/06/1824. *Letters of Edward John Trelawny*, p.83.

18 Leigh Hunt to Bess Kent, July 1824. *Correspondence of Leigh Hunt*, I, 224–5.

19 Leigh Hunt to Bess Kent, 01/09/1824. *Correspondence of Leigh Hunt*, I, 227.

20 Bess Kent to Leigh Hunt, 01/09/1823. Bodleian MSS Shelley adds. d. 5. ff. 47–8.

21 *Flora Domestica*, p.xiii.

22 *Blackwood's* (August 1818), in *The Romantics Reviewed: Part C*, I, 92.

23 Elizabeth Kent to John Clare, 19 September, year unknown. British Library. MSS Egerton 2250, fol. 244.

24 *Recollections of Writers*, pp.37–8.

25 Vincent Novello to Leigh Hunt, ?23/06/1824. David Cheney Collection. Box 19, file 28.

26 *The Journals of Mary Shelley*, II, 482.

27 Mary Shelley to Leigh Hunt, 02–05/10/1823. *MWS Letters*, I, 393.

28 Mary Shelley to Leigh Hunt, 20/10/1823. *MWS Letters*, I, 396.

29 Mary Novello to Leigh Hunt, 19/10/1823. *Correspondence of Leigh Hunt*, I, 209–10.

30 Leigh Hunt to Vincent and Mary Novello, 09/01/1824. *Recollections of Writers*, p.226.

31 Marianne Hunt to Mary Shelley, 04/10/1823 – 27/11/1823. Bodleian MSS Shelley adds. d. 5 ff. 42–3.

32 Leigh Hunt to Vincent Novello, 16/06/1825. *Correspondence of Leigh Hunt*, I, 246.

33 Leigh Hunt to Bess Kent, 22/27/09/1825. *Correspondence of Leigh Hunt*, I, 246. See *Leigh Hunt: A Life in Letters*, pp.175–6 for clarification of the date of this letter.

34 In 1824, when Mary moved to Kentish Town, it was still a country hamlet, linked
    to London only by the most rudimentary public transport. Its rural qualities
    were one of its main attractions, for both Mary and the day-trippers for whom it
    provided a convenient escape from town.

35 Leigh Hunt to John C. Claris, 12/03/1825. *A Life in Letters*, p.165.

Chapter Eleven: The Past

1 Charles Brown to Leigh Hunt, 21/12/1836. *The Letters of Charles Brown*, p.341.
2 *The Keats Circle*, ed. Hyder Rollins, II, 54.
3 George Keats to C.W. Dilke, 12/04/1828. *Keats Circle*, I, 313–14.
4 *Lord Byron and Some of His Contemporaries*, p.vi.
5 *Lord Byron and Some of His Contemporaries*, p.23.
6 *Lord Byron and Some of His Contemporaries*, pp.64–5.
7 *The Quarterly Review* 37 (March, 1828), 403.
8 *The Autobiography of Leigh Hunt*, II, 91.
9 Mary Shelley to Leigh Hunt, 14/12/1838. *MWS Letters*, II, 305.
10 *Poetical Works of Percy Bysshe Shelley* (1839), I, xii.
11 *Poetical Works of Percy Bysshe Shelley* (1839), III, 163.
12 Susan Wolfson, 'Editorial Privilege: Mary Shelley and Percy Shelley's Audiences',
    p.42.
13 Trelawny to Claire Clairmont, 19/03/1875. *The Letters of Edward John Trelawny*,
    p.247.
14 Silsbee Collection. Box 7, file 3.
15 Carl H. Pforzheimer Collection of Shelley and his Circle, The New York Public
    Library, Astor, Lenox and Tilden Foundations. Uncatalogued MS, filed in Claire
    Clairmont to Lady Mountcashell, 24/09/1822. For ease of reading, I have not
    transcribed Claire's deletions and rewritings. These occur frequently in a manuscript
    which was evidently an early draft of a projected longer work.
16 *Footsteps*, p.181.
17 Quoted in William St Clair, *Trelawny: The Incurable Romancer*, p.197. St Clair
    notes that not only did Trelawny misquote Shelley (following Mary Shelley's
    transcription), but that he also considered rewriting his friend's poetry so that
    it better described their relationship, and read as follows: 'These are two friends
    in life devided/ Death has united, so let their memory be/ Now that they have
    glided under their grave/ Let not their bones be parted/ For their two hearts in life
    were single hearted'. 'I doubt', St Clair writes, 'if many people would find this an
    improvement on Shelley's verse even if the sentiment accords better with the facts'
    (p.230).

Select Bibliography

A comprehensive bibliography of biographical and critical studies of the writers discussed in this book would fill a book of its own, and indeed does so every year, in the shape of the annual *Keats-Shelley Journal Bibliography*, published by the Keats-Shelley Association of America. The aims of the bibliography provided here are more modest. It provides full details of primary and secondary material cited in the Notes, as well as details of a small number of additional works which have informed my thinking significantly. It also encompasses a highly selective list of works by individual members of the Shelley/Hunt circle. Here, I have focused on authoritative editions, works written in the period covered by this book, or on works which are directly related to that period.

1) Selected works of the Shelley/Hunt circle

Byron, George Gordon, *Complete Poetical Works*, ed. Jerome McGann, 7 vols (Oxford: Clarendon Press, 1980–93).

Cowden Clarke, Charles, *An Address to that Quarterly Reviewer who touched upon Mr Leigh Hunt's Story of Rimini* (London: R. Jennings, 1816).

Cowden Clarke, Mary, *The Life and Labours of Vincent Novello* (London: Novello and Co., 1862; repr. 1864).

—— *My Long Life* (T. Fisher Unwin, 1896).

Cowden Clarke, Charles and Mary, *Recollections of Writers* (Sussex: Centaur Press, Ltd, 1969; first published 1878).

Hazlitt, William and Leigh Hunt, *The Round Table* (Edinburgh: Constable, 1817).

Hazlitt, William, *Selected Writings*, ed. Duncan Wu, 9 vols (London: Pickering and Chatto, 1998).

Hogg, Thomas Jefferson, *Memoirs of Prince Alexy Haimatoff* (London: T. Hookham, 1813).

—— *The Life of Percy Bysshe Shelley*, 2 vols (London: E. Dowden, 1858).

Hunt, Leigh, *Juvenilia* (London: J. Whiting, 1802).

—— *The Descent of Liberty* (London: Gale and Fenner, 1815).

—— *The Story of Rimini* (London: John Murray, 1816).

—— *Foliage; or, Poems Original and Translated* (London: C. and J. Ollier, 1818).

—— *The Literary Pocket Book*, 5 vols (London: C. and J. Ollier, 1819–1823).

—— *Lord Byron and Some of His Contemporaries*, 3 vols (London: Henry Colburn, 1828).

—— *The Autobiography of Leigh Hunt*, ed. Roger Ingpen, 2 vols (London: Constable and Co.,1903; first published 1850).

—— *Selected Writings*, ed. Robert Morrison and Michael Eberle-Sinatra, 6 vols (London: Pickering and Chatto, 2003).

Keats, John, *Complete Poems*, ed. Jack Stillinger (Cambridge, Mass.: Harvard University Press, 1978; repr. 2003).

Kent, Elizabeth, *Flora Domestica: or, The Portable Flower-Garden; with Directions for the Treatment of Plants in Pots; and Illustrations from the Works of the Poets* (London: Taylor and Hessey, 1823; repr. 1825).

—— *Sylvan Sketches; or, A Companion to the Park and The Shrubbery* (London: Taylor and Hessey, 1825).

Lamb, Charles and Mary, *Tales from Shakespeare*, ed. Marina Warner (London: Penguin, 2007).

Lamb, Charles, *Elia and the Last Essays of Elia*, ed. Jonathan Bate (Oxford: Oxford University Press, 1987).

Peacock, Thomas Love, *The Genius of the Thames: A Lyrical Poem* (London: T. Hookham, 1810).

—— *Rhododaphne, Or, The Thessalian Spell* (London: T. Hookham, 1818).

—— *Nightmare Abbey*. ed. Raymond Wright (Harmondsworth: Penguin, 1969; first published 1818).

—— *The Four Ages of Poetry*, ed. H. F. B. Brett-Smith (Oxford: Basil Blackwell, 1921; first published 1821).

—— 'Memoirs of Percy Bysshe Shelley' in *Memoirs of Shelley and other Essays and Reviews*, ed. Howard Mills (London: Rupert Hart-Davis, Ltd, 1970).

Novello, Mary, *A Day at Stowe Gardens* (London: John and Henry L. Hunt, 1825).

Reynolds, John Hamilton, *Peter Bell: A Lyrical Ballad* (London: Taylor and Hessey, 1819).

—— *The Garden of Florence and Other Poems* (London: John Warren, 1821).

Shelley, Mary Wollstonecraft, *History of a Six Weeks Tour*, ed. Jeanne Moskal, in *Novels and Selected Works*, ed. Nora Crook (London: Pickering and Chatto, 1996; first published 1817), VIII.

—— *Frankenstein; or, The Modern Prometheus* (1818), ed. Marilyn Butler (Oxford: Oxford University Press, 1998; first published 1818).

—— *Frankenstein; or, The Modern Prometheus* (1831), ed. M. K. Joseph (Oxford: Oxford University Press, 1969; repr. 1998; first published 1831).

—— *Matilda*, ed. Pamela Clemit in *Novels and Selected Works*, ed. Nora Crook (London: Pickering and Chatto, 1996), II.

—— *Valperga; or, The Life and Adventures of Castruccio, Prince of Lucca*, ed. Michael Rossington (Oxford: Oxford University Press, 2000; first published 1823).

—— *The Last Man*, ed. Morton D. Paley (Oxford: Oxford University Press, 1994; first published 1826).

Shelley, Percy Bysshe, *Posthumous Poems*, ed. Mary Wollstonecraft Shelley (London: John and Henry L. Hunt, 1824).

—— *Poetical Works*, ed. Mary Wollstonecraft Shelley, 4 vols (London: Edward Moxon, 1839).

—— *The Poems of Shelley*, ed. Geoffrey Matthews and Kelvin Everest, 3 vols (London: Longman, 1989–).

—— *Poetry and Prose*, ed. Donald Reiman and Neil Fraistat (New York, New York: W. W. Norton and Company, 1977; repr. 2002).

—— *Prose Works*, ed. E. B. Murray (Oxford: Oxford University Press, 1993).

Smith, Horace and James, *Rejected Addresses, or, The New Theatrum Poetarum* (London: J. Millar, 1812).

Trelawny, Edward John, *Adventures of a Younger Son*, 3 vols (London: Henry Colburn, 1831).

—— *Recollections of the Last Days of Shelley and Byron* (London: Constable and Robinson, 2000; first published 1858).

—— *Records of Shelley, Byron and the Author*, 2 vols (London: Basil Montagu Pickering, 1878).

2) Periodicals and newspapers

Blackwood's Edinburgh Magazine, 1817–1824.
The Courier, 1822.
The Examiner, 1808–1825.

The Indicator, 1819–1820.
The Liberal, 1822–1823.
The Monthly Review or Literary Journal, 1822.
The Quarterly Review, 1819, 1828.
Theatrical Observer, 1823.

3) Manuscript collections and privately printed sources

Bodleian MSS Shelley adds d. 4, adds d. 5, and [Abinger] Dep. e. 196–227, Dep. b. 221/3(a), Dep c. 524, Dep. c. 516, Dep. c. 533. The Bodleian Library, University of Oxford, Oxford.

British Library MS Ashley 906; MS Egerton 2250; MS Add 38108. British Library, London.

Silsbee Family Papers, Series III. James Duncan Phillips Library. Peabody Essex Museum, Salem, Mass.

David R. Cheney Papers, Series I. Ward M. Canady Center for Special Collections. The University of Toledo, Ohio.

The Luther Brewer Leigh Hunt Collection. The University of Iowa Libraries, Iowa City, Iowa.

The Henry W. and Albert A. Berg Collection of English and American Literature. The New York Public Library, Astor, Lennox and Tilden Foundations

The Carl H. Pforzheimer Collection of Shelley and His Circle. The New York Public Library, Astor, Lenox and Tilden Foundations.

Shelley and Mary, ed. Lady Shelley, 4 vols (privately printed, 1882).

4) Published primary texts

Beavan, A. H., *James and Horace Smith* (London: Hurst and Blackett, Ltd, 1899).

Bennett, Betty T., ed., *The Letters of Mary Wollstonecraft Shelley*, 3 vols (Baltimore, Maryland: Johns Hopkins University Press, 1980–88).

Blessington, Marguerite, Countess of, *Conversations of Lord Byron*, ed. Ernest J. Lovell, Jr (Princeton, New Jersey, 1969; first published 1834).

Brewer, Luther, ed., *My Leigh Hunt Library: Holograph Letters* (Iowa City, Iowa: University of Iowa Press, 1938).

Djabri, Susan Cabell and Jeremy Knight, eds, *The Letters of Bysshe and Timothy Shelley and Other Documents* (Horsham: Horsham Museum Society, 2000).

Erdman, David, *Childe Harold's Pilgrimage: A Critical, Composite Edition* (New York, New York: Garland Publishing, 1991).

Feldman, Paula R., and Diana Scott-Kilvert, eds, *The Journals of Mary Shelley, 1814–1844*, 2 vols (Oxford: Clarendon Press, 1987).

Fogle, Stephen F., ed., *Leigh Hunt's Autobiography: The Earliest Sketches* (Gainsville, Florida: University of Florida Monographs, 1959).

Forman, H. Buxton, *The Letters of Edward John Trelawny* (Oxford: Oxford University Press, 1910).

Gates, Eleanor, ed., *Leigh Hunt: A Life in Letters* (Essex, Connecticut: Falls River Publications, 1998).

Gay, H. N., 'Unpublished Diary of Mrs Leigh Hunt', *Bulletin and Review of the Keats Memorial Association*, 2 (1913), 69–77.

Gigliucci, Contessa Valeria, ed., *Clara Novello's Reminiscences* (London: Edward Arnold, 1910).

Godwin, William, *Political Justice* in *Political and Philosophical Writings of William Godwin*, ed. Mark Philip (London: Pickering and Chatto, 1993), IV.

—— *Collected Novels and Memoirs*, ed. Pamela Clemit, Maurice Hindle and Mark Philip, 8 vols (London: Pickering and Chatto, 1992).

Gray, Duncan and Violet W. Walker, 'Benjamin Robert Haydon on Byron and Others', *Keats-Shelley Memorial Bulletin*, 7 (1956), 14–26.

Griggs, Earl Leslie, ed., *Collected Letters of Samuel Taylor Coleridge*, 6 vols (Oxford: Clarendon Press, 1956–71).

Guiccioli, Teresa, *Lord Byron's Life in Italy*, ed. Peter Cochran, trans. Michael Rees (Newark, New Jersey: University of Delaware Press, 2005).

—— *My Recollections of Lord Byron*, trans. Hubert E. H. Jerningham, 2 vols (London: Richard Bentley, 1869).

Haydon, Benjamin Robert, *Correspondence and Table-Talk, with a Memoir by his Son, Frederic Wordsworth Haydon*, 2 vols (London: Chatto and Windus, 1876).

Holmes, Richard, ed., *A Short Residence in Sweden and Memoirs of the Author of 'The Rights of Woman'* (Harmondsworth: Penguin, 1987; *Residence in Sweden* first published 1796, *Memoirs* first published 1798).

Hunt, Thornton, 'Shelley', *Atlantic Monthly* XI (1863), 184–204.

Hunt, Thornton, ed., *The Correspondence of Leigh Hunt*, 2 vols (London: Smith, Elder and Co., 1862).

Jerningham, Hubert E. H., *Reminiscences of an Aattaché* (Edinburgh: William Blackwood and Sons, 1886).

Jones, Frederick L., ed., *The Letters of Percy Bysshe Shelley*, 2 vols (Oxford: Clarendon Press, 1964).

Jones, Frederick L., ed., *Maria Gisborne and Edward E. Williams. Shelley's Friends. Their Journals and Letters* (Norman, Oklahoma: University of Oklahoma Press, 1951).

Joukovsky, Nicholas A., ed., *The Letters of Thomas Love Peacock*, 2 vols (Oxford: Clarendon Press, 2001).

Marchand, Leslie, ed., *Byron's Letters and Journals*, 12 vols (London: John Murray, 1973–94).

Marrs, Edwin, ed., *Letters of Charles and Mary Anne Lamb*, 3 vols (Ithaca, New York: Cornell University Press, 1975–8).

Massey, Irving, *Posthumous Poems of Shelley: Mary Shelley's Fair Copy Book* (Montreal: McGill-Queens University Press, 1969).

Medwin, Thomas, *Conversations of Lord Byron*, ed. Ernest J. Lovell Jr (Princeton, New Jersey: Princeton University Press, 1966; first published 1824).

—— *The Shelley Papers* (London: Whittaker, Treacher and Co., 1833).

—— *The Life of Percy Bysshe Shelley*, 2 vols (London: Thomas Cautley Newby, 1847).

Moore, Thomas, *Letters and Journals of Lord Byron: With Notices of his Life*, 2 vols (London: John Murray, 1830).

Morley, Edith J., ed., *Henry Crabb Robinson on Books and their Writers*, 3 vols (London: J. M. Dent, 1938).

Norman, Sylva, ed., *After Shelley: The Letters of Thomas Jefferson Hogg to Jane Williams* (London: Humphrey Milford, 1934).

Pope, Willard Bissell, ed., *The Diary of Benjamin Robert Haydon*, 5 vols (Cambridge, Mass.: Harvard University Press, 1960–63).

Pope, Willard Bissell, ed., *Invisible Friends: The Correspondence of Elizabeth Barrett Barrett and Benjamin Robert Haydon, 1842–1845* (Cambridge, Mass.: Harvard University Press, 1972).

Prothero, Rowland E., ed., *The Works of Lord Byron: Letters and Journals*, 6 vols (London: John Murray, 1899).

Reiman, Donald, ed., *The Romantics Reviewed: Part C: Shelley, Keats and London Radical Writers*, 2 vols (New York, New York: Garland Publishing, 1972).

Reiman, Donald, et al, *Shelley and his Circle*, 10 vols to date (Cambridge, Mass: Harvard University Press, 1961–).

Robinson, Charles, ed., *The Frankenstein Notebooks*, 2 vols (New York, New York: Garland Publishing, 1996).

—— ed., *The Original Frankenstein, by Mary Shelley (With Percy Shelley)* (Oxford: Bodleian Library, 2008).

—— ed., *Mythological Dramas: Proserpine and Midas* (New York, New York: Garland Publishing, 1992).

Rolletson, Maud, *Talks with Lady Shelley* (London: George G. Harrap and Co, 1925; first published 1897).

Rollins, Hyder, ed., *The Letters of John Keats*, 2 vols (Cambridge, Mass.: Harvard University Press, 1958).

Rollins, Hyder, ed., *The Keats Circle*, 2 vols (Cambridge, Mass.: Harvard University Press, 1948).

Rossetti, William M., ed., *The Diary of Dr John William Polidori* (London: Elkin Matthews, 1911).

Rossetti, William Michael, 'Talks with Trelawny', *The Athenaeum*, 2855–2858 (1882), 78–9, 144–45, 176–77.

Sadler, Thomas, ed., *Diary, Reminiscences and Correspondence of Henry Crabb Robinson*, 3 vols (London: Macmillan and Co., 1869).

Scott, Grant, ed., *Joseph Severn: Letters and Memoirs* (Aldershot: Ashgate, 2005).

Scott, W. S., ed., *New Shelley Letters* (London: The Bodley Head, 1948).

Sharp, William, ed., *The Life and Letters of Joseph Severn* (London: Sampson Low, Marston and Company, Ltd, 1892).

Shelley, Jane, *Shelley Memorials* (London: Smith, Elder and Co., 1859).

Smiles, Samuel, *A Publisher and his Friends: Memoir and Correspondence of the Late John Murray*, 2 vols (London: John Murray, 1891).

Staël, Anne Louise Germaine, *Corinne; or, Italy*, trans. Avril Goldberger (New Brunswick: Rutgers University Press, 1987; first published 1807).

Stillinger, Jack, ed., *The Letters of Charles Armitage Brown* (Cambridge, Mass: Harvard University Press, 1966).

Stocking, Marion Kingston, ed., *The Journals of Claire Clairmont* (Cambridge, Mass.: Harvard University Press, 1968).

Stocking, Marion Kingston, ed., *The Clairmont Correspondence*, 2 vols (Baltimore, Maryland: Johns Hopkins University Press, 1995).

Stocking, Marion Kingston and David Mackenzie, 'New Shelley Letters in a John Gisborne Notebook', *Keats-Shelley Memorial Bulletin* 31 (1980), 1–9.

Sykes, Herschel, ed., *The Letters of William Hazlitt* (New York, New York: New York University Press, 1978).

Wollstonecraft, Mary, *A Vindication of the Rights of Woman*, ed. Miriam Brody Kramnick (Harmondsworth: Penguin, 1975; repr. 1992; first published 1792).

Wordsworth, William, *The Major Works*, ed. Stephen Gill (Oxford: Oxford University Press, 2002).

Wordsworth, William, and Samuel Taylor Coleridge, *Lyrical Ballads*, ed. R. L. Brett and A. R. Jones (London: Routledge, 1991; first published 1798).

5) Selected secondary reading

Bakewell, Michael and Melissa, *Augusta Leigh: Byron's Half-Sister* (London: Chatto and Windus, 2000).

Barnard, John, 'Leigh Hunt and Charles Cowden Clarke, 1812–1818' in *Leigh Hunt: Life, Poetics, Politics*, ed. Nicholas Roe (London: Routledge, 2003) pp.32–57.

Bate, Walter Jackson, *John Keats* (Cambridge, Mass.: Harvard University Press, 1963).

Bieri, James, *Percy Bysshe Shelley*, 2 vols (Newark, New Jersey: University of Delaware Press, 2004–5).

Blunden, Edmund, *Leigh Hunt: A Biography* (London: Cobden-Sanderson, 1930).

—— 'The Keats-Shelley Poetry Contests', *Notes and Queries*, December (1954), 546.

Butler, Marilyn, *Peacock Displayed: A Satirist in his Context* (London: Routledge and Kegan Paul, 1979).

—— 'Myth and Mythmaking in the Shelley Circle', in *Shelley Revalued*, ed. Kelvin Everest (Leicester: Leicester University Press, 1983), pp.1–20.

Cochran, Peter, 'Trelawny, Edward John (1792–1881)', *Oxford Dictionary of National Biography*, Oxford University Press, 2004 [http://www.oxforddnb.com/view/article/27687, accessed 13 May 2008].

Cox, Jeffrey, *Poetry and Politics in the Cockney School* (Cambridge: Cambridge University Press, 1998).

—— 'Leigh Hunt's *Foliage*: A Cockney Manifesto', in *Leigh Hunt: Life, Poetics, Politics*, ed. Nicholas Roe (London: Routledge, 2003), pp.58–77.

Crompton, Louis, *Byron and Greek Love: Homophobia in Nineteenth-Century England* (London: Faber and Faber, 1985).

Donovan, Jack, Headnote to *Laon and Cythna* in *The Poems of Shelley*, ed. Kelvin Everest (London: Longman, 2000), II.

Dowden, Edward, *The Life of Percy Bysshe Shelley*, 2 vols (London: Kegan Paul, 1886).

Elwin, Malcolm, *Lord Byron's Wife* (London: John Murray, 1962).

Gittings, Robert and Jo Manton, *Claire Clairmont and the Shelleys, 1798–1879* (Oxford: Oxford University Press, 1992).

Grylls, Rosalie, *Claire Clairmont: Mother of Byron's Allegra* (London: John Murray, 1939).

Holmes, Richard, *Shelley: The Pursuit* (London: Harper Collins, 1974; repr. 1994).

—— *Footsteps: Confessions of a Romantic Biographer* (London: Hodder and Stoughton, 1985).

—— 'Death and Destiny', *The Guardian*, January 24th, 2004.

Lee, Hermione, *Biography: A Very Short Introduction* (Oxford: Oxford University Press, 2009).

MacCarthy, Fiona, *Byron: Life and Legend* (London: John Murray, 2002).

Marchand, Leslie, *Byron: A Biography*, 3 vols (London: John Murray, 1957).

Mayne, Ethel Colburn, *The Life and Letters of Anna Isabella, Lady Noel Byron* (London: Dawsons, 1969; first published 1929).

Mellor, *Mary Shelley: Her Life, Her Fiction, Her Monsters* (London: Routledge, 1998).

Motion, Andrew, *Keats* (London: Faber and Faber, 1997).

Origo, Iris, *The Last Attachment* (London: John Murray, 1949; repr. 1971).

Paul, Charles Kegan, *William Godwin: His Friends and Contemporaries*, 2 vols (London: H. S. King, 1876).

Pereira, E., 'Sonnet Contests and Verse Compliments in the Keats-Hunt Circle', *Unisa English Studies: Journal of the Department of English*, 25, No. 1 (1987), 13–23.

Rajan, Tilottoma, 'Introduction', *Valperga* (Ontario: Broadview Press, 1998), pp.7–42.

Reiger, James, 'Introduction' in Mary Shelley, *Frankenstein* (Chicago: Chicago University Press, 1974), pp.xi-xxvii.

Robinson, Charles, *Shelley and Byron: The Snake and Eagle Wreathed in Fight* (Baltimore, Maryland: Johns Hopkins University Press, 1976).

Roe, Nicholas, *John Keats and the Culture of Dissent* (Oxford: Clarendon Press, 1997).

—— *Fiery Heart: The First Life of Leigh Hunt* (London: Pimlico, 2005).

—— ed., *Leigh Hunt: Life, Poetics, Politics* (London: Routledge, 2003).

Russell, Gillian and Clara Tuite, eds, *Romantic Sociability* (Cambridge: Cambridge University Press, 2002).

Seymour, Miranda, *Mary Shelley* (London: John Murray, 2000).

Smith, Johanna M., '"Hideous Progenies": Texts of *Frankenstein*', in *Texts and Textuality: Textual Instability, Theory and Interpretation*, ed. Philip Cohen (New York, New York: Garland Publishing, 1997), pp.121–40.

St Clair, William, *The Godwins and the Shelleys* (London: Faber and Faber, Ltd, 1989).

—— *Trelawny: The Incurable Romancer* (London: John Murray, 1977).

Stillinger, Jack, *Multiple Authorship and the Myth of Solitary Genius* (Oxford: Oxford University Press, 1991).

Stout, Alan Lang, 'Knights of the Burning Epistle', *Studia Neophilologica* 26 (1953–54), 77–99.

Sunstein, Emily, *Mary Shelley: Romance and Reality* (Baltimore, Maryland: Johns Hopkins University Press, 1989; repr. 1991).

Todd, Janet, *Death and the Maidens: Fanny Wollstonecraft and the Shelley Circle* (London: Profile Books, 2007).

White, Newman Ivey, *Shelley*, 2 vols (New York, New York: Alfred Knopf, 1947).

Wolfson, Susan, 'Editorial Privilege: Mary Shelley and Percy Shelley's Audiences', in *The Other Mary Shelley: Beyond* Frankenstein, ed. Audrey A. Fisch, Anne K. Mellor, and Esther H. Schor (Oxford: Oxford University Press, 1993), pp.39–72.

Worthen, John, *The Gang: Coleridge, the Hutchinsons and the Wordsworths in 1802* (Yale, New Haven: Yale University Press, 2001).

Acknowledgements

Anyone currently working on the Romantic writers explored in this book owes a substantial debt of gratitude to the biographers and literary critics who have revolutionised the study of Romantic lives and letters over the past few decades. I would like to acknowledge the inspiration I have drawn from biographies of Shelley by Richard Holmes and James Bieri; of Mary Shelley by Emily Sunstein and Miranda Seymour; and of Leigh Hunt by Nicholas Roe. I have been influenced by several key studies of Romantic sociability, chief among them Marilyn Butler's *Romantics, Rebels and Reactionaries*, Jack Stillinger's *Multiple Authorship and the Myth of the Solitary Genius*, Charles Robinson's *Shelley and Byron: The Snake and Eagle Wreathed in Fight*, and Jeffrey Cox's *Poetry and Politics in the Cockney School*.

I am also indebted to those who have undertaken the Herculean task of editing Romantic letters and diaries. I particularly wish to acknowledge Betty T. Bennett's volumes of Mary Shelley's letters; Marion Kingston Stocking's editions of Claire Clairmont's letters and diaries; and the Pforzheimer Collection's *Shelley and his Circle* volumes, edited by Kenneth Neill Cameron, Donald Reiman, Doucet Fischer and others. I am most grateful to Timothy Webb, who shared with me some of the findings relating to his forthcoming edition of Leigh Hunt's *Autobiography* and to David Cheney, whose work on a complete edition of Hunt's correspondence ceased only with his death. I have made substantial use of Dr Cheney's typescript and thank the

University of Toledo for allowing me access to his papers, and his widow, Pat Cheney, for making me welcome during my visit to Ohio.

Throughout my research on the Shelleys and the Hunts I have been fortunate to be able to draw on the support and advice of many individuals. In Cambridge Leo Mellor, Raphael Lyne and Heather Glen have provided much encouragement, and I am very grateful to the President and Fellows of New Hall for awarding me a Bye-Fellowship to support my work. I am also grateful to Nigel Leask, who supervised my doctoral thesis on literary collaboration in the Shelley circle. My agent, Clare Alexander, has been a wonderful advocate and a source of much wisdom, and Michael Fishwick at Bloomsbury and Paul Elie at Farrar, Straus and Giroux have been generous and incisive editors. It has been a pleasure to work with Margaret Stead, who copy-edited the book, and Anna Simpson, who saw it through production.

For help with particular questions I would like to thank Bruce Barker-Benfield, Peter Cochran, Nicholas Roe, Michael Rossington, William St Clair and Heather Tilley. I would also like to record my gratitude to the late Marion Kingston Stocking, who answered several questions about the papers of Claire Clairmont, and to Candia McWilliam, who very kindly scrutinsed a set of proofs. In archives and libraries I have been aided by Sid Huttner, Nana Diederichs, Kathy Flynn, Isaac Gewirtz, Elizabeth Denlinger and Charles Carter, as well as by the staff of the Brotherton Collection, Leeds, the British Library, the London Library, the Bodleian Library, and Cambridge University Library. I owe special thanks to Paul Howard, for his translations of the manuscript letters of Alexander Mavrocordato, and to Barbara Floyd and Sandra Rice, for the warm welcome they extended to me during my stint at the University of Toledo's Canaday Centre. Jessie and Johnny Saunders, Jane Deuser, and Liz and Matthew Edwards were all wonderfully hospitable during my travels to archives in Britain and the United States. Doucet Fischer has guided me at every stage as I have attempted to unravel the complexities of the Pforzheimer Collection manuscripts, and has done so with unflagging wit and good humour. Above all I am indebted to Nora Crook, who has read the book in draft, saved me from my own inaccuracies on numerous occasions, and who, over the past few years, has generously revealed to me the fathomless depths of her knowledge of all things Shelleyan. All mistakes are, of course, my own.

I could not have written this book without the support of my friends and my family, and am very grateful to them all for listening. In particular, I thank Polly Mackenzie and Aoife Ní Luanaigh for their advice; my sister, Marianna Hay, for her support; and my father, Michael Hay, for his unwavering faith in my abilities and for much quiet good sense along the way. I have discussed this book at every stage of its development with my mother, Amanda Mackenzie Stuart, and feel exceptionally fortunate to have been able to draw on her expertise as I have put my narrative together. Most of all, I would like to thank my husband, Matthew Santer, who has lived with the Romantics for as long as he has lived with me. He has accompanied me on fact-finding missions in England and Italy, has read drafts and been the source of many sensible suggestions and, on one notable occasion, sat beside me in an archive in Salem, Massachusetts, searching near-illegible nineteenth-century notebooks for references to Shelley, as we raced the clock towards closing time. I cannot thank him enough for his support.

I also gratefully acknowledge the support of the London Library Trust, provided through the award of Carlyle Membership of the library.

Index